Inside Book Publishing

Now fully revised and updated for its seventh edition, *Inside Book Publishing* is the classic introduction to the book publishing industry.

The book provides excellent overviews of the main aspects of the publishing process: commissioning authors, product development, design and production, marketing, and sales. Angus Phillips and Giles Clark offer authoritative and up-to-date coverage of all sectors of the industry from commercial fiction to educational publishing and academic journals. They reveal how publishers continue to adapt to a fast-changing and highly interconnected world, in which printed books have proved resilient alongside ebooks and the growth in audio. The topics explored include AI, social media in marketing, sustainable book production, open access for research, and diversity, equity and inclusion. International case studies from industry experts give perspectives on, for example, comic books, children's picture books, women in Indian publishing and the Korean literary wave.

As a manual for those in the profession and a guide for the publishers of the future, this book remains a seminal work for anyone with an interest in the industry. It will also be of interest to authors seeking an insider's view of this exciting industry.

The book is supported by online resources, including a glossary, a further reading list and links to a range of online resources, available at www.routledge. com/9781032516554.

Angus Phillips is Director of the Oxford International Centre for Publishing Studies at Oxford Brookes University, UK.

Giles Clark was formerly Co-Publishing Adviser at The Open University, UK.

Inside Book Publishing

Praise for previous editions

'The definitive text for all who need to learn about the publishing industry.'
Publishing Training Centre

'This book was invaluable to me when I set up And Other Stories without having worked for any publishing company. To understand the industry, this is your book. It's an MA in itself!'
Stefan Tobler

'An excellent book ... I recommend this book to everyone.'
Gillian Clarke, *Editing Matters*, magazine of the Chartered Institute of Editing and Proofreading

'A crucial title if you are looking to enter the industry.'
Suzanne Collier, bookcareers.com

'Seen as the definitive book about the industry, which is used as a recommended textbook on a number of publishing courses. It will help you understand how the industry works and the responsibilities of each department or sector.'
Society of Young Publishers

'Unless you can confidently claim to have a well-rounded understanding of publishing, this is a great book for when you want to check what a bit of jargon means, or beef up the financial case for a marketing idea by refreshing your memory of how a book's P&L is calculated. Fabulous to have as a shelf reference whatever your department.'
Rachel Maund, Marketability

'An excellent introduction to anyone with a professional interest in publishing. It is the most clear and specific guide to publishing I have ever read. Although it focuses on British publishing for its examples, any reader would get a good grounding in what publishing is all about, with a lot of useful detail about every aspect of the business. It provides a comprehensive overview and answers so many questions about why publishing works the way it does. No writer equipped with this book need ever feel like an ignorant outsider again.'
Chris Holifield, WritersServices

'Approachable and entertaining as well as highly informative. No one embarking on a career in publishing should fail to read it – and even those with a few years' experience will find useful things in it.'

Nicholas Jones, Strathmore Publishing

'A mainstay adoption on publishing courses throughout the UK and abroad ... No matter your age *Inside Book Publishing* makes for a pleasant reading experience.'

Jason Mitchell, *InPrint*

'An excellent introduction to the subject, managing to be both comprehensive and concise ... worth reading for budding authors and publishers alike ... There are shelves of books available on the subject of publishing (and in particular self-publishing), but I think it's worth reading something that takes a serious-minded, academic approach to the core of the subject, and this book fills that role perfectly.'

The Fiction Desk

'The text for many publishing courses and to where one directs all those enquirers keen to get into publishing. Routledge have completely redesigned the book and made it a real joy to look at and use.'

Publishers Association Bulletin

'At its best when talking about the internet and the complexities of publishing and controlling intellectual property in a digital age ... well-worth reading as an overview of the global industry and publishing process.'

Thomas Woll, *Publishing Research Quarterly*

'A publishing textbook which punches through all the competition ... In short, this volume merits the accolade of being "essential": anyone who wants to get a good grip on the way publishing works should read it. New students following publishing courses will find the balance of practical advice and academic rigour perfect for underpinning classroom sessions, and those beginning a career in the industry will do well to keep a copy at hand as a quick reference guide.'

Samantha Rayner, *BookBrunch*

'This is one of the best and most comprehensive overviews of the publishing and book industry currently on the market ... One of my new MA Publishing students refers to this book as her "bible" and carries it around with her at all times.'

Debbie Williams, *Logos*

Inside Book Publishing

Angus Phillips and Giles Clark

Seventh Edition

Routledge
Taylor & Francis Group

LONDON AND NEW YORK

Designed cover image: Jelena Stevkovikj / iStock via Getty Images

Seventh edition published 2025
by Routledge
4 Park Square, Milton Park, Abingdon, Oxon, OX14 4RN

and by Routledge
605 Third Avenue, New York, NY 10158

Routledge is an imprint of the Taylor & Francis Group, an informa business

First edition published by Blueprint 1988
Sixth edition published by Routledge 2020

British Library Cataloguing-in-Publication Data
A catalogue record for this book is available from the British Library

Library of Congress Cataloging-in-Publication Data
Names: Clark, Giles N. (Giles Noel) author. |
Phillips, Angus, 1961– author.
Title: Inside book publishing / Angus Phillips and Giles Clark.
Description: 7th Edition. | New York, NY: Routledge, 2025. |
Includes bibliographical references and index.
Identifiers: LCCN 2024027236 (print) | LCCN 2024027237 (ebook) |
ISBN 9781032516530 (hbk) | ISBN 9781032516554 (pbk) |
ISBN 9781003403289 (ebk)
Subjects: LCSH: Publishers and publishing. |
Publishers and publishing—Vocational guidance. |
Publishers and publishing—Great Britain.
Classification: LCC Z278 .C557 2025 (print) | LCC Z278 (ebook) |
DDC 070.5—dc23/eng/20240621
LC record available at https://lccn.loc.gov/2024027236
LC ebook record available at https://lccn.loc.gov/2024027237

ISBN: 978-1-032-51653-0 (hbk)
ISBN: 978-1-032-51655-4 (pbk)
ISBN: 978-1-003-40328-9 (ebk)

DOI: 10.4324/9781003403289

Typeset in Scala
by codeMantra

Access the Support Material: www.routledge.com/9781032516554

Contents

Expert, focus and skills boxes

Illustration credits

The publisher and authors would like to give thanks for the following images:

Sources for quotations in sidebars

Preface to the seventh edition

In this seventh edition, appearing over 35 years since the book's first appearance, we cover the characteristics, dynamics, and core functions of the business, including: the diversity by sector; the continuing growth in globalization; the strategic concentration in ownership and the dynamism of smaller firms; the move from the sale of products to the provision of services; and how publishers operate within the digital world. We show the new ways in which they produce, market, sell and distribute books in print and digital formats to benefit readers, authors and shareholders. We equip students and recent entrants to publishing with the knowledge and understanding to navigate the industry. The book also gives an insight into the industry for authors working with publishers, as well as authors who self-publish.

The seventh edition captures major changes in the industry since the publication of the sixth edition in 2019. For example, the sale of printed books has proved resilient while audiobook sales are growing fast. Encouragingly, children's publishing continues to prosper. Self-publishing grew enormously yet publishers retained their authors. The success of BookTok has driven the sale of genre fiction and backlist titles. Diversity in authorship, readership and amongst the industry workforce remains an issue for the industry. The challenge of climate change has led publishers to re-examine their supply chains. In the USA, the major college textbook publishers faced disruption in their sale of new printed books and have had to cut their prices and transition more quickly to digital learning and assessment. In journal publishing the growth in open access publication whereby articles are made freely available to readers has been largely co-opted by the major publishers – OA is now moving into the area of academic books. The issue of research integrity is exercising publishers.

We are immensely grateful to Lizzie Cox (Editor, Journalism and Media, Routledge), Ann Klein (Production Editor, Routledge), and Hannah McKeating (Editorial Assistant, Routledge) for seeing the book through to publication. We thank them greatly.

April 2024

Preface to the previous editions

The history of this book's publication reflects the dramatic changes in publishing over the decades. Since its conception in the 1980s, the copyright of *Inside Book Publishing* has passed through six changes of outright publishing ownership, has appeared under five publishing imprints and been worked on by eight editors. This story is not unique in publishing today.

In the 1980s, the Society of Young Publishers (SYP) asked Giles Clark to write a book for the benefit of its members, to give an overview of publishing and the careers available. His employer, The Open University, supporting the project, gave him special leave to undertake the primary research: over 150 publishing managers were interviewed. The first contract was with Allen & Unwin, a long-established, family-owned publisher of medium size and diversity most noted for its general list, including the classic works by J. R. R. Tolkien – *The Lord of the Rings* and associated titles. This publisher also had a respected school textbook list, and higher education and professional titles in the earth sciences and the social sciences. By the time Giles had pulled together his research, Allen & Unwin had been taken over by another privately owned company and became Unwin Hyman. The first editor Adam Sisman left the restructured company (later going on to write a well-received biography of A. J. P. Taylor), and the new editor cancelled the contract and paid compensation. Unwin Hyman was then bought by HarperCollins, the international book publishing imprint of Rupert Murdoch's News Corporation. The Tolkien classics joined the ranks of other famous dead and living authors of HarperCollins and were to become in the next century reissued bestsellers tied in to the international film series, but at the time of purchase the staff were surplus as were the more specialist titles. A few of the Unwin Hyman managers formed University College London Press, which was later acquired by Taylor & Francis, and the social science titles were acquired from HarperCollins by Routledge, the respected academic imprint of the International Thomson Organization.

Giles was thankfully saved from the wilderness of being unpublished by Gordon Graham, then President of the Publishers Association and Chief Executive of Butterworths (legal and technical publishers) and subsequently the founder of the renowned publishing journal *Logos*, who introduced him to Dag Smith of the Book House Training Centre (renamed the Publishing Training Centre), who in turn contacted Blueprint Publishing – a new small publisher spearheaded and owned by Charlotte Berrill. She successfully focused on books on publishing and printing. Giles' work was adapted to the brief they drew up. The first edition of *Inside Book Publishing* (1988) was energetically published and sold by Blueprint.

Blueprint Publishing was later acquired by Chapman & Hall, the scientific and professional book imprint of Thomson. In 1993, Vivien James (the publisher in charge of the Blueprint list) needed a thoroughly revised second edition, which duly appeared in the autumn of 1994. German translation rights were sold to Hardt Wörner, which published their edition in 1996. During the summer of 1995, International Thomson conducted a reorganization which included combining the business and management lists of Routledge and Chapman & Hall into a new company, the International Thomson Business Press, and the transfer of Blueprint to the media studies list of Routledge under the editorship of Rebecca Barden. By the autumn of 1995 the first printing of the second edition of *Inside Book Publishing* had fortuitously sold out, enabling the reprint to appear under the Routledge imprint. A management buy-out of Routledge occurred in 1996, supported by the venture capitalist Cinven. In 1998, the UK journal and book publisher, Taylor & Francis bought Routledge. The third edition appeared in 2001, reprinted three times and was translated into Vietnamese. In May 2004, Taylor & Francis and Informa merged under the public listing of Informa to provide specialist information to the global academic and scientific, professional and commercial communities via publishing, events and performance improvement.

The publication of the fourth edition in 2008 marked a step change in the book's development with the aid of a new co-author Angus Phillips and a redesign. Why? When first published in 1998, the book was never conceived as a textbook but over the years it had become an 'accidental textbook'. It was widely adopted by lecturers as a key set text on the growing number of respected courses on publishing, and student purchasing kept it alive. Textbook publishing is long term. Publishers need to issue new editions of successful books to keep them current, to fend off competition and to overcome the attrition in sales from the used book market. They also face the possibility that the original author may not have the time to undertake yet another new edition alone, or more problematically, be able to consider their work afresh. Katrina Chandler, the development editor at Routledge, found for Giles Clark a new co-author, Angus Phillips of the Oxford International Centre for Publishing, who brought significant new ideas for additional content, structural reorganization, publishing knowledge, and teaching and illustrative approaches. One of his innovations was to commission contributions from a wide range of industry experts; he also recruited specialists to review the content. Aileen Storry succeeded Katrina and saw the book through to publication. The redesign of the book in a larger textbook format to match market needs and the finding of a new co-author of complementary strengths to work alongside the original author in a highly productive way, are good examples of a publisher adding value, a theme which runs throughout this book. By a happy coincidence he also succeeded Gordon Graham as editor of *Logos*. An ebook edition was published after the publication of the printed edition. The rise in importance of Asian publishing was reflected by translation into Korean and Chinese; other translation interest included a Romanian version.

The fifth edition came out in 2014. A good publisher guides, supports and invests in authors. Christoph Chesher (then Group Sales Director of Taylor & Francis Group, which includes Routledge) suggested to the authors that the new edition should be more international in scope and that was subsequently reflected in increased export sales. Niall Kennedy, our development editor, took the now enlarged edition through to publication.

Between the publication of the fourth edition (2008) and that of the fifth (2014) publishers faced a perfect storm. The prolonged recession in Western markets, which lowered book sales and revenue, coincided with unprecedented technological disruption and innovation which challenged their businesses. The large technology companies, particularly Amazon, saw opportunities in the area of books, and the newly arrived Kindle reading device, first launched in the USA in 2007, was to drive the purchase of ebooks by the public and create a new distribution channel for self-published authors. Some commentators and publishers imagined that ebook sales would soon surpass print sales, that Amazon would control the entire industry, and that many authors would abandon their publishers and self-publish. The uncertain economic climate helped to accelerate change across many dimensions as publishing houses searched for efficiencies. Nevertheless, the industry proved to be both resilient and adaptive, and publishers continued to operate successfully and profitably. Angus's international connections brought translations into Croatian and Lithuanian. The sixth edition (2019) brought a greater emphasis on digital developments, open access publication, consumer insight, self-publishing and the growth of audiobooks.

Special thanks are therefore due on the first edition to all Giles's friends in the SYP, to The Open University, Gordon Graham, Dag Smith and Charlotte Berrill; on the second edition to Vivien James; on the third edition to Rebecca Barden; on the fourth edition to Katrina Chandler and Aileen Storry; on the fifth edition to Christoph Cheshire and Niall Kennedy; and on the sixth edition to Natalie Foster, Margaret Farrelly and Jennifer Vennall. Furthermore we are indebted to the many dozens of people who have helped with *Inside Book Publishing* over the last 30 years.

Professor **Angus Phillips** is Director of the Oxford International Centre for Publishing at Oxford Brookes University. He has degrees from Oxford and Warwick Universities, and many years' experience in the publishing industry, including running a trade and reference list at Oxford University Press. He has acted as consultant to a variety of publishing companies, and trained publishing professionals from the UK and overseas in editorial, marketing and management. He is the author of *Turning the Page: The evolution of the book*, and the editor, with Michael Bhaskar, of *The Oxford Handbook of Publishing*. His most recent book is *Is This a Book?*, with Miha Kovač. His books have been translated into eight languages. He is the editor of the premier publishing journal *Logos*.

Giles Clark, with a family background in publishing, and educated at University College London, worked at The Open University UK, where he was the Co-publishing Adviser. He organized co-publication arrangements between the university and a wide range of publishers from small to large, across most academic disciplines. The partnerships forged with commercial publishers extend the university's readership internationally, reduce its costs and give it entrepreneurial income. He now chairs the Graham Greene Birthplace Trust in Berkhamsted, serves on other charities and works on business ventures.

Acknowledgements

We are indebted to the cartoonist John Taylor for his wit and to the staff at Routledge for producing, marketing and selling this book.

A number of friends and colleagues have given their help with the new edition. The following read chapters in draft and offered many useful comments on the text: Naomi Bacon, Lionel Bolton, Adrian Bullock, Suzanne Collier, Nitasha Devasar, Chris Jennings, Lynette Owen, Philip Shaw, Craig Taylor and Jeremy Trevathan. The illustrations are credited separately but in all cases there was a cheerful and prompt response to the authors' requests. A variety of people helped the search, including Rachel Abbott, Georgia Buckthorn, Mary Cannam, Sam Derby, Hilary Fine, Sarah Franklin, Barry Gibson, Katie Idle, Christopher MacLehose, Alenka Kepic Mohar, Nigel Newton, Richard Ogle, Juliet Pickering, Jenny Ridout, Bahar Siber, Louise Swannell, Beverley Tarquini, Cheryl Thomas, Jeremy Trevathan, Zool Verjee, Simon Winder, Alex Wright, Smit Zaveri and Barbara Zitwer.

All the contributors of the boxed panels deserve our gratitude for their readiness to have their arms twisted to write for the book.

Angus would like to thank Ann, Matthew, Charlotte and Jamie for their patience and support during the writing of this and three previous editions. More recent encouragement has come from Charlie and Rich; with a level of exuberance added by Anouk, Lily, Gabriel, and Winnie. Giles would like to thank Julia, the sausage dog and two black and white moggies for their humour and perseverance over many editions.

Book publishing
An introduction

The book industry is notable for both its economic impact and its wider influence. The business is international and digital access means that books have a ready global market. Yet the printed book remains resilient whilst offering a reliable business model for publishers, and some publishing markets have so far not made the transition towards digital products. The book industry has special features such as subsidies from national governments, a favourable tax regime in many countries, and general agreement that the book retains an important place as the carrier of culture, knowledge and information.

This book provides detailed analysis of the main aspects of the publishing process: commissioning authors, product development, design and production, marketing, sales and distribution. There is coverage of all sectors of the industry, from commercial fiction and non-fiction to educational publishing and academic journals. The text reveals how publishers continue to adapt to a fast-changing and highly interconnected world, and explores important themes such as digitization, globalization, sustainability, and diversity and inclusion. The development of artificial general intelligence (AGI) is seen as highly probable in the next few years, and in the meantime the arrival of AI models poses many questions for the work of authors and publishers, as well as for the copyright environment.

WHAT PUBLISHERS DO

Book publishing serves the million-copy brand author and the specialist author with sales of under 300 copies. Books can be published profitably for tiny markets which though limited in scale are many in number. As a long-established industry, publishing developed over time a worldwide distribution system through which its output of physical books could be traded in a regulated and controlled way. This ecosystem now coexists with digital distribution through which content can be sold and distributed right around the world on to mobile devices such as smartphones and tablets. Whilst this offers an exciting opportunity, at the same time publishers have to compete vigorously against other forms of entertainment, learning processes and information sources.

The primary definition of 'to publish' given in the *Oxford English Dictionary* is 'to make public'. In a world where anybody can post content on their blog or

DOI: 10.4324/9781003403289-1

Facebook page, is this enough of a definition? Michael Bhaskar suggests the following thought experiment: 'you write a novel, and leave it on a park bench. Is this a published novel? Let's say you print 1,000 copies, leaving them on 1,000 park benches. How about now?' (2013, page 18). Professional publishers go much further and undertake a range of activities. Publishers are not printers or mere 'middle men' interjecting themselves between authors and readers while creaming off the profits. They both add value to authors' works and protect the value of their copyrights. If they are doing their job well, they will develop an author's career and make a market for their works. Publishers commission authors, confer the authority of their brand on authors' works, project manage the publishing process, risk finance the production and marketing, and sell the works in multiple forms and ways wherever possible. Additional income benefiting the publisher and author may be made from various licensing arrangements that enable other organizations to exploit the work in different ways, media and languages.

Unless the publisher can add sufficient value to the author's work over and above the costs to make a profit from revenue received, the publisher will go out of business. Publishers' business models and the ways in which publishers add value to authors and shareholders are explored in Chapters 3 and 4. There are differences in models and approaches between the various sectors of book publishing.

Whilst the specialist staff of large publishers carry out many activities, some work (such as the detailed editing of books) is often contracted out to freelancers or possibly to other firms. Smaller publishers may not have the resources to employ their own sales staff or to distribute the books themselves so they may use larger publishers, or specialist firms. Apart from the decision to publish a book and raising the finance, all the other work can be outsourced, to freelancers nearby or separate firms overseas. Publishers of all sizes have increasingly outsourced work in order to reduce their overhead costs, a process that began in the editorial and production departments. But there are potential drawbacks: the publisher may have less control over the way the books are produced, leading to a diminution of quality; lose the marketing emphasis projected by its own employees committed solely to its books; run the risk of outsourcing core competences; and contribute to the profit margins of sub-contractors.

In discussing publishing we see publishers creating books but also content in different forms. The so-called 'book publishing industry' encompasses significant non-book publishing operations, such as the publication of scholarly journals and database reference works. Moreover, the definition of what constitutes a 'book' has become increasingly elusive. In the physical world, children's publishers stretched the definition through their publication of 'novelty books' for babies and toddlers and upwards. In the digital world, content is published as ebooks and audiobooks or on websites and social media. However, for many publishers the sale of printed books still constitutes their largest source of sales and revenue.

Publishers have traditionally defined themselves through the printed book: an icon conveying authority, prestige and great cultural significance over the ages. Publishers have shifted from simply selling physical products to licensing digital content, for example, in the form of ebooks. This is a fundamental change affecting workflows and the whole mindset of the organization. Another way of defining publishers is to say that they are traders of intellectual property (IP). The author creates the IP, and under copyright owns it, and is able to give it away for free or to sell it, usually via a publisher by means of an exclusive publishing licence – a publishing contract. The contract between the author and publisher not only conveys the right to the publisher to sell the work as a book, in whole or in part, but also other rights which enable the publisher to exploit and sell the work in many different ways. In the transition from printed books to digital publishing, the ways in which authors' works can be sold are multiplying. The 'book' as a printed container of content represents a too restrictive view especially with the widespread adoption of the ebook and audiobook.

'So many books, so little time.' Frank Zappa (1940–1993)

Demand and supply-side publishing

Demand-side publishing is based on two main assumptions. First, the publisher at its own risk and expense undertakes the production, marketing and the selling of the work: services that are usually provided free to authors. Second, the publisher attempts to earn its revenue from the demand-side, the market, with a view to making a profit. The assumption underlying most publishing is that publishing is a service to both authors and readers.

There is an alternative: supply-side publishing. The authors or their sponsors pay for the cost of publishing at their risk and expense, and the resulting product may be given away for free or charged for, usually at a low price. The receipt of revenue from market demand may be of little or of no consequence. For instance, in some countries, ministries of education pay publishers to produce textbooks for schools: the publishers earn their profit from the service provided. Universities subsidize the publication of scholarly works through their own presses and libraries. In this century, some supply-side publishing models have been growing, enabled by digital technologies. In the USA and subsequently elsewhere, there has been an enormous growth in authors self-publishing books at their own risk and expense, and paying author services companies for distribution and often for production and marketing. In journal publishing, under the gold open access model the research funders pay the publishers for the cost of publication. When publishers or service companies charge for their work, they primarily provide a service for their customers (authors or sponsors), rather than readers. The creation of content abundance usually underpins the business model of supply-side firms.

MARKET SECTORS AND PUBLISHER SIZE

The publishing industry is divided into various market sectors within which the publishers specialize. The general or consumer publishers produce books for the public. They have historically been called *trade* publishers because their business was and still is mainly conducted through the book trade.

Non-consumer publishing embraces other significant sectors based around readers' places of study and work. The educational publishers produce textbooks and other instructional resources for schools and higher education. However, educational publishing is usually more narrowly defined as serving primary and secondary schools. Educational publishing is mainly non-international and defined by countries or sub-national regions. In North America, school publishing is referred to as El-Hi (Elementary-High School) or K-12, i.e. an abbreviation of kindergarten (4–6-year-olds) to 12th grade (18–19-year-olds). English Language Teaching for all age-groups, both American and British English, is a significant international market and is called ELT publishing.

The publishers serving higher educational and professional markets are differentiated into overlapping sectors. Academic publishers concentrate on the arts, humanities and social sciences (AHSS); and STM publishers focus on science, technical and medical areas. In the educational context, STEM refers to science, technology, engineering and mathematics. All these publishers produce a wide range of products and services, such as textbooks and digital content for students, resources for lecturers, high-level books and reference works for researchers and practitioners, and learned journals. The professional publishing sector for practitioners' research, reference, and training overlaps with academic and STM publishing, and additionally includes law, accountancy and business information. Sometimes it may overlap with 'trade', such as through the publication of books on management and business.

Subsequent chapters in this book expand on this topic. The key points here are that publishing is a very diverse industry, that there are significant differences between the sectors, and that the business models operated by publishers differ markedly. Overall, publishing is one of the most important creative industries, and it has a prominent place in the UK economy: 'Publishing is the bedrock of the UK creative industries as a whole, with top films, TV shows and plays inspired first and foremost by books' (publishers.org.uk, accessed 24 January 2024). In 2023, the UK publishing industry had total revenues of £7.1 bn.

Moreover, many kinds of organizations, such as corporates, not-for-profit enterprises, universities and societies publish books and employ staff who undertake the publishing work described in this book. It is common for authors to self-publish their work. Their activities may not appear in publishing statistics – not least because they publish and sell directly to their communities.

The global publishers

The publishing business is highly international with its ownership dominated by European and US corporations and those from China and Japan. While the news media and publishing blogs give much coverage to the consumer book publishers, the industry's giants are RELX (UK/NL), Thomson Reuters (US), Pearson (UK) and Walters Kluwer (NL), all of which are non-consumer publishers. Elsevier (part of RELX) is the world's leading STM publisher, while Thomson Reuters and Wolters Kluwer concentrate more on professional markets. These three companies derive much of their revenue from publishing high-priced content and services on subscription to a relatively small number of organizations.

Global 50 ranking of publishers, 2023

Rüdiger Wischenbart, journalist and consultant

In 2022, the 50 largest publishing groups worldwide accounted for combined revenues of €62,729 m (up from €51,100 m in 2017, and €48,935 m in 2008), of which the 10 largest groups alone controlled well over half (55 per cent). From 2008 to 2023, a remarkable degree of continuity was seen among the top tier of the industry: Pearson, RELX, Thomson Reuters, Bertelsmann, Wolters Kluwer, and Hachette have figured in the top six for one and a half decades.

Further down the ranks, however, several companies have disappeared, notably due to industry consolidation, such as the American group Houghton Mifflin Harcourt or De Agostini Editore in Italy. Furthermore, the academic heavyweight Springer Nature, formed by the German Holtzbrinck Group in 2015, and the continually expanding Chinese Phoenix Publishing and Media Group have accessed the top 10.

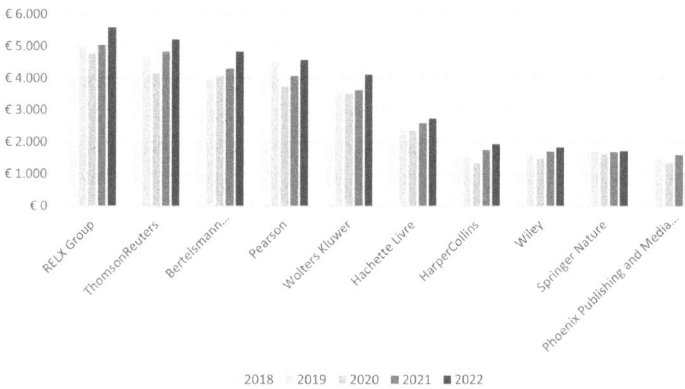

Global 50 2023: Top 10 evolution 2018 to 2022 (revenue in fiscal 2022, mEUR)

The top ten largest publishing groups worldwide, and their respective turnover between 2018 and 2022

Source: Global 50 Publishing Ranking, 2023.

Among those ten leading publishing corporations, well over half of all revenue has been generated by professional and STM publishers (scientific, technical, and medical), which also includes academic journals, while turnover from trade or consumer books accounts for less than one third.

Share of revenue in trade, STM and educational publishing

Publishing sector	% share
STM/Professional	54
Trade	31
Educational	15

In the decade between 2001 and 2010, a process of consolidation and restructuring, coinciding with the move from print to digital, and from selling individual publications to offering subscriptions for securing recurrent income to the publishers, had already reframed the segment of science, technical and medical (STM) publishing. This shift also started to transform the educational publishing sector, albeit only by the end of the following decade, and with an acceleration triggered by the COVID-19 pandemic of 2020. In the consumer book sector meanwhile, ebooks had been added as a new, digital publication format after Amazon's introduction of the Kindle platform in 2007. In most English language markets, ebooks from traditional publishers plateaued around 2013 with a share in revenues between 15 and 20 per cent. However, these numbers do not include the segment of self-publishing, which had been kicked off with the launch of the Kindle Direct Publishing model that accompanied e-reading devices.

The largest traditional consumer book corporations include Penguin Random House, owned by the German Bertelsmann media group, with a turnover of €4,223 m in 2022, the French Hachette group (which include strong book divisions in the USA and the UK) at €2,748 m, and the US company HarperCollins at US$2,191 m (€1,936 m). The Chinese Phoenix group, focusing on a mix of consumer and educational publications, reports revenues of 12,692 m RMB (€1,760 m).

The year 2023 was a watershed year for international consumer book publishing. In the USA, a bid by Penguin Random House to acquire the prestigious trade publisher Simon & Schuster was rejected by a court on competition concerns, resulting in the takeover of the publisher by the private equity group KKR in a $1,620 bn all-cash transaction. In France, there occurred the biggest and most dramatic shake-up in publishing ever between competing billionaires, each focused on gaining a dominant position in media. The cross-media corporation Vivendi, led by Vincent Bolloré, acquired the country's by far largest publishing group Hachette from Arnaud Lagardère after an epic battle which started in 2021, and resulted in a hostile takeover by Vivendi in 2023. Vivendi sold off Editis, the second-largest French publishing group, to Czech billionaire Daniel Křetínský, to avoid concerns from European competition authorities. Křetínský is also invested in the retail chain Fnac Darty, in numerous French magazines and in the daily *Le Monde*.

For the rapidly expanding sector of 'non-traditional' publishing platforms, no comparable financial figures are publicly available so far. However, according to various estimates, sales on a similar scale to the largest conventional publishing groups are achieved in diverse non-traditional publishing platforms. Yuewen, for instance, a publicly listed subsidiary of the Chinese media and entertainment giant Tencent, reports revenues of US$1 bn just from producing and disseminating 'online literature' and derivative narrative content in other formats such as animated movies.

Note: The Global 50 ranking is researched by the author, with annual updates published by international professional book trade publications, namely *Bookdao* (China), *The Bookseller* (UK), *Buchreport* (Germany), *Livres Hebdo* (France), and *Publishers' Weekly* (US). More at wischenbart.com

Consumer book publishers

The ownership of international consumer book publishing is dominated by
continental European publishers, mainly the French, German and Spanish, and by
a few US corporations. Today, two major publishers dominate: Penguin Random
House (PRH), owned by the German media company Bertelsmann (privately held
by the Mohn family and trusts); and Hachette Livre, owned by the French media
company Lagardère. The consumer book publishers derive most of their revenue
from the copy sale business model, selling books at low prices to very large
numbers of people. Publishers give most marketing and sales attention to their
important new books (*frontlist* titles), whilst significant sales revenue comes from
established titles – their *backlist*. The success of BookTok has brought backlist titles
back into prominence, sometimes to the surprise of their publishers.

Holtzbrinck (Germany), founded by Georg von Holtzbrinck, is family-owned
and active in over 80 countries. It publishes across the sectors of consumer,
education, STM and professional – and newspapers. Outside Germany, its
well-known English language imprints include the trade publishers Farrar, Straus
and Giroux in the USA and Pan Macmillan in the UK, Macmillan Education
and the academic publisher Palgrave Macmillan, and the major science brands
Springer Nature and *Scientific American*. Scholastic (US) is the world's largest
publisher and distributor of children's/young adult (YA) books, including via its
book clubs and book fairs based in schools.

Grupo Planeta (Spain) is the world's leading Spanish language book
publisher, operating in Spain, Portugal, France, and Latin America with more than
100 imprints. (The USA has many Spanish speakers but most read their books in
English.) The Italian publisher De Agostini also publishes part-works, trade and
educational books; Mondadori is the largest trade and education book publisher
in Italy, with a market share approaching 30 per cent in trade books. Bonnier
(Sweden) and Egmont (Denmark) are leading Scandinavian media companies
spanning trade books, magazines and new media products. Both are especially
strong in children's publishing and related products and services.

Small and medium-sized publishers

While the trend is towards larger publishers, there will always be room for
innovative and entrepreneurial small publishers that are more agile compared
to larger competitors overburdened with bureaucracy and complexity, or slow to
respond to fast-changing markets and technological developments. The larger the
giant publishers become, the more niches they leave open for smaller publishers
to exploit. Small publishers must work hard at choosing and marketing their titles
carefully, and at developing authors and books that endure on the backlist. Small
publishers run the risk of losing their successful authors to larger publishers yet
they often offer a more personal service to authors, who can receive less special
attention from the larger publishers.

A sign of a vigorous industry is the frequent start-up of new firms – compared
with many industries, publishing needs only a little equipment and a relatively
small amount of investment capital. The entry costs have become lower with the rise
of digital publishing and printing. Across all sectors, there are a number of serial

publishing entrepreneurs: individuals who create new publishers and sell out or move on repeatedly. A good example in the UK is Anthony Cheetham, who founded Century (1981), Orion (1992), Quercus (2004), and Head of Zeus (2012). Some of the small and medium-sized publishers grow at a much faster rate than larger companies. In comparison to the large corporate publishers, the smaller publishers are often far more open to discussing their innovations and sharing experiences.

The medium-sized publishers are arguably in a more difficult position because they have neither the scale and financial benefits of major publishers nor necessarily the agility and focus of smaller publishers. They are prime targets for takeovers by larger publishers provided they have valuable backlists which fit the objectives of the larger organization, and increasingly, if they possess digital publishing assets. These will include content and IP, and digital capital such as brand recognition and an established community of authors and readers. One of the fascinating aspects of publishing is that publishers do not need to be the size of Pearson, Elsevier, or Penguin Random House to be successful in the home market, to reach world export markets and to apply innovatory technology to expand sales and services.

CSR AND ESG

CSR or corporate social responsibility relates to whether an organization operates in a fair and ethical manner, and is essentially a framework developed to ensure the company is a good corporate citizen and is socially accountable to its stakeholders (Phillips and Bhaskar, 2019, page 149). ESG is more data-driven and offers criteria (environmental, social and governance factors)

by which external investors can view performance. Publishers are keen to be responsible global citizens and take action in support of the UN's Sustainable Development Goals (SDGs). The SDG Publishers Compact was launched in 2020 and has attracted support from many publishers. Publishers have set targets for becoming carbon neutral across not just their core activities (scope 1 and 2 emissions) but also their whole supply chains (scope 3 emissions). They are conscious of the need to diversify their talent pipelines for both employees and authors, and ensure their products appeal to all sections of society. In terms of what they publish, the Compact says that signatories 'have to actively promote and acquire content that advocates for themes represented by the SDGs, such as equality, sustainability, justice and safeguarding and strengthening the environment' (internationalpublishers.org, accessed 24 January 2024).

Industry targets are to halve greenhouse gas emissions by 2030, to attain net zero by 2050 at the latest and to reduce waste. Every part of the business is affected, and the environmental impact of book publishing has to be measured in terms of its carbon footprint and acted upon; or, if not in direct control of the publisher, offset to partner schemes which have a positive climate impact. Publishers source the paper for books directly, or indirectly via printers, from responsible sources (such as in Scandinavia or Canada). However, a newer focus has been on the paper manufacturing process itself which is energy-intensive and requires careful waste management.

The reduction of transport emissions and rationalizing supply chains form another important area of change. For example, publishers have had books printed in China, the stock of which is shipped to the UK warehouse and then shipped back to fulfil orders in Asia and elsewhere. The trend is now towards globally

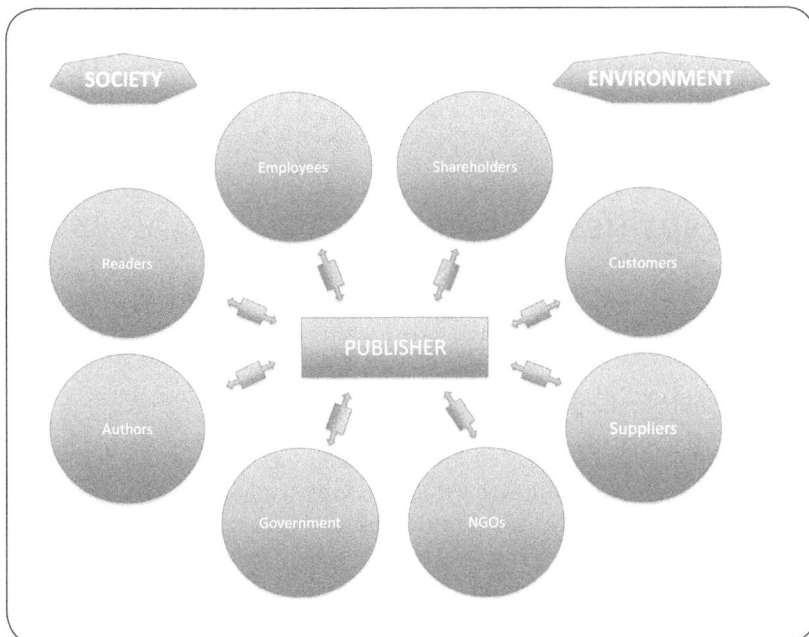

Map of the stakeholders of a publisher

distributed printing. Books are digitally printed in a country to fulfil local demand. Localized printing lowers the publisher's carbon impact by reducing inbound and outflow movements while offering speed to market.

Whilst academic publishers may not hold any stock at all, relying on print to order, consumer publishers aim to be more efficient in their operations, for example, using quick reprints. In the past, trade publishers were prone to over-production of books printed. The publisher's aim was to secure as much space as possible for their titles in bookshops and other retailers. In turn, the booksellers over-bought only to return unsold copies to the publisher. Such returns historically reached more than 20 per cent of books actually sold. Generally advance orders in the trade have reduced over time, and the booksellers have reduced the level of returns.

Additionally, there are ethical and social concerns to be taken account of in respect of planning a book's end of life. Publishers rid themselves of overstocks by pulping or selling to remainder dealers. Some of the attractive cover finishes make the recycling of cover board materials difficult. Books that cannot be recycled may end up in landfill.

In the area of DEI (diversity, equity and inclusion), publishers have set themselves targets around the composition of their workforces and their publishing programmes; they are also keen to build a more inclusive culture within their organizations. There are a set of broader questions around how publishing operates in its communities. Scholars in the Global South want to read content written by their own colleagues, rather than just from the main Western countries. The rise of reading in English in many countries has stimulated export sales from the USA and the UK, but is there a risk of domestic publishing industries being weakened? If AI programmes are being trained on Western, English language content, will their outputs sufficiently represent the world as a whole?

'Books can provoke change, but they can also provide escape and solace.' Leila Mottley

It is estimated that at least 87 m people in Europe are living with a disability. There are residual barriers for them to access books. The European Accessibility Act 2019 requires that publishers must make accessible versions of their ebooks available by June 2025; and e-readers must be available with a text-to-speech facility.

MAJOR BUSINESS TRENDS

There are a number of trends which affect the business of publishing around the world.

Tectonic shifts in the world economy

US and European publishers of all sizes are looking beyond their traditional and mature markets of North America and Europe to the faster-growing markets of the East and of the South. These countries have sizeable populations, are investing heavily in education and research, and have expanding middle classes – people who are interested in self-improvement and business books, international fiction and non-fiction, and children's books. In respect of geographical organization,

Women in Indian publishing

Nitasha Devasar, Managing Director and Commercial Lead, India, South Asia and Sub-Saharan Africa, Taylor & Francis Group

E★PERT

India is the third-largest English language market in the world and Indian publishing is a $8 bn industry with double-digit growth. Given the fact that 95 per cent is educational publishing, catering to over 55,000 higher education institutions and 41 m students, and with an internet penetration of 50 per cent, it is not difficult to understand its resilience and growth. The presence of women has always been palpable in the ranks of employees and increasingly at more senior levels, but despite rich anecdotal evidence, data remains sketchy.

Indian publishing, now in its seventy-seventh year, has its roots in family businesses that evolved from book distribution to publishing. These often passed from one generation of males to another. Alongside were the colonial and post-colonial entrants, international publishers attracted by the size and potential of the market. They have in recent years brought global DEI (diversity, equity and inclusion) practices to interact with local patriarchy. The rich landscape of independent publishers proliferating in the market has been dominated by women, from the earliest feminist publishing initiatives to the most recent children, tribal, Dalit, and alternative publishing start-ups. Clearly entrepreneurial spirit and business acumen are not an issue even though women seem to flock to the creative, publishing and design end of the industry spectrum. These are vital jobs that need measurement and recognition.

In the wider ecosystem, in 2022, there were more women authors than men globally but in India, non-fiction authorship (books available on Amazon India) continued to be dominated by men. Of the 100 bestsellers in 2023 across 13 categories, only 4 per cent were by Indian women. Not surprising then that 85 per cent of endorsements for non-fiction books were also by men. More widely, women on boards in listed Indian companies have grown thanks to laws mandating their presence. According to a 2022 EY report, the number has tripled in the last decade. Almost 95 per cent of NIFTY500 companies have one female board member, up from 69 per cent in 2017. The percentage for the media and entertainment sector (including publishing) was 23 per cent in 2022, up from 14 per cent in 2017. The growth though was skewed and uneven with a few companies exceeding mandates and, of course, India lags far behind Europe.

What we need is more metrics – objective measures of contributions and the presence of women in Indian publishing. How many books published in India were commissioned/written by women? How many became bestsellers, won accolades? What is their presence in senior management and boards? What is the gender pay gap? It is telling that no study on Indian publishing in the last five years has covered gender. What is measured can be acknowledged and enhanced. We need objective measures of collective impact and for women to be visible and vocal beyond individual success stories, pushing boundaries and using their articulate voices for building metrics and driving change.

Anglo/American publishers usually divide the world into vertical hemispheres: the Americas; Europe, Middle East and Africa (EMEA); and Asia. Meanwhile, Asian and Latin American publishers are growing and are looking to expand exports to the North and the West.

Globalization of publishing

The publishing industry used to be rather narrowly defined by geography and limited by language, by nation states and empires. From the nineteenth century, the British publishers published in English and exported books to a worldwide empire and to America (later setting up offices), the French publishers to their colonies in Africa and elsewhere, and the Spanish to Latin America. The large German publishing industry exported to neighbouring countries where German was spoken. Meanwhile US publishers benefited from a home market that became the world's richest and largest. In the postwar era, the USA dominated popular culture, science and technology, grew exports and became a major source of college textbooks that were sold to overseas markets or adapted. The UK, the USA, France and Spain are still the main exporters. UK publishers owned by US and continental European publishers are sometimes used to expand the parent's international English language reach, helping to make the UK one of the world centres of international publishing expertise.

While national and regional markets are still defined by language (less so in science and technology, where English is the world's language), the international publishers operate in many countries. They publish original books in the local language and may export a selection in one or more of the main transnational languages of English, Spanish and French; and they translate or adapt selected imported books, which they have originated and published elsewhere. Smaller publishers that do not own their own overseas companies are able to export by selling their books though networks of other companies and have them translated by other publishers. In addition, ebooks can now reach all parts of the world. There is a significant market opportunity for publishers with the growth of the English language and reading in English in many countries.

The globalization of the supply side of publishing means that books may be printed in China or Hong Kong, or printed for sale in local markets using distributed printing. The outsourcing of editorial, design and typesetting, for example, in academic publishing, may lead to publishers merely retaining a project management function at their headquarters. Parallel developments have been the rise of global booksellers (Amazon), distributors (Ingram) and aggregators (EBSCO and ProQuest).

Strategic concentration

Major publishers have progressively sold off publishing operations that do not fit with the main sectors in which they operate. The aim has been to be a major player in some sectors and markets, and to exit the other areas. From the 1980s,

Anglo/American managements especially concentrated on sectors. Since the turn of the century, most of the owners of the trade publishers have sold off their educational, academic, STM and professional publishing interests. The STM and professional publishers divested remnants of their trade book publishing operations which they saw as lower margin and higher risk businesses, or educational publishing units requiring significant scale and technological investment, or if in professional publishing, print publishing units which are not amenable to the development of digital services. There are examples of a counter-trend, such as the consumer book publisher Bloomsbury, which re-invested profits from the Harry Potter books into a series of acquisitions of academic and professional publishers.

Consolidation and scale

The scale of the largest publishers gives them economic advantages over smaller publishers: the benefit of spreading costs over a larger revenue base; the clout to purchase materials and services at lower cost; the employment of a greater number of publishing and technology specialists, along with the payment of top salaries to attract the best people; and greater visibility in the worldwide market place. In the related media industries, the digital era is aiding the concentration of market dominance by a few companies.

The major publishers have raised their market share in their chosen sectors through organic growth and by acquiring or merging with similar publishing companies, or those serving adjacent markets or new geographies. They may also acquire technology companies or start-ups which are disruptive of their business models. For example, in 2008, Springer bought the publisher BioMed Central which at that time was pioneering open access. They like to search for companies which add value (including those providing related services), can be easily absorbed, and do not create or introduce undue risk. They try to avoid companies that are over-priced, passing peak value, or which are not conducive to digital publishing and exploitation. In each Western market sector, three to four major publishers have come to dominate and together may account for more than half of a market sector's revenue, with the leader accounting for around one-quarter or more.

Collaboration

In a fast-changing business environment, impacted by technology, there is a greater need for publishers to collaborate with other firms, even if they are competitors. Experimentation in new areas forges partnerships, for example, a publisher collaborates with a software developer or games company to produce new products. The importance of scale in the aggregation of content encourages publishers to form alliances with other publishers to strengthen their marketing and sales in existing or new markets, or those overseas. The cost of developing new technologies and software prompts publishers and partners to share costs, for example, in the development of platforms or machine learning. The challenges facing educational and professional organizations, and the publishers serving them, forge partnerships between them. Common goals to improve the user experience (UX), such as enabling an ebook to be portable across platforms and readable on different devices, or a researcher to hyperlink to citations in an article, drive publishers to support the development of universal standards. The third party infringers of IP, unauthorized copying and changes in copyright law in respect of digital content, necessitate the sharing of information among publishers to reduce such risks and their support of organizations that defend IP rights globally.

Government intervention

Publishing is affected by public policy in a number of different ways. Across the world national governments interfere in the freedoms of authors and publishers, from China to Iran and Turkey. Books are confiscated and destroyed, writers and publishers investigated and intimidated, and some end up in prison. This is perhaps no surprise to many, but there also cries of censorship in the school system in the USA. In the 2022–2023 school year, PEN America recorded 3,362 examples of book bans in public school classrooms and libraries:

> Authors whose books are targeted are most frequently female, people of color, and/or LGBTQ+ individuals. Amid a growing climate of censorship, school book bans continue to spread through coordinated campaigns by a vocal minority of groups and individual actors and, increasingly, as a result of pressure from state legislation. (Pen America, 2023)

'Reading fiction is important. It is a vital means of imagining a life other than our own, which in turn makes us more empathetic beings.' Ann Patchett

One of the International Publishers Association's (IPA) primary objectives is to fight censorship and to safeguard the fundamental freedom of expression, freedom to publish and freedom to access information. There are also challenges to copyright, sometimes promoted by technology companies or educational activists. The decision of policy-makers that the publication of research should be freely available under open access mandates affects the publishing ecosystem. The rise of personal data privacy laws, especially in the EU, affects publishers' operations, not just in relation to online marketing but also regarding the use of online student reading data to aid learning, for example.

DIGITIZATION OF PUBLISHING

Digitization is the mega trend of the age and affects every aspect of the publishing process from authors to readers. Book and journal publishers have largely remained viable whilst investing in the digital transformation of their businesses. The penetration of the digital varies by sector of publishing but the global pandemic of COVID-19, which began in 2020, accelerated the need for digital content for education. The closure of bookstores encouraged consumer sales of ebooks and audiobooks, and, in turn, their reopening led to many readers returning to print.

The professional reference and STM publishers realized early on the threats and potential opportunities of digital publishing. From around the mid-1990s onwards, the STM publishers applied digital methods to the peer review process and to the production of journal articles, and made their printed journal content available online to researchers, via libraries, in PDF format. From around 2006, the main consumer book publishers began to digitize their new books and selected backlist books.

The death of the printed book has been announced each time a new format has gained prominence, and the industry has seen repeated convulsive episodes with the arrival of CD-ROMs, ebooks and apps. But the demise of print is not expected in the foreseeable future as purchasers still appreciate the appearance, collectability, usability and permanence of the physical object. The cyberattack on the British Library in 2023, which took down many of its services, brought into relief the risks around relying purely on digital preservation of content. One observer commented that 'the only silver lining of the attack was that students and researchers were having to reacquaint themselves with printed catalogues and the experience of finding a book on a shelf' (*New Yorker*, 19 December 2023).

Reading devices, ecosystems and walled gardens

In the late 1990s, dedicated ebook reading devices came on to the market though ebook sales were limited to enthusiasts. The launch of Amazon's Kindle in the USA in 2007, and subsequently in the UK and elsewhere in 2010 had a dramatic impact on the public's purchase of ebooks. In order to forestall the widespread piracy which had bedevilled the slow-moving music industry, the publishers moved quickly in supplying their books to Amazon. Amazon is credited with creating the first ecosystem that encouraged people to buy publishers' ebooks easily and legally.

Apple launched the iPad in the USA in 2010 along with its iBookstore for purchasing ebooks. This led to an explosive growth in the purchase by consumers of tablet computers with the connectivity to consume all kinds of media. The increased availability of the new reading devices, linked to compelling websites for ease of purchase, drove ebook demand. The sharp rise in the use of mobile phones or smartphones on which people read books continues worldwide.

Lying behind the impact of the reading devices on ebook uptake are the very different business models of the technology firms. Amazon is primarily a retailer of products and services, intent on increasing the value of the user's shopping basket. It develops software and sells hardware at cost. Apple, by contrast, is primarily a hardware firm, that requires content to help sell its high margin products. Other companies, such as Sony and Kobo, developed reading devices with ebook stores. The business model of Google and Facebook are based primarily on attracting advertising revenue deriving from the search technologies of the former and the social network of the latter. It is in Google's interests for content to be kept outside paywalls and to be freely searchable.

During this brief period of technological change, the importance of an entire proprietary ecosystem with a social component has emerged. In this respect,

Amazon and Apple stand out. Both have developed *walled gardens* of content and services. Their customers benefit from the ease of remaining within their favoured system but the proprietary software locks them into the system in various ways. The printed book, in contrast, has a universally available and non-proprietary operating system.

Disruption

The invention of the web and more recently the trend to mobiles are often described as 'disruptive technologies', a term devised by Clayton Christensen in 1997, who subsequently preferred 'disruptive innovations'. Such innovations do not just disrupt the business models of technology firms but those engaged in the publishing business, along with many others. Christensen also developed the theory of 'disruptive competitors' – those firms which start by selling inferior goods at low margins in areas ignored by incumbents operating on high margins, but which move up the value chain to eventually challenge and possibly replace the incumbents.

The main disruptors in the world of publishing are the big tech companies – Amazon, Apple and Google. Amazon is arguably more of a disrupter than Apple and Google because for many publishers it controls the main retail channel to consumers. Amazon started in 1995 as a mail-order discount bookseller, a direct to consumer (D2C) business. At that time, mail-order bookselling was generally seen as a low margin if not loss-making area of business and was ignored by large incumbents. Through the application of innovatory technology and its diversification into other products beyond books, Amazon overtook the US chain Barnes & Noble and expanded internationally. It provided a self-publishing service to authors most of whom would not receive a contract from a traditional publisher; and installed digital printing technology to manufacture books.

Amazon rapidly became the leading online retailer of printed books through a focus on excellent customer service and a long-term strategy to gain market share. Amazon wields considerable power in the book market and over 50 per cent of print sales, both in the UK and the USA, are now online. In previous eras, the publishers have faced similar concentration and buying power from bricks-and-mortar retailers. Paradoxically, the smaller publishers, who rarely negotiate directly with Amazon, have a direct route to market and benefit from a more level playing field compared to the high street, where shelf space is limited.

In the context of audio, Amazon made some far-sighted purchases. In 1985 it purchased the audiobook publisher Brilliance Audio, which through technical innovation is credited with revolutionizing the burgeoning US audiobook market in the mid-1980s since it made unabridged books affordable. The 2008 purchase of Audible drove audiobook sales, making it the western world's largest seller of audiobooks, and through Audible Studios the largest producer.

In addition to founding the ebook market, many of Amazon's earlier bookselling innovations, such as the sales ranking of titles (1998), personalized book recommendations (1999), and Look Inside the Book (2001) have aided publishers' sales of new and backlist books, in home and export markets. Disruptive initiatives included Amazon Marketplace (2002), the launch of the self-publishing platform Kindle Direct Publishing (2007), and the purchase of AbeBooks (an online used book market) in 2008 and of the UK competitor Book Depository (2011).

Amazon's greatest disruption was its impact on bricks-and-mortar bookselling. During the last decades of the twentieth century and into the first decade of the twenty-first, most physical retailers (including the bookselling chains in the USA and the UK) spent their resources investing in new and ever larger stores with more staff, in expensive real-estate locations with high foot-traffic. However large their stores were, the shelf-space to display titles was limited. Amazon, in contrast, did not invest in high cost real-estate but in technology. It had no limits on the number of titles it could display on its website. Provided it could sign up the supplying publishers, the inventory of titles on its website was limitless. Another key advantage, lost on other retailers of the time, is that retailing is about enticing and retaining customers, but also about collecting data on those customers in order to sell them more products and services.

The online retailers offered convenience, speed of delivery, discounted prices and greater title availability. Internet selling aided the smaller specialist publishers since physical booksellers did not stock their titles. It gave them greater reach into export markets. The overall book market widened and deepened. During the long recession in Western markets and subsequently, the online booksellers (predominantly Amazon) increased their market share against the physical stores. There are several reasons for the decline in physical bookselling but among the chief ones are the ease of online ordering and delivery of printed books; the use of smartphones in store to check comparative prices (showrooming); and the growth in the purchase of ebooks, especially in some fiction genres, including self-published titles. The decline of book display and sales also occurred in other stores such as supermarkets, which had previously stocked books as a sideline.

The business model of consumer publishers traditionally relied on their ability to sell and distribute large quantities of printed books to physical retailers. The retail exposure fosters the discovery of books, encourages impulse purchases, aids the launch of new writers and provides a venue for Christmas gift buying. As the physical consumer book retail market is disrupted and reduced, the business model of consumer book publishers is being disrupted and potentially weakened. The key challenge is to aid discoverability of both frontlist and backlist.

For decades the educational, STM and professional publishers have supplied their products directly to end-user organizations, cutting out suppliers, and increasingly do so via their own platforms, though various kinds of intermediaries still exist. The word 'disruption' is overly used in the technological context. But the impact on business models is of equal significance. For instance, in the 1990s, the journal publishers introduced electronic journals which enabled the publishers to sell large bundles of journal titles to libraries rather than individual titles in print; and subsequently to charge funders to make researchers' articles freely available under open access. In contrast, higher education textbook rental companies in the USA (e.g. Chegg, launched in 2007) lowered the cost to students, thereby adversely affecting the publishers' retail sales of new printed books. There is now interest in inclusive access models whereby students access textbooks through payment of a course fee, benefiting from a discount through bulk purchasing.

Disintermediation

The internet lowers transaction costs in the supply chain, for instance, the cost a publisher incurs when handling orders from booksellers, which once were handwritten and which are now processed electronically with fewer people. Moreover, the Internet offers the potential for *disintermediation*, the removal of entire businesses in the supply chain from author to reader. Many specialist intermediaries punctuate the linear supply chain. All of them, such as authors' agents, publishers, printers, wholesalers and booksellers, add costs and profit to their activities. The internet and other digital technologies revolutionize the ways in which books are produced and sold. Books can be published faster and cheaper. Some publishers initially feared the rapid growth of self-publishing might lead to their demise. Large publishers opened their own self-publishing units while others bought self-publishing companies. Penguin bought Author Solutions in 2012 but it was subsequently sold in 2016 by Penguin Random House.

All parts of the traditional supply chain are under pressure: each is prone to disintermediation. There are many examples. Authors self-publish stories and cut out agents and publishers. Librarians act as university publishers. Printers may supply customers direct; wholesalers may act as printers. Publishers cut out wholesalers and retailers. And online retailers act as publishers, printers, aggregators and libraries, thereby attempting to disintermediate everyone in order to create a total vertical business from author to reader. For example, Amazon has its own publishing operations in fiction, non-fiction and children's books, alongside a world literature imprint, Amazon Crossing. Could authors be replaced? Already some newspaper content is automatically generated and the mainstreaming of AI has seen the proliferation of new titles using the technology. In 2023, Amazon introduced a rule 'limiting the number of books that authors can self-publish on its site to three a day, after an influx of suspected AI-generated material was listed for sale in recent months' (*Guardian*, 20 September 2023).

Scarcity and abundance

Before the digital age, books were scarce and costly to reproduce. There was a scarcity of publishers that had the resources to produce, print and distribute them. The publishers were the gatekeepers that made books available to readers. The booksellers were the gatekeepers of the retail channel to market; guarding the shelf space on which books were displayed and sold to readers. Libraries were the gatekeepers through their selection of titles, as they had limits of funding and of shelf space to store books for reference and lending. Scarcity helped the publishers to control pricing.

The coming of the web broke down over time the barriers to the scarcity of content and information, and abundance emerged. The connectivity afforded by the internet has given rise to a range of free-to-end-user business models that are used by businesses and organizations outside the publishing industry. Free sources of information, such as Wikipedia, eroded the sales of printed reference titles; and sites with user-generated content, such as TripAdvisor, challenged the publishers of printed travel guides. Amazon and others facilitated the resale of used books and enabled the growth of self-publishing. Classic books that were out of

UNESCO Cities of Literature include Angoulême, Kozhikode, Montevideo and Nanjing copyright (in the public domain) were digitized and made freely available. Piracy of in-copyright titles is a growing problem though far less prevalent than in the film and music industries. Freemium selling, whereby readers can sample the content before purchase, is a variant of the user-free model. Amazon's Look Inside the book and Google search have opened up the contents of books to readers that helps publishers sell to global audiences. As Mike Shatzkin notes, in 1990, there were around a half a million English language titles in print. Today Ingram holds 20 m titles in its print on-demand database which amounts to a forty-fold title increase over the period. Publishers have long since lost their moat around the launch of new books and face a multitude of competitors (idealog.com, accessed 11 April 2024).

There is also a philosophical shift around how content is created and appraised. Rather than rely on a few gatekeepers to assess the value of content, why not put it up for everyone to see, review, and offer their reaction? This shift is reflected in the huge growth in user-generated content and extends to the peer review of papers in some academic journals post publication.

In a world of abundance, agents and publishers offer a vital service in selecting authors and developing their content to meet readers' needs. They manage the authors' brands and focus readers on the books they have selected. That service is worth paying for when time is scarce. To attempt another definition, the publishing process may be described as managing the scarcity of good authors and content to drive profitability.

'The part of the mind that reads a story is also the part that reads the world.' George Saunders

Communities and connectivity

Publishers have always published books for people sharing common interests, termed vertical communities. The non-consumer publishers have the advantage over the consumer publishers in that the places and objectives of work or study define communities of interest. The internet and the development of social media have fostered the development of vertical communities, and the connectivity between readers, authors and publishers. The increase in vertical connectivity affects every aspect of the publishing business, whatever its size. Furthermore, strength in a vertical community offers the opportunity to provide new product types and related services. This is strongly market-focused and derives scale from selling different types of product to the same customer base.

In most markets with digital services as products (mobile data, film, TV and music) that are distributed at near zero marginal cost, the trend is for consumers to change from the purchase of digital goods to accessing them via subscriptions or renting. This major trend is occurring in publishing, especially in the areas of audiobooks, higher education and among publishers serving vertical communities.

Aggregation and curation

The *aggregation* of content is the assembly of different objects from different sources to form a whole. In the publishing world, the largest aggregators are the online booksellers, wholesalers and library suppliers, and technology companies, such as Google. The larger the amount of content they gather, the greater the benefit they offer to their customers, the greater amount of customer data they collect, and the greater their commercial prospects. Amazon is the premier aggregator in the world of books and dominates the consumer market in many parts of the world. Publishers too benefit from the aggregation of content, for example, in the area of journals and databases – one important reason behind their merger and acquisition activity.

The term *curation* (borrowed from the museum world) is the appraisal and selection of content. Mike Shatzkin writes about the connection between curation and aggregation:

> The concept [of curation] in the digital content world means the selection and presentation of these disparate items to help a browser or consumer navigate and select from them. Aggregation without curation is, normally, not very helpful. Curation creates the brand. (idealog.com, accessed 22 March 2024)

A number of players in the value chain carry out curating activities. Authors' agents act as gatekeepers and curators of the authors they represent. They curate the projects of their authors for submission to selected editors at publishing houses. Authors too may be described as curating publishers in that they appraise and select the publishers to whom they submit their ideas and projects. They want publication in an aggregation of similar books, such as an imprint, or, if a research scientist, in the most prestigious journal in their field – journals are curated, peer-reviewed and branded aggregations. In turn, the editors curate authors and projects through their decision to publish a very small number from a large number of projects submitted. Agents and publishers sort the wheat from the chaff. The publishers curate projects and then publish, whereas the practice on the internet is to publish first and curate afterwards.

The aggregation of published book titles forms the publisher's imprint (a list of books within a publisher's overall publishing programme). Publishers pay great attention to building trusted brands in the minds of consumers, both of authors and imprints. The curation of projects to fit the objectives and personality of the imprint creates the brand. Michael Bhaskar comments:

> Publishing is messy. Chance plays an outsized role. Every aspect of list-building represents an over-determination of factors. Company hierarchy, personal taste, the backlist and trajectory of the firm, individual aspiration, tradition, finances ... all tie together in an intricate knot that is ultimately impossible to unpick. (Phillips and Bhaskar, 2019, page 233)

'Reading is important. If you know how to read, then the whole world opens up to you.' Barack Obama

The booksellers are of course both aggregators and curators. Physical stores curate titles by displaying them on shelves devoted to subject categories or by placing bestsellers in the window or on tables at the front of the shop. The online booksellers use the metadata (data about data, e.g. book title, author, cover, description) supplied by the publishers to place books in subject classifications or to populate the algorithms which create recommendations for consumers.

Finally, readers are curating content on the web, and a good example is Maria Popova with her blog *The Marginalian* – 'a record of [her] reading and reckoning with our search for meaning: sometimes through science and philosophy, sometimes through poetry and children's books, always through the lens of wonder' (themarginalian.org, accessed 24 January 2024).

Granularity and personalization

The container of the printed edition of the book or journal fixes its content and presentation. The economics of print production necessitate boundaries on length: short books or very long books are problematic and uneconomic to publish. Digital publishing reduces or removes such boundaries. Additionally, it gives the opportunity for users to download a single chapter or article – the container is chunked at the granular level. The publisher is able to offer users the ability to personalize content for themselves or, if a teacher, to customize resources for students.

There are broader issues connected with the granularization of content – how easily can the rights be licensed in a piece of IP (say, an image or extended piece of text), when the value of the transaction may be quite low? The system of digital object identifier (DOI) – common in journal publishing – has not yet reached the rest of publishing.

The application of data analytics technology and the development of machine learning (or AI) when applied to users interacting with online content enable publishers to curate custom solutions for them. Examples are adaptive learning programs or platforms, and the research tools developed for researchers, medical practitioners and lawyers. Related to these is the growing use of big data to understand the behaviour of users.

Digital printing

Digital printing is a transformative technology that developed at the turn of the century and which was pioneered by Lightning Source, owned by the US wholesaler Ingram. Books have traditionally been printed on offset litho presses, which require print runs of at least 500 copies. A publisher, in advance of publication of a new book, estimates the quantity that could be sold in, say, one year, and places the order with the printer. The printed copies are stored in the publisher's warehouse and dispatched over time to fulfil customers' orders. The publisher ties up its cash in the stock, which may not sell or be damaged, and pays for storage. Digital printing, by contrast, enables the production of just one copy and that copy can be printed after the customer order has been received: pure print on demand (POD). Digital printing also enables economic short print runs of, say, 10–500 copies. Formerly, backlist titles selling only small quantities went out of print and became unavailable because the publisher could not afford to reprint them using litho presses. As digital printing improves in cost-effectiveness and quality in comparison with litho and storage costs, the trend is from long litho print runs to short digital runs and POD. The quality and economies of digital colour printing are also improving.

THE FUTURE

Every aspect of the publishing process is changing. Publishers are finding authors in new ways and are responding directly to the market trends developing on social media. They are developing streamlined digital workflows that enable the work to be published in a variety of formats. Content management systems are used to hold the publisher's IP in codified and retrievable form. The abundance of content on the internet makes it progressively difficult to capture readers' attention. The publisher's signal has to rise above the noise. People discover or come across books in many ways, and their behaviour is constantly changing. The influence of book reviews in the traditional media has been in decline. Retail shelf space devoted to books remains important for discovering consumer books and new writers through browsing. Word-of-mouth recommendations among readers remain as important as ever.

Digital marketing offers the publisher new routes to interact with consumers and to make books visible within search and communities. Social media and the success of BookTok in particular are bringing new audiences to books. Authors too are adapting by building an online profile through their own website and social media presence – today a key factor in winning a book deal. There are dramatic changes in some publishing markets, for example, in China: 'Online sales now account for 84% of all book sales and social media bookselling in the form of short videos has revolutionized publishing in China' (*Publishers Weekly*, 20 April 2023).

Metadata helps computers and readers discover books and content in the online environment. Data analytics informs publishing decisions: real-time sales data and engagement levels on social help the analysis of the effectiveness of marketing; data about readers guides the creation of new content and the way publishers interact with users across the whole value chain.

The velocity of change affects every aspect of the publishing process. Former methods of working become uneconomic, ineffectual or redundant. Flexibility is key. Enduring business models that were once profitable begin to fade. Constant experimentation forms an important part in navigating successfully the transition from print to digital publishing. Business models may vary from giving content away free to encourage subscriptions, to pricing ebooks cheaply to attract new audiences, to bundling content together into a service.

The move from simply the creation and sale of products to the provision of services and solutions is apparent across all publishing sectors. Many of the services related to content are designed to make it more useful, personal and valuable to users. Services supplied to authors help them publish and build their brand. Services supplied to teachers help their professional development and teaching through using the publisher's content. Online assessment services provided to students aid their learning outcomes. Tools supplied to researchers and professionals improve the speed of searching for relevant content, and aid their productivity and competitiveness. In some areas, the addition of services to the core business of publishing content is a way of occupying more of the value chain to gain new sources of revenue. All such services are examples of investment in developing the value of online vertical communities.

Publishers have seen increases in the staff categories engaged in digital production, marketing and selling, along with investment in technology, digital distribution and services. AI tools will be accessed in many areas of the business, such as in the creation of marketing copy and its adaptation to different purposes. The formerly distinct activities of editorial, production, marketing and sales are overlapping, and merging into new job roles. Disruption and opportunity occur not only in the external environment but on a constant basis within the organization. It is essential for publishers to alter their mind-set to focus more clearly on the end-user and how they would like to interact with the product or service, whether they are reading for pleasure, teaching a class, or consulting must-have information. One of the key success factors for all organizations is to be able to manage change successfully.

AI (artificial intelligence) is set to revolutionize and disrupt many industries and professions: 'AI has been climbing the ladder of cognitive abilities for decades, and it now looks set to reach human-level performance across a very wide range of tasks within the next three years' (Suleyman and Bhaskar, 2023, page 9). We cannot be sure of the implications for publishing but there are already books written by AI, and we can imagine content created for individual need alongside highly targeted marketing. Workflows will be reimagined and companies are planning for efficiency gains. The copyright environment is being challenged and new policies are required from national governments and through international agreement. What sets publishers apart from the social media channels is that they take responsibility for their content and strive to ensure its high quality and authenticity. The arrival of AI and the consequent availability of fake and unvalidated content highlight the opening for publishers to stress their brand values; just as the growth of user-generated content on the web was an earlier opportunity.

Now read this

Angus Phillips and Michael Bhaskar (eds), *The Oxford Handbook of Publishing*, Oxford University Press, 2019.

Sources

Naomi Baron, *How We Read Now*, Oxford University Press, 2021.
Michael Bhaskar, *The Content Machine: Towards a theory of publishing from the printing press to the digital network*, Anthem Press, 2013.
Michael Bhaskar, *Curation: The power of selection in a world of excess*, Piatkus, 2016.
Richard Charkin, *My Back Pages*, Marble Hills, 2023.
Clayton M. Christensen, *The Innovator's Dilemma: When new technologies cause great firms to fail*, Harvard Business School Press, 1997.
PEN America, *Banned in the USA: The mounting pressure to censor*, 2023.
Angus Phillips and Miha Kovač, *Is This a Book?*, Cambridge University Press, 2022.
George Saunders, *A Swim in a Pond in the Rain*, Bloomsbury, 2021.
Brad Stone, *The Everything Store: Jeff Bezos and the age of Amazon*, Little Brown, 2013.
Mustafa Suleyman and Michael Bhaskar, *The Coming Wave*, Bodley Head, 2023.

Web resources

https://www.digitalbookworld.com Digital Book World (USA).
https://www.thebookseller.com/futurebook Blog from *The Bookseller* (UK).
www.idealog.com Blog from Mike Shatzkin.
https://internationalpublishers.org International Publishers Association.
https://sdg.internationalpublishers.org/cop26-accelerator/ The Publishing
    2030 Accelerator has three workstreams: calculating the carbon footprint
    of an individual book, distributed printing, and reimagining the
    accounting of revenues.
https://scholarlykitchen.sspnet.org Blog of the Society for Scholarly
    Publishing.

CHAPTER 1

The development of modern trade publishing

This chapter gives an overview of the development of modern trade publishing in the UK. Broad themes include the vertical integration of the hardback and paperback publishing houses, an increase in scale through merger and acquisition, the democratization of authorship, and the growth of digital sales. Running alongside is the change in culture from a product-led to a market-led business, and the need to diversify the talent pool for both authors and publishing staff to match the composition of society as a whole.

STABILITY AND EXPANSION

In the 1950s, book publishing was broadly based with around 50 medium-sized UK firms each employing around 50 staff and issuing several hundred titles per year, usually in hardback. The publishers were privately owned, usually by family members who held a majority share. They concentrated on fiction and non-fiction – termed 'general' or 'trade' or, more recently, 'consumer books' – although they also developed educational and academic lists alongside the general imprints.

The 1960s brought great optimism as in other cultural industries such as music and fashion. Rayner Unwin (1925–2000) of George Allen & Unwin talked of the 'informal, almost casual, publishing that was still possible during the sixties' (Unwin, 1999, page 238). For example, work on the travel writer Eric Newby's book, *Grain Race* (1968), took place in Unwin's flat in the evenings. Censorship was dealt a blow with the publication of the unexpurgated version of D. H. Lawrence's *Lady Chatterley's Lover* on 10 November 1960 – a victory for Penguin, which had won the right to publish the previously banned novel against a charge that it was obscene. The first print run of 200,000 sold out on the first day and within a month Penguin had sold 2 m copies. 'The trial was a turning-point, and after it was over previously forbidden works like *The Ginger Man* and *The Kama Sutra* were finally published in this country' (Lewis, 2005, page 333).

Throughout the 1960s and 1970s, apart from during the recession of the early to mid-1970s, much of the publishers' fast-growing prosperity was based on readers' affluence and increasing public expenditure (Table 1.1). Sales of hardback adult and children's books were underpinned by generous government funding of schools and libraries. Mass-market paperback publishing grew substantially and was carried

The prosecutor in the *Lady Chatterley's Lover* trial asked the jury: 'Is it a book that you would even wish your wife or servants to read?'

DOI: 10.4324/9781003403289-2

Table 1.1 Number of titles published in the UK from 1950 to 1980

Year	Number of titles and new editions
1950	17,072
1960	23,783
1970	33,489
1980	48,158

Source: Norrie (1982), page 220.

out by separate firms. In the main they acquired reprint paperback rights from the houses that originated titles in hardback. Literary agents, who increasingly began to represent the interests of fiction and non-fiction authors, were resented by some traditional publishers, who saw them as unwarranted intruders into the publisher–author relationship. New publishers arose producing highly-illustrated non-fiction books in full colour at low and affordable prices – viewed by traditionalists as 'down-market'. Paul Hamlyn (1926–2001), the greatest exponent of affordable illustrated books, made a series of fortunes from illustrated book publishing.

The publication of *The Reader's Digest Great World Atlas* (1961), which had double-page spreads displaying superb full-colour graphics, and extended captions not unlike those found in magazines, and the *Treasures of Tutankhamun*, tied-in to the British Museum exhibition (1972), were inspirational to some embryonic book packagers. They went on to produce highly illustrated full-colour information books which they presold to publishers around the world to be marketed and distributed under the publishers' imprints. In the late 1970s, the highly illustrated publishers brought colour books into the supermarkets by producing own brand books for them at very low prices.

By the end of the 1970s, the era of the 'gentleman publisher' was fast disappearing. The phrase had been used to describe grand publishers of literary fiction, typically derided as gentlemen who ran their companies by the seat of their pants, who adopted a paternalist management style, or who, according to some literary agents, exhibited ungentlemanly behaviour in their contractual arrangements with authors. Some of the foremost publishers, who had personally built great publishing companies, had reached the end of their careers. Some of their descendants, given senior management positions, were either incompetent or ill prepared for the changes to come.

The stable and expansionary publishing world of the 1960s and 1970s was rudely shattered by the recession of 1980 which forced publishers to cut their lists and overheads – making redundant both older staff and the weaker staff sucked in during the era of fast growth. Reductions in public funding adversely affected the publishing and availability of some kinds of books, including hardback fiction destined for public libraries and children's books supported by school libraries.

MERGERS AND ACQUISITIONS

The rise of European publishers through their purchase of US publishing began in the 1970s. The UK banking, investment and publishing group Pearson, owner of the *Financial Times*, bought the UK publisher Penguin in 1970, and the New York-based Viking Press in 1975. The German media group Bertelsmann broke out of Europe through the purchase of the US publishers Bantam Books in 1980, Doubleday in 1986, and Random House in 1998. By 2013, Penguin had merged with Random House to create the world's largest consumer book publisher (Penguin Random House) with its headquarters in New York. In 2017, Pearson sold part of its stake in the company to Bertelsmann to make a 25:75 ownership split; and, in 2020, Bertelsmann increased its stake to 100 per cent, ending the British ownership of any of the so-called 'Big Five' English language book publishers.

In the UK, the 1980s were an important period of mergers and acquisitions that restructured the publishing industry and saw, as in the USA, its ownership largely transferred overseas. Three large international publishing groups eventually came to control a large part of the UK home market; long-established, medium-sized British-owned firms were to become a rarity. The deregulation of financial markets led to the increased availability of equity and debt financing, allowing the large players to take over medium-sized publishers, and small publishers to expand or start in business. Book publishing was attractive to investors who could see that the industry had consistently, that is until 1987, returned pre-tax profits and return on capital above the average level of all industries. News International, having acquired the US publisher Harper & Row, took control of the UK publisher Collins in 1988 and created HarperCollins. Random House, at the time in American ownership, bought Cape, Chatto, Virago and Bodley Head in 1987, Century Hutchinson in 1989, and subsequently Secker & Warburg and Heinemann before it itself was purchased by Bertelsmann in 1998. Around that time the German Holtzbrinck media company acquired Macmillan. From 2004 to 2006, Hachette (owned by the French media corporation Lagardère) purchased the UK trade publishers of Hodder Headline, Orion and John Murray; and the US trade publishers owned by Times Warner which included Little, Brown and the paperback publisher Grand Central Publishing. The century's second decade was marked by further significant acquisitions. In 2014, News Corp bought the romance publisher Harlequin (including Mills and Boon) which became a subsidiary of HarperCollins. Hachette bought publishers including Perseus in 2016 and Bookouture in 2017. In 2021, US publishing consolidated further: HarperCollins completed its purchase of the Houghton Mifflin Harcourt trade group and Hachette Livre bought the Workman Publishing Company.

The purchase of US publishers gave the continental European publishers access to the world's largest and richest nation and the ability to grow quickly their dominant market share of English language book publishing worldwide. The steady earnings growth derived from book publishing in US and UK markets is attractive to mainland European publishers, some with a strong history of family ownership; in France and Germany companies have historically been less exposed to the vagaries of the stock market and activist shareholders.

The major publishers are driving the globalization of publishing. Hitherto the publishers catered principally for Anglophone countries and benefited from the growing use of English worldwide. Now they are extending into countries where English is the second or even third language through publishing local authors and translation. For example, Penguin Random House (PRH) is active in more than 20 countries.

Founded in 1929, Faber & Faber remains an independent publishing house. William Golding's *Lord of the Flies* was published by Faber in 1954

VERTICAL INTEGRATION

The restructuring of UK book publishing in the 1980s affected all types of publishing but its effects were most dramatic in consumer publishing. Ownership was traditionally divided between the hardback publishers and around a dozen separate mass-market paperback houses. In 1969 the top paperback houses included Penguin, Pan, Fontana, Corgi and Panther.

The publishing strategy was to establish a book in hardback at a high price and subsequently to reissue it, around a year later, in a paperback format at a lower price to a wider audience. Mass-market paperbacks were fast-moving books published in monthly batches, with each month headed by lead fiction and non-fiction titles, with various genre category titles forming the remainder. Paperbacks were published in A format – 'pocket' or 'rack-sized' books. Printed in large quantities on cheap paper, they reached a wider retail market beyond bookshops and were sold in a way more similar to that of magazines, mainly through merchandising wholesalers which stacked the racks in outlets at monthly intervals.

The respective character of hardback and paperback publishers was very different. The hardback publishers inhabited their fine but slowly decaying Georgian houses in Bloomsbury, around Bedford Square, and in other high-class central London locations. The mass-market paperback reprinters occupied office blocks in cheaper London locations. Theirs was a sales driven operation.

When Tom Maschler decided to pursue a career in publishing in the 1950s, he went to see André Deutsch (1917–2000), who was to publish in hardback some of the most important names in post-war fiction, including John Updike, V. S. Naipaul, and Philip Roth. When Deutsch told him that he had no openings, Maschler responded that the salary was not important. 'At that he asked when I could start. We settled for the following Monday' (2005, page 39). The editors were very much in control and women were in the majority in the publishing workforce. Diana Athill, who also worked with André Deutsch, writes in her memoir *Stet*: 'All publishing was run by many badly-paid women and a few much better-paid men: an imbalance that women were, of course, aware of, but which they seemed to take for granted' (2000, page 56). The production staff, who hired the printers to produce the books, and the marketing and sales staff were crammed in smaller offices in the basement and the attics.

Stet (2000) by Diana Athill is a memoir of her fifty years in publishing

The hardback publishers played their traditional role of nurturing new writing talent and working closely with authors on manuscripts. Their backlists were complete with great and loyal authors, and some enduring money-spinning books. Their formidable reputation ensured that new books were reviewed (literary editors ignored paperbacks), that the public librarians would automatically order sufficient quantities, and that the compliant independent booksellers would display and stock their titles. However, by the early to mid-1980s, hardback publishers found themselves making hardly any profit from selling copies themselves. They derived their profit and laid off risks by making rights and co-edition sales to others: to paperback publishers, book clubs, US publishers and foreign language publishers. While the hardback publishers employed highly talented editors, they also had editors who favoured their pet projects and authors who produced books which few wanted to buy.

The false dichotomy between hardback and paperback publishing could not survive. The book market was rapidly changing, readers' expectations were altering, competition between publishers to secure bestselling authors was intensifying and literary agents were far more adept in extracting maximum advance payments for their authors from publishers. Bookshops had steadily increased the display space for paperbacks, and publishers such as Penguin had provided free paperback shelving for bookshops.

Since authors derived most of their income from paperback sales (and sometimes US sales), it made sense for agents to cut out the hardback publisher's share of such sales. Agents looking to maximize income would license the book separately to an independent hardback publisher, a paperback publisher, and a US publisher, thereby obtaining advances from each party and full royalty rates for their authors (less the agent's commission). The general publishers, which owned both hardback and paperback firms (vertical integration), paid authors full royalty rates on each edition and were therefore better positioned to capture the leading authors. Paperback and hardback publishers without a hardback or paperback arm became increasingly desperate – sometimes they entered alliances in order to bid for the big books jointly.

Another strand leading to the amalgamation of consumer book publishing, again reaching back to the late 1970s, was the weakening polarization between the traditional formats. Readers' expectations created a new market for certain books and authors to be published in the larger B format – quality or trade paperback. The move was begun with the launch of Picador by Macmillan in 1972. Literary fiction and a range of non-fiction could be published at higher prices in B format. Peter Mayer (1936–2018), Chief Executive of Penguin from 1978 to 1996, applied the idea to more commercial fiction, such as M. M. Kaye's *The Far Pavilions*, which was to sell 400,000 copies within six months of its publication in paperback in 1979.

The second wave of the feminist movement in the 1960s and the subsequent rise of women's studies courses in the 1970s and 1980s not only created a new market for books but also inspired the foundation of women-run, women-centred publishing houses whose range and diversity reflect the multiplicity of female experience and writing. Virago was founded in 1973 by Carmen Callil, and later (in 1995) sold to Little, Brown. Its series of Virago Modern Classics, launched in 1978 with *Frost in May* (1933) by Antonia White, was instrumental in the rediscovery of a forgotten female tradition. Persephone Books, established in 1999, reprints neglected fiction and non-fiction by mid-twentieth-century (mostly women) writers.

By the end of the 1980s and early 1990s, most of the formerly independent hardback houses were part of the major publishing corporations. Each had the capability of publishing and acquiring rights in all formats: mass-market paperback, trade paperback and hardback. Their imprints were gathered together in modern London offices. The new owners combed through the old contracts entered into by their hardback houses with the paperback publishers and the titles which had, from other takeovers, fallen into the hands of rival paperback imprints and the termination dates of the licences. In due course they would claw back the paperback rights to those books for their own paperback imprints, much to the consternation of the bereft paperback houses, and some authors and agents. Most of Graham Greene's novels were published from the 1920s by the hardback publisher Heinemann and from the 1960s by The Bodley Head, and sublicensed in paperback to Penguin. Then Random House, having subsequently purchased the hardback publishers, reverted the paperback rights from Penguin and reissued his major works under the Vintage Classics imprint.

The hardback general book publishers held an increasing rarity value and at the peak of the merger boom commanded high prices. As for the staff of the newly taken-over general publishers, the outlook for many was bleak. If not made immediately redundant, they found themselves entering the world of corporate publishing. They carried with them a set of values quite often at odds with those of their new employers, which emphasized sales and profit and sometimes demanded clean and tidy desks, clear of manuscripts and books, in an open plan environment. Some editors blamed the accountants for preventing them from doing the books they wanted to publish. It was not the accountants per se: the whole culture had changed. The nature of consumer book publishing had changed from being product-led to being market-driven. As Alan Bartram noted at the end of the twentieth century,

> the practice of financing a potential poor-seller by profits from successful books, as a publisher such as Victor Gollancz would do because he, personally, believed it deserved publishing even if it cost him money, or as university presses considered it their duty to do – behaviour once considered normal practice – has almost disappeared. (Bartram, 1999, page 9)

Editorial individuality is still present in the large corporations. Some major publishing groups have attempted to regain some of the advantages of the smaller publisher by retaining or creating individual imprints. It is vital for innovation that they can lead the market by introducing new authors, publishing books in different formats, and marketing and selling them in different ways. In a world of brand authors, changing business models, and digital experimentation, publishers are hiring new kinds of staff, sometimes from other media industries. They want publishers who are entrepreneurial, can manage talent, and develop properties into brands suitable for licensing or direct investment across games, film and other media. Francesca Dow, of Penguin Children's, talked of thinking beyond the book:

> Part of our strategy is to develop brands in ways so that we are moving away from being a publisher to an owner and investor in new content… As a very strategic move, we acquired media rights in *The Snowman* – that is part of our strategy to grow in a new way beyond books. (*The Bookseller*, 11 October 2013)

Once the major consumer book publishers had sister imprints on both sides of the Atlantic, the obvious move was to acquire world English rights in the works of bestselling authors. However, this is still constrained by US and UK literary agents, who continue to license UK and US editions separately.

THE RESHAPING OF RETAIL

While trade or consumer publishing was being restructured, the increased availability of finance in the 1980s also aided the transformation and concentration of UK bookselling. Traditionally, UK bookselling had meant the major chain WHSmith (which had its roots in station bookstalls and high street stationery outlets), small independently owned chains, and a large number of independent or small bookshops. In the 1980s and 1990s, large bookselling chains, principally Waterstones and Dillons in the UK (Barnes & Noble, Borders and Waldenbooks in the USA), brought a new kind of bookselling – large well-stocked bookshops, stocking up to 50,000 titles in the UK, three to four times the size of many independents. Amazon began its operations in the USA in 1995 and in the UK in 1998. The US bookstore chains started to discount bestselling hardbacks, as did the UK chains from the late 1990s, thereby reducing sales of mass-market paperbacks. In the immediate aftermath of the collapse of the Net Book Agreement (NBA) in 1995, under which publishers set minimum prices for books, consumer spending on books bottomed out in the spring of 1996, and then staged a steady recovery to a new peak in 1998 – a vintage year for bestselling titles. Heavy discounting by retailers of the new, most popular hardback titles became the norm. As John Thompson writes: 'The financial formula that had underpinned the industry in the 1950s and 1960s was being turned on its head: increasingly it was the frontlist hardcover, not the backlist paperback, that was the engine of growth for the industry' (2012, page 378).

The independents lost market share. The new chains expanded aggressively and argued that they needed higher discounts from publishers and extended credit periods (the time to settle invoices). In the USA, the Robinson-Patman Act (1936) has prevented producers (e.g. publishers) favouring particular customers since they have to offer the same wholesale terms to everybody in order to protect small merchants. The consumer book publishers benefited from the well-stocked and branded bookshops displaying their books, and agreed to better discounts, easier credit and the continued right to return unsold books. The power relationship between publishers and booksellers, for so long weighted in the publisher's favour, began to tip towards the major retailers, as is common in most consumer goods industries. Furthermore by the mid-1990s, the major supermarkets were devoting more space to bestselling books and were intent on driving down book prices to the consumer, and their costs of supply. The decades either side of the new century marked the high point of the physical retailing of books. Subsequently the growth in online retailing of print and the arrival of ebooks reinforced the dominance of Amazon compared to physical book stores.

The low company valuations of the consumer book publishers in the 1990s were in marked contrast to the boom of the 1980s. While most of the owners persevered, Reed decided to sell its consumer imprints in order to concentrate on STM and professional publishing, recording a massive write-off in the process. Nevertheless, newer independent UK publishers, such as Fourth Estate (later bought by HarperCollins), Orion (Hachette) and Piatkus (Little, Brown) grew strongly. Bloomsbury was established with ambitious plans for growth. By the end of the century, the main consumer publishers had mostly recovered their levels of profitability, and WHSmith paid what was considered by some competitors to be a high price for Hodder Headline. The commercial logic of a retailer owning a publisher was to come under question (the publisher was sold on in 2004 to Hachette), although in 2011 Amazon began its own publishing operation including Amazon Crossing, which became a leading player in translated fiction.

The first Waterstone's was opened in 1982 by Tim Waterstone in Old Brompton Road, London

The first book sold by Amazon, on 3 April 1995, was *Fluid Concepts and Creative Analogies* by Douglas Hofstadter

The founding of Bloomsbury

Nigel Newton CBE, Founder and Chief Executive

I conceived the idea of Bloomsbury in February 1984 whilst on leave from Sidgwick & Jackson Publishers following the birth of my first daughter, Catherine. I decided to start a new, independent, medium-sized publisher of books of editorial excellence and originality with high standards of design and production. It would publish literary authors of the highest quality and sales potential.

BLOOMSBURY

During the London Book Fair in March 1985, David Reynolds, a publisher with Shuckburgh Reynolds, joined me and we began meeting early each morning to plan the detail of the company, before going off to our day jobs. By May 1986 and with advice from Mike Mayer, a venture capitalist who later became a non-executive director on the Board of Bloomsbury, we wrote a business plan which served initially as a fundraising document and, to this day, as an operating manual for the company. It incorporated several unique ideas, including the creation of the Bloomsbury Authors' Trust, which was to own 5 per cent of the company on behalf of the future authors of Bloomsbury whose books were to be published between the founding of the company and its flotation on the stock market in 1994.

The name Bloomsbury was chosen not only as Bloomsbury Way was the street where my previous employer was based and because I liked the name, but also because it was the neighbourhood associated with traditional publishing at a time when the industry was being taken over by foreign-owned multinational conglomerates, who were moving out to more distant parts of London. An intimation of the Bloomsbury Group was not the idea, but did no harm.

The first investors were approached in May 1986 as we sought £1.75 m initial funding. Alan Wherry of Penguin become the first Marketing Director of Bloomsbury, also responsible for sales and publicity, and Liz Calder of Jonathan Cape became Editorial Director in charge of all fiction publishing and some non-fiction. David Reynolds would commission the main non-fiction list.

Three investors, Caledonia Investments, the lead investor, ECI, and Legal and General Ventures, came on board. The four publishers set about conceiving a logo for the new company. Liz Calder suggested Diana, Goddess of Hunting, and Newell & Sorrell, the designers, came up with our colophon and a specially designed typeface for the company name. During August 1986, the four of us resigned en masse on the same day from our existing jobs. By late September, a day was chosen when briefings about the new publishing house would be given in secret to Louis Baum, Editor of *The Bookseller*, and Rodney Burbeck of *Publishing News*, and to journalists from *The Times* and *Guardian*. All four stories appeared on the same day and the existence of Bloomsbury was announced to a surprised publishing industry. Baring Brothers Hambrecht & Quist was secured as the final investor, duly impressed that the company had been launched earlier that day.

A stand had already been booked at that October's Frankfurt Book Fair and the company simply had to exist by the following week when the Fair was to begin. Five days after the press announcement, the four of us were standing on the beautifully designed stand with not a single book on it. At the same time, Liz Calder signed up Bloomsbury's first book, *Trust* by Mary Flanagan, and David Reynolds acquired the first titles in the non-fiction programme. The industry came to visit the Frankfurt stand in fascination that the five-day-old publisher had quarter bottles of Bollinger to offer, but as yet no books!

mary flanagan

Trust

B L O O M S B U R Y

Premises were found above a Chinese restaurant in Putney and the company was based there for three months as further colleagues were recruited, including Kathy Rooney, who founded the company's reference list, and the Finance Director Nigel Batt. Caroline Michel was appointed Publicity Director and Lucy Juckes Sales Manager. Alan and Lucy began recruiting a sales force which included David Ward, who later became Sales Director. They negotiated discounts and opened accounts with some 2,000 booksellers around the world and stockholding agents in the Commonwealth such as Allen & Unwin in Australia. Other colleagues were hired for rights (Ruth Logan), publicity (Sarah Beal) and production (Penny Edwards). All three rose to head their departments in later years.

The company entered a mode of vertical take-off with tremendous conviction as it commissioned its first year's list and at the same time prepared to publish it only six months later. In April 1987 *Trust* came out together with *The Land That Lost Its Heroes* by Jimmy Burns, a book about Argentina and the Falklands War which went on to win the Somerset Maugham award. There was a tremendous launch party that night at the Braganza restaurant in Soho. *Trust* went straight into the *Sunday Times* bestseller list at number 5.

Design innovations made the look of each Bloomsbury book quite distinctive, ranging from a reading ribbon in each novel, which was Reynolds' idea, to wide flaps on the jackets, and the high standard of paper, typography, and book production. The ISBN prefix 747 was chosen as £747,000 was the company's profit target in its 5-year business plan.

Highlights of the company's first Christmas season included *Presumed Innocent* by Scott Turow and *Marilyn Among Friends* by Sam Shaw and Norman Rosten. Liz Calder signed up Jeanette Winterson and Margaret Atwood and, in short order, John Irving, Joanna Trollope, Brian Moore, Jay McInerney, Nadine Gordimer, and Michael Ondaatje. These authors were to win literary prizes from the Booker to the Pulitzer and the Nobel in the years ahead. Calder's list of brilliant literary authors was to become the soul of the new Bloomsbury. By December 1987, the company finished its first full year with a staff of 26, a turnover of £2,231,198 (which rose to £342.7m and a staff of 1,000 by the financial year ending in February 2024) and a vibrant new presence in publishing.

The financial crisis of 2008 led to a long period of declining printed book sales (mitigated to some extent by the rapid rise of ebook sales) and book price deflation (Phillips, 2017). Legacy practices of the NBA era endure in the world of print. Consumer publishers still display the price on the book's cover, and author royalties are usually based on the recommended price, albeit with let-outs for sales at high discounts. The arrival of ebooks brought a new dynamic with the ability to change prices at will, both by publishers and retailers, whereas previously printed stock had to be restickered in the warehouse. With Amazon leading the development of internet sales and the ebook market, publishers struggled to maintain prices at the levels they considered reasonable whilst attempting to create alternative models for the business relationship with intermediaries. A further factor impinging on publishers' ebook prices in some fields was the rapid growth of self-published titles at low prices.

The recession also led to new categories of publishing such as thrift lit alongside interest in serious political and economic titles about the causes of the financial crisis. The global pandemic, which began in 2020, led to the closure of book stores and fresh impetus for ebook, audio, and other digital products such as for home learning. In turn, the reopening of shops revitalized sales of print as consumers rediscovered the pleasure of browsing in a physical store. Cost pressures such as rising paper prices pushed publishers to raise their prices – any revenue gains in 2023 largely came from rising prices rather than volume increases.

Wholesale and agency models

Consumer publishers use the *wholesale* pricing method when they trade through all kinds of intermediaries, such as retailers, to reach consumers. The use of the word 'wholesale' in this context is different from 'wholesaler' – an intermediary between a publisher and a retailer. Under the wholesale pricing method, the retailer buys the book from the publisher at a set price and is free to sell it to a consumer at any price. The price to the retailer is arrived at by deducting the percentage discount from the recommended retail price which is set by the publisher. The percentage discount (referred to as the 'trade discount') in the UK is the outcome of the negotiation between the publisher and the retailer. The greater the buying power of the retailer in terms of the quantity of books ordered

Fixed book prices

Various forms of fixed pricing exist in some mainland European countries, including France and Germany. Governments there are supportive of their cultural heritage expressed through their indigenous publishing industries and are also keen to see the continued existence of physical bookshops. Fixed prices are regarded as helpful to smaller and independent bookshops, as well as to all bricks-and-mortar stores, which face competition from the lower prices of internet retailers. At the beginning of 2012, a law came into force in France allowing publishers also to fix the prices of ebooks. The French government banned the free delivery of books in 2014, to help smaller booksellers compete with Amazon, and in response to the introduction by Amazon of a very low delivery charge, mandated a minimum payment of €3. There are no fixed prices for books in the UK following the collapse in September 1995 of the Net Book Agreement (NBA) or resale price maintenance (RPM). There are differing levels of tax applied to books around Europe. For example, in the UK in 2023, both print and ebooks were totally exempt; in France, a reduced rate of 5.5 per cent applied to both paper books and ebooks; in Germany, the equivalent rate was 7 per cent.

FOCUS

or its market share in relation to other retailers, the higher the discount it can extract from the publisher.

The UK and US book trade is characterized by some retailers offering consumers deep discounts off the publishers' recommended published prices. The practice shifts large quantities of selected titles. This sales model is in contrast to the 'fixed retail price' book trade of the important European markets of France and Germany. In the quickly developing market for ebooks, the internet retailers offered consumers deeply discounted prices. The high trade discounts won by the dominant physical retailers and Amazon were transferred to embryonic ebook sales and became established.

As an alternative to the wholesale model, the alternative *agency* model for ebooks came to a controversial fore with Apple's launch of the iPad and its iBookstore in 2010. At the time, Amazon enjoyed almost complete domination of ebook sales in the USA with a market share of 90 per cent. To the chagrin of the big trade publishers, their hardcover bestsellers, typically priced at say $25.00, were sold by Amazon as ebooks to consumers at the heavily discounted price of $9.99. Apple, in contrast, offered the major trade publishers the agency model under which the publisher sets the price of the ebook to the consumer and appoints the retailer which acts as its agent to sell the ebook to the reader. The agent takes a sales commission on the sale, in this case, 30 per cent. The major publishers in the USA, which published most of the biggest authors and titles, were at the time called the 'Big Six': Hachette, HarperCollins, Macmillan, Penguin, Random House and Simon & Schuster. With the exception of Random House (the largest), the other five accepted the agency model. The agency contract with Apple included an unusual 'most favoured nation' (MFN) clause which allowed Apple to sell ebooks at least as cheaply as others. Random House by delaying its own decision to transfer to agency pricing gained a competitive advantage and escaped being targeted by the regulators (the US Department of Justice and the European Commission). The regulators

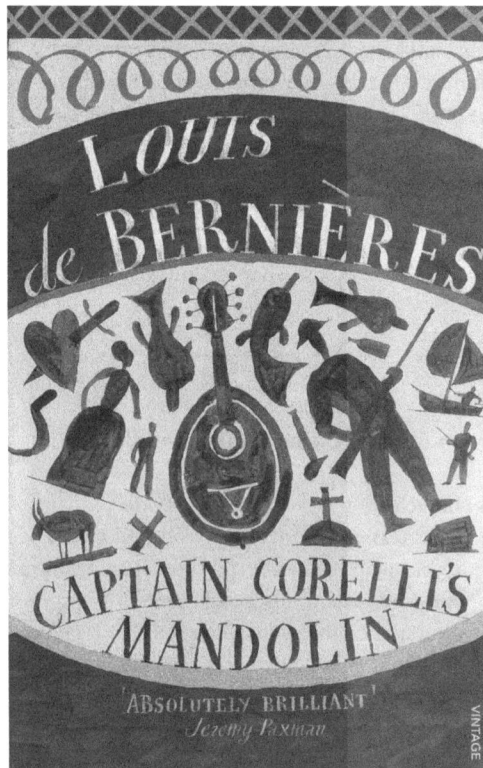

Few book covers have the iconic status of album covers. One example, however, is the 1995 design for *Captain Corelli's Mandolin* by Louis de Bernières

launched investigations in 2011 as to whether there was collusion between Apple and the five publishers to conspire to fix the prices of ebooks. By the end of 2012, the regulators concluded their investigations and began to sue Apple and some of the publishers. The legal cases were settled with the publishers and compensation paid.

After the settlement the major publishers switched to the so-called 'agency lite' model, which prevents publishers dictating the price to consumers; but they do set the list price to retailers, from which some discounting is allowed. The 'non-agency' publishers continued with the wholesale model and their ebooks were subject to aggressive retailer discounts off the publishers' list prices. But by now, as Mike Shatzkin comments:

> Amazon was essentially done with the strategy of discounting big publishers' ebooks. And big publishers are left wondering whether they should be glad they got what they wished for. Let's remember that those discounts from Amazon came from their share of the price; now with agency protocols, publishers can only discount ebooks by reducing their own take! (idealog. com/blog, accessed 24 March 2024)

This led to a decline in ebook sales from the mainstream publishers, and a rebalancing in the market in favour of print.

A CHANGE IN PUBLISHING STRATEGY

From the late 1990s, the major publishers were to reverse their former 'scatter-gun' strategy of publishing as many titles as possible in the hope that one or two would be hits. Facing increasing polarization in the market between the bestselling titles and the also-rans (the 'winner takes all' maxim common in the creative industries), they cut their new title output progressively to concentrate on books and authors considered marketable, especially those that would fit the retailers' promotional plans.

The so-called 'midlist' authors were casualties, not that publishers admit publicly to having a midlist. Writers whose works had been well received within the writing community, who were previously supported by publishers over a number of books – awaiting their sales breakthrough – could be seen as on their way out much earlier and were rejected after only their first few books. Some moved to smaller and welcoming, independent publishers while others were dropped by their agents too.

The major publishers' other strategies – apart from reducing the advances and royalty income of less-favoured authors – included giving greater emphasis to brand authors and series. They also entered into 'licensed' partnerships with television and film companies to merchandise their properties, and marketing and distribution partnerships with smaller publishers. In the decade following the financial crisis of 2008, publishers displayed caution, investing in brand authors and debut authors of promise – but generally the level of advances was reduced.

Trends in fiction and non-fiction – a US perspective

Edward Nawotka, Senior International Editor, *Publishers Weekly*

The US market is geographically, demographically, economically and culturally vast, and accordingly the subjects covered by general trade fiction and non-fiction are equally diverse. When you include self-published titles, there are several million books published in the United States a year. It is an astonishing figure.

The past decade has seen the internet and self-publishing cater to ever more niche interests, particularly in genres like romance, paranormal and crime. Name your fetish and it will be catered to online. Trends in popular fiction come and go quickly: one year chaste Christian romance novels are all the rage, the next, sexually daring new adult 'romantasy' novels might top the bestseller lists, or hybrid. Always though, you have the stalwarts: thrillers and detective novels in which the lone-wolf hero decides to take matters into their own hands. Likewise, in literary fiction, it is often the same: an individual battling an unacknowledged threat, acting counter to the prevailing trends in society.

Why? Americans are, generally speaking, raised to resent or rebel against authority. It was the founding principle of the country. Characters at the heart of the bestselling American fiction tend to reflect this attitude. This applies to non-fiction as well as fiction. Where, previously, one would have to be viewed as a credentialled expert to publish a book, the democratization of media has meant you will see more and more personal narratives published from writers who have otherwise developed a platform of followers, typically on social media. This focus on individual empowerment means the best literature Americans produce is largely character-driven, rather than driven by a 'theme' or agenda, presenting a series of events through the prism of an individual, rather than a family, group or a larger movement.

That said, US publishing has also sought to broaden its appeal and put increased attention on formerly marginalized individuals, people whose literary identity is presented as being different than, but equal in importance, to those of the majority racial and sexual patriarchy. This new emphasis on diversification has empowered these individual writers to serve as stand-ins for a larger group and their collective experience.

Finally, it is a common refrain to say that Americans are parochial readers, disinterested in 'foreign books', in translation. Why? Because America largely contains a significant percentage of people who, though they may have been born abroad, now consider themselves as Americans. Look at the number of assimilation narratives produced in the USA: hundreds of books a year tell the story of several generations of an immigrant family where the parents adhere to the values of the 'old country' and the children live by the rules of their new home. These books might be set in New York, Milwaukee, or Dallas and feature families from India or China, Russia or Brazil. As a consequence, the USA generally translates less foreign fiction than almost any nation on earth, largely because it already contains peoples from much of the world within its borders. Still, this literary cultural myopia too is falling away, and among the most dynamic publishers in the USA are those that are focused on literary translation.

All said, if there's one thing that can reliably said to be unchanging of trends in American reading habits, it is this: they like novelty.

Books are firmly positioned in genres and categories (see Table 1.2 and Table 1.3), whether crime or fantasy in fiction, or home and garden, history, or popular science in non-fiction. This is reflected in the cover design and associated marketing. The success of the erotic trilogy *50 Shades of Grey* encouraged other publishers to boost their profile in this market category; later this was followed by a boom in romance sales stemming from the genre's prominence on BookTok. Crime is perennially successful as a genre and has the ability to change with the times – cosy crime came back into vogue with such authors as Richard Osman, Richard Coles and Janice Hallett. Publishers came to recognize that prolific readers (those who buy more than 20 books a year) are eclectic in their taste and happy to move between genres. The boundaries between crime, horror and romance, for example, blurred into different subgenres for the general reader.

Table 1.2 Top five book genres for adult fiction and non-fiction

	Fiction	*Non-fiction*
1	Crime/mystery	Auto/biography
2	General fiction	Self-help/popular psychology
3	Thriller/suspense	History
4	Romance	Cookery/food/drink
5	Historical fiction	Mind/Body/Spirit

Source: 2022 data from Nielsen's UK Books & Consumers Survey.

Table 1.3 Top five book genres for men and women

	Genres bought for men	*Genres bought for women*
1	Crime/mystery	General fiction
2	Thriller/suspense	Crime/mystery
3	Auto/biography	Romance
4	General fiction	Thriller/suspense
5	Self-help/popular psychology	Auto/biography

Source: 2022 data from Nielsen's UK Books & Consumers Survey.

MARKET SHARE

If the consolidation of the consumer book publishers in the last quarter of the twentieth century was about the vertical restructuring of an archaic industry, the next wave of consolidation was about gaining market share in the face of ever more powerful retailers and the increasing internationalization of consumer publishing. The market shares of the leading publishing groups in 2023 are shown in Table 1.4 – the top four groups (the Big Four) have approaching half of the market, and the top 10 just over 60 per cent.

In a market increasingly dominated by powerful retailers and bestsellers, publisher size is crucial, especially in a large market segment like fiction. This was a factor behind the merger of Random House and Penguin, alongside the search for cost savings in back office operations, including production and distribution. Both Hachette (acquired by Vivendi in 2023) and Bertelsmann adopt a decentralized approach to the management of their publishing groups. Literary agents are encouraged to submit projects to editors across their imprints, even to the extent that their constituent publishing companies may be in direct competition against one another. Philip Jones (*The Bookseller*, 2 March 2018) noted that the profit margin in 1995 of HarperCollins was 6 per cent, Penguin 9 per cent, Hodder Headline 6 per cent, and Little, Brown 7 per cent. Only Transworld regularly bettered those numbers, with its 15 per cent margin. Consolidation and globalization have improved profitability: for example, the profit margin for Hachette in 2022 was 11 per cent and for Penguin Random House 16 per cent.

There is a notable polarization between the big players and a large number of much smaller firms – in between there are only a small number

Table 1.4 Market shares of publishers for consumer sales 2023

Publisher	Market share (%)
Penguin Random House	20
Hachette	14
HarperCollins	9
Pan Macmillan	5
Bloomsbury	4
Simon & Schuster	3
Bonnier	2
Scholastic	2
Usborne	1
Oxford University Press	1

Source: Nielsen BookScan.

Note: the market share for the Independent Alliance of 18 independent publishers was 13 per cent.

of medium-sized companies. The middle-ranking publishers lack the scale of operation and deep backlists of the large players and are sometimes too small to resist the pressures from the large retailers for improved terms of trade, at the expense of their margins. They also face greater risks in publishing brand-named authors on whom they depend to give them access to the main retailers. If, for example, they are in competition to buy a potentially huge book, they may be outbid by an advance on royalties from a larger publisher. Alternatively, if they won the book and its sales were disappointing, the failure of their prime investment would have severe consequences on their profitability. In contrast, a major publisher could afford to purchase six potentially huge books, of which the chances are that three or four turn out to be winners. The biggest authors migrate to the largest publishers – even those who achieve their early success with a smaller publisher, or start out by self-publishing, are likely to be tempted away by larger advances. The smaller publishers, which cannot compete against the large corporations in terms of advances, concentrate on bringing forward new writers, or those overlooked writers who may not have agents or have been rejected by larger publishers. They may opt to build a stable of authors who will work for one-off fees instead of royalties – common in the field of highly illustrated books.

Although consumer book publishing is dominated by the existing majors, there are other large publishers in the UK, including Bloomsbury, Simon & Schuster (owned by private equity firm KKR), Bonnier, and Oxford University Press. Quarto is a sizeable player in the illustrated book field. Medium-sized independents include Atlantic, Canongate (in Edinburgh), Faber & Faber, Profile Books, and the art publishers Phaidon, Thames & Hudson and Tate Publishing.

The recession associated with the financial crisis of 2008 onwards had an impact on consumer spending in many countries, and led to redundancies at publishers, tight control on costs, and reduced advances to authors. This latter effect to some extent levelled the playing field for the smaller independent publishers, priced out of the major auctions. As the larger publishers lowered their level of risk, agents could see advantages for their authors from being published by smaller, fleet-footed companies with an adventurous streak. Also Amazon offers a platform for smaller publishers to reach a global market across formats.

Peepal Tree

E★PERT

Jeremy Poynting, Founder and Managing Editor, Peepal Tree Press

Peepal Tree aims to bring readers the very best of international writing from the Caribbean, its diasporas and the UK. Our goal is to publish books that make a difference, and though we want to achieve the best possible sales, we are most concerned with whether a book will still be alive in the future.

Peepal Tree is about bringing different goals and contexts together. It has always been a very personal mission, but one that depends on a team without whom nothing would happen, about there being a network of people invested in what we do and our attempt to create a family of authors and committed readers. It's about finding individual voices and writing talents that collectively contribute to a continuing conversation. It's about working with political, cultural and aesthetic goals that are marginal in an economic environment that is market-driven and has huge discrepancies of economic and cultural power. I like the analogy made by a brilliant Caribbean thinker, Sylvia Wynter, about the difference between the plantation, which was part of a world-economic system of trade and exploitation, and the plot, where enslaved people grew their own crops, made something that was theirs, found a space for cultural continuities in at least the growing of food, and, quite literally, sometimes plotted. But the plot was also about self-exploitation since plots were given to enslaved people to save the owners of the plantation the trouble and expense of importing food. Now at one level the analogy is absurd because there can be no comparison with the suffering and exploitation of enslaved people and the very willing self-exploitation of the kind of people who run small independent publishing firms, but the truth remains that the plot has to operate in the same market-driven, hugely unequal economic system as the plantation.

I think that over the years my perception of what Peepal Tree does or can do has changed. Initially, it was very much about giving voice to Caribbean writers in an environment that had lost interest in them. This was the 1980s when changes in the ownership and control of publishing were taking place – where independent medium-sized publishing houses were disappearing into the conglomerates – including the publishers who had been interested in writers from the Caribbean such as André Deutsch, Allan Wingate, McGibbon and Kee and others – and the closing down of ventures such as the Heinemann African Writers series and the dwindling of their Caribbean Writers Series. In the process, only a handful of already internationally known Caribbean writers were getting published in the

UK – a parallel to the way that British media in general lost interest in what was happening in the postcolonial Caribbean, except for disasters – climatic, political or criminal. Because places which, not so long before, we had thought of as British, and where British fortunes had been made, were so many thousands of miles away, we forgot about our own Deep South.

Now I see more clearly that the process of decolonization has to take place not only in the Caribbean (where the recognition now exists that you can't undo hundreds of years of colonialism in just a few decades) but also in Britain itself where we have recognize that amnesia won't do, that we need to acknowledge how much the creation of our elites, our prized heritage of grand country houses, our ways of seeing, including our self-perceptions, our language and culture have been shaped by over four hundred years of colonial and imperial presence in the world. Over sixty years ago the Barbadian novelist George Lamming wrote an important book called *The Pleasures of Exile* where he called for a treaty of understanding between the children of Prospero and the children of Caliban. Peepal Tree has been about that conversation.

Peepal Tree Press gratefully acknowledges Arts Council of England support.

There are many smaller specialist publishers producing adult or children's books. Today the independent publishers are a thriving part of publishing, signing up exciting new authors, exploring diverse voices, and picking up established authors discarded by the larger publishing groups. Examples of smaller presses are Oneworld, Fitzcarraldo, and Jacaranda Books. Their books are also winning major literary prizes. For example, *The Seven Moons of Maali Almeida* by Sri Lankan author Shehan Karunatilaka won the Booker Prize in 2022 and was published by Sort of Books, an independent publishing venture set up by Mark Ellingham and Natania Jansz, founders of the Rough Guide travel series.

CHILDREN'S AND YOUNG ADULT PUBLISHING

By the late 1970s the outlook for publishers of children's books, especially those producing quality hardbacks, appeared grim in the UK. Many bookshops, other than WHSmith, were hardly enthusiastic buyers, public and school libraries were cutting back their expenditure, and the birth rate was forecast to fall. In that the vitality of children's publishing creates the book buyers of the future, there were serious worries about the demise of book reading, foreshadowing the end of publishing itself. Between 1981 and 1990 the population of 5- to 14-year-olds did indeed fall by 13 per cent but the inventiveness of authors and illustrators, of existing publishers, of new publishers such as Walker Books, and book packagers transformed children's publishing into arguably the most dynamic sector of the industry. Retail sales per child rose by nearly three times, and the number of new titles doubled to around 6,000. Between 1985 and 1990, the sales of children's publishers rose in real terms by 26 per cent while their adult general publishing counterparts achieved growth of only 7 per cent.

The publishers found new ways of reaching the home market via supermarkets (often titles appeared under a supermarket's own brand label),

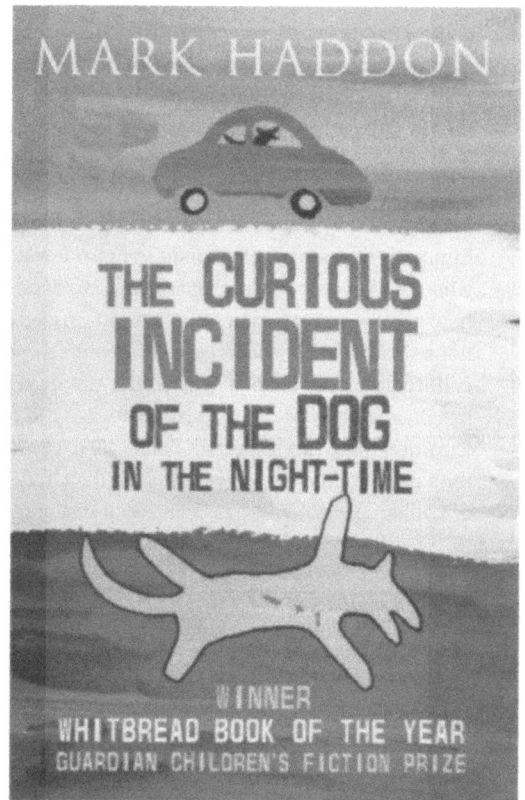

Mark Haddon's *The Curious Incident of the Dog in the Night-Time* was published in separate editions for adults (*left*) and children (*right*)

toyshops and direct sales – including book clubs and school book fairs. They sold international co-editions to US and European publishing partners, enabling picture books and highly-illustrated non-fiction or information books to be published at low and affordable prices worldwide. Paperback sales grew enormously and in volume terms came to dominate the market. Teenage fiction lists were established.

The recession of the early 1990s saw a reversal in sales of around 13 per cent yet the publishers continued to increase their title output through to 1995 when it stabilized at around 8,000 titles. The UK market for children's books declined from 1990 through to 1997, as other new products competed for children's attention and parents' spending. However, in 1998–1999, the market staged a substantial recovery. Government policy to give greater emphasis to literacy in primary schools was a fillip to some children's publishers, encouraging school and library sales. Some titles became more answerable to the needs of the National Curriculum, although this did create a tension between the book as entertainment and as a learning aid. It is important to note that the children's publishers sell their books through many different distribution channels beyond booksellers, such as direct to schools.

By the end of the twentieth century an explosion in new children's fiction was apparent. This was led by J. K. Rowling's Harry Potter books, which not only rocketed the independent publisher Bloomsbury up the charts for retail sales in the UK, but also became international bestsellers and widely translated. They were attractive to a cross-over market – read by children and adults – and stimulated consumer interest in children's books across the board (and interest from film companies in children's book properties). In fiction, the importance of the branding of authors, such as Jacqueline Wilson, Philip Pullman and Francesca Simon, strengthened. Publishers were keen to develop series based around the fictional characters, which could lead to sales of associated merchandise. In the early years of the new century, children's publishing became a vibrant sector with publishers willing to invest in both authors and marketing in search of the next bestseller, and it continues to display healthy sales growth.

Beyond binaries, beyond borders: on diversity in children's picture books

Bijal Vachharajani, Commissioning Editor at Pratham Books and Author

Smit Zaveri, Consultant Editor – Children's

When #WeNeedDiverseBooks first started trending on Twitter (now X) in 2014, it not only led to the formation of a not-for-profit that promotes diversity in children's literature, but sparked a movement that changed publishing structures and operations. Ten years later, diversity is not just a buzzword bandied around in strategy meetings. It's part of the spine of publishing when it comes to books, creators and marketing. But boundaries need to be pushed, especially the ones that box diverse children's literature into hegemonic identities.

E★PERT

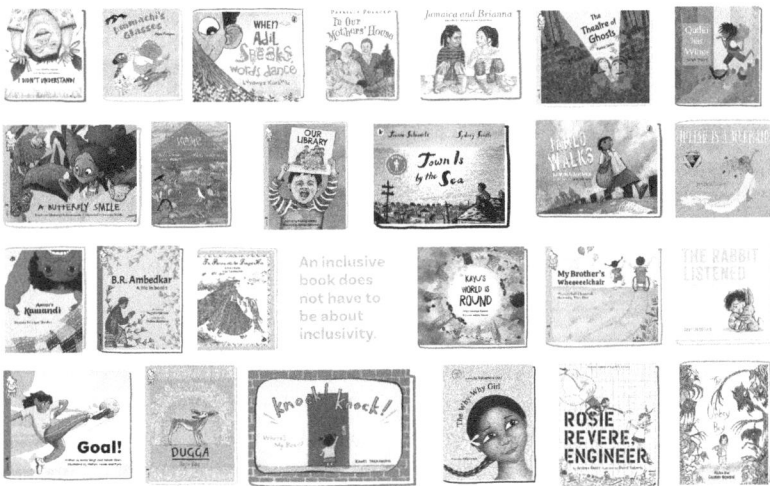

Diversity, for instance, in Indian picture books published abroad, often centres Hindu festivals such as Diwali or Holi, where spices and saris spill across the pages and of course heaps of samosas too. Global literature is evolving, but hegemonies continue to hold sway across stories of identities and colour. PEN America reported that out of the 1,648 titles banned in schools in 2022, 41 per cent addressed LGBTQ+ themes and 40 per cent contained 'protagonists or prominent secondary characters of color'. While the diversity efforts by mainstream publishing houses are well-intentioned, the lines between tokenism and representation need to be examined.

For instance, Scholastic USA wanted to license Maggie Tokuda-Hall's picture book *Love in the Library* (Candlewick Press, 2022), but asked for the omission of large swathes of her author's note to remove any mentions of racism in America towards the Japanese, even though that formed the very crux of her story. Scholastic later apologized, but it opened a can of worms about diversity in publishing.

Children's picture books around the world have always been bold – challenging gender stereotypes, tackling issues of divorce, depression, championing mixed families, and creating equal spaces for all genders. But authenticity comes when writers and illustrators create from a place of lived experience. Where they can find spaces for their voices to be amplified and tell stories that are not boxed in, but the ones they want to tell.

In 2017, Deepa D wrote in the Indian newsmagazine *Caravan*, 'Having people of dominant castes and classes tell and draw stories about disadvantaged communities is just one more way to uphold the narratives of the status quo.' The article titled 'That's How I See Things: Looking for the Adivasi and Dalit presence in Indian children's literature', was a mirror being held up to Indian publishing, an industry that should be about the many Indias. A reflection that needs to be examined by editors, art directors, copy-editors, designers, every person who plays a role in shaping the literary landscape of children's books in India as well as globally.

Recent years have seen the likes of Knights Of and Kumusha Books in the UK and Pratham Books, Duckbill Books, and Adivaani in India create globally inclusive, diverse books that are also commercially viable. These publishing houses have become the torchbearers in championing lived experiences, with catalogues that aren't just tick boxes of representation but are joyfully diverse without being fenced in by identity. Iconic picture book maker Ruth Krauss wrote in *How to Write a Book*, 'You can write books about anything ...' That should be true for all creators. They should not have to write and draw just their identity. But about anything and everything.

Notable is the spectacular success of the YA (young adult, 13–18) category of fiction, spurred on by the success of Harry Potter and then the vampire romance Twilight series of books from Stephanie Meyer. Next came dystopian fiction and in 2012, the year the film was released, around 3 m copies of the Hunger Games trilogy were sold in the UK – both print and ebook. Supplanted to an extent by strong interest in middle grade books (aimed at the 8–12 age group), YA is showing signs of renewed vibrancy with success for authors such as Holly Jackson and Jenny Han.

This is alongside the success of new adult (NA) titles aimed at the 18–25 age group – with content suitable for more mature audiences.

The main children's imprints are part of the major adult consumer publishers which have been consolidated over time, such as Puffin, Ladybird and Dorling Kindersley (now part of PRH). Others in the UK include Bloomsbury and Oxford University Press. There are specialist children's publishers such as Scholastic (USA), which are not part of adult book publishing groups, and in the UK many independents, such as Knights Of, Nosy Crow, Usborne and Walker Books. Egmont Books UK was purchased in 2020 by HarperCollins from the Danish Egmont Group and rebranded as Farshore. Along with Phidal (Canada), the publisher features licensed character book publishing in conjunction with the originating film and game companies.

The diversity of US children's books has been tracked regularly by the Cooperative Children's Book Center (CCBC) at the University of Wisconsin. There has been some improvement in recent years and by 2022:

> This year's statistics show the continuation of some positive trends. After a long period of relative stagnancy, the number of children's books the CCBC received by BIPOC [Black, Indigenous, and People of Color] authors and illustrators and about BIPOC characters began to increase starting around 2015. By 2020 – only five years later – the number of books the CCBC received that were by or about a person of color had tripled. (ccbc.education. wisc.edu, accessed 25 January 2024)

A list of Carnegie Medal winners over a ten-year period is given in Table 1.5. The prize drew controversy in 2017 over its lack of diversity:

> The UK's oldest prize for children's literature, the Carnegie medal, has promised long-term change following a review of its lack of diversity, which one respondent said stemmed from the fact that 'literature in the UK is an unapologetic bastion of white privilege'. The independent diversity review was prompted by outrage at the all-white, 20-author longlist for the 2017 Carnegie. The prize was established in 1935 but has never been won by a black, Asian or minority ethnic writer. (*Guardian*, 27 September 2018)

Table 1.5 Yoto Carnegie Medal winners, 2014–2023. The medal is awarded by children's librarians for an outstanding book for children and young people

Year of award	Author	Title	Publisher
2014	Kevin Brooks	*The Bunker Diary*	Puffin
2015	Tanya Landman	*Buffalo Soldier*	Walker Books
2016	Sarah Crossan	*One*	Bloomsbury
2017	Ruta Sepetys	*Salt to the Sea*	Puffin
2018	Geraldine McCaughrean	*Where the World Ends*	Usborne
2019	Elizabeth Acevedo	*The Poet X*	Electric Monkey
2020	Anthony McGowan	*Lark*	Barrington Stoke
2021	Jason Reynolds	*Look Both Ways*	Knights of
2022	Katya Balen	*October, October*	Bloomsbury
2023	Manon Steffan Ros	*The Blue Book of Nebo*	Firefly Press

In 2019, the slam poet Elizabeth Acevedo became the first writer of colour to win the award. As a teacher of primarily Latino students,

> [she] realized that all these stories I had been telling in class and these poems I had been writing didn't necessarily end up on their bookshelves. And so I began writing the Poet X almost as a response to what my students were asking for. (epicreads.com, accessed 10 August 2023)

KEY DEVELOPMENTS IN TRADE PUBLISHING

There have been a series of overlapping developments which have impacted trade publishing in the most recent period. Many are part of the rise of digital in the area of consumer publishing, with growing sales of ebooks and audiobooks. The issue of sustainability is covered in Chapter 8. The following are key developments:

- Arrival of large technology players
- The rise of self-publishing
- Growth of ebooks and audio
- Digital product development
- Diversity and inclusion

Arrival of large technology players

The landscape of publishing changed significantly with the entrants of major players including Amazon, Apple, and Google. This kickstarted and then accelerated the move towards ebooks with the devices, from the Kindle to the iPad, facilitating a high-quality user experience, and digital content being made widely available. Amazon's strategy of aggressive pricing opened up the market for ebooks and audio, and publishers encouraged the other players in the market in the hopes of easing the internet retailer's domination. Publishers had to learn to work with the technology companies, encountering differences in culture and mind-set.

The rise of self-publishing

Authors have always published themselves, without publishers, but with some difficulty and expense. In the pre-digital world, the so-called vanity presses manipulated authors' often life-long desire to be published by charging them large sums for printing their books in considerable quantity, typically delivered to their homes, where the stock remained. However, from the turn of the century, the availability of print on demand (POD) technology enabled new companies, such as Lulu Enterprises, to offer production and distribution platforms for authors to self-publish their own books at much lower cost than hitherto. Today Amazon sells millions of print copies from self-published or indie authors; as well as ebooks through Kindle Direct Publishing (KDP). The number of self-published titles is enormous, especially in the USA, where in 2021 over 2 m ISBNs were issued to self-published authors. Self-published authors captured around half of the total unit sales of ebooks in that year (*Publishers Weekly*, 17 February 2023). Amazon in the UK released figures on bestselling book series, across print and digital, and up to May 2022, the second most successful series was from self-published crime author L. J. Ross, behind the Jack Reacher books from Lee Child.

The supply-side business model is the opposite to the curatorial/ risk-investment model of the trade publishers. It is founded on creating content abundance, charging authors a small percentage on sales made through their own platform or through other sales channels, and through offering authors charged-for-services, such as copy-editing, design and marketing. Critics have called it the monetization of the slush pile. While physical booksellers do not stock self-published authors, the advent of ebooks gives authors direct access to the reading public. Some kinds of authors are no longer dependent on securing the services of a literary agent and a contract from a publisher to reach readers: authorship has been democratized.

The self-published authors and the author services companies disintermediated literary agents, publishers and physical bookstores from the supply chain. The authors grew their market share against the trade publishers, mostly in terms of title output more than in sales revenue. A small number of *indie* authors, as they came to be known, especially prolific writers of genre fiction topped the US ebook charts. Other indie authors, termed *hybrid* authors, both self-publish some titles and publish other titles through the mainstream publishers.

Online entertainment sites, such as Wattpad, emerged for writers to reach and communicate freely with readers. Wattpad launched its own book imprints such as Wattpad Books, publishing 'the most popular and diverse voices', and WEBTOON Unscrolled, 'the home for WEBTOON books in North America'. Community sites offer authors the facility to publish fan fiction (their take on a TV series or a novel) or original web fiction, sometimes in serial form. Authors can use such sites to build a fan base or try out stories.

However, the once-feared supposition that there would be a mass migration of authors away from the traditional publishing houses has yet to materialize. For publishers the presence of self-publishing is, they hope, an opportunity to stress the value they add to the author's work. The aim of some indie authors is indeed to achieve a contract from a publisher. The self-publishing websites and forums form talent pools for publishers, agents and scouts to spot new writing talent. Furthermore, the communities which develop around their writing provide a ready-made audience for the publisher to build greater sales success.

Growth of ebooks and audio

Most ebooks are replicas of the print edition – so-called *vanilla* ebooks. The sale of ebooks rose steeply after the introduction of Amazon's Kindle in the USA in 2007; and in 2010 in the UK, along with devices and online bookstores from other international retailers such as Apple, Kobo, and Sony. Barnes & Noble launched its Nook reading devices in 2009 and began to sell them in the UK in 2012. The UK initially lagged behind the USA by one to two years in the availability of devices and consequent ebook sales. The devices were popular Christmas presents and ebook sales spiked at New Year. However, the growth of self-published ebooks and that of Amazon's own proprietary publishing imprints was hidden.

The traditional pattern of hardback to paperback was disrupted by the arrival of ebooks, and the new convention was that the ebook should be published simultaneously with the first print edition to maximize marketing exposure and reduce piracy. Sometimes there was *digital first* publication, and later on *digital-only* imprints and publishers, especially in the area of genre fiction (e.g. Canelo, acquired by Dorling Kindersley in 2024). Consumers expected ebooks to be priced lower than print editions, while the publishers wanted to hold up prices as long as possible. The biggest early shifts in the purchase of ebooks occurred in the area of fiction, and genre fiction in particular. In 2012, publishers were reporting ebook sales of up to 50 per cent on some individual new fiction titles, and the UK print market for crime alone fell by 25 per cent. Sales in the UK for the Big Six of trade houses (Hachette, PRH, HarperCollins, Pan Macmillan, Bloomsbury, Simon & Schuster) reached a peak of 55 m ebooks (by volume) in the pandemic year of 2020, falling back to 44 m in 2023 (*The Bookseller*, 2 February 2024).

A major problem arises from the online retailers, such as Amazon or Kobo, not releasing regularly their sales data for publication. As a consequence, ebook sales made by smaller publishers, digital first publishers and indie authors, along with the publishing imprints of Amazon and others, are not reported. Exposure of that hidden data in the USA comes from Bookstat.com which in real time scrapes

In 2011 Stieg Larsson became the first author to sell 1 m ebooks on Amazon. In all formats 120 m copies of his books have been sold in over 50 publishing territories.

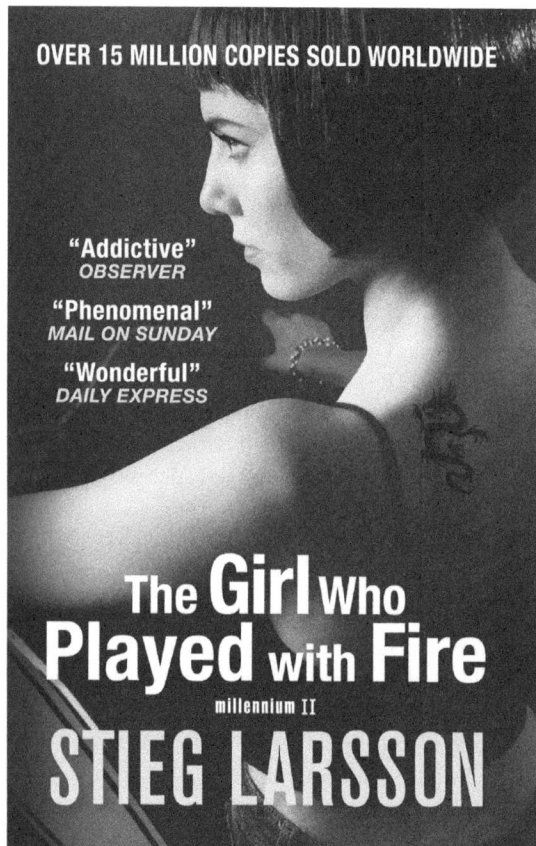

Amazon and the other main online retailers and claims it captures more than 90 per cent of US online sales across print, ebook and audio. For 2022, online unit sales were 403 m for print, 526 m for ebooks, and 188 m for audiobooks. In revenue terms, print and audio each generated higher overall income compared to ebooks because of the difference in pricing (*Publishers Weekly*, 17 February 2023). Ebooks have seen a high level of sales for genre fiction such as romance and erotica, and crime and mystery, and as noted above there are significant sales for self-published authors.

Mike Shatzkin interviewed Paul Abbassi of Bookstat (now owned by Podium Audio), who stated:

> In general, the strongest indicator for how fast sales in a particular book genre will transition to online retailers and digital formats is typical reader 'voracity' in that genre. A three-book-a-year reader is usually picking up their three books in hardcover in airports or brick-and-mortar bookstores (or receiving them as holiday gifts). But most fifty-book-a-year genre fiction readers are, by now, buying those books online, and most probably as ebooks – which usually means that half or more of them are self-published purchases. (idealog.com/blog, accessed 12 March 2024)

Publishers' revenue from ebook sales is derived mainly from the copy sales business model, enacted through licences with resellers. Amazon started its subscription service Kindle Unlimited in 2014 and now offers over one million ebook titles, plus thousands of audiobooks.

Audiobooks

The fast growth in sales and revenue from audiobooks – supercharged by Amazon's Audible – reflects the earlier surge in the uptake of ebooks. The Audio Publishers Association (APA) reported in 2023 that revenue in the US market grew by 10 per cent in 2022 reaching $1.8 bn, with continuous growth seen over the previous decade. A study conducted for the APA by Edison Research found that

> half of the 18+ U.S. population has ever listened to an audiobook, and listeners are likely to be young: 57% are age 18–44. Listeners are also as diverse as the U.S. population, with 29% of audiobook listeners identifying as either African-American or Hispanic, compared to 27% of the U.S. population. (edisonresearch.com, accessed 10 August 2023)

In the UK, sales growth has been equally robust, albeit from a small base. In 2020, audiobooks had a market share of around 6 per cent across book sales in all formats, in both volume and value terms (*Publishing Perspectives*, 30 November 2021). Nielsen carries out regular research into the audiobook consumer, and they find that: 'consumers are increasingly likely to buy audiobooks on subscription, at 38 per cent of all audiobook consumers in 2020 ... rising to over 80% of heavy buyers and nearly all heavy digital buyers' (Nielsen, 2020). The audiobook format remains popular with younger males; whilst heavy buyers are increasingly likely to be female.

More retailers have entered the market, such as Kobo, Google, BookBeat (Bonnier) and AudioBooks.com, and Apple has audiobooks in Apple Books. The streaming market is served by Spotify, and by Storytel in a number of European markets. In Sweden, audiobooks have an impressive 57 per cent share of the book market by volume (Gustafsson, 2021).

The major publishers have their own audio divisions and production facilities, and smaller publishers are increasing their capabilities, though they may sell the rights onto large players. There are also independent audio publishers such as W. F. Howes that buy rights and create original audio content. However, the major force is Audible which bids aggressively for audio rights.

Trends in audio

Richard Lennon, Audio Publisher at Penguin Random House UK

One major trend in audio over the last decade has been a lack of verifiable data on audiobook consumption and purchasing. All the available data sources are either based on incomplete data, or from consumers self-reporting their habits. The following piece thus relies on a mix of those sources and on anecdotal or observed trends from my experience in the field. With that caveat in place, there are four trends we should discuss.

First: growth. Audiobooks have experienced a transformative period of growth over the past decade. Until recently most consumers saw audiobooks as a way of making books available for consumers living with visual impairment or some form of print disability. They are now the fastest-growing area of the market and a hot topic at book fairs and in the trade press. Revenues have exploded, with Nielsen BookData's UK Books & Consumers Survey estimating that UK consumers purchased 28.4 m audiobooks in 2023, up from 8.6 m in 2014. So too have the number of readers for whom audio is now a choice rather than a necessity. Alongside this is a rapid increase in the volume of audiobooks coming to market. A far greater proportion of frontlist titles than ever before now have audiobook editions, often published simultaneously with first format. This is helping drive consumer demand as well as revenues and royalties.

Second: retail diversity. Listeners can access audiobooks through a diverse range of retailer platforms, offering a broad range of commercial models. Players in the space range from some of the world's biggest technology companies to independent start-ups with curated selections of books and/or innovative business models. By contrast to the ebook market where retailer diversity has diminished over the past few years, the audio market offers more choice to the listener regarding where they buy and access content and at the time of writing this choice is increasing rather than diminishing.

E★PERT

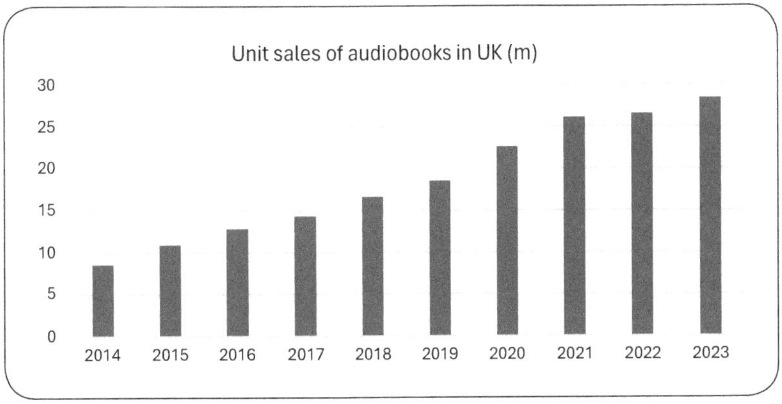

Third: a maturing consumer profile. Ten years ago Nielsen data indicated that only around 2 per cent of the UK adult population had an Audible subscription, and that this audience was more likely to be younger, male, educated to degree-level or higher and to live in an urban setting than the average book-buyer. In 2024 that profile has shifted away from that classic early-adopter digital audience to a demographic somewhat closer to the rest of the book market – the split between male and female listeners now hovers around 50:50 and the average age has increased. It is notable that the audience in audio is still more likely to be young and male than in other formats, which feels significant given this is an audience that the publishing industry has struggled to reach.

Fourth (and arguably most significant): greater engagement from authors with audiobooks. This engagement can manifest in a multitude of ways: more direct involvement in the casting and production process; more creative input into how the recording might be enhanced, for example, with music or sound design; creating extra content which is exclusive to the audio edition, often in the form of recorded conversations. We have also begun to see authors writing with the audio edition in mind from the start. This is particularly true of non-fiction, especially where the author may also have a presence as a podcaster, but can also be true in fiction.

Digital product development

The development by Apple of its app store in 2008 and the launch of the iPad in 2010 opened up an opportunity for publishers to produce, often in collaboration with app developers, titles which contained rich media along with interactive features, similar to those developed by Dorling Kindersley in CD-ROM form over a decade earlier. In retrospect we can see that the lessons of the CD-ROM revolution had been forgotten – no mass market appeared for the products and

Seamus Heaney is one of Ireland's best-loved poets. Considered by many to be the most important Irish poet since Yeats, he was awarded the Nobel Prize in Literature in 1995. He has published more than fifty works of poetry and fiction and is a leading expert in Anglo-Saxon literature. He lives in Dublin.

Seamus Heaney

Encountering Eliot's poetry for the first time

The process of reading Eliot ✓

Reading the end of 'The Fire Sermon'

Reading 'Death by Water'

Paul Keegan

Eliot and illness

Eliot's collaboration with Ezra Pound and Vivienne Eliot

Eliot's legacy

I.   The Burial of the Dead

April is the cruellest month, breeding
Lilacs out of the dead land, mixing
Memory and desire, stirring
Dull roots with spring rain.
Winter kept us warm, covering
Earth in forgetful snow, feeding
A little life with dried tubers.
Summer surprised us, coming over the Starnbergersee
With a shower of rain; we stopped in the colonnade,
And went on in sunlight, into the Hofgarten,
And drank coffee, and talked for an hour.
Bin gar keine Russin, stamm' aus Litauen, echt deutsch.
And when we were children, staying at the arch-duke's,
My cousin's, he took me out on a sled,
And I was frightened. He said, Marie,
Marie, hold on tight. And down we went.
In the mountains, there you feel free.
I read, much of the night, and go south in the winter.

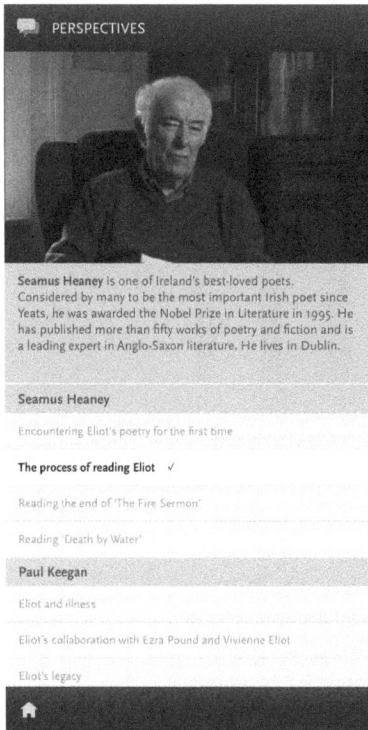

A screenshot from *The Waste Land* app from Faber and Touch Press (released in 2011; Seamus Heaney died in 2013)

the publishers could not cover their high development costs. The development of apps again proved very costly, initially with six-figure investments. Touch Press, in partnership with publishers such as Faber & Faber, produced some notable titles for adults – Steve Jobs used the *Solar System* app in his launch of the iPad 2 in 2011. However, the world of apps is populated with large numbers of free apps, apps sold on a freemium model, and paid-for apps available at very low prices. Most publishers scaled back or abandoned the production of content app titles for adults, but continued modest developments of story book apps for children and young adults. In today's world, most effort is devoted to the world of AI rather than the development of smartphone apps.

Digital publishing breaks the economic constraints of the printed book container, enables faster publication, and updates. In the print-only era, short stories (typically up to, say, 20,000 words) were published only in collections or anthologies, and their sales were modest. Novels often had to be at least 40,000 words, and novellas fell somewhere in between. Amazon at the start of 2011 launched its Kindle Singles programme and kickstarted a new channel for short-form digital fiction and non-fiction, published at low prices, up to $2.99 or £2.50, to drive impulse purchase. Writers may self-publish their short fiction or via their publishers. Short fiction and serial release may be used to promote a future novel through generating pre-orders; or help readers discover and sample established or new writers. Today authors are experimenting with audio-first publication alongside the tremendous growth in podcasting, an area which draws in authors and seeds book projects.

Comics: a phenomenon that crosses borders and transcends literary genres

Marie-Laurence de Rocher, Asfored, Paris

For nearly a decade now, comics – in all their different forms – have been gaining recognition and readership around the world. They can be found in almost every bookcase, have started appearing on major media platforms and have found their way into academic research. For some, this is due to comic books' roots in popular culture; for others, it's due to their unique way of blending visual and textual elements in today's highly visually oriented society. The fact remains that comics have transcended borders to become a truly global phenomenon in the publishing industry. This form of storytelling has evolved to resonate with readers from different cultures, languages and demographic groups: no longer read only by the traditional adult male reader, or considered for children only, comics are now available for all audiences, at all ages.

In France, for example, comics (all genres combined: traditional Franco-Belgian comic strips, manga, graphic novels, superhero comics, etc.) now account for 1 in every 4 books purchased. The sector has overtaken children's books to become the second-largest segment in terms of market share, second only to general literature.

On a global scale, manga – which originated in Japan and appeals to the younger generation with its low prices and serial format – now dominates the market, while Korean webtoons, both in their digital form and as print adaptations, are establishing themselves ever more firmly in the publishing landscape. Yet these publishing trends from Asia are not only being spread around the world, but they are also generating new forms of appropriation. To stand out from the extreme competition in this segment, and given the increasing scarcity of blockbuster titles in a global licensing war, publishers are being forced to innovate in order to continue to serve their audience. They are therefore opting to add original creations to the translation of foreign works, which are increasingly difficult to source. Therefore, you can now find *manfra* (French manga), American *webcomic* that adopts the visual style and format commonly associated with Korean *manhwa*, and so on.

On the European side, classic Franco-Belgian comic strip series are in slight decline in specialist bookshops, as they face increasing competition from documentary or reportage graphic novels: through comic strip adaptations, the publishing world seems to have found a way to enhance the success of its essays. Indeed, the non-fiction comics segment has also been growing steadily over the last ten years. This phenomenon is fairly easy to explain: in today's society, people are more likely to read the latest comic book by Jean-Marc Jancovici and Christophe Blain (*World Without End*, translated into 11 languages in its first year of publication) than the latest scientific reports on the ecological crisis. These adaptations are not the only ones on

E★PERT

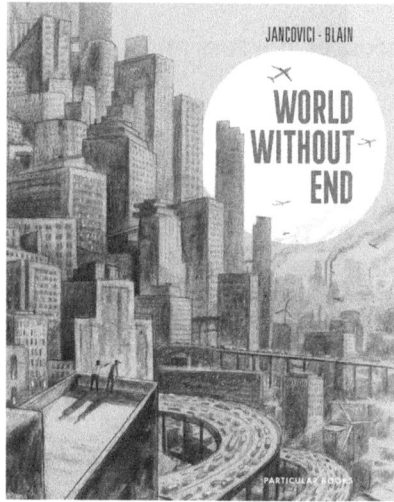

the rise. Classic literary works are also being turned into graphic novels. They appeal particularly to female readership and are now part of many school programmes.

Another major societal development is the emergence of AI in the comics industry. Whether we use this new technology to produce new comics – an ongoing controversy – or to facilitate editorial processes for accessibility, which are still very complicated in the comics field, it is certain that this will be one of the hot topics of the future.

One area of growth is that of manga and digital comics. Manga originated in Japan and Osamu Tezuka (1928–1989) is regarded as the father of the modern manga and anime industries. Not only has manga become mainstream in print, but there are also a variety of online services such as ComiXology, Crunchyroll, and Shonen Jump. Webtoons, which originated in Korea, are a type of digital comic that can be easily read on a smartphone.

In 2020, webtoons' combined sales topped 1 trillion won (£684.6 million) for the first time, representing a year-on-year increase of over 64%. Today, webtoons stand as a foundation of Korean storytelling industries, having become an inexhaustible source of inspiration for K-drama, cinema, musicals and computer games. (vam.ac.uk, accessed 10 August 2023)

Diversity and inclusion

There have been huge changes in society over the period covered by this chapter. In the UK these include the decriminalization of homosexuality and the introduction of equal pay for women. The global phenomenon of the Black Lives Matter movement has highlighted the issue of racial inequality.

There is a high proportion of women in publishing, particularly London consumer book publishing, and two-thirds of the workforce is female. In senior management the position of women has improved at board level and there are a number of prominent women in senior positions across the industry. However, the UK government's survey of the gender pay gap (the difference between the average hourly earnings of men and women) in companies with more than 250 employees revealed a national median figure of 18.5 per cent. Some large publishers were above or below that median (*The Bookseller*, 23 March 2018).

Diversity has many dimensions from gender to class and ethnic background, and it can be examined across the workforce, a company's publishing output, authorship, and the pool of translators for works from other languages. An industry study (*Writing the Future*, Kean, 2015) found that only 8 per cent of UK publishing employees came from a black, Asian and minority ethnic background. Not only did this not reach the proportion within the UK as a whole (14 per cent from an ethnic minority), but also did not reflect the ethnic make-up of London (40 per cent), where many consumer publishers are based. Progress has undoubtedly been made to rectify the imbalances in the composition of the workforce, and publishers are keen to go further. They are actively pursuing initiatives to improve diversity and inclusivity in their workforce, from internships and apprenticeships to blind recruitment processes and the building of networks to support staff throughout their career. In the UK, Creative Access helps young people from under-represented communities to secure paid training opportunities in creative companies, and support them into regular employment. Publishers have opened up regional offices outside London to help recruit from different parts of the country, and to help those employees who can't afford to live in London without considerable sacrifice.

> 'I hate the feeling of being read just because somebody's trying to tick off a diversity check box.' Rebecca Kuang

The 2020 UK study *Rethinking 'Diversity' in Publishing* examined how writers of colour are affected by the practices of the publishing industry, concluding that:

> The core audience for publishers is white and middle-class. The whole industry is essentially set up to cater for this one audience. This affects how writers of colour and their books are treated, which are either whitewashed or exoticised in order to appeal to this segment. (Saha and van Lente, 2020)

There is clearly an opportunity for publishers to increase their inclusivity and broaden the readership for their books. Again progress has been made in the industries on both sides of the Atlantic. In the USA the number of Black authors increased by 22 per cent between 2014 and 2020, although most of this gain occurred in the final year of the survey (wordsrated.com, accessed 29 January 2024). Diana Evans writes:

> The feeling arises that with the ebbing of immediate outrage, the energy for change is in danger of stagnating, owing to deep-rooted structural inequalities. Although we are seeing a broader range of subject matter, there exists a penchant in acquisition and marketing departments for 'risk-free' books by writers of colour – such as the slave narrative or the racial identity narrative or the gritty urban tale. (*Financial Times*, 27 January 2024)

Table 1.6 Composition of the workforce in UK publishing

	% of workforce	% of national population (England and Wales)
Female	66	51
Ethnic minority groups	17	18
LGB+	15	3
Disability or long-term health condition	16	18
Privately educated	17	7
Educated to degree level or above	82	34

Source: 2022 data from Publishers Association, Publishing Workforce report.

Now read this

John B. Thompson, *Book Wars: The digital revolution in publishing*, Polity, 2021.

Sources

Diana Athill, *Stet*, Granta, 2000.

David Barker and Cat Mitchell, 'The Thursday Murder Club: Launching a megabrand author', *Logos* 33:1 (2022).

Alan Bartram, *Making Books: Design in British publishing since 1945*, British Library, 1999.

Karl Berglund and Ann Steiner, 'Is Backlist the New Frontlist?', *Logos*, 32:1 (2021).

Helena Gustafsson, 'The Market for Audiobooks', *Logos*, 32:2 (2021).

Danuta Kean (ed.), *Writing the Future: Black and Asian writers and publishers in the UK market place*, Spread the Word, 2015.

R. F. Kuang, *Yellowface*, HarperCollins, 2023.

Jeremy Lewis, *Penguin Special: The life and times of Allen Lane*, Viking, 2005.

Tom Maschler, *Publisher*, Picador, 2005.

Nielsen, *Understanding the UK Audiobook Consumer*, 2020.

Ian Norrie, *Mumby's Publishing and Bookselling in the Twentieth Century*, 6th edition, Bell & Hyman, 1982.

Angus Phillips, 'Have We Passed Peak Book?', *Publishing Research Quarterly*, 33:3, September 2017.

Matthew Rubery, *The Untold Story of the Talking Book*, Harvard University Press, 2016.

Anamik Saha and Sandra van Lente, *Rethinking 'Diversity' in Publishing*, Goldsmiths Press, 2020.

John B. Thompson, *Merchants of Culture*, Polity, 2012.

Rayner Unwin, *George Allen & Unwin: A remembrancer*, Merlin Unwin Books, 1999.

Web resources

https://www.audiopub.org Audio Publishers Association (USA).

www.carnegiegreenaway.org.uk Carnegie and Kate Greenaway Children's Book Awards.

https://www.edisonresearch.com Research into consumer behaviour across media.

http://blogs.guardian.co.uk/books/ *Guardian* blog about books and the book trade.

CHAPTER 2

Publishing for educational, academic and professional markets

Non-consumer publishing encompasses the educational, academic, and professional publishing sectors, including the publication of learned journals. The major publishers strive to gain scale in the sectors in which they specialize – across the world. Their markets are open to disruption from both large technology players and start-ups with no legacy business, and Apple's Steve Jobs expressed his aim to crack open the school textbook market: 'Jobs had his sights set on textbooks as the next business he wanted to transform. He believed it was an $8 bn a year industry ripe for digital destruction' (Isaacson, 2011, page 269). Nevertheless, many years later publishers have made significant advances themselves in terms of the creation of digital materials and the move from product to service. Sectors such as journal publishing have been in the advance of digital developments, and well over 90 per cent of journals are now available online. Content has been both aggregated into large searchable databases, and disaggregated so that individual articles and chapters can be purchased. Whilst governments around the world continue to experiment with the introduction of digital content into schools, some publishers are looking to own the whole value chain in educational and academic markets by providing learning, testing and examination services. Developments in artificial intelligence (AI) are taking shape with the technology embedded in products and services. Publishers are keen to embed the UN Sustainable Development Goals (SDGs) into their mission and their operations, including the areas of inclusive and equitable quality education and combating climate change. There remain challenges around research integrity in academic publishing with paper mills pushing fabricated articles into the system of scholarly communication.

In terms of ownership, consolidation has continued apace in the twenty-first century. Private equity groups have played a significant role in reassembling publishing imprints and assets, both by purchasing them and selling them on in new forms. Major drivers for consolidation have been the migration to digital formats and services, the high costs involved in making the transition, and the decline in old business models and the adaptations to new models. There are also threats to publishers from the growth of open access (OA) models, first in journals and now in books. The success of rental schemes in the college textbook market has prompted a response from publishers with subscription services for digital content for both institutions and individual students.

DOI: 10.4324/9781003403289-3

The centre of gravity of international publishing is shifting eastwards towards the growth markets of India and China. China is now the largest producer of research articles, having overtaken the USA, and overall the Global South is seeing strong growth in the output of scientific research. Research bodies are looking to equity and social justice when making funding decisions; and readers are keen to access diverse content from non-western researchers.

CONSOLIDATION

The consolidation of industry players has taken place over a long period. Pearson, well known for its Longman imprint purchased in 1968, acquired the US publisher Addison-Wesley in 1988, and then in 1998 acquired Simon & Schuster's educational operations – including Prentice Hall – and the US Macmillan Publishing from its parent Viacom. It created the world's largest educational (textbook) publisher. Pearson led the way in its purchase of companies which offered to educational organizations services in assessment, elearning, and student recruitment and support. Its many acquisitions included in 2007, Harcourt Assessment from Reed Elsevier, and eCollege, a US provider of elearning, enrolment and student support services to higher education; in 2009, Wall Street English, a provider of English language training in China; and in 2010, a division of Sistema Educacional Brasileiro (SEB), giving it a strong presence in *sistemas* ('learning systems') for preschool, primary and secondary schools in Brazil.

A significant shake-up of publishers occurred around the turn of the century. In 1995, the Macmillan family had sold a majority stake in Macmillan Publishers (whose interests included the journal *Nature*) to the German publisher Holtzbrinck. The remaining shares were purchased by Holtzbrinck in 1999. Taylor & Francis floated on the London Stock Exchange in 1998 and shortly after more than doubled in size with the acquisition of the Routledge group of publishers. It has since acquired numerous academic and STM publishers on both sides of the Atlantic, enabling it to enjoy both economies of scale and synergies in areas such as marketing.

In 1999, the German family-owned Bertelsmann – primarily a consumer-focused media group – bought a controlling interest in the (German family-owned) STM publisher Springer before selling it on to private equity. Springer and the academic and STM publishing operations of the Dutch publisher Kluwer were merged in 2003. Subsequently in 2015, Holtzbrinck and the private equity owners of Springer agreed a merger to form Springer Nature, second only to Elsevier in the STM market.

The opening decades of the century were challenging to the educational and college textbook publishers, especially in the USA, and triggered many changes in ownership, and in some cases the debt re-financing of loss-making publishers. In 2002, a private equity consortium bought the major US educational publisher Houghton Mifflin, which then in 2006 underwent a reverse takeover by the smaller Irish educational software company Riverdeep. In 2007, Reed Elsevier, the world's biggest publisher of information for professional users operating in the markets of science, medical and legal, having previously bought the US publisher Harcourt in 2001, decided to sell its school educational imprints (including Heinemann in the UK) to Pearson, while keeping the higher education and medical publishing businesses. Likewise the other major information and professional publishers decided to concentrate on providing digital content and services to professionals, rather than compete in education against Pearson. In 2007, the Dutch information and health publisher Wolters Kluwer sold its school publishing assets (including Nelson Thornes) to private equity, in order to concentrate on its professional businesses. In the same year, the Canadian family-owned Thomson Corporation sold Thomson Learning, a division focused on higher education (second only to Pearson in the US college market), again to private equity, to form Cengage, and bought Reuters. Running against the trend of European purchases of US publishers, in 2007, the family-controlled US publisher John Wiley purchased the family-owned Blackwell, based in Oxford, which published books and journals for STM, humanities and social science markets. In 2008, Cengage Learning was combined with the College Division of Houghton Mifflin.

Following the financial crisis beginning in 2008, merger and acquisition activity in the industry was subdued until 2013 when McGraw-Hill Education was divested from McGraw-Hill Financial (S&P Global) and purchased by private equity. It was rebranded as a learning science company to show investors that it was making the transition from primarily a printed textbook company to a provider of digital content and technology-enabled learning, such as through the use of adaptive learning systems. Also in 2013, Cengage Learning, overburdened by debt and facing declining printed textbook sales, filed for bankruptcy under Chapter 11; it operates today under the name Cengage Group. In 2022, Houghton Mifflin was acquired by the private equity firm Veritas Capital.

All the major educational publishers in the USA, especially at the college level, experienced severe financial stress and the viability of their core business model of selling big printed textbooks to students at high prices came into question. The American college textbook market is several times the annual turnover of the entire UK publishing industry. It is described as counter-cyclical in that during an economic recession student enrolments increase and conversely reduce as employment opportunities increase. After the financial crisis of 2008 the US economy recovered and student enrolments fell. But there were deeper and long-standing problems facing the publishers. Some analysts argued that the publishers were too slow in migrating to digital formats which explained their declining profitability. However, there were many reasons. Students facing rapidly rising college fees were highly critical of the high prices of the new textbooks they were asked to buy by their professors.

Many American students had long turned to buying second-hand copies, and in a defensive move the publishers (as a result of falling new book demand) issued new editions at escalated prices all too frequently, say, every three years, frustrating teachers and students. Custom textbook publishing was a feature of the higher education landscape in the 1990s and 2000s. Furthermore from around 2006, textbook rental through third-party companies such as Chegg, and through campus bookstores, grew quickly, placing more pressure on the publishers' margins. In the USA, rental companies buy a printed book, rent it at a lower cost to students repeatedly (say 4–5 times), and do not recompense the publisher and author. (Such unlicensed renting is prohibited in the UK where copyright legislation differs.) In 2012, Amazon – which at that time had around 30 per cent of US textbook sales, overtaking sales through campus bookstores – launched its own printed textbook rental offer. It was to be nearly a decade later that publishers began to offer their own rental schemes for printed and ebooks, and deeply discounted the retail price of ebook formats. This strategy was superseded by the promotion of digital texts on an all-you-can eat model in return for a monthly subscription. Access for students might be through their institution or as an individual subscription. Such a service is Cengage Unlimited and by 2022 the number of its subscribers was approaching 5 m. Amazon's rental service for printed textbooks closed in 2023 but still rents digital texts.

Another big issue for the US college textbook publishers was the re-importation into America of the foreign editions of their printed texts by third party arbitrage traders, who took advantage of the price differential between high US prices and the lower prices in Europe, Asia and Australia. In 2013, the US Supreme Court ruled in favour of a Thai trader, reselling books in the US market, in the *Kirtsaeng vs John Wiley* case. Such parallel importation affects all kinds of publishing and has occurred for decades in the print world wherever significant price differentials exist between nation states. The ruling resulted in publishers implementing global price hikes, which further reduced demand for printed copies.

The big textbook publishers bought edtech companies, sometimes at inflated prices, that offered the prospects of higher growth, but which in some cases were unrealized or were diversifications that added little value to the publishing ecosystem. The publishers recorded digital growth but that was outweighed by the significant disruption from the used market in physical textbooks.

The world's largest educational publisher Pearson was badly affected by the decline in the USA of its traditional printed textbook market and that of its testing business, and reported a loss of \$3.3 bn (£2.6 bn) in 2016. Like others, it refocused its investment in digital learning outcomes, rationalized its complexity and numerous IT systems, adopted new business models, reduced the prices of retail and rental ebooks, and cut staff numbers by many thousands. It shut previously acquired technology businesses; sold off businesses which did not fit, such as the bricks-and-mortar Wall Street English; and in 2017 announced that it would sell its K-12 courseware publishing in the USA and the UK (a sector slow to adapt to digital learning). The company sold off thousands of titles to other publishers such as Taylor & Francis. It had previously raised cash by selling the *Financial Times* and its 50 per cent stake in *The Economist,* and continued to reduce its stake in Penguin Random House. Pearson returned to profit in 2018, and sold its remaining stake in PRH to Bertelsmann in 2020.

The migration to digital formats drives consolidation, not least in the ability enabled by size to invest in technology. Economies of scale along with the formation of large aggregations of content are critical in academic and STM publishing. The big players can afford to make the necessary large investments in online scientific journals and accompanying tools to aid researchers, and in building ebook collections for libraries. The larger the publisher's content and the greater their control over the intellectual property, the greater is the leverage of the aggregation. It is argued by the large publishers that it is easier for academic libraries and their purchasing consortia to deal with just a few publishers and to use their platforms providing online content and services – rather than have to negotiate with dozens of publishers and intermediaries.

EDUCATIONAL PUBLISHING

Schools publishing

Educational markets worldwide are subject to the influence of government, politics and regulations at the state, regional and local levels more than any other publishing sector. Generally speaking, the greater the amount of content prescription and regulatory control, the narrower the range of published material and that tends to favour large publishers over smaller publishers. The UK market is influenced by curriculum and assessment strategies, the vagaries of government expenditure, organizational and funding changes to the state school system, and the performance metrics applied to schools. The government's emphasis on academic qualifications or vocational training reverses periodically. The main educational publishers usually cover schools, sixth form colleges and further education colleges. Changes in demographics over time affect market size, for example, the number of live births in the UK fell from 730,000 in 2012 to 605,000 in 2022 – this will feed through into enrolments. The global pandemic accelerated the move towards digital access and services, as schools and parents sought home-learning resources and tools. Digital sales represented 17 per cent of the total in 2022, as compared to 8 per cent in 2017.

In comparison to the consumer book publishers, the educational publishers are less affected by the powerful retailers since many sales are direct to schools:

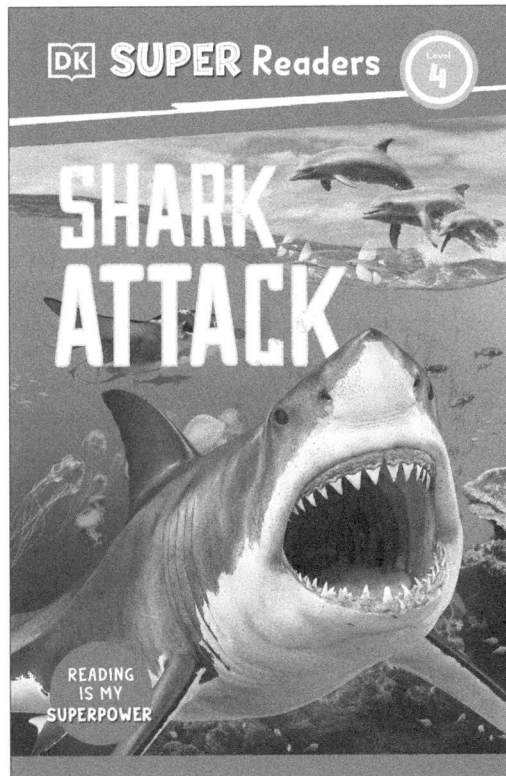

DK Super Readers help young readers to practise their reading skills typically more than 50 per cent. Sales through Amazon and educational suppliers are significant routes to market. But their business is affected by the interest of the technology companies in this market, increased use of tablets and of free internet content, and teacher-generated content. For example, lesson plans or activities can be easily downloaded from the internet. Publishers' lists of books, learning resources and services can take longer to build and their sales, though more steady and generally more profitable than in consumer publishing, are subject to periodic downturns. Publishers have invested in research into children's learning, and for example Oxford University Press has conducted studies on the word gap in education:

> For our Oxford Language Report we carried out market research with more than 1,000 teachers. Over half of those surveyed reported that at least 40% of their pupils lacked the vocabulary to access their learning. 69% of primary school teachers and over 60% of secondary school teachers believe the word gap is increasing. (Oxford Language Report, 2018, page 2)

An important subsector of educational publishing is referred to as 'trade' or 'consumer' education. This area embraces study and revision guides aimed at students for home study and the parental anxiety market, and self-study products, some of which are published online. It is referred to as 'trade' since historically such product lines were purchased by parents through booksellers (including Amazon) and not by schools for class use, although they may be used in schools. The independent Cumbria-based publisher Coordination Group Publications leads the major publishers in this area: 'CGP has a firm grip on the UK's study guides market. Nearly £1 in every £2 spent through Nielsen BookScan's School Textbooks & Study Guides category in the past year was on a CGP book' (*The Bookseller*, 9 June 2023). The back to school (BTS) retail market occurs in England in August and September.

Overall, educational content has become progressively localized and therefore less exportable to overseas countries than hitherto. However, the major companies invest in local publishing and apply their technologies and approaches across their international operations. Some specialize in publishing for the English-medium education market with its international qualifications. The for-profit schools are growing in emerging economies, cover international curricula and offer their students the prospect of entry to world-leading universities. The first overseas subsidiaries of UK publishers were opened in the late-nineteenth and early-twentieth centuries in Australia and Canada, and in the 1960s the educational and academic houses opened subsidiaries in the newly formed African Commonwealth countries and exported large quantities of UK-based textbooks. The educational systems there were based on UK curricula or examinations.

The UK Bribery Act, which came into force in 2011, holds UK firms accountable for bribery, whether committed directly and on their behalf, in the UK or overseas. Publishers have to take care how they regulate their international businesses in order not to fall foul of this legislation. There have been unfortunate incidents, and in 2011, Macmillan was

> ordered to pay £11.3m for 'unlawful conduct' related to its education division in East and West Africa. The High Court order was made after the Serious

Fraud Office (SFO) began an inquiry last year following a report from the World Bank. The report said Macmillan had made 'bribery payments' to secure a deal to print textbooks in South Sudan. (bbc.co.uk, accessed 19 January 2024)

This initiated a significant retreat by the publisher from a number of African countries. OUP faced similar charges in Kenya and Tanzania, and was fined nearly £2 m in 2012.

The first wave of publisher consolidation occurred during the 1980s when UK school pupil rolls declined, and the number of significant educational publishers decreased from around 30 to 15. By the early 1990s, the top three publishers commanded 50 per cent of sales to schools; and the top seven over 75 per cent. The remaining publishers concentrated in specialist areas or subjects. Consolidation amongst publishers proceeded more slowly until 2007, when Reed Elsevier decided to sell its education interests (Harcourt, including Heinemann) to Pearson; and Wolters Kluwer decided to divest its educational publishing assets (Nelson Thornes and other European publishers) to private equity. In 2013, Nelson Thornes was sold to Oxford University Press – a rare example of an acquisition by a university press. The main players include:

- Pearson
- Hodder Education (Hachette)
- Oxford University Press
- Collins (News Corporation)

There are other significant players, for example, Cambridge University Press, whose publishing (along with resources from Pearson and OUP) includes materials for international qualifications such as the IGCSE (International General Certificate of Secondary Education) and IB (International Baccalaureate); Macmillan Education concentrates on international markets. Other publishers serving UK primary schools and the school library market are children's publishers such as Penguin Random House, Usborne and Scholastic.

Schools have seen the application of technologies and business models first developed in higher education, such as the introduction of learning management systems (LMS), online testing linked to learning resources, and the growth of online resources. Digital innovation is also driven by the major technology companies, such as Google and Microsoft, and specialist edtech companies, many of which have venture capital investment.

The use by publishers of subscription models for digital course materials, adaptive learning systems and testing services continues to grow. The first generation of interactive textbooks was published for the iPad in 2012. The secondary market for publishers is still based on the sale of printed textbooks, but for some subjects (e.g. in science) the proposition is blended with digital elements delivered by a platform rather than a website. Other materials include workbooks, online revision resources, and digital content for front-of-class teaching. There is a continuing rise in the number of teachers using interactive and digital content around the world, and for example during the pandemic publishers increased the provision of PDF versions of textbooks – these could be used at home when the schools were closed. Teachers and students also have access to a vast amount of free content available on the web.

Major investments have been made, especially in adaptive learning systems, initially funded by US government grants targeted at K-12 learning in mathematics topics to mimic a personalized tutor. Houghton Mifflin Harcourt, the leading publisher in the US pre-K-12 market, purchased the edtech business of Scholastic in 2015. Digital tools available to teachers include Kahoot!, which gamifies learning, and Google Classroom, which promotes paperless classrooms. Adaptive learning products, utilizing AI, are being applied to language learning, and to the more rule-based subjects such as maths and science subjects. In the UK in 2023, the government announced an investment of

> up to £2 million in Oak National Academy, which was established to support teachers with high-quality curriculum resources online, to create new teaching tools using AI – marking the first step towards providing every teacher with a personalised AI lesson-planning assistant. (www.gov.uk, accessed 17 January 2023)

ELT Publishing

The publishing of English Language Teaching (ELT) course materials engages very large investments and a worldwide marketing strength for this predominantly export-orientated field. The publishers enjoyed strong growth from export sales through the 1990s but in 1997 it began to falter. Although the quantity of books exported rose, prices fell in sterling terms and the real value of turnover decreased. The strength of sterling, the Asian economic crisis, and the problems in Brazil and Argentina (important ELT markets) took their toll. Then in the years following the financial crash of 2008, publishers experienced difficulties in traditional European markets such as Greece and Spain. The adoption of smartphones and tablets is helping to push digital sales in emerging markets in Asia and the Middle East. The share of digital sales for UK publishers rose to 12 per cent in 2022 from 7 per cent in 2017. The main publishers include:

- Oxford University Press
- Pearson
- Macmillan Education
- Cambridge University Press
- Richmond Publishing

Oxford University Press (OUP) is the largest international ELT publisher and this part of the business accounts for a significant portion of its sales and profit. It maintains market leadership in British English (especially in Europe) while also publishing in American English. Pearson is the biggest player in the American English market. It added the important American English lists of Addison-Wesley (in 1988) and Prentice Hall (1998) – thereby leading the markets in Latin America and Asia – to its original mainly British English Longman imprint. Cambridge University Press (CUP) built its business without acquisition, and benefited from its close association with the University of Cambridge Local Examinations Syndicate (UCLES) under the brand Cambridge

Assessment, which operates the internationally recognized examinations. In 2021, Cambridge University Press and Cambridge Assessment came together to form Cambridge University Press & Assessment, with a turnover of £1 bn across all parts of the business. Macmillan Education developed its ELT business through the purchase of Heinemann ELT in 1998. It was a pioneer in ELT digital publishing and developed from 2002 the Macmillan English Campus, a complete learning management system, and Onestopenglish for teachers. Since then, other ELT publishers have developed their own subscription platforms serving millions of students and communities of registered English language teachers. Some overseas ELT publishers have taken advantage of UK expertise and have established UK operations, for example Richmond Publishing owned by the Spanish publisher Santillana. Founded in 1992, it has a strong emphasis on materials for Spanish and Portuguese markets, including Mexico and Brazil. Other major publishers, such as Cengage and Collins, have ELT lists, and there are smaller, niche publishers in the UK, and also packagers which offer editorial, design and production services to the major players – often their former employers. National Geographic Learning is part of Cengage Learning: 'Access to National Geographic Society's high impact photography, storytelling and other content provides tools to teach the English language in ways that celebrate global citizenship and diverse cultures rather than focusing on so-called native speaker individual cultures' (Maguire, 2022).

From the standpoint of the major players, ELT publishing is a distinct field of publishing needing its own publishing operations, typically based in the UK and the USA to produce British and American English materials; plus other publishing centres, such as those in Spain, Asia, Latin America and Eastern Europe, to commission or adapt the courses to national or regional markets; and marketing sales offices elsewhere. In some countries, ministries of education have to approve the courses. Part of the strategic importance of ELT is that as a growing market worldwide it provides the publisher with a local or regional foothold in non-English areas of the world, through the opening of local companies or marketing offices, or through the acquisition of local publishers. Although the major publishers dominate the international provision of course materials, they have faced increasing competition from indigenous local publishers; private language school chains with publishing operations; and online providers.

The convention that children learn their native language and subsequently learn English as a foreign language (EFL) or second language is increasingly being challenged in some countries where children learn their local language and English simultaneously. English is being taught from pre-primary school in many countries, offering significant new opportunities to the international players and local companies.

ACADEMIC, STM AND PROFESSIONAL PUBLISHING

The internationalization of academic, STM and professional book publishing occurred earlier than in consumer book publishing, and is far more extensive. High-level books and journals in English, especially in STM, have an international currency throughout the world and remain important drivers of academic reputations and careers. Their publishers do not have to contend with the retention of territorial and other rights by literary agents: they invariably acquire all rights in authors' works, including electronic rights worldwide. The journal and reference publishers were the first to embark on the transition from print to digital publishing in the last century. Later, the larger players that provide textbooks for higher education, such as Pearson, McGraw-Hill, Cengage, and Wiley, aimed to transition from the supply of discrete printed products or ebook equivalents to the provision of interactive digital products and learning solutions, including video and audio.

Again the pandemic shifted institutional purchasing and student preferences further towards digital access even though there is evidence that the printed page supports more effective learning. Anna Mangen suggests:

> an interesting finding in some of the empirical studies is that we tend to overestimate our own reading comprehension when we read on screen compared to on paper. Some studies have shown that we believe we have understood the text better, when we read from a screen. However, it has been found that we tend to read faster on screen and consequently understand less compared to when reading from paper. (cited in Torhelm, 2018)

While learned journal articles are mainly delivered online, the fixed page PDF print layout endures as the dominant format used by researchers for their citations. Publishers have to contend with a range of consumer preferences in a world which is nevertheless moving towards mobile and interactive engagement. Learning and research are also transformed by search, with Google at the centre of the workflows of both students and researchers.

The fortunes of academic and STM publishers and the kinds of books and other products they produce are inextricably linked to institutional spending on research worldwide, especially in relation to library budgets in the developed world (generally static) and to faster growth in emerging economies (e.g. India and China); to the numbers and wealth of full-time and part-time students; to the behaviour of librarians, researchers, administrators, teachers and students; and to policies on the open access publishing of research in the form of journal articles and monographs (especially in Europe). Professional publishing in the areas of law or finance has traditionally been highly profitable. The trend has been towards online content and services. For example, LexisNexis, part of RELX and founded 200 years ago, is the leading global provider of legal, regulatory and business information and analytics. During the 1970s, it pioneered the electronic accessibility of legal and other documents. The move from product to service is exemplified by Elsevier's ClinicalKey AI, which gives doctors access to the latest research. The tool combines 'evidence-based clinical content with conversational search powered by generative AI to support clinicians in delivering high-quality patient care' (elsevier.com, accessed 4 March 2024).

Funders of research have policies on diversity, equity and inclusion (DEI) and there is impetus to address inequities within scholarly communication and the wider research environment. In the area of biodiversity, the involvement of local researchers is seen as key to finding workable solutions. Yet,

> Most scientific publications in tropical ecology and conservation are led by authors from just a handful of countries, with researchers and scientific institutions based in the Global South remaining underrepresented. This publishing bias is often accompanied by parachute research, in which foreign scientists researching in or about the tropics fail to involve local counterparts and share scientific outcomes and practical resources from their studies with stakeholders in the study area. (Ocampo-Ariza et al., 2023)

Major publishers dominate the fields of academic and professional publishing on a worldwide scale. The market sectors are diverse in respect of the character of the publishing operations. Two giant publishers occupy either end of the spectrum. Pearson Education (part of the UK-listed company Pearson) is a significant higher education publisher, primarily focused on teaching and learning resources. Elsevier (RELX) is the world's leading STM publisher, with a focus on scientific journals and the supply of information to health and pharma markets, with associated book businesses, including some textbook, academic and professional book publishing.

The leading publishers are diverse in their discipline span and the character of their operations. Springer Nature majors in research publishing, especially in STM, and through its common ownership by Holtzbrinck, is associated with technology operations and Macmillan Education. Wolters Kluwer offers information and services to professionals in the areas of law, taxation, finance and health care. The operations of Wiley, another leading STM publisher with important journals, include the area of arts, humanities and social sciences (AHSS) and textbook, academic and professional publishing. Taylor & Francis (part of Informa, and including the imprints of Routledge and CRC Press) has a broad spread of journal and book publishing and a large book title output. SAGE Publications (named after its founders SAra Miller and GEorge McCune), covering books and journals, is privately owned. It began as a social science publisher but has since diversified and grown organically as well as through the acquisition of other companies.

In the UK, other academic publishers include Bloomsbury Academic (as part of its diversification from trade into academic) and Emerald (acquired in 2022 by the Cambridge Information Group), alongside smaller companies such as Edward Elgar, Pluto, Polity, and other specialists, such as the professional publisher Kogan Page, and Rowman & Littlefield International (acquired by Bloomsbury in 2024). In addition, there are numerous not-for-profit scholarly societies and museums that publish academic works.

The not-for-profit university presses are significant book and journal publishers. Oxford University Press, which publishes more than 6,000 titles per year, competes alongside the leading private-sector publishers. It supports financially the university. OUP spans most academic disciplines at the higher level of academic and scholarly publishing, and includes textbook, reference and journal publishing. It acts as a print and digital distributor for smaller presses. In 2011 it developed University Press Scholarship Online (UPSO): an aggregation of OUP content and that of other university presses. It was overtaken in turnover by Cambridge University Press, which has a similar spread of activities, with the merger of CUP and the exams group Cambridge Assessment in 2021. The mid-size UK university presses – Liverpool, Manchester, Edinburgh, Bristol (developed out of the Policy Press) and Wales – account for the publication of hundreds of titles and dozens of journals, typically in AHSS subjects. Such UK university presses are expected to be commercially self-sustaining, unlike many US presses which are financially supported by their universities or have endowed funds such as Princeton and Harvard. The US university presses are also represented in the UK, notably Yale and Princeton, which have local commissioning operations. The editors of university presses actively commission authors from other universities. Likewise many authors favour the publication of their books through university presses other than that of their own institution in order to gain third-party endorsement. Academics have freedom of choice to publish through university presses or commercial publishers (academic and trade) wherever in the world.

Library publishing expanded in the USA from around 2010 and was taken up in the UK. In some cases university presses were folded into libraries, although in most instances libraries extended their operations beyond managing their institutional depositories of content to include publishing services for faculty and students, and publishing journals for learned societies. Most are small-scale publishing operations. Library presses are experimenting in new forms of scholarly communication. For example, UCL Press was founded in 2015 by University College London as the UK's first fully open access university press: a model typically used by library publishers. It is subsidized by its host university to enable OA publishing and it delivers significant impact for the university. Broadly speaking, university presses of all kinds are moving closer to the objectives of their host institutions, especially in the aim of sharing and wider dissemination of research while trying to maintain sustainability. In so doing they are differentiating themselves to some degree from commercial publishers.

All publishers specialize in publishing books or journals in particular academic disciplines or groups of allied disciplines. Not even the largest would claim to publish in all disciplines. Their output can be divided into three broad categories:

- textbooks (course materials)
- monographs and reference books
- journals

TEXTBOOKS

The US core textbook model has moved towards digital delivery focused on learning outcomes. The publisher's aim is to create scalable products to improve learning outcomes worldwide. This model was initially applied to the arguably more defined and quantifiable or rule-based subjects – mainly the hard sciences, mathematics, psychology, business and economics – but is extending to other subjects.

In the USA, publishers traditionally analyse and synthesize curriculum needs across the continent, recruit the best teacher creators who are supported by teams of writers, reviewers and publisher professionals, and craft printed textbooks of up to 1,000 pages with high design values and special learning features. The US professors adopt one book per course, from which they, or more likely their instructors (post docs in science or adjunct faculty, part-timers contracted to teach on less favourable employment terms), usually teach chapter by chapter. In view of the large class sizes and the high value of adoptions generated from sales to students, US core textbook publishing became a very large, competitive and highly profitable business until the first decade of this century. The publishers became engaged in a virtual arms race. In order to secure adoptions of their books they competed to offer the instructors additional and free supplementary material to help them teach the course. The material, which started out in the late twentieth century as a marketing device to persuade faculty to use the publisher's books,

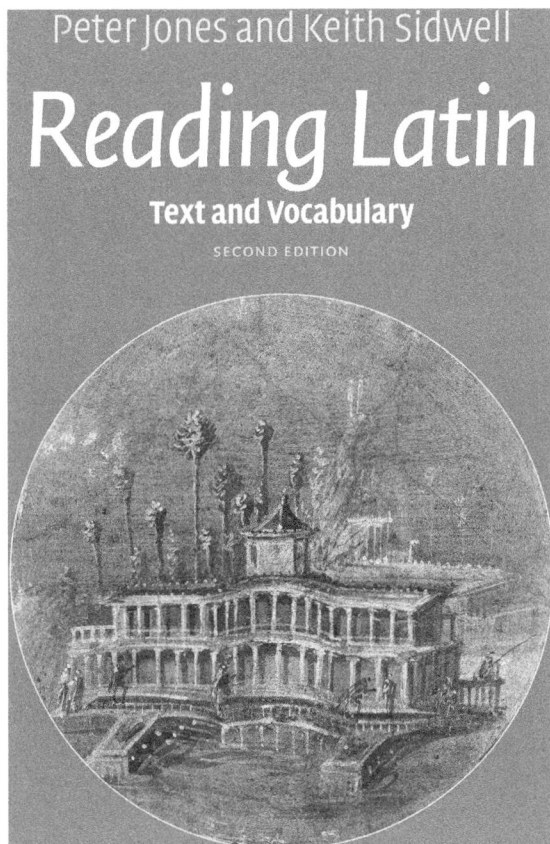

Peter Jones and Keith Sidwell

Reading Latin

Text and Vocabulary

SECOND EDITION

An example of a higher education textbook published by Cambridge University Press grew in scale and complexity. As part of these supplements, the publishers built test banks of thousands of multiple choice questions to support their big texts. The delivery of the supplementary packages has gone through every development of technology: print, video tape to disk, overhead projection to PowerPoint. With the advent of online delivery and connectivity, the supplements were renamed 'digital resources' or 'bonus content' and from around the turn of the century they came to embrace publisher technology support.

Pearson scored a major success from around 2011 with the innovative and interactive homework platform MyLab, first associated with its mathematics textbooks. Such homework platforms were developed for wider use in classroom teaching. Pearson is now incorporating generative AI tools into its content, for example, students are able to engage in conversations to help them understand key concepts. Other publisher initiatives include WileyPLUS – an online product that combines electronic versions of texts with media resources and tools for instructors and students (including for tracking student progress and providing targeted feedback) – and the mobile adaptive learning technologies pioneered by McGraw-Hill Education among others. Institutions use a learning management system (LMS), such as Blackboard or the open source Moodle, through which publishers' products can be used. Some publishers offer institutions their own LMS, providing a distribution channel for online content and services. Publishers claim that their high-end digital products aid student performance and retention and reduce teaching costs.

Publishers are taking their services further, for example, in respect of data analytics, such as analysing data collected from student usage of their products to aid a teacher or institution, through to emerging big data collected on a world scale. Some publishers offer institutions Online Program Management to develop online degrees and certificates. This can include instructional design, marketing and student registration, and sometimes joint venture investment.

In order to address the affordability issue of textbooks, publishers are discounting their ebook prices, producing cheaper paperback editions, producing for lecturers customized editions and coursepack material, and experimenting with new business models. Cengage launched an online subscription service which offered students, per semester, access to the entire catalogue at roughly the price of just one major text. The major publishers (and platforms such as VitalSource and RedShelf) launched an inclusive access model to ensure every student on day one of a course has access to the adopted course materials at affordable prices – or included in the tuition fee, funded by the university. The model ameliorates problems such as the used book market and illegal imports. Such a model is not generally applied to publishers' higher priced courseware: computer software usually with the textbook embedded, and including interactive features such as auto-graded homework, student and instructor dashboards, and personalization tools.

Although some of the online resources from publishers are freely available on companion websites for marketing purposes, the rich material is restricted to code access. This enabled publishers, for so long separated from students by intermediaries (e.g. campus bookstores), to make the direct link with them and derive rich data from how students use content. Publishers were keen to make the transition from the free supply of online content and services (on condition of textbook adoption) to licensing premium content and services.

In the UK, the teaching tradition differs, and lecturers are far less likely to adopt only one book for a course, or even if they do, to teach from it chapter by chapter. The blockbuster textbooks may be criticized as being too long, exhaustive and expensive, and UK-originated books are cheaper. However, the US-originated core texts are still used extensively. Texts in management studies and the social sciences are usually versioned or localized in the UK for the European market, and by other publishing centres elsewhere, not least to deter importation into the USA.

UK-originated publishing largely avoids competing directly against the US core textbooks, but nonetheless is extensive in title output. The major texts developed in the UK also deploy online resources and assessment. Covering a variety of subjects, they take account of the different approaches of UK academia, and extend up through the undergraduate levels to the very specialist graduate courses. Although rarely finding a significant US market, some UK-originated textbooks are highly exportable elsewhere. There is innovation and enormous diversity in UK teaching that finds expression through publishers.

Supply-side-funded Open Educational Resources (OER), available for free on the internet under Creative Commons licences (see Chapter 4), were pioneered by MIT in 2002. Subsequently many universities worldwide (including The Open University in the UK) and other agencies have invested millions in producing OER which can be configured by users. They are funded by philanthropy or endowments, or indirectly by tuition fees or taxpayers, and mainly self-published by the institution. Rice University, supported by philanthropy, launched the OpenStax platform in 2012 and produces peer-reviewed textbooks that are available online for free, though students can buy printed copies.

MONOGRAPHS AND REFERENCE BOOKS

This title embraces all kinds of books used in academic institutions for teaching and research, and by practitioners in the workplace. These include supplementary paperbacks with some adoption potential, reference works, handbooks, readers (compilations of previously published content), conference proceedings, multi-authored original volumes on research topics; and academic monographs (original research) published in hardback and as ebooks at high prices and destined for the libraries mainly in the UK and the USA, and in other research centres worldwide. Such book categories are rarely customized (other than through translation) for different markets, but can be disaggregated: the publisher sells individual chapters.

Books with a trade sale may be categorized as academic/trade. Such titles include subject guides or primers, polemical or topical paperbacks and in-depth researched non-fiction in areas such as history or literature. Some titles are adopted for teaching – from a publisher's standpoint becoming 'accidental textbooks' and bought by students. For many of the smaller academic publishers, including most university presses and museums, printed book sales to libraries

A research
monograph from
Cambridge University
Press

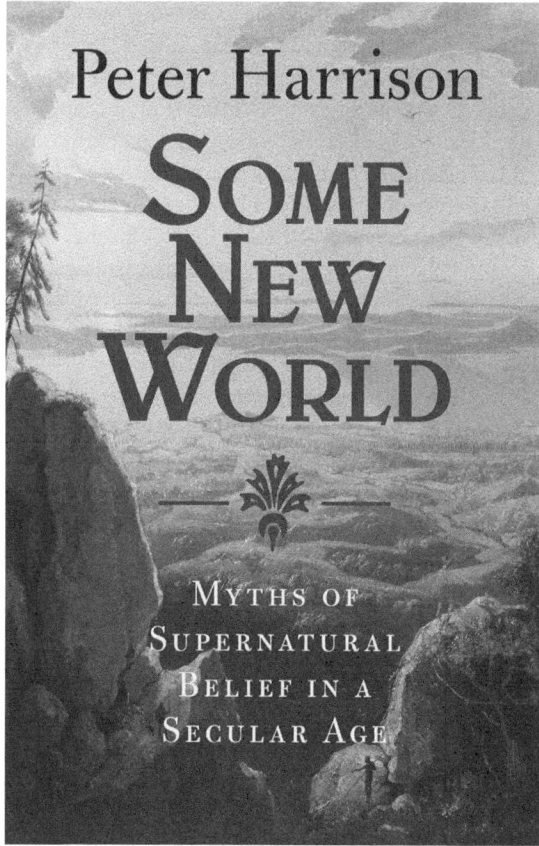

Peter Harrison

SOME
NEW
WORLD

MYTHS OF
SUPERNATURAL
BELIEF IN A
SECULAR AGE

and individual still account for the majority of sales revenue. However, ebook sales have increased through etailers (mainly Amazon), direct to libraries, and through licences to third-party aggregators; publishers have also aggregated texts into online services, sometimes alongside journals. Some publishers, such as Palgrave and CUP, have experimented with the quick publication of shorter texts as ebooks with paper copies printed to order. For some publishers digital sales have reached 60 per cent of their total revenues.

Monographs – peer-reviewed original research by one author in book form (or in the sciences sometimes by multiple authors) – have for a long time been the cornerstone of commercial academic publishing and of the university presses briefed to disseminate works of scholarship as part of their mission. The characteristics of monographs range from the publication of high-quality titles with very low sales potential, through to titles of wider appeal and greater reach. Since the 1980s, their economic viability has been questioned and their demise often predicted. Monograph publication remains especially important to AHSS academics for tenure and career progression in the same way that article publication in a prestigious journal is to scientists. Although the supply-side research output has increased worldwide, paid-for institutional demand per title in the West has declined. Library cutbacks and changing purchasing behaviour, such as the switching of book budgets to the subscription of journals and other electronic resources, the greater use of inter-library lending and the growth of library consortia, have progressively reduced print sales quantities. For example, sales of monographs fell to very low numbers, from, say, 1,500 copies worldwide in the 1980s down to as low as 200 copies by 2022. There is little scope for publishers to raise prices further in this market. The advent of digital printing has aided the continuance of the publication of highly specialist titles, and the strategy of Springer Nature is only to print books to order. Leading monograph publishers, such as OUP, CUP, Routledge (Taylor & Francis), and Palgrave Macmillan (Springer Nature), have maintained their publishing programme by reducing the costs of production and increasing title output – confounding the so-called crisis in monograph publishing. A 2020 survey of monograph publishing found that: 'The total output identified by the 25 respondents was 32,600 titles. Of these the nine commercial publishers released 28,409 titles (87% of the total) and the university presses 4,191 titles (13%)' (Shaw et al., 2023, page 387).

In comparison to the consumer book publishers, the AHSS and STM publishers have developed a far greater range of demand-side business models for their digital products. In addition to print sales made via Amazon, and to some extent direct from publishers' websites, ebook sales to libraries are important – often as part of collections. The greater the amount of content offered in terms of aggregation and of linked data, the greater the digital opportunity and business value. While scholars mostly access journal articles from libraries, they make significant purchases of books for personal use, and this is facilitated further with the availability of ebooks. While the sales revenue from ebooks has steadily increased, it has not kept pace with the decline in revenue from print sales.

The *site licence* business model, applied to licensing online content (at the outset reference and learned journals) to universities and other organizations, is fundamental and many other business models stem from it. The university is responsible for the authentication of its members and the security of its network, and thus provides controlled access to the publisher's licensed content. It is a form of digital rights management (DRM). The terms applying to such site licences are among many negotiated between publishers and library consortia at the regional or national level. In the UK, Jisc provides a central role in negotiations with publishers, and facilitates the use of digital resources and services, and the progress towards open access publishing. Throughout the world, libraries join consortia in order to negotiate savings and other benefits from suppliers, but they also buy books independently.

Supply-side-funded open access (OA) business models, which developed in STM journal publishing, are spreading to monograph publishing. They have developed faster in Australia, Canada and Europe than in the USA. An early push to OA in the UK was that researchers were mandated by their university or funders to place their doctoral theses in digital repositories from which they are freely available under a Creative Commons licence, called green OA. Such mandates mean that authors have to significantly develop and change their work to attract a publisher to invest in and publish a monograph based on their research. As yet in the UK there is no requirement for those monographs submitted to the Research Excellence Framework in 2029 to be OA.

The OA publication of professionally produced monographs is sometimes funded by universities (usually through their libraries), other agencies and philanthropy as part of their primary objective to maximize the dissemination of research (referred to as Platinum OA). Knowledge Unlatched, founded in 2012, created an alliance of libraries around the world to help finance publishers' costs and subsequently promoted OA more generally (it was acquired by Wiley in 2021). Generally speaking, the commercial publishers such as Bloomsbury Academic, De Gruyter Brill, Palgrave, Taylor & Francis, SAGE and Springer developed their OA programmes faster than the university presses in the UK and the USA. The main business model is based on charging authors (usually their research funders) a book processing charge (BPC) or other subvention to publish the book; and to make it available online for free immediately (referred to as Gold OA). Additional revenue can be gained by using the freemium model whereby other formats (such as print) or services incur a charge. This model can work in the publisher's favour: they receive a subvention towards publication costs whilst the ready availability of the digital edition acts as promotion for the print edition. However, AHSS subjects are poorly funded compared to research funding in STM. BPCs from publishers vary greatly and often exceed £10,000. OA books may cost more to publish than non-OA books because third-party rights holders are likely to object to the use of their material or charge premium rates for its open reproduction, and the marketing costs may be paradoxically higher since the support of profit-driven supply chains is absent. Such books are published under Creative Commons (CC) licences.

Detractors of OA monograph publishing argue that its long-term sustainability is problematic: it diverts resources from research budgets; and runs the risks of exacerbating inequality among authors in their access to funds, lowering quality, and concentrating the power of the large publishers whilst weakening smaller publishers and societies. Advocates of OA publication stress the wider dissemination and impact. For example, a study by Springer Nature of its OA publishing found that this route can lead to 10 times more downloads, 2.4 times more citations, 10 times more online mentions, and reach 61 per cent more countries compared to publishing a book through the non-open access route (springernature.com, accessed 18 January 2024).

JOURNALS

The publishing of refereed or peer-reviewed learned journals (or serials), sold mainly through subscription to libraries and corporates, is a highly profitable sector of publishing. STM journal publishing especially grew strongly facilitated by the internet, digital publishing, global growth in research and the packaging of content in the form of Big Deals negotiated with library consortia.

In late 2021 there were around 25,000 English language active peer-reviewed journals. 'Just over 30 per cent of all scholarly articles are published as paid-for Open Access, accounting for just over 7 per cent of the total journal publishing market value' (*STM Global Brief*, 2021, page 12). In STM publishing, the revenues far outweigh those from book operations. Historically, the higher net profit of journal publishing (up to 30 per cent) has in effect cross-subsidized book publishing operations, which earned lower profits (10–15 per cent) – however, some larger players can achieve rates from books approaching 25 per cent. The major international journal publishers are Springer Nature, Taylor & Francis, Elsevier, Wiley and SAGE, each of which publishes more than 1,000 journals, followed by a significant group of publishers such as De Gruyter Brill, OUP, CUP, Emerald and MDPI. Additionally there a thousands of smaller publishers, many of which publish just a few journals. Half of all journals are owned or controlled by learned societies. They may have their journals produced and marketed for them under contract by the publishers, or they may publish the titles themselves. Prominent amongst the latter are, in the USA, the American Chemical Society (ACS), the American Institute of Physics (AIP) and the Institute of Electrical and Electronics Engineers (IEEE); and in the UK, the Institute of Physics (IOP), the Royal Society and the Royal Society of Chemistry (RSC). For many societies, journal publishing has traditionally kept them afloat financially.

Science journal publishing reaches back to the publication in 1665 of both *Le Journal des sçavans* in France and the *Philosophical Transactions of the Royal Society of London*. For over three centuries, the number of articles published each year and the number of journals have grown by about 3 and 3.5 per cent respectively, along with a similar annual rise in the number of researchers. The two leading countries in research are China and the USA (Table 2.1); both India and China display high growth rates for the number of scientific publications. The inequalities in the global publishing landscape are highlighted for Africa by David Mills et al.:

> As the number of academic publications and journals continues to increase, many African researchers find themselves at the margins of this economy, negotiating a global knowledge system dominated by 'Northern' journals and global publishing conglomerates. Bibliometric data on Africa's share of global scientific publishing shows a slow increase to just over 3% of all indexed articles, but this is mostly dominated by South Africa, Egypt and Tunisia. (Mills et al., 2022, page 2)

The endurance of journals as the primary source of research communication is attributed to four key functions:

- *Registration*: third-party establishment by date-stamping of the author's precedence and ownership of an idea
- *Dissemination*: communicating the findings to its intended audience usually via the brand identity of the journal
- *Certification*: ensuring quality control through peer review and rewarding authors
- *Archival record*: preserving a fixed version of the paper for future reference and citation.

Table 2.1 The top 10 countries by research outputs in the sciences (2023)

Country	Share of total (%)*
China	22.0
USA	20.5
Germany	4.4
UK	3.7
Japan	3.0
France	2.2
Canada	1.7
South Korea	1.6
Switzerland	1.4
India	1.4

Source: nature.com, accessed 18 January 2024.

Note: *Time period, 1 August 2022 to 31 July 2023.

To these might now be added a fifth function, that of navigation, that is, providing filters and signposts to relevant work amid the huge volume of published material – increasingly to related material, such as datasets (Ware and Mabe, 2015).

Some of these functions are weakening. For example, in physics, researchers publish their new research as preprints (unrefereed author's original manuscript) on the pre-print (e-print) server arXiv (Cornell University) in advance of journal publication. There are similar preprint servers for biology (bioRxiv) and health sciences (medRxiv). The open research platform F1000Research (purchased by Taylor & Francis in 2020) offers immediate article publication and the sharing of underlying data; it operates post-publication peer review with the details published of reviewer names. Nevertheless the endurance of journal publishing is underpinned by the integration of the functions through the publishing process. Journal publishing is fundamentally maintained by academic behaviour in their peer groups, and tenure and promotion committees and research funders attach great importance to a researcher's reputation manifest by their publication record and the citations to their articles in highly rated journals. Since researchers' career prospects and funding opportunities are often evaluated on the basis of their publication record, they try to be published in the highest-ranked journals in their subject they can attain. Moreover, researchers make a qualitative evaluation of the journals to which they submit their work.

While the journal is the container, the article is the primary object transmitted, via the institution, to the users. The PDF remains an important format for articles but there is experimentation with the form of display of HTML versions with value added, for example, articles are enriched with supplementary datasets and extra functionality to produce graphs or tables.

Broadly speaking, a journal's academic editor, or editor-in-chief, backed up by an academic editorial board, with input from the publisher, steers the policy, direction and focus of the journal, which is usually aimed at a well-defined community of researchers. Peer review prior to publication is central to quality control and the selection of articles, readership impact and the branding status of journals across all subjects. The brand value of journals is reflected by their perceived or measured rank in a hierarchy. There are many ways journals are measured to indicate their impact and quality. In science especially, the journal impact factor (IF) – a measure of the average citations to a particular journal over the previous 2–3 years – is of great significance (published annually by Clarivate Analytics). The impact factor of a journal is calculated using this formula:

$$\text{2023 impact factor} = \frac{\text{Citations in 2023 to articles in the journal from 2021 and 2022}}{\text{Number of 'citable items' in the journal in 2021 and 2022}}$$

It should be appreciated that different disciplines use citations in different ways. Some of the highest-rated and most profitable journals are published by societies and not-for-profit publishers, not by commercial publishers. Nevertheless, the strength and value of a commercial publisher's business are expressed by the number of leading journals it has created over long periods. Some learned societies outsource their publishing by entering into contracts (say, for 5 years) with publishers which undertake the production, marketing, sales and distribution on their behalf while they retain their editorial independence.

There are enormous differences in authorship between disciplines, ranging from multiple contributors per article in some sciences to sole authors in the humanities. Furthermore, the output of researchers is highly skewed. A small fraction of researchers are highly productive and publish one or many articles per year, while the great majority hardly at all, say, one article in a career. The leading scientists heading large research groups score very high citation counts, and the major research universities dominate article output.

There are many forms of peer review. To summarize the traditional method: the journal editor determines which of the papers received will be checked for plagiarism (such as through the Crossref Similarity Check), will be editorially rejected or selected for peer review, and selects the reviewers who assess it. In double-blind peer review, the identities of the author and the reviewers are not revealed to each other during the review process. The editor, who also takes into account research novelty and likely impact, assesses the reviews and sends them with recommendations to the author for revision. The revised paper is either rejected or accepted. The article is contracted with the author, produced, published (called the version of record that is citable) and archived. This peer review process is complex and expensive to manage, even though reviewers work for free. The highest-ranked journals have the highest rejection rates (up to and sometimes above 90 per cent) and incur the highest peer review management costs for the publisher, which usually pays for the costs of the editorial office. Peer review is pressured by the increasing receipt of articles, worldwide, and faster publication times demanded by authors: timeliness of publication differs across disciplines.

Journals benefit from network effects or positive externalities, a business model on which social media companies are founded. The value of the product or service increases the more it is used, creating a positive feedback loop, a virtuous cycle. For example, the greater the visibility and usage of a journal within its research community, the higher are its citations and IF, and the greater the receipt of better and available papers, which in turn further increases the IF, visibility and readership.

The market imbalance between the ever-increasing supply of articles versus declining library budgets in proportion to total university expenditure culminated in the serials crisis from the late 1980s to the early 1990s. The catalogue prices for journals were increasing as print circulations fell due to subscription cancellations – in turn, caused by the universities coming under increasing financial pressure to reduce costs. It created a negative feedback loop that pushed up publishing costs, increasing prices further. Moreover, the leading journals containing the best research are not substitutable, and are in effect mini monopolies that command high prices – their demand is price inelastic (see Chapter 9). The crisis overlapped with the initial development of electronic journals and led to the development of the *Big Deal* business model, whereby publishers offered bundles of journal titles in electronic format to library consortia and other major customers at discounts off the print catalogue prices. The model gathered momentum from the mid- to late-1990s onwards and although initially welcomed by academia – researchers gained access to far more content and their institutions benefited from reducing average unit costs – it later came under fierce criticism from libraries locked into fixed-term agreements of, say, three years and facing fast-rising prices on renewal. In response they formed consortia to negotiate the terms of the deals, giving them greater bargaining power, and began to criticize some of the harsher clauses of contracts – such as non-disclosure to third parties of the financial terms.

As the Big Deals absorbed a higher proportion of their budgets, the libraries had to reduce purchases of book titles. The major publishers, wielding their must-have premier journals bundled up with aggregations of lesser journals, and with their international marketing strength, captured greater visibility for their product, furthering network effects. These companies accrued a range of benefits from purchasing the operations of smaller journal publishers. They could strip out costs, add more value into their journal packages and databases, and increase their revenues and market share (and shareholder value). The site licence and Big Deal model aided publisher concentration, enabled large publishers to deal directly with institutions (marginalizing the subscription agents which used to serve libraries), and hastened the great decline in individual subscriptions, especially to society journals whose members could instead access articles remotely via their library.

The journal publishers use a variety of business models: institutional subscription and site licence; personal subscription (in severe decline); pay per view (article downloads to readers whose institution does not subscribe to the journal); and engage with and sell through aggregators and subscription agents. Some printed journals attract advertising revenue (e.g. in health sciences).

Workflows and usability

Journal publishers, especially in STM, have been at the forefront in applying new technologies to digital publishing and the provision of services, either free or sold on subscription. Innovations and investments are made largely by the major commercial publishers, and the larger not-for-profit publishers, for example, the main learned societies, and OUP and CUP. They have not waited for the large technology players to impose their solutions on them. From the mid- to late-1990s, the publishers also developed web-based manuscript submission and peer-review management systems. Today publishers are still trying to improve manuscript submission and tracking systems to make them more author-friendly, and the majors are acquiring specialist companies.

Of wider significance to the publishing industry as a whole, the journal publishers pioneered in the 1990s *digital first* production systems: a central concept of which is structured content. It involves tagging the textual elements (such as the article title, author, affiliation, abstract, keywords, headings), enabling the file to be output to multiple file formats. Digital workflows reduce costs and speed publication. Articles can be released when ready rather than waiting for a complete issue to be paginated and published. Journals contain increasing amounts of rich metadata. The addition of the semantic metadata to articles to reveal meaning that computers can understand aids search within databases or through web browsers. The inclusion of research datasets alongside journal articles facilitates data mining – the investigation of patterns across large volumes of data. Virtually all journals are published in electronic formats (mainly PDF, HTML and increasingly other screen reflowable formats). Print distribution has shrunk in importance, and printing has been shifted from the producer to the user.

The major publishers developed their own content delivery platforms. For instance, in 1997 Elsevier launched the first large-scale platform, or full-text scientific database, ScienceDirect, which by 2024 gave access to over 19 m journal articles and book chapters. Publishers compete on the usability of their platforms, such as reliability, speed, and ease of use, search and linkage to other data. However, the strength – and overall brand – of the platform are based on the brand value of the individual journals and books, and the size of aggregation. The major publishers are large enough to deal directly with the institutional librarians or purchasing consortia (some at state or nation state level), through which the institution's subscriptions to journals and ebook collections are negotiated. Publishers without their own platforms use third parties for distribution, notably Atypon, which at the time of purchase by Wiley in 2016 hosted 7,000 journals from significant publishers (and now has over 200 clients). The major US aggregators of journals and content databases, such as EBSCO and ProQuest (Clarivate), provide library access to the output of publishers.

In the print-only era, publishing journals and publishing books were distinct operations, with different systems, channels to market and business models. This was reflected in a publisher's internal organization into book and journal silos for its staff and systems. In the transition to the digital era, the readers (researchers, practitioners, teachers and students) increasingly want to access and use content across former boundaries, and across a range of devices including smartphones and tablets. The channels to market are converging as are the business models. The publishers are reorganizing their systems and staff to reflect the convergence. Researchers also need to demonstrate that their findings are reaching a wider audience, so, for example, journal articles may be connected up to their presence on social media.

The major publishers are aiming to occupy more of the value chain within the fields of scholarly communication, research management, expert information, and analytics. Their suites of tools from manuscript submission through to archiving reflect features – advantages to users, network effects, and institutional and personal lock-ins – comparable to those engendered by the earlier Big Deals. Publishers offer editing services to help non-native English authors, and in 2023 Springer Nature announced a new AI-powered writing tool, Curie, to help researchers whose first language is not English. The research workflow product range for Elsevier includes manuscript submission and tracking (Aries Systems), academic social networks facilitating sharing and collaboration (Mendeley), altmetrics (Plum Analytics), OA pre-print server (SSRN), services to showcase research in library repositories (bepress), and analytic services for research managers.

Journal publishing benefits from many standards and systems developed through collaboration among the publishers and with the research community and funders. For example, CrossRef (launched 2000) enables readers to link from article references or citations to the cited article. COUNTER (launched 2002) facilitates the recording and reporting on the usage of online content (journals, books, databases) which helps librarians, publishers and intermediaries to operate more efficiently. The ORCID iD (Open Researcher and Contributor ID, launched in 2012) uniquely and persistently identifies authors and contributors. CHORUS launched in 2014 is supported by most publishers of funded research. It provides a suite of services for agencies and publishers to monitor and deliver open access to published articles reporting on funded research.

Publishers have invested heavily in recent years in research integrity, employing staff in this area and developing best practice for journal editors and authors. Issues can range from straightforward plagiarism through conflicts over authorship to the scientific rigour of a dataset. Controversy surrounded the growth of some OA publishers through the practice of recruiting large volumes of articles for guest-edited special issues. Journal publishers have acted to retract published papers after doubts about the propriety of the peer review conducted. In 2021, Wiley bought the open access publisher Hindawi for $298 m, expanding their portfolio of OA journals. The acquisition was followed by questions over the editorial practices at Hindawi journals – these included peer review 'rings', where editors and reviewers worked closely together to approve articles for publication. By the end of 2023, Wiley had decided to drop the use of the Hindawi name.

The use of generative AI to write papers challenges publishers to come up with a response and effective policies. In 2023, the organization STM prepared a set of guidelines for authors:

> Using publicly available GenAI as a basic tool that supports authors in refining, correcting, formatting, and editing texts and documents is permissible. Authors must disclose any use of GenAI that transcends those use cases so an editorial decision can be made as to its legitimacy. (stm-assoc.org, accessed 4 March 2024)

The organization COPE (Committee on Publication Ethics) is active in the area of publication ethics (publicationethics.org).

OPEN ACCESS

Central to journal publishing, and now significant for monograph publishing, are business models based on open access. The advent of the internet gave rise to electronic journals and to the concept of open access (OA): the free and unrestricted online access to peer-reviewed research articles in journals, made available under Creative Commons licences. OA was in contrast to the paid for and restricted content, or toll access (TA), provided by the publishers of the time. The OA movement was defined by the Budapest Open Access Initiative (BOAI) in 2002. It reflected an overall societal trend towards free access, such as open content and data, and OER and MOOCs (massive open online courses). Advocates criticized the major toll-access publishers for creating what they saw as an unsustainable and high cost journal subscription system from which they extorted immense profits from academia and tax-payers; and the secrecy surrounding their deals with libraries. OA publishing would not only provide broader accessibility and the greater sharing of research, they argued, but would deliver scholarly communication at far lower cost, disrupt incumbents, and foster new entrants and means of communication. But OA publishing developed in unexpected ways.

Published research standards are maintained through peer review and the retraction of bad articles post publication. However, such defences do not protect the research publishing system from the rise in populist distrust of experts, big government and its agencies; the growth in fake news and fake science, and of scam OA predatory publishers. The issue of paper mills has become more prominent, described as 'the process by which manufactured manuscripts are submitted to a journal for a fee on behalf of researchers with the purpose of providing an easy publication for them, or to offer authorship for sale' (COPE and STM, 2022, page 4). The ease of manufacture of articles will only increase in an age of AI. OA and TA publishing is often presented in the media as a conflicting dichotomy which is too simplistic. They are both forms of publishing that overlap and coexist. There are many forms of OA publishing and many forms of TA publishing. Governments are wishing to extend and speed up OA publishing such as in the UK (the Finch Report of 2012 advocated the use of gold OA) and the EU's commitment to make all research freely available. Governments and their agencies are increasing mandates on authors and publishers to OA publish in various ways.

From a business standpoint, however, there is fundamental difference. OA publishing is predominately supply-side funded (e.g. government funding agencies, major foundations and universities), whereas TA publishing is largely demand-side funded by a larger number of market purchasers worldwide (e.g. university libraries).

OA publishing has taken some decades to establish but has grown considerably over the last decade from a low base, and in 2024 the Directory of Open Access Journals listed over 20,000 titles (doaj.org, accessed 18 January 2024). New OA journals have been launched; some former subscription journals have flipped to OA entirely, while others incorporate a mix of OA and TA models (hybrid). New players such as Frontiers and MDPI have given impetus to the growth of OA publishing, offering a full OA model and speed of publication for authors: 'MDPI and Frontiers are not the ideal destination for every paper of every author, but at one point, they combined for about 500,000 papers (annualized), while growing at a rapid pace' (Petrou, 2023).

After initial opposition, the publishers quickly adapted to the new business model, and for instance, in 2008 Springer purchased the pioneering OA publisher BioMed Central and today Springer Nature is the world's largest OA publisher. There is a shift from closed to open content. Furthermore there are degrees of openness in respect of user and author rights. There is also a growth in mandates made by institutions, funding agencies and governments on researchers to make their work available in OA in different ways. OA publishing has become increasingly complex and difficult to define.

Open access publishers adopt many business models to finance their operations. For example, universities may totally subsidize their own publishing through research groups or libraries (usually small scale and especially prevalent in AHSS), and research funders and philanthropies may finance publishing operations. Such models where no fees are charged to authors and readers are described as the *platinum OA* model but it is difficult to scale. Some OA publishers may form membership organizations to lower and share the cost of publication. Some start-up journals will waive charges altogether to gain momentum, and most publishers will waive charges for authors from developing countries.

The *green OA* route is when an article is deposited to a disciplinary or institutional or funder repository. The publisher's concern here is that if the article is made freely available too soon, libraries would cancel their subscription to the relevant journal. Alternatively, authors may choose to publish in a delayed access OA journal, without charge, and deposit their accepted manuscript of the article in a repository, subject to the embargo period set by the publisher or mandated by the research funder. The embargo periods vary by subject and journal – say, 6–12 months or longer – and STM journals usually have shorter embargos than AHSS titles and are designed not to compromise subscription sales. Many leading society journals adopt the delayed OA model.

However, most OA journals published by commercial and not-for-profit publishers and societies charge a fee to authors (an article processing charge, APC) after peer review and acceptance which enables *immediate OA publication*. It is called *gold OA* or the 'author or funder pays' model. The author's university or the research funder normally pays the charge, say, £2,500, though charges vary widely by publisher and journal, and geography. Premium journals which incur the largest costs in curation and peer review usually charge much higher APCs (the APC for *Nature* in 2024 was £8,890). Through the payment of APCs, the entire journal can be fully OA. Librarians usually have the task of managing the payments from funders to publishers. By 2022, the percentage of articles published in subscription journals had fallen to 51 per cent compared to 73 per cent in 2012. The level of gold OA had reached 35 per cent of articles (stm-assoc. org, accessed 18 January 2024).

Hybrid OA is used on many subscription journals: some articles are made OA immediately on publication provided the APC is paid, whilst other articles published at the publisher's expense remain behind a paywall. In many high-quality hybrid journals the APC rates are subsidized by the subscription revenue. Some publishers were criticized for double dipping, in that they charged for both subscriptions and APCs without offsetting the latter from the subscription price.

Overall, OA publishing has been driven by the interests of the health and biosciences. In STM areas author teams publish numerous articles and have access to large-scale research funding, whereas lone AHSS researchers have far less direct access to publication funding. Since the main research universities have the highest output of articles, they are exposed to the greatest costs under the gold OA model while continuing to subscribe to substantial journal collections. On the other hand, teaching universities and large corporations are arguably beneficiaries.

Gold OA publishing favours the large publishers over smaller publishers, such as the societies, and promotes further industry concentration. The major publishers have a global reach, derive economies of scale in production and distribution, and own themselves, or under contract, many leading brands with vertical communities. Supply-side-funded publishing businesses are focused primarily on servicing authors (and in this context their funders) rather than the market; and the creation of abundance over content selectivity. Three developments in journal publishing, encouraged by OA, were the arrival of mega journals, the concept of cascade publishing and transformative agreements.

In 2006, the not-for-profit US Public Library of Science (PLOS) launched the first gold OA mega journal *PLOS ONE*. In contrast to the highly selective subscription journals designed to serve small vertical communities, *PLOS ONE* publishes very large numbers of articles of scientific and medical research submitted from that broad horizontal community. The traditional role of the editor-in-chief, to steer and curate for a vertical community and to attain high impact, is redundant in this context. To speed publication and reduce iterations, it adopts a light peer-review process prior to publication by concentrating on scientific rigour, rather than on novelty and impact that are left to be assessed post-publication. It is thought that the mega journals have levelled off at around 2–3 per cent of articles published and have become a niche business that publishes technically correct articles.

The cascade model developed in OA and TA publishing. If rejected by a premier journal (with a high rejection rate), an article may be automatically submitted for publication to a lower-ranked journal (with a lower rejection rate) within the publisher's vertical stable of titles, and the peer review process is not repeated, leading to cost savings and faster publication for the author. The publisher therefore retains manuscripts which might otherwise have been transferred to competitors on rejection. The larger publishers have the cascade capacity while smaller publishers are likely to lose submissions. In some cases, the cascade ends in a low-rated gold OA journal.

From around 2014/2015, some of the national library consortia (such as in Germany, the Netherlands, Finland and Sweden) challenged the notion that Big Deals were too big to cancel while pursuing their aim to flip subscription journals to OA. New OA Big Deals were negotiated with some publishers: called read and publish (RAP). The price for accessing the publisher's journals includes a provision which enables authors to publish OA articles in the publisher's hybrid and OA gold journals, thereby saving them time to find APC funding, though the consortia may pay more overall for the OA Big Deal to the chosen publishers. The flip from subscription to OA is very complicated and protracted, requiring collaboration between funding bodies, government agencies and publishers. Lisa Hinchcliffe defines such transformative agreements as: 'a contract is a transformative agreement if it seeks to shift the contracted payment from a library or group of libraries to a publisher away from subscription-based reading and towards open access publishing' (scholarlykitchen.sspnet.org, accessed 18 January 2024). The drive to such transformative agreements was accelerated by the EU's Plan S, launched in 2018, with the aim of requiring publications resulting from public funding to be published in OA journals. Such models ensure efficiencies within the ecosystem of journal publishing and enable lower APCs or equivalents to be charged.

The danger of the supply-side business models is their tendency to diminish quality in the drive for APC volume. Furthermore there is growth of *predatory* publishers which take advantage of academics seeking a home for their article, with echoes of the vanity press in consumer publishing. Such scam publishers offer authors the pretence of quality, do not undertake peer review but charge them APCs. A further threat comes from so-called black open access sites that pirate subscription content, such as the popular Sci-Hub which hosted in one place many million articles from multiple publishers. The site has been blocked in many countries but its success did suggest the desire for a single source of search and retrieval.

The trend towards gold OA has disappointed those advocates of green open access who view their ideal of content freely available to all as now tainted by compromise and co-opted by publishers. The debates over OA range across business models, the costs and who pays, and sustainability issues; author and user rights, and the licences under which content is made available (e.g. the Creative Commons Licence, CC-BY); increased state control over research (via funding agencies) and the effect on academic freedom to research and publish; and emerging inequalities between disciplines, individuals, institutions and geographies. The debates have overshadowed other ways to make research hidden behind paywalls available more widely, for instance, through extending licences to public libraries.

Overarching the OA debates are the impact of ever-changing technologies on research, the increased focus on user experience, and the ways in which research and increasingly data can be linked and communicated, all of which provide many opportunities for publishers and other players. The sharing of research data through open data is seen as a way of speeding up the pace of scientific discovery and encouraging public trust in research. The growing importance of AI is creating new businesses which can draw on OA articles and data. For example, diagnostic systems in health care are being developed based on the machine reading of a vast array of content.

Sources

Bill Cope and Angus Phillips, *The Future of the Academic Journal*, 2nd edition, Chandos, 2014.

COPE and STM, *Paper Mills: Research report*, June 2022.

Albert N. Greco, *The Business of Scholarly Publishing*, Oxford University Press, 2020.

Albert N. Greco, *The College Textbook Publishing Industry in the US 2000–2022*, Palgrave Macmillan, 2023.

Walter Isaacson, *Steve Jobs*, Little, Brown, 2011.

Jennifer Maguire, 'Large, Global ELT Publishers Innovate to Meet Evolving Needs', 2022. bridge.edu, accessed 17 January 2024.

David Mills, Patricia Kingori, Abigail Branford, Samuel Tamti Chatio, Natasha Robinson and Paulina Tindana, *Who Counts? Ghanaian academic publishing and global science*, African Minds, 2022.

Carolina Ocampo-Ariza et al., 'Global South Leadership towards Inclusive Tropical Ecology and Conservation', *Perspectives in Ecology and Conservation*, 21 (2023).

Christos Petrou, 'Reputation and Publication Volume at MDPI and Frontiers', *Scholarly Kitchen*, 18 September 2023.

Philip Shaw, Angus Phillips, and Maria Bajo Gutiérrez, 'The Death of the Monograph?', *Publishing Research Quarterly* 38 (2022).

John B. Thompson, *Books in the Digital Age*, Polity Press, 2005.

Maria Gilje Torheim, 'Do We Read Differently on Paper than on a Screen?', https://phys.org/news/, accessed 26 October 2018.

STM Global Brief, STM, 2021.

Mark Ware and Michael Mabe, *The STM Report*, 4th edition, STM, 2015.

Web resources

http://blog.alpsp.org Blog of Association of Learned and Professional Society Publishers.

https://creativecommons.org Details the licences under which OA content can be published.

https://doaj.org Directory of Open Access Journals.

https://www.journalofelectronicpublishing.org Forum for research and discussion about contemporary publishing practices.

https://scholarlykitchen.sspnet.org Blog established in 2008 by the Society for Scholarly Publishing.

CHAPTER 3

The characteristics of the main publishing sectors

Chapters 1 and 2 have traced the development of the book publishing industry across its various sectors. Themes shared across publishing sectors include the growth of digital publishing, experimentation in business models, changes in publishing processes, and the search for fresh and diverse voices.

All kinds of publishers can be described as serving niche markets. Attaining a critical mass in a particular field, right down to a list of books or journals on the narrowest subject area, is vital to publishers of every size. It allows the employment of editors who understand and have contact with authors and associates in a particular field, and who can shape projects for their intended markets. A respected list attracts authors. Furthermore, a list of books needs to generate sufficient turnover to allow effective marketing and selling, which in turn feeds new publishing.

Although common themes can be identified, there remain differences in the ways books are published for different markets. Publishers specialize in reaching particular markets, and each market has a separate dynamic and key drivers. The skills of their staff, the activities they perform and the structure of the business are aligned accordingly.

UK PUBLISHING

Table 3.1, using figures from the Publishers Association (2022), gives the scale of the UK publishing industry in 2022 based on companies' sales. In addition to the sales of £3.8 bn of physical books, there were invoiced sales of over £3.1 bn of digital products (including academic journals), giving a combined total of £6.9 bn (£6.6 bn in 2021). Export sales were 60 per cent of total sales (58 per cent in 2021) and digital sales were 45 per cent of total revenues in 2022. The size of the domestic consumer book market was estimated at £2.5 bn in terms of end-purchaser prices, with 348 m units sold. By volume, paperbacks represented 52 per cent of sales, ebooks 21 per cent, and audiobooks 8 per cent. Self-published ebooks are a part of the market for which there are no official figures available. It is estimated that self-published books take up over 25 per cent of the overall ebook market but the likely revenue figure will be small, given the low prices of many self-published titles.

DOI: 10.4324/9781003403289-4

Table 3.1 UK publishers' sales (£m) in 2022

	Physical	Digital	Total
Sales	3,800	3,100	6,900
Percentage	55	45	100

Source: Publishers Association (2022).

Table 3.2 Number of titles published in the UK, 2005–2020

Year	Number of titles and new editions
2005	111,000
2010	170,000
2015	173,000
2020	186,000

Source: Nielsen BookData.

Table 3.3 Share by sector of digital sales in 2022

Sector	% share 2022	% share 2017
Consumer	18	15
Fiction	39	29
Children's	6	4
Schools	17	8
ELT	12	7
Academic books	44	22
Journals	83	84

Source: Publishers Association (2022).

A total of 153,000 new titles was reported in 2022. Books and ebooks in the UK are zero rated for VAT alongside newspapers, magazines published at regular intervals (more than once a year), and printed music. VAT is charged on digital products such as audiobooks, online content and CD-ROMs, as they are classified as supplies of services.

CONSUMER PUBLISHING

The consumer or trade publishers are the most visible part of the industry. Their titles are displayed prominently in high street bookshops and other outlets, receive considerable mass-media coverage and are aimed mainly at the indefinable 'general reader', and sometimes at the enthusiast or specialist reader. They form the mainstay of public libraries, and in some cases penetrate academic markets. In 2022, consumer sales in the UK market (fiction, non-fiction and children's) totalled £1.4 bn compared to £1.5 bn in 2021 (Publishers Association, 2022). Digital sales (ebooks and audiobooks) in 2022 were 18 per cent of the total, and 39 per cent of fiction sales.

Most publishers are in London, giving them ready access to authors, agents, other publishers, social venues, journalists and producers of the mass media, and other influential people who decisively affect the life of a nation. The remaining publishers are spread around the country, with concentrations in Oxford and Edinburgh, and tend to be more specialized.

Consumer book publishing is the high-risk end of the business: book failures are frequent but the rewards from 'bestsellers' – some of which are quite unexpected – can be great. The potential readers are varied, spread thinly through the population, difficult to identify, and have tastes and interests that can be described generally but are not easily matched to a particular book. Publishers bet to a great extent on their judgement of public taste and interests – notoriously unpredictable. During testimony in the USA in the case to decide on whether Penguin Random House could take over Simon & Schuster (this was refused), 'Penguin Random House executives said that just 35 per cent of books the company publishes are profitable. Among the titles that make money, a very small sliver – just 4 percent – account for 60 percent of those profits' (*New York Times*, 19 August 2022).

Sometimes the publication of a book creates its own market. And the authors whose work arouses growing interest can develop a personal readership, thereby creating their own markets – perhaps attaining a 'brand name' following, especially in fiction. Publishers compete fiercely for their books. Few other consumer goods industries market products with such a short sales life. Generally speaking, for a book to flourish, it is vital for the publisher to secure advance or subscription orders from booksellers before publication and for the response to the book to be good in the opening few weeks post-publication. The peak sales of most new books occur well within a year of publication though the advent of internet bookselling has lengthened the life of some titles. Most adult hardback fiction and paperback titles are dead within three months or just weeks, while paperback fiction written by famous authors may endure for long periods. Compared to the non-consumer book publishers, the trade publishers earn a higher proportion of their revenues from their frontlist publishing. With the increasing focus on the lead titles that are part of bookseller promotions and receive online exposure, frontlist revenues are vitally important. Some publishers' lists are very frontlist weighted, while others keep their backlists alive from their new book programme and by relaunching older books in new covers or special editions. An energetically promoted backlist provides retailers with staple and more predictable stock, should earn good profits for the publisher, and keeps authors' works alive. The success of BookTok has stimulated sales of some backlist titles, often to the surprise of the publisher.

Spare by Prince Harry is the UK's fastest-selling non-fiction book of all time, with 750,000 sales in its first week on sale in January 2023

Many readers mistakenly believe that the large price differential between hardbacks and paperbacks is due to the extra cost of binding a book in hardback; it is also argued that ebooks should be cheap since there are no costs of physical production. There are cost differences between editions but the price differentials tend to reflect how publishers traditionally sought to maximize the revenue from a title by segmenting the market through different formats and price points. Furthermore, some titles of minority appeal would not recover their investment if first published at lower price ranges – meant for books with higher sales potential.

With ebooks in the mix it is harder for publishers to tread the well-worn sequential path of hardback, trade paperback, and then mass-market paperback. A fiction title might still be launched first in hardback at a high price to satisfy eager readers, but there is a market expectation that a lower-priced ebook is available. Over time it has become harder to sell many categories of book in hardback, and some titles may be published first as a paperback or ebook original. The fast growth in audio is encouraging new projects developed for that market. Audio continues to grow, reaching £108 m sales in 2022.

In 2022, non-fiction sales (invoiced to the publisher) were £1 bn whilst fiction sales totalled £798 m (up 9 per cent from 2021), with £494 m of home and £304 m of export sales (Publishers Association, 2022). A longer-term decline in sales of literary fiction was highlighted in a 2017 report from the Arts Council, which concluded:

> There is only a small 'long tail' of novels that sell in sufficient quantities to support an author; all bar the top 1,000 writers (at a push) in the country sell too few books to make a career from sales alone. (Arts Council, 2017, page 2)

The key characteristics of consumer publishing are shown below.

The reference work *Who's Who*, now published by Bloomsbury, is available both in print and online. It has been published annually since 1849

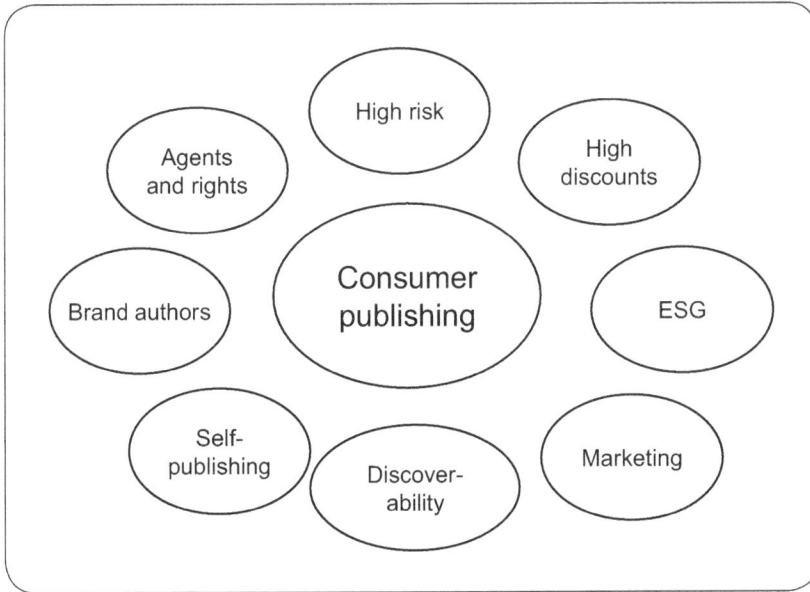

High risk

The business is high risk since it is difficult to forecast the sales potential of new books, and large sums may have to paid out to authors for advances. The cash return, however, can also be large. The major publishing groups can afford to gamble on a variety of new projects.

Agents and rights

Publishers are squeezed to a far greater extent by agents (on behalf of their authors), who look to negotiate higher royalty rates and advances, compared to non-consumer publishers The major trade houses may pay out up to 25 per cent of their sales revenue to authors (more than twice the percentage paid out by non-consumer publishers). Agents restrict rights granted to publishers to exploit the work in all forms of media, languages and territories.

There is usually greater scope in consumer publishing to sell rights in the author's work to other firms (e.g. in translation), and to set up co-edition deals with overseas publishers, especially for highly illustrated titles.

Brand authors

Consumer publishers give greater emphasis to top authors in terms of advances, promotional expenditure, sales effort and high-profile publication dates – author brands help to sell books.

Self-publishing

Self-published ebook authors erode the market share of publishers but can provide a source of new talent.

Discoverability

Publishers depend to a great extent on retail exposure to aid book discovery and sell their books, and on gift buying for adult and children's books (the pre-Christmas period is of immense importance). The main customers and channels to market for physical books are diverse, including internet retailers, bookselling chains, independent bookshops, and direct distribution channels. The growth in online retailing (dominated by Amazon) disrupted the business model of sales through physical stores, and raised the issue of how readers discover books in the online environment.

Marketing

Publicity in the media makes a significant difference to visibility and sales, along with social media marketing. A large promotional spend is often necessary to secure large orders from key retailers. Publishers have attempted to shift to B2C marketing, and have invested in online vertical communities and the provision of services.

ESG (environmental, social and governance)

Publishing houses are keen to increase the diversity of their authors and books, alongside the creation of a diverse and inclusive workplace. The aim is to match more closely the changing demographics of society at large. They are also responding to the climate emergency, with the aim to increase the sustainability of their business, becoming climate-neutral in both their direct operations and in their global value chain.

High discounts

Publishers are squeezed by the large retailers ratcheting up the discounts granted to them. The discounts granted to the book trade, essential to gain exposure in the shops, can reach over 60 per cent of the recommended price of a book in the UK, at least 10–20 per cent higher than those granted by the non-consumer publishers. Trade publishers suffer from returns of unsold books from physical retailers and wholesalers.

CHILDREN'S AND YOUNG ADULT PUBLISHING

The area of children's publishing has been resilient in recent years. Children's books recorded £429 m of sales in 2022 (£425 m in 2021), made up of £285 m home and £144 m in export sales; digital sales were £24 m compared to £23 m in 2021 (Publishers Association, 2022). Children's books are published by the specialist children's divisions of the major consumer book publishers (e.g. Penguin Random House and HarperCollins) and by independent publishers (e.g. Bloomsbury, Usborne and Walker Books). The vitality of children's publishing creates the book buyers of the future. The text and illustrations of children's books must excite, and appeal to, children of different age groups, and at different levels of reading skill and comprehension. They must also appeal to adults in the supply chain (the major non-book and book retailers) and to adults who buy or influence choice (parents, relations, librarians and teachers). Many titles are in full colour yet have to be published at low prices, and these often need co-edition partners in the USA, in Europe and elsewhere in order to attain economies in printing.

The books are usually aimed at age bands reflecting the development of reading skill. The bibliographic information supplied by publishers to the book trade is formalized through the Book Industry Communication (BIC) Children's Book Marketing Categories standard which denotes amongst other things, the title's intended age range (bic.org.uk). These are divided up as follows:

A   0–5
B   5–7
C   7–9
D   9–11
E   12 upwards

The 0–5 age group from babies to toddlers may be described as the parent pointing stage. Included here are the so-called 'novelty books' (which extend above the age group), a category of ever-widening inventiveness, such as board books

The seventh volume in the Harry Potter series, *Harry Potter and the Deathly Hallows*, was published on 21 July 2007: it sold 2.6 m copies in the UK on that day alone

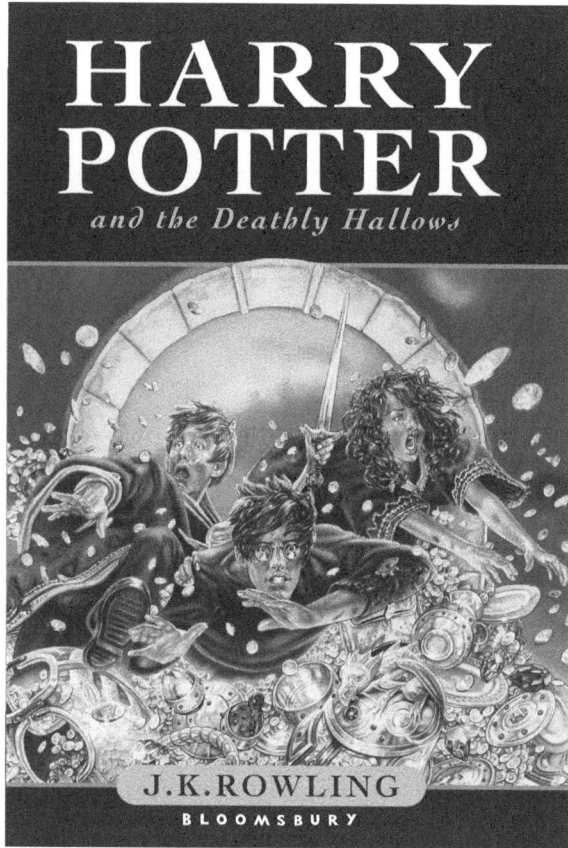

and bath books (introducing page turning), colouring and activity books, question and answer books, pop-ups; and the lower end of picture books. Books for the very young need to be durable and often use cloth, plastic or hardback binding. The production departments of children's publishers are particularly concerned with product safety. The apps produced for this age group include reading experiences and games.

The 5–7 age group may be described as the starting to read, as well as the reading to children stage. Picture books figure prominently: these books, invariably in full colour, tend to be 32 pages long, display strong narrative and may include just a few words up to possibly several thousand. They may be created by an illustrator or writer (or one controlling mind), and often need co-edition partners. Publishers have experimented with augmented reality, accessed through a phone or tablet, to create immersive story worlds.

The next stage, of young fiction, may have from 2,000–7,500 words of text, and may be published in paperback in smaller formats; these titles are designed for children reading their first whole novels. There are major series produced by

Some character
brands have an
international reach:
the Turkish edition
of *Horrid Henry
and the Abominable
Snowman*

many of the main trade publishers as well as reading schemes by the educational publishers. Moving up, and through, the 9–12 age group, longer-length novels of up to 35,000 words come into play as well as the more recent mass-market genre series. Above this age group, there are the teenage or young adult, fiction titles. Much middle grade (roughly 8–12) and young adult fiction is published straight into paperback. Non-fiction, sometimes highly illustrated, spans the age groups as do home learning series, reference titles (such as dictionaries), anthologies and character books (some which are tie-ins to films).

Children's books often receive less window or promotional space in general bookshops; and children's publishers of quality books earn a higher proportion from backlist sales. The children's and young adult (YA) market is subject to crazes for particular authors and series (from Twilight to the Hunger Games), which can be prompted by word of mouth or film releases. Anthony Horowitz said that his 'success, and that of at least half-a-dozen other children's fiction writers, rests entirely on J. K. Rowling. We just happened to be around at the right time' (*Guardian*, 14 September 2013). There are also international influences with, for example, manga becoming mainstream in the UK. Whilst the penetration of digital across the whole of children's publishing remains low, there may be higher figures for young adult titles. The Hunger Games trilogy sold over 1 m ebooks in 2012 in the UK, around one-third of the total sales. The market for YA fiction has become buoyant again after a period of saturation.

Echoing developments in adult publishing, children's publishers have little time to build authors slowly. The focus is on promotable debut authors, established adult authors or celebrities writing for children, and media tie-ins. Author branding and the development of branded series are notable features of children's publishing. As in adult publishing, the gender differentiation of books for male and female markets is evident, in part influenced by consumer advertising of other products to children.

The Yoto Player is a screen-free audio player for children, initially funded through a Kickstarter campaign

Children's publishing in the UK continues to push out the frontiers of book availability into a wide range of retail outlets, including grocery stores, toy-shops, and garden centres, reached via the wholesalers. Such retailers, and some of the book clubs, tend to concentrate on books for the younger age groups. Internationally, the Bologna Book Fair held in the spring is the world's meeting-place of children's publishing. The UK publishers and packagers have for long dominated the international trade in the selling of overseas co-edition rights and, like their adult counterparts, they import far less.

NON-CONSUMER PUBLISHING

The educational, academic, STM, and professional book publishers have a number of advantages by comparison to firms operating in consumer markets:

- Their markets are more defined into vertical communities.
- Their authors and advisers are largely drawn from the same peer groups as their customers.
- Customers can be reached and engaged through their place of work.
- Backlist sales, especially if textbook and reference, account for a major proportion of their business.
- Institutional and business purchasers are far more amenable to buying digital formats.
- Subscription and site licence business models are more prevalent.

EDUCATION

Schools publishing

The total value of school book sales in 2022 was £355 m (£328 m in 2021), comprising £182 m of home and £173 m of export sales; digital sales totalled £61 m – compared to £58 m in 2021 (Publishers Association, 2022). Educational publishers provide materials for schools: print textbooks and digital media for use by teachers and students, both in class and at home. Ancillary printed materials include teacher guides and workbooks.

The key characteristics of schools publishing are set out below.

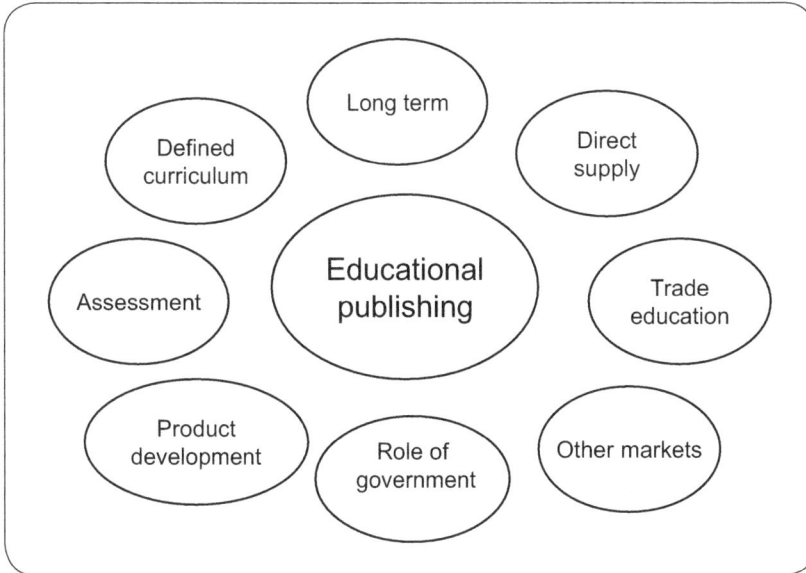

Long term

Compared with consumer book publishing, educational publishing is for the long term. Schools can ill afford to dump adopted texts frequently and there is tight pressure on school budgets. Yet there is an active programme of new publishing, for both primary and secondary education, driven by curriculum change and the need to be up to date. This type of publishing calls for a large amount of working capital – the liquid assets of a company – invested over a long time. The development costs of digital resources are also very high.

Defined curriculum

The books are market-specific, i.e. precisely tailored to the government set curriculum, examinations, academic levels and age groups. While to some extent the broad content is predetermined, educational publishers and their external advisers and authors give great attention to the pedagogy. They help raise the quality of teaching. Links have been developed between publishers and the examination boards, for example, Pearson with Edexcel (Pearson bought the examination body in 2005). In addition, publishers produce publishing to support specific exam board specifications.

Assessment

A key feature of educational publishing is a focus on low-stakes assessment and preparation, or practice for high-stakes assessment.

Product development

Understanding the market is vital to the creation of a new textbook course or digital content for schools. Primary research may include visits to the classroom, sending out questionnaires to teachers or the use of focus groups.

Many books are highly illustrated, printed in colour, and involve the publisher in considerable development work. Yet they must be published at competitive prices and the cost of developing associated digital materials can be high. The use of e-textbooks and other digital resources continues to grow – to aid home learning and exam revision, or to enliven lessons – along with the provision of services to aid the professional development of teachers. Popular learning platforms in schools are Dynamic Learning from Hodder Education, which enables access to a variety of multimedia content, ActiveHub from Pearson, and Kerboodle from Oxford University Press. Some schools have introduced tablets for all pupils, and the major tech players are keen to integrate their technology into the classroom.

Role of government

Publishing is dependent on demographics and school budgets, and influenced by government policies. The latest education minister can have a big impact on the curriculum and how schools are run.

Other markets

Some educational publishers produce books for further education (especially for vocational qualifications) and reference (for home or school library use).

In 2022 export accounted for 49 per cent of the sales of school books. Primary school titles in the areas of reading schemes and literacy have an international market. UK-orientated textbooks at secondary level have reduced export potential (other than to the international schools) but there is increasing scope to develop materials for local markets.

Trade education

With the increased concentration on testing of pupils, there is a healthy trade market for self-study and revision books, sold through bookshops or directly to the more affluent parents and pupils. Personalized online learning materials are at the leading edge. Teachers can influence this parental anxiety market through their recommendations, and there is a growing market for home tuition from specialist companies, often delivered over the internet.

Direct supply

New and backlist titles are promoted directly to teachers and by publishers' sales consultants in schools and at exhibitions. Teachers scrutinize products before adopting them. Textbooks are mainly supplied directly to schools, or via booksellers, specialist school contractors and local authority direct purchasing organizations, and may be stocked by booksellers for parental purchase. The direct supply route to schools provides valuable marketing information to publishers.

ELT publishing

Many people come to the UK each year to learn English and although the business was affected by the global pandemic, the level of arrivals had recovered significantly by 2023. The publishing of English language teaching (ELT) or English as a foreign language (EFL) course materials is primarily export-orientated. In 2022, sales of ELT books were £276 m (£220 m in 2021) with £268 m of export and £8 m of home sales of physical books; digital sales were £34 m – compared to £27 m in 2021 (Publishers Association, 2022). The pandemic led to an acceleration in the provision of digital resources, for example, in PDF and ebook formats, to facilitate home learning.

There are around 1.5 bn learners of English worldwide

The traditional main markets have been in Southern Europe (e.g. Spain, Italy and Turkey), Eastern Europe (Poland), Japan, the Far East and South East Asia (China, Taiwan, Korea, Thailand), Latin America (Argentina, Brazil and Mexico) and the Middle East. The ELT publishers have set up companies, opened offices or acquired publishers in such areas, or have copublishing links with local publishers, or local marketing arrangements. Recent high-growth markets include India where companies are keen to provide digital learning in a country where there is high mobile phone usage.

The mixed media ELT courses are major investments and may be orientated or versioned to regional cultural distinctiveness and are sometimes produced for ministries. Digital coursebooks may be supplied alongside print, together with the provision of an online environment to support face-to-face tuition.

The courses serving primary, secondary and adult sectors are backed up with supplementary materials (such as reading books, dictionaries and grammars) with a broad international appeal. They are sold to the Private Language Schools (PLS), from primary to adult, primary and secondary state schools, and sometimes to universities. In the UK there are specialist booksellers that supply the local and export markets.

Whereas previously UK publishers could rely on the same course to sell well around the world, there are now separate needs for different markets, which raise the costs of product development. The big change has been the growth of the state school market – for example, in Italy, Spain, Argentina and Eastern Europe – which has probably overtaken the PLS market. A state syllabus has its own demands, specific to the country, and offers an opportunity for local publishers to enter the market. Some countries, such as Argentina, may insist on using locally produced materials. A key competence in ELT publishing is the ability to network with local schools and educational authorities.

AHSS, STM AND PROFESSIONAL PUBLISHING

The terms 'academic' or 'professional' publishing are used loosely and interchangeably. Academic books tend to be associated with the arts, humanities and social sciences (AHSS). Research monographs of primary research are described as 'academic' and are often vital to career progression. Professional books usually have an applied focus to aid practitioners directly in their work, for example, schoolteachers, health care workers, engineers, architects, managers, and those working in law and finance. STM, reference and information books usually fall into the professional book publishing area. Some academic/professional titles may be designed for vocational or continuing professional development courses and be adopted. Their pricing level varies widely, depending on the target audience's ability to pay and whether they are purchased by the individual or the employer. Sales of academic and professional books totalled £1.2 bn in the UK in 2022 (£1.1 bn in 2021), with £651 m of home and £531 m of export sales; digital sales totalled £514 m or 44 per cent – compared to £440 m or 39 per cent in 2021 (Publishers Association, 2022).

Publishing has seen some fundamental changes, with the impact of technology, the move from product to service, and the increasingly bespoke nature of tools and platforms. Nitasha Devasar, Managing Director of Taylor & Francis, India and South Asia, commented in 2018:

> As the boundaries between content and platforms are disappearing, we are seeing transformation in the arena of services. We are witnessing a lot of dynamic changes—variety in formats, the splicing and dicing of content to aid continuous learning, translation on tap, testing applications, audio, and video, and much more! The arena of action has simultaneously shifted from the mature markets of the Western world to this side of the globe, throwing countries like China and India into focus. (editage.com, accessed 12 February 2024)

The business models are subject to change. Institutions may want to buy directly from publishers, for example, to provide content as part of the tuition fee for a university degree. The publisher's brand role of quality assurance and accuracy in the supply of information is supplemented by the direct provision of services and tools to end-users. A key added value is to provide users with access tools to the content they need quickly, and in a form they want, at the point they need it in their workflow, be they researchers or lawyers in their offices, or medical practitioners on the move. AI is helping to revolutionize search and the supply of essential information. Elsevier developed Scopus AI, which offers 'easy-to-read topic summaries based on trusted content from over 27,000 academic journals, from more than 7,000 publishers worldwide, with over 1.8 bn citations, and includes over 17 m author profiles' (elsevier.com, accessed 4 January 2024).

Not even the largest publisher could claim to be equally strong in all disciplines, or even those in science alone. Publishers concentrate on particular subjects, and vary in the emphasis given to different categories of book. The books for professional or practitioner use which have a wider market beyond teaching institutions tend to be those in the applied sciences for researchers or practitioners in industry and government agencies; and those serving professional sectors, for example, law, medicine, management, accounting, finance, architecture. Such high-priced titles are bought by the wealthy (offices, commercial libraries and individuals). Special sales channels include booksellers, aggregators or training companies serving corporations, agencies and individuals; dedicated business, computer and medical book distributors and aggregators reaching end-users directly; conference and exhibition organizers; and companies which take bulk orders of titles as promotional items.

The legal and financial publishers sell a high proportion of their materials directly to end-users, not via booksellers. Publishers migrated their businesses to digital information services, and their products are usually licensed directly to libraries and businesses on subscription or by use of a site licence. Key abilities of such publisher are to identify information needs and the way that information is used in the workplace, and to translate that knowledge into the creation of products, tools and services using the appropriate media and technologies.

Traditionally Europe and North America have been the strong export markets but recent years have seen strong growth in Asia, for example, in India and China. For many publishers, mainland Europe is the single most important market with the Scandinavian and Benelux countries featuring as significant markets for English language textbook adoptions, and for professional lists. Southern Europe, for example Spain and Italy, is a market for high-level professional texts; undergraduate texts exist in translation or are published locally. The sale of translation rights to Eastern Europe and more recently to China and Korea, for example, has grown.

High-level textbooks, AHSS, STM and professional titles are sold to the USA, the largest and richest market, via a sister company. A UK firm without a US presence may develop a copublishing link with a US firm, or license rights to a variety of publishers, or sell directly through importers. Sales to less-developed countries tend to be dependent on aid agency funding. Publishers may on their own account arrange for special low-priced editions of some of their textbooks to be published in less-developed countries, either through their own local companies or through sublicensing editions to local publishers. At the minimum, such editions have different covers in order to reduce the possibility of their penetrating developed markets through conventional and internet traders.

AHSS and STM publishers are mostly outside central London with a high concentration in Oxford, and their output includes major textbooks (both print and digital); higher-level textbooks for more advanced students through to graduate; edited volumes of reprinted or commissioned articles for students or academics; research monographs; books for professional use; reference titles (online) and learned journals (print and online). These broad categories are not clear-cut, for example, high-level 'textbooks' may incorporate original research.

Textbooks

There is no commonly accepted definition of what constitutes a 'textbook'. Indeed, there are plenty of examples of books of different kinds that are never written or intended as textbooks but which subsequently become adopted by lecturers for teaching and bought by their students (such as this book, first published in 1988). However, from a publishing standpoint, a higher education or 'college' textbook is commissioned, designed, timed and priced at the outset to meet teaching and learning needs in a defined area and at a particular level, and is marketed to lecturers with the intention that they adopt the book for use on a course, resulting in the purchase of multiple copies by students. The global pandemic highlighted the need for students to have digital access and print volumes have been replaced in favour of ebook editions.

There are many factors affecting textbook purchasing in the UK, including student use of the internet, competing financial demands, the rise in published prices above the rate of inflation, changing behaviours about the sharing of books, and the rise of the used book market. Broadly speaking, textbooks are published in paperback, though some for professional training (e.g. medicine, law) may be hardback. The high-level supplementary texts occasionally have a short high-priced print run for libraries, issued simultaneously with the paperback. Conversely, textbooks, printed in larger quantities, may become established and are reprinted for annual student intakes and revised through new editions when appropriate.

Publishers promote (and sometimes sell directly) their books to lecturers, researchers and practitioners (mainly by mail, email and telephone) and compared with consumer book publishers usually have smaller sales forces calling on a limited range of booksellers, and sometimes campuses, or attending exhibitions. However, some firms publish titles of wider general interest and of bookshop appeal, in which case, booksellers may be granted higher 'trade' discounts. These include more titles in the humanities, especially history, than the social sciences, some technical books (e.g. on computing) and medical works (e.g. personal health) supplied through specialist wholesalers.

Other titles, sometimes referred to as 'supplementary texts', may include the author's original research or commissioned edited collections. These can be priced for student and individual academic purchase, and can be published economically in small quantities – from around 1,500 copies in paperback. Paradoxically, if an author's primary research were to appear in a textbook, it could seriously damage saleability through being seen as idiosyncratic or too advanced. The highly saleable textbooks usually reflect a mainstream view of current teaching and assessment. Other kinds of books, such as edited collections and anthologies, may be bought by students and academics.

The key characteristics of textbook publishing are shown below.

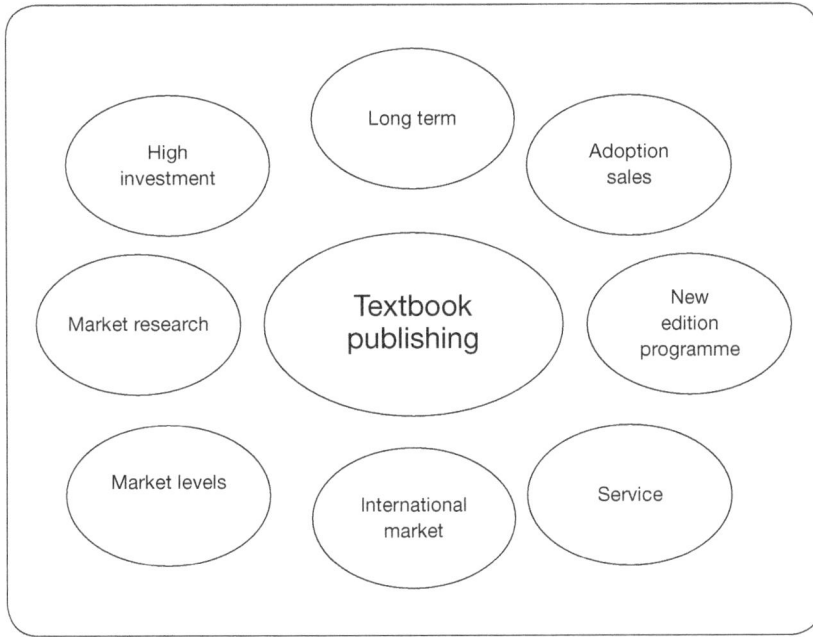

Long term

Initiating and developing a textbook list requires planning and sufficient attention to product development. Textbooks require development editors to control the authoring, schedule and budget.

High investment

Some textbook projects require high levels of investment, and there are growing demands to fund digital content and services.

Market research

Just as in educational publishing, a major investment in a new textbook requires comprehensive research into the market and competition.

Market levels

There will be different levels in the market, from first-year undergraduate through to graduate. More introductory texts may have a larger potential sale but will encounter fiercer competition.

International market

For some subjects there may be a large international market. For example, a business textbook may be used around the world, and some business schools in non-English-speaking countries may teach in English. Successful textbooks may be localized in different markets. For example, Kotler et al.'s *Principles of Marketing* is available in a European edition. The adaptation of textbooks for particular regions of the world aids local sales and inhibits their exportation to other higher-priced regions.

Service

Alongside the market growth of etexts, the publishers producing major textbooks for subjects with high student intakes adopt US practices, such as a periodically updated companion website carrying data, activities, test banks of questions, website links, and lecturers' guides; and develop adaptive learning products. The large publishers offer lecturers the ability to customize – personalize – the book's content to meet their specific teaching needs (assuming sufficient numbers of students). The publisher creates a unique product for the particular institution.

New edition programme

In order to ensure that texts are up to date, and also to minimize lost sales from the used book market, textbooks regularly go into new editions.

Adoption sales

The successful sale of a textbook involves persuading the lecturer to adopt it, the bookseller to stock it and the student to buy it. US publishers have developed 'all you can eat' models for digital access to textbooks for a monthly subscription.

AHSS, STM and professional specialist titles

Specialist titles, including research monographs, are usually high-priced and published mainly for libraries and individual researchers and practitioners. They are printed in small quantities and will be available as ebooks. Some publishers are moving towards holding no stock and simply printing to order. Publishing books with very low sales forecasts is not risk-free – the profit may come from the sale of the last 50 copies. Individual titles or collections of ebook titles are sold directly by publishers to libraries, or via aggregators, using a variety of models based on the site licence. The models include perpetual access, PDA (patron-driven acquisition), short-term loans under rental agreements, pay per view, and subscription. The sale of ebook collections to libraries comes ever closer to the usage and business models of journals. The OA (open access) agenda is relevant to monograph publishing as OA publication may be required by funders and for research audits.

JOURNAL PUBLISHING

If sales to UK publishers of books total over £4.5 bn, a further contribution of £2.4 bn comes from journals publishing; digital sales in 2022 were 83 per cent of the total (Publishers Association, 2022). Worldwide, it is a huge business with sales of $10 bn just in the area of STM publishing. The content of learned journals, as distinct from magazines, is not predetermined (commissioned or written in-house), and contributors submit papers of original research to an academic editor-in-chief for refereeing and inclusion. Refereed journal articles are a primary information source and serve the research community. The publishing system sorts and assesses the research outputs, and aggregates content in the form of brands – the journal title. It provides quality assurance, visibility and usability. Generally speaking, learned journals are not dependent on advertising for their viability; their revenue is mainly derived from subscriptions, and to a growing extent through various forms of open access (OA) publishing models. Some publishers produce journals for professional use that are supported by advertising.

Journals are published by not-for-profit societies and research institutes – a few of which run substantial journal and book publishing operations – and by divisions of academic and STM publishers including the university presses, and especially in OA by a variety of subsidized publishing operations, usually university and research agencies. The commercial journal publishers initiate journals, or produce and market journals for societies and others under contract. The provision of such services to societies can be a significant proportion of some publishers' business.

Virtually all journals are available electronically though print is maintained for subscription journals. Researchers, students and industry practitioners mostly access journal articles online away from the library. Librarians are able to check the value for money of a subscription from user statistics on articles downloaded. Many authors assign the copyright in their article to the journal publisher or society. Authors and referees are not paid, but academic journal editors may be paid – some only expenses, some handsomely. However, the cost of funding the academic editorial office is considerable. The higher the rejection rate, the higher the cost.

There are more STM journals than in other academic areas. They are promoted by mail and at academic conferences, and sold mainly through institutional subscriptions (and those made with consortia), via site licences with academic libraries worldwide (either directly from the publisher's platform or through intermediaries) and to individuals (although this is increasingly rare). Journals of applied science, management, economics and law also sell to industrial and commercial libraries. Members of societies may receive a journal free as part of their membership fee, or at a reduced rate. Other income arises from pay-per-view article downloads, advertisements, inserts and reprints (especially in STM). The income from the licensing of back files to institutions and consortia can be significant on long-established journals. The Big Deal business model (the bundling of content) became a dominant method of sales.

The impact of OA is felt in a number of ways, including the use of delayed OA (articles are freely available after an initial embargo period), the deposit of articles in disciplinary or institutional repositories on publication (green OA), and the rise of gold OA – whereby authors (or mainly their funders) pay APCs to have their articles made OA immediately on publication. Some subscription journals allowing paid-for OA are called hybrid journals. Subscription-only journals traditionally took a long time to break even – up to 5 or 7 years – and often required a high level of investment. By contrast, journals using the gold OA model can generate income more quickly, provided they attract a sufficient supply of publishable articles. New journals are usually bundled into existing packages to help them gather momentum.

The key characteristics of journal publishing are set out below.

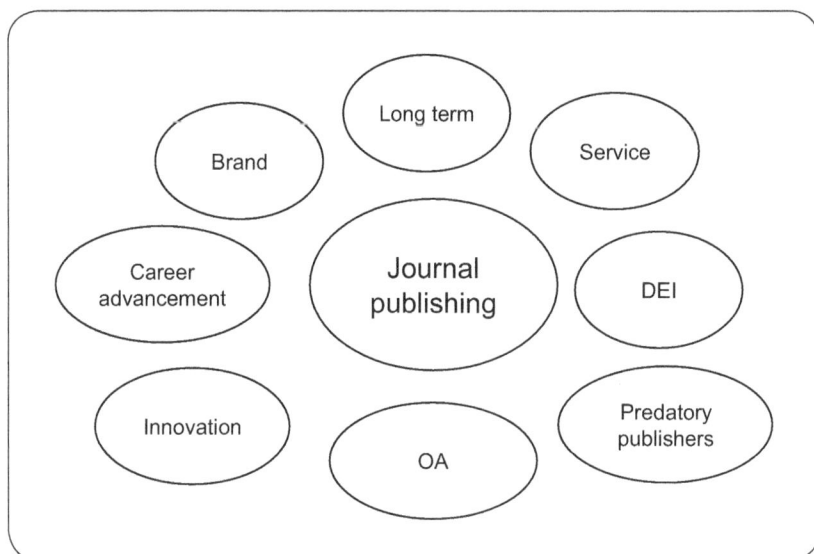

Long term

Journals take a long time to establish but over time the sales pattern and revenue are more predictable than for books, the demand for capital lower (as are staff overheads), and the value of sales per employee is higher.

Brand

Long-established and successful journals, such as *Nature*, become high-profile brands, attracting the best submissions from authors. Their content is essential in their relevant communities and the curated aggregation benefits from network effects.

Career advancement

Publication in high-ranking journals can establish or enhance the academic standing of authors – counting towards their personal and institutional research funding and their promotion prospects.

Innovation

There are many examples of innovation, some of which reach the other sectors of publishing, from aggregation to the breaking down of content into small chunks. The arrival of OA has prompted a search for efficiencies in the peer review system and new methods of measuring impact. Mega journals are not limited by size and will accept articles according to quality standards around the methodology; cascade models allow articles rejected by top-quality journals to be referred to lower-ranked journals within the same stable. The use of AI will affect many parts of the workflow and what kind of services are offered. An example is Scopus AI, a search tool amongst the scientific literature, powered by generative AI which synthesizes search results into clear summaries.

OA (open access)

The open access movement argues that access to journal articles should be free to the end-user. There are a number of OA models in existence, from 'author/funder pays' to the institutional repository. The policies of government and research funders to promote open access are driving change, including the introduction of transformative agreements, often at national level.

Predatory publishers

The growth of OA has encouraged their existence, and these publishers prey on scholars seeking publication. A fee is charged to authors but quality standards are low, whether in the peer review or editing.

DEI (diversity, equity and inclusion)

Of importance to research funders and within research communities, DEI initiatives are seeking to challenge the hegemony of the US and UK publishing system. Many in the Global South are keen to see content authored by a broader spectrum of scholars.

Service

Journal publishing has been at the forefront of online publishing. The large players have invested huge sums in online platforms, enabling them to sell direct to their customers, usability design, and in back file conversion of long-established journals. The migration to digital has meant the transition from a physical product industry to a digital service. Journal publishers constantly strive to improve the service they offer their customers – including access, search, usability and product range. The growth in open access publishing has placed greater onus on publishers to help authors meet the obligations set by their funders. Publishers offer research institutions a set of tools to help them manage and record workflows.

Now read this

Chapter 4, Creating and protecting value in publishing

Sources

Arts Council, *Literature in the 21st Century: Understanding models of support for literary fiction*, Arts Council, 2017.
Frania Hall, *The Business of Digital Publishing: An introduction to the digital book and journal industries*, 2nd edition, Routledge, 2022.
Angus Phillips, 'Have We Passed Peak Book?', *Publishing Research Quarterly*, 33:3, September 2017.
Publishers Association, *Industry Insights*, 2022.

Web resources

https://www.thebookseller.com *The Bookseller* trade magazine.
https://www.publishers.org.uk Publishers Association.

Creating and protecting value in publishing

The aim of a book publisher is to publish and sell at a profit. Even a not-for-profit publisher will want to at least break even, covering their costs, unless they receive a subsidy from their sponsor or parent organization. A publisher might previously have cross-subsidized less popular titles from the profits of its top sellers. That approach has largely been abandoned although the high-risk element of consumer publishing does mean that bestsellers compensate for titles with poor sales. Of course, a book may acquire value as a collectable object or a great literary work to be admired and studied by future generations, but this chapter will concentrate on the creation of monetary value by publishers as commercial enterprises. How publishers add value is of interest to both authors and readers in an age when self-publishing is quick and inexpensive, and consumers expect digital content to be available at lower prices than physical products.

VALUE CHAIN

Taking the raw material – the author's text – the publisher aims to add sufficient value so that it sells the final product at a higher value than the costs that have been incurred. A number of activities are undertaken in order to take the author's text and make it available as an attractive product that consumers will want to buy. These activities are shown below (Cope and Phillips, 2006, page 48). Each of the publishing functions is described in more detail in the relevant chapter.

Once a book is acquired from an author, it has to be edited, designed, produced, marketed to the book trade and readers, and sold to bookshops or the

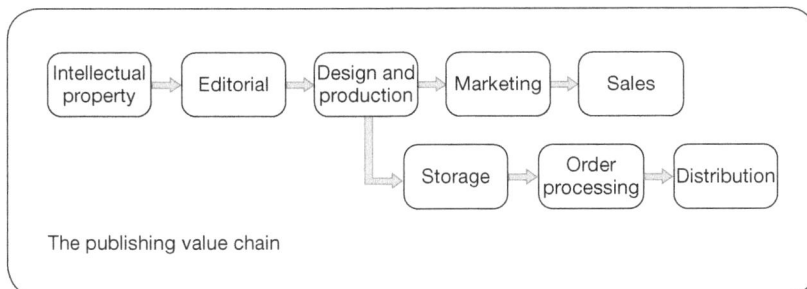

The publishing value chain

DOI: 10.4324/9781003403289-5

end-purchaser. Once produced, it has to be stored in print form or the digital file made available through key intermediaries, orders are taken from retailers or consumers, and the book is then dispatched from the warehouse, downloaded on to a device, or made available through a cloud service. Publishers can choose which elements of the value chain they undertake themselves, and which are outsourced to third parties. For example, while commissioning new titles is usually done in-house, copy-editing and proofreading are typically carried out by freelance editors or by suppliers which provide an entire production service. The key elements of the value chain are the curation and acquisition of intellectual property, editorial, design and production, marketing, and sales, and most publishers will control these functions directly. Publishers can look to combine stages of the value chain, for example, editorial, design and production may be combined into one function; the posts of production editor and project manager are common.

Publishers seek to gain competitive advantage in the market, and this is done through acquisition and control of the best intellectual property and that creates a virtuous circle in attracting the best authors. The late Peter Mayer (1936–2018), former CEO of Penguin, said that 'Publishing is what you publish. That's how you are really successful' (*Guardian*, 19 May 2018). Having the best possible people in the commissioning roles will be the key to the success of many publishers.

Other parts of the value chain also offer the opportunity to add value. For example, a larger publisher will be able to negotiate from a stronger position with printers and paper suppliers, and with key retailers and wholesalers. 'In the experience of two independent trade publishers, on absorption into large groups they found their print bills reduced by more than 25%' (de Bellaigue, 2004, page 192). There are economies of scale in production if co-edition orders can be added to the print run. Using digital printing to produce smaller quantities, or selling ebooks, may minimize or eradicate investment in stock. Some publishers build up expertise in the area of design. Everyman's Library, owned by Random House, offers editions of literary classics in hardback editions with high production values that contrast with a cheap paperback or free ebook. Smaller publishers often benefit from speed to market – commissioning and publishing faster than their larger rivals. Selling direct, rather than through intermediaries, enables a publisher to keep more of the price paid by the end customer.

There is less competitive advantage to be found for a publisher in the physical distribution of books, since the levels of service are now high across the industry. Nevertheless a larger publisher benefits from economies of scale in distribution in such areas as investment in IT systems, the number of units shipped in one order, negotiation over carriage costs with shippers, and the collection of money from customers. In digital distribution the larger publisher benefits from the greater aggregation of its intellectual property, and has deeper pockets to invest in innovation and technology.

Adding value

Publishers add value to an author's work in a variety of ways – these reflect both creativity and business acumen. Embedded throughout the book, they are summarized here.

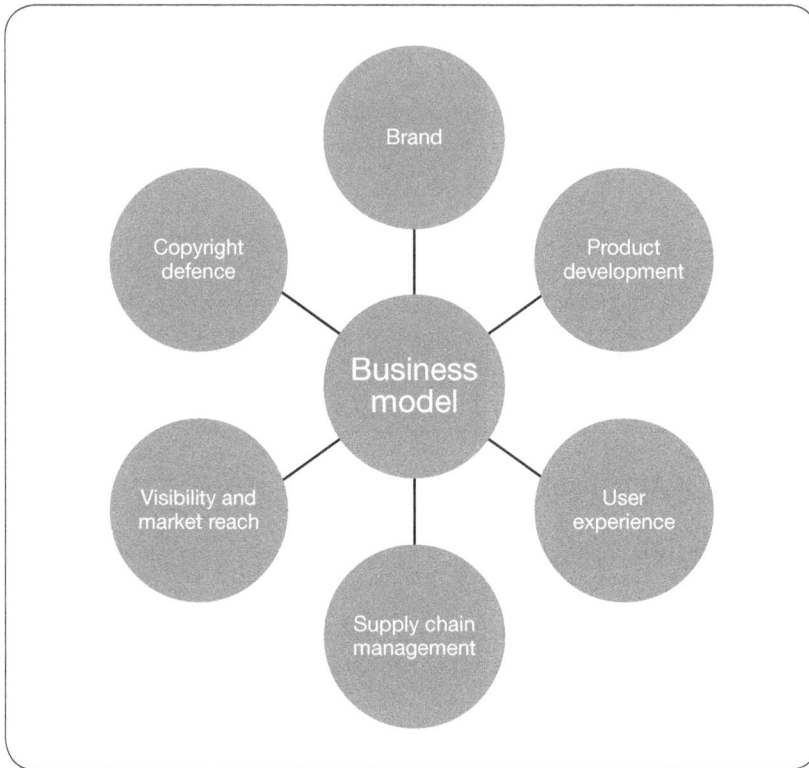

Brand

In consumer publishing publishers offer the service of developing and managing the brands of leading authors. Most consumer book publishers are B2B firms and their imprints are called trade brands, recognizable by the trade but not by consumers; however, publishers serving vertical communities (B2C) develop consumer brands which are recognizable by readers.

By lending its brand or imprint, the publisher is making a statement about the value of an author's work – it is worth publication by an investor, i.e. the publisher. Emphasis has been placed on the role of the publisher as the curator of excellent content: the brand (or imprint) adds value and endorsement. In trade publishing the payment of an advance (risk capital) gives the author the time and resources to research and write. The flavour or character of an imprint is understood by authors and agents, informed sections of the media, trade buyers in the supply chain in the UK and overseas, and by other media companies and overseas publishers.

In non-consumer book publishing, an imprint's status is recognized by associated peer groups (e.g. teachers) and those in the market channels, including institutional (such as librarians) and corporate purchasers. Major textbook brands offer authors a platform to show their approach to teaching is more effective than existing texts, and the advantage of online support services. Highly rated academic and professional publishing brands offer authors peer group recognition worldwide and personal career advancement.

The advent of AI has given us a world in which content – text, pictures and video – can be easily created. The veracity of that content is open to doubt when fakes are so simple to construct. The brand of the publisher is influential in identifying quality content:

> Online content will no longer verify itself, so who posted something will become as important as what was posted. Assuming trustworthy sources can continue to identify themselves securely – via urls, email addresses and social-media platforms – reputation and provenance will become more important than ever. (*The Economist*, 18 January 2024)

The age of AI in book publishing

E★PERT

Michael Bhaskar, writer, publisher and co-author of the bestselling book about AI, *The Coming Wave*

Artificial intelligence (AI) is here. It's impacting almost every industry, but has especially come for the core product of publishers: words, now produced in utter abundance, automatically by machines. The book publishing industry is hence about to undergo a seismic shift, with AI emerging as the next in a long sequence of transformative forces. But with a difference.

Although technologies have always transformed publishing's business model, never before has one so radically altered the nature of the process of producing books themselves. From primary writing and editing to marketing and distribution, AI is already transforming the way books are created, published, and consumed, and will do so in ever greater degrees over coming years and decades. Writing and communication have just been automated. No one involved in the book business can afford to ignore what this means. The implications of this revolution, both positive and negative, will eventually leave little unchanged.

The use of AI in writing and editing is perhaps the most significant development in the publishing industry in recent years. AI-powered writing tools can generate text based on a set of prompts, helping writers overcome writer's block and generate ideas without limit. The process of writing has just been made much easier. But at the same time this powerful natural language capacity also holds out the promise of books written with no human involvement; indeed, Amazon has already been spammed with thousands of books generated by ChatGPT (with considerable manual help, it should be said), and changed policies as a result. AI-powered editing tools can analyse text and suggest improvements to readability, coherence, and style. All these tools can increase efficiency and consistency in the writing and editing process, but also raise questions about originality and authenticity. Drawing on data covering sales trends, pricing, writing style and reader demographics, publishers could automatically micro-target segmented audiences with precisely tailored content generated on the fly. Get ready for AI-authored literature, of every conceivable kind, and soon.

Just as AI can craft and edit customised tales, it may transform publishing's central workflows – assessing submissions, copy-editing manuscripts, managing sales data and more. Its analytical breadth offers gains in efficiency, cost and accuracy.

Yet adoption faces hurdles. No algorithm can yet fully replace subjective human judgement of a book's artistic, cultural or even scholarly merits. There are also many practical constraints around integrating AI smoothly alongside staff and existing processes – designers, for example, may not be happy to see their core value being automated away (images as much as words can be seamlessly generated by AI).

AI will also transform marketing. AI algorithms can analyse vast amounts of data to identify trends, recommend books to readers, and optimise marketing campaigns. They can generate bespoke adverts surgically catering to niche books and audiences on the fly. This data-driven approach can again help publishers make informed decisions about what books to publish and how to reach their target audiences. However, it also raises concerns about data privacy and the potential for AI to perpetuate biases in the publishing industry.

As AI becomes more prevalent, there are deep implications for intellectual property and copyright. For example, if an AI-generated text is published, who owns the copyright? Is it the AI developer, the person who prompted the AI, or the AI itself? And that's before you get to the most contentious question of all, the idea that large technology groups have 'trained' their AI systems on vast numbers of in-copyright texts, effectively using writers' and publishers' intellectual property to build systems of immense power and value. Do these algorithms also infringe IP rights by reproducing protected text snippets? What are the legal implications if they remix this data into new synthetic creations?

The stakes are monumental. Tech giants claim AI output counts as fair use - even if it echoes copyrighted source material. Yet creators argue this denies consent, payment or attribution. Caught in between, publishers recognise AI's potential but fear ruinous lawsuits if courts side against its unfettered use and strongly object to the use of their IP in any context without due authorisation and remuneration. Deciding this in the courts will be a major milestone on what AI means for publishing. These questions raise ethical and legal concerns that will need to be addressed as AI continues to shape the publishing industry.

Striking a balance between fostering innovation through access to diverse training datasets and respecting the intellectual property rights inherent in those datasets will be an ongoing challenge. While most publishers, authors and rights holders have a clear anti-AI view on the copyright question, the evolving discourse on copyright in the context of AI underscores the need for a nuanced legal framework that can accommodate the dynamic nature of

AI-driven content creation while safeguarding the rights of content creators. Suffice to say, getting this balance right is neither easy nor simple.

Moreover, AI has the potential to disrupt the traditional publishing model, with self-publishing becoming more accessible and cost-effective. AI can automate many aspects of the publishing process, such as formatting, layout, and even cover design. This could democratise publishing further and provide opportunities for diverse voices to be heard, as well as providing a boost to traditional publisher bottom lines - costs can be saved at any part of the value chain. However, it also poses a threat to some traditional publishers who may struggle to adapt to this new landscape. Much will depend on how organizations approach and manage the transition. The recent record on ambition and competence integrating pioneering technologies and business practices is mixed ...

As with every previous technological revolution, the age of AI in book publishing presents both opportunities and challenges. Ethical, legal, creative, practical and economic concerns cannot be dodged - by either writers, publishers or tech companies. As the industry navigates this new landscape, it will be crucial to strike a balance between leveraging the benefits of AI and preserving what publishers have always managed best: the unique contributions of human creativity and expertise. Ultimately, the success of AI in publishing will depend on how well the industry navigates these complex issues and harnesses the power of AI to create a more inclusive, innovative, and sustainable future for books and literature.

But make no mistake, AI is a paradigm shift. Writing is no longer the province of human beings. Vast portions of the publishing workflow may now happen at the touch of a button. Moreover, this is only the beginning. AI will dominate the discussion and practice of publishing for years or decades to come. Its integration into book publishing holds promise for efficiency gains, enhanced decision-making, and novel creative and communicative possibilities. And yet it also brings commercial challenges, legal ambiguities, ethical worries, and the potential dilution of human creativity. It needs careful reflection and ongoing scrutiny. Buckle up.

Product development

The publisher invests its staff resources and technological infrastructure to produce, market and sell the book on the author's behalf. Their knowledge and judgement of current markets and future trends add value to those authors who are commissioned and selected by the publisher. Authors are helped through the creative development of the proposal to match market and user needs, including filling gaps in the market (also of course imitating the competition) and realizing opportunities, and through the provision of other guidance and advice. Editorial expertise helps writers craft their work, from advice on structure through to line-by-line editing. The value of editorial intervention is evidenced by the purchase of stylistic and other editing tools by some self-published authors.

User experience

Another creative expertise of the publisher is to design and present the author's work to best effect in a saleable printed book: length, size, format, usability, fitness for purpose, quality and accuracy of content, feel and look (design and production values), especially the cover to sell it. A hardback art book, for example will be produced to a very high standard and sold at a high price. An inexpensive paperback or ebook will be produced with lower production values. The publisher organizes and manages the workflow to deliver the book. Digital distribution breaks the link between the contents and the physical packaging, for example facilitating the download of a book chapter or journal article. Users of travel content may want access in print, on mobile devices or through voice-activated virtual assistants. Because readers access digital content through a variety of distribution channels and devices, attention is given by the publisher to the user experience (UX) of the product and service in their personal context.

Supply chain management

The publisher orchestrates the production of the book or journal through the procurement and management of a range of external services from individuals – freelance editors, designers – and companies – typesetters, printers, paper suppliers, technology companies. The outsourcing and procurement of services extend to marketing, sales and distribution worldwide. The publisher has an extensive sales network of representatives, agents, distributors, wholesalers and retailers. From a publisher's perspective, authors are critical suppliers and their 'management' is arguably the most challenging.

Visibility and market reach

The publisher sets the time of publication of the author's work in order to maximize sales. It may be related to a specific marketing and sales opportunity or need, to the publication of the publisher's other books, to competitors' publishing schedules, or be subject to the demands of the retailers. The realization of connecting a readership to a book and consequent sales depends largely on the effectiveness of the publisher to promote the work in a variety of formats, to maximize discoverability through metadata and search engine optimization (SEO), and to sell it and distribute it through the channels to market. Reaching the high street trade is difficult for self-published authors and a key selling-point of mainstream publishers.

  The founder of O'Reilly Media, Tim O'Reilly argues that the publisher must offer more visibility and sales than the author can achieve on their own. Specifically, he says: 'your job as a publisher is to do things for authors that they can't do for themselves: things that require special expertise; that require scale; that are expensive, that require marketplace leverage; things that are boring and time-consuming' (O'Reilly, 2010).

Copyright defence

Through the author contract, the publisher acquires from the author an exclusive licence to exploit the intellectual property rights in the author's work for an agreed term and in the agreed markets and languages. The publisher's responsibility and expertise are to exploit the rights granted to the fullest in print and electronic forms (and when available, to license others to do so), and to protect the author's rights against infringement by others using technical and legal means. The latter is very important in an age of AI, file-sharing and book piracy.

BUSINESS MODEL

Ultimately a publisher has to operate a profitable business model that delivers sufficient return to enable the publication of authors' works, and offers authors remuneration in terms of readership, money and status. Changing patterns of authorship, readership, and distribution mean that there are a multitude of business models and constant experimentation. Content may be sold as discrete products, bundled into a service sold on subscription, or given free to users to encourage sales of higher value products. Authors may earn a royalty, a fee or a share of the profits from a title.

The potential financial worth of the author's work is assessed by the publisher at the outset. The publisher envisages in advance the product package, its price, the potential demand over a time period and the projected sales income, balanced against the estimated costs of production and the payments to the author, resulting in the publisher's forecast profit. The publisher takes the risk decision based on multiple factors as to whether to invest in the author's work or not. When the publisher issues the contract to the author, it confers financial value on the author's work.

Impact of the internet

The internet offers publishers and self-publishing authors opportunities for value creation. It has speeded up communication and encouraged a global market in design, typesetting and print, which has led to lower costs. Whilst authorship has become democratized, bestsellers are selling in larger quantities than ever, creating a top tier of brand authors. There is also a global market of readers to be reached with digital content, and this is an opportunity in particular for English language publishers of many types of book, from educational books to trade fiction. The challenge for many publishers is to become direct-to-consumer businesses, rather than simply reaching their markets through intermediaries. As ebooks became popular, some publishers were able to save on the costs of producing and distributing the physical book and established a direct relationship with their readers. The internet provides a means of marketing books – both promoting them and identifying individual consumers. Value can be created through making brands work directly with book readers, through building communities around content, and from involving readers in the creation of content (e.g. suggesting ideas for new titles). Digital tools such as social networking facilitate the creation of this digital capital (Phillips, 2014, page 93).

Providers of digital content can create extra value by adding the element of service. Electronic services can be created using a wide range of content, offering users on demand up-to-date and searchable content (including pictures,

Brand

Digital capital

Community

Co-creation of value

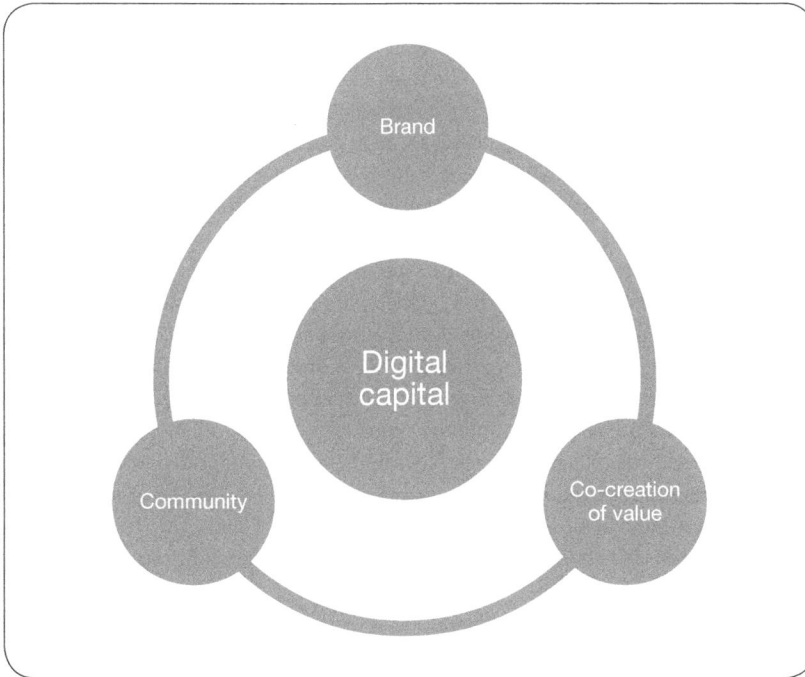

video and animation) from a range of different sources. Such services may be highly profitable once established, but the initial costs can be significant.

The internet also offers a new set of issues. First, there is a vast range of information for free. This has had a major impact on travel or reference publishing, for example. Can consumers see the value of publishers' products when there are free sources of 'good enough' information on the web? How do publishers compete with user-generated content? In a relatively short space of time, Wikipedia (founded in 2001) has come to dominate online searches for information – users can write entries and edit the content. In 2023. the English Wikipedia contained over 4 bn words. By comparison, the 32-volume print set of the *Encyclopaedia Britannica* (2007) had 44 m words. User-generated content also covers social platforms such as YouTube, WhatsApp, Instagram, Facebook and TikTok. Wattpad and Scribd have developed large communities around writing and reading. The business model of Google is to offer search for free content and generate revenues from advertising (Google Ads and YouTube Ads). Search becomes ever more sophisticated with new features powered by AI. At the same time, AI-generated content is turning up in search results and on social media, from text to video. As Erik Hoel writes, 'Increasingly, mounds of synthetic A.I.-generated outputs drift across our feeds and our searches. The stakes go far beyond what's on our screens. The entire culture is becoming affected by A.I.'s runoff, an insidious creep into our most important institutions' (*New York Times*, 29 March 2024).

It becomes difficult to price digital products if there is an expectation that content on the internet should be free. Publishers have developed good business models for online services sold to an institutional market of companies and

In 2024, Wikipedia contained around 6.8 m articles

libraries, and have developed strong brands, but how do you sell to consumers reluctant to pay for content? A further issue is how to price ebooks when consumers expect digital content to be cheaper than print.

If there is a strong demand for a particular author, what is to stop the author taking ownership of the online market for their own writing? A service such as Substack offers authors the opportunity to make money from paid subscriptions. In 2000, the wine writer Jancis Robinson set up her own subscription site, offering articles, podcasts, wine reviews, a member's forum and exclusive access to *The Oxford Companion to Wine* (jancisrobinson.com), before selling out to Recurrent Ventures in 2021. In 2012, J. K. Rowling launched the Pottermore site to sell ebooks of the Harry Potter books and create an online experience with games and other content (pottermore.com). Publishers need to differentiate clearly the service they can offer to brand authors, from editorial work through to running their websites or financing promotional apps.

There are other issues connected to online publication. Transferring print brands to the internet is not straightforward, which has led some publishers to create new brands for the Web. Many publishers do not control the full rights to their books, and this can hinder the transfer of illustrations, for example, into digital products and services.

Dale Dougherty of O'Reilly Media coined the term Web 2.0 – popularized by Tim O'Reilly

In the world of the printed book, authors and publishers devote a great deal of thought and effort to the creation of a physical entity – the bound volume which is sold as a complete package of information. Readers usually have to buy the entire book, even if they only want part of it. In the digital world, the focus has shifted. As John Thompson writes, publishers have increasingly realized that it is the 'content, and the control of the copyrights that governed what they could do with the content, which was in some respects their key assets, not the books themselves' (Thompson, 2012, page 9). Innovation in style and content is encouraged by digital publishing, from the use of multimedia to new ways of structuring texts. The world of digital content and search unravels the content packaged in printed books. Content may be purchased at different levels of granularity, and consumers may wish to purchase by the chapter or even in smaller chunks such as by the page or illustration. Alongside the fear that consumers will cherry-pick the best chapters and sales of the complete work will be cannibalized, there are the potential benefits for publishers – additional purchases may come from those who are not considering buying the whole book. The implications of the digital world for the control of intellectual property are discussed in detail later in the chapter. The advent of AI is seen as an inflection point similar to that created by the internet.

Risk

In the traditional business model for book publishing – where transactions are based on the physical copy – there are issues around risk, the power of retailers to ask for high discounts, and the fact that returns of unsold books can take some months to materialize. There are different risk levels according to the publishing sector and, for example, consumer publishing is riskier than academic publishing. Paying a large advance to a celebrity whose star may not be shining so brightly when the book is published is a risky venture. The investment in a large print run or a highly illustrated work bears the associated risk that the book will simply not sell. In order to secure the book's availability in the shops, cash will need to be spent on promotion and high discounts will have to be given to retailers. Money is paid out and only recouped some weeks after publication – retailers will demand a period of grace (the credit period) before they have to pay for the stock. By contrast, traditional journal publishing (as distinct from OA) has been a more secure and profitable model. Subscribers pay licence fees to receive a bundle of journals, and demand for a premium collection does not drop significantly if prices are raised.

Booksellers have sought a higher share of the value created for trade books, asking for higher discounts off the recommended price. But at the same time price competition has lowered the prices paid for books by consumers. Just as publishers try to capture more value by selling direct, retailers have been investing in their own publishing operations – an example of vertical integration. The US bookstore Barnes & Noble has done this for a number of years, joined by Amazon from 2009 with a series of imprints.

The sale of ebooks lowers the risk from holding printed stock, and on the face of it margins should be higher without the physical cost of production. This is largely true but publishers struggled to keep prices as high as they would like when the dominant player in the market, Amazon, was driving the market with competitive pricing. Authors also expect a higher royalty rate, and consumers expect that digital products should be cheaper. Audiobooks may be bought by consumers by title or as part of a subscription service.

New business models abound and subscription services are in place for ebooks and audiobooks - and also physical books. In the case of Audible, whilst consumers feel they are part of a subscription service, publishers are still selling individual titles that are downloaded. Streaming services offer new opportunities but also the risk of reduced revenues (to both publishers and authors) from any model based on usage. There has been a growth in the popularity of print subscription boxes, such as from Illumicrate or FairyLoot, often offering special editions or books in particular genres such as SF or fantasy: 'The boxes have plugged into a new way of consuming books – you don't just read a book, you pose with it and post it online' (*Sunday Times*, 17 March 2024). The crowdfunding of projects has grown in popularity through sites such as Kickstarter. In the UK the publisher Unbound was set up in 2011 to support the crowdfunding of new books. Authors appeal directly to their readers to secure the necessary financial support to go ahead and write and produce their books; the selection of books is first curated by Unbound's editorial team.

It is estimated that there are over 130 m titles in print around the world

Financial performance

From a financial viewpoint, a publisher strives to increase the rate of return on the company's capital, and to improve the profit margin to finance expansion and pay a dividend to the owners. The management aims to do the following:

- Invest in quality content and IP.
- Maximize the income and minimize the production costs.

- Contain royalty rates while keeping competitive. In consumer book publishing it is important to monitor the amount of money and level of risk tied up in authors' advances.
- Control stock levels by selling a high proportion of the print stock on publication or soon after, and storing only adequate stock of backlist titles. Digital printing has changed the dynamic and some academic publishers no longer aim to hold stock in a warehouse, simply printing to order.
- Monitor pricing on a regular basis and for key titles almost on a real-time basis for ebooks.
- Re-price backlist titles regularly in line with current prices and exchange rates.
- Exercise tight control over the firm's overheads (e.g. staff and office costs) while maintaining effective management. If profits fall, overheads may have to be reduced.
- Take all available credit from suppliers, whether paying printers after a certain period or deferring royalty payments to authors through annual or six monthly cycles.
- Keep discounts as low as possible and minimize returns while maintaining stock levels in retail outlets.
- Collect debts quickly from customers.
- Obtain the best terms from capital providers such as banks.
- Invest in innovation including the establishment of communities around content, new digital products and services, and experimentation around business models.
- Invest in fixed assets (such as IT systems) only if a favourable return can be shown in comparison with subcontracting or leasing. In the longer term the company will look to minimize any investment in the warehousing of physical products.
- Sell off underused or underperforming assets, whether buildings or publishing lists.
- Buy complementary (or competing) businesses at home and abroad.
- Forecast regularly the cashflow (the flow of money payments to, from, or within the firm) over time; even a profitable publisher can exceed its borrowing requirement before profits are earned and run the risk of going bust.

One planning tool is the compilation of a financial plan showing a profit target for the medium term (say, three years). It is built up partly from the historic costs of running the business and from forecasts – the estimated costs of producing the new titles and the revenue from estimated sales of new and backlist titles made through various channels at home and abroad. Departmental managers will prepare budgets for carrying out their activities. Actual performance can be compared with the plan at monthly intervals, and with the performance of the previous year; and the plan itself is updated. Some publishers compile rolling plans for up to five years ahead. The annual profit and loss statement of a publisher reveals the financial performance of the business as a whole. This will differ according to the publisher and the publishing sector. The following figures give an impression.

Table 4.1 Average overheads of publishers

Overhead costs	% of sales
Editorial	5–7
Production and design	2–4
Marketing and sales staff	5–10
Advertising and promotion	3–6
Order processing and distribution	8–12
General and administrative expenses	7–12

Table 4.2 Bloomsbury Publishing accounts to 28 February 2023

	£000	%
Revenue	264,102	
Cost of sales	119,191	45.1
Gross profit	144,911	54.9
Marketing and distribution costs	32,529	12.3
Administrative expenses and other costs	81,096	30.7
Operating profit	31,286	11.8

The total sales revenue is the sum of money the publisher receives from home and export sales after discounts have been deducted from the recommended prices (and returns of unsold books have been taken into account). Taking the net receipts as 100 per cent and subtracting from that the production costs of the books (around 20 per cent, plus or minus 5 per cent) plus the write-off of stock unsold (2–10 per cent) and the cost of royalties (10–15 per cent), leaves the publisher with a gross margin of 50–60 per cent. High sales of ebooks for a title will reduce the physical cost of production; at the same time the market rate for royalties on ebooks is 25 per cent to the author. There continue to be editorial and design costs whatever the format. A consumer book publisher may suffer from the write-off of unrecoverable authors' advances, but it may benefit from greater rights sales income. From the gross margin, the publisher's overhead costs are deducted, and will roughly total 30–50 per cent (see Table 4.1). When deducted from the gross margin, this leaves the publisher with a net or operating profit (before interest charges on borrowing and tax are deducted) in a target range of 9–12 per cent (compare the figure in the accounts shown for Bloomsbury in Table 4.2). After interest and tax, a dividend may be paid to shareholders and the remaining profit re-invested in the business.

Valuing a company

The worth of a publisher can be measured in terms of its physical assets – buildings and stock – but more importantly by the intellectual property it controls. Richard Charkin, former Executive Director at Bloomsbury, comments, 'What really matters, in my opinion, is the building up of publishing assets–the author contracts in filing cabinets (or preferably on a secure hard disc), the licenses, the distribution arrangements, the brand value of imprints' (*Publishing Perspectives*, 31 October 2018). Valuations of publishing companies – how much they are bought and sold for – tend to be based on the revenues of the companies and the sector in which they operate. This is partly because the balance sheets of companies, which show their assets, can be difficult to interpret. Debts owing to the company may include advance payments to authors which will never be earned out, and the value of stock may be inflated by books in the warehouse that will never be sold. Hidden liabilities could include an overseas distributor having the right to return tens of thousands of books for credit. Companies with interests in, say, legal or STM publishing are likely to be bought for a higher multiple of sales than companies publishing for consumer markets. This reflects the varying degree of control over intellectual property – higher in legal and STM publishing with, for example, the easier acquisition of world and subsidiary rights – and the lower levels of risk. There tend also to be higher levels of profitability. Increasingly there is value to be measured in the service offered and its number of users.

Tech companies developing AI are keen to harvest data to train their products. The evidence is that the larger the dataset, the higher the performance of LLMs. It was revealed in 2024 by the *New York Times* that Meta, which owns Facebook and Instagram, had discussed purchasing Simon & Schuster in order to gain access to long works for developing its AI models (6 April 2024).

Publishers create value through innovation, coming up with new ideas and variations on existing titles. Larger publishers strive to maintain innovation with the maintenance of small imprints with their own distinctive profile. Smaller publishers may be more likely to try out new authors and formats. Innovation is encouraged by the system of copyright, which creates value in intellectual property and provides a mechanism to protect that value. Reflected in a company's value are the intangible assets, such as their publishing licences and goodwill. Goodwill is the term for those elements that contribute to the company's competitive advantage, including its brand, publishing relationships and employees. It is given a monetary value if the company is taken over when there is an opportunity to value the worth of the company over and above the net assets shown on the balance sheet. The goodwill then appears on the balance sheet of the acquiring company. The publisher's licences and brand will be protected by intellectual property rights.

> In 2024 HarperCollins agreed a deal to license non-fiction titles for training an LLM

Selling and valuing publishing assets

Natalina Bertoli, Partner, Bertoli Mitchell LLP

Why are publishing assets sold? Possible triggers for sale include: the business is at a growth inflexion point and requires access to resources and/or capability outside of the existing organization; or, in the case of large publishing organizations, when a strategic review has determined that parts of its publishing portfolio no longer fit with the areas in which it wishes to plant its flag in the long term; or the proprietors may simply want to exit and capitalize their assets.

E★PERT

How are publishing businesses sold? Most successful publishing sales are achieved through a discreet competitive process. An Information Memorandum (IM) is usually the bedrock of an effective competitive sale process, and must map the performance and profile of the assets being sold in detail, especially revenue and margin data by product, likewise the status of the forward plans. The IM is distributed to interested parties who have signed non-disclosure agreements and who are set an Offers Date by which to submit offers in writing. All prospective buyers should be marched to the same deadlines.

When, after negotiations, a preferred bidder emerges, that party may be granted an exclusivity period in which to complete its investigations and finalize contracts. From start to finish the sale process will typically take six months or more. The process will often be run on behalf of the seller by a specialist advisory firm like Bertoli Mitchell LLP. Of course, not all publishing businesses are saleable and at any given point many will be worth more to hold than to sell.

How are publishing assets valued? The principal drivers of value – over and above fit with the buyer's strategic plans and priorities – include business momentum and scalability. Buyers will pay a premium price for assets which fit exactly with their own strategic priorities, be they subject priorities, capability priorities, or geographical priorities (e.g. increased market penetration in North America). Cultural and/or mission fit between the parties, and synergy benefits from a combination also play their part. Premium prices are paid for publishing companies/assets which are scalable in the new owner's hands and which confer a market position that the buyer would not otherwise achieve so quickly or effectively.

At the operating level, drivers of value include quality and reliability of income streams (with recurring revenue business models attracting the highest value, especially where they are high growth), typical profitability and market growth potential (with businesses with a genuine multinational total addressable market typically also commanding a premium). Valuations at the level of individual companies will vary according, *inter alia*, to market position, scarcity, scale (larger businesses command higher multiples), growth profile and outlook, perceived macro and micro risk levels, revenue mix, forward pipeline and quality of intellectual property rights.

The drivers referred to above are reflected in the different 'Sales Multiples' paid for assets in different publishing sectors – the Sales Multiple being what buyers have typically paid to buy a pound (£) of sales in companies they have purchased (e.g. £1.5 m paid for a company with £1 m sales represents a Sales Multiple of 1.5). Typical ranges by sectors are: Consumer Publishing 0.5 to 1.5 x sales; Educational and Academic Book Publishing 1 to 2.5 x sales; high level Academic and Professional Journals Publishing 3 to 5 x sales.

INTELLECTUAL PROPERTY AND PROTECTING VALUE

Although copyrights need not be registered in the UK, trademarks need to be protected by registration

The intellectual property (IP) owned or controlled by a publisher includes its copyrights and licences. The publisher may own some copyrights outright, for example in the case of reference works, or have acquired licences from their authors. Other IP may be brands which could be registered as trademarks. Trademarks can cover words, logos, or pictures used as identifiers for goods and services, and must be renewed every 10 years in order for them to stay in force. Examples of trademarks are Penguin and the Penguin logo, Beatrix Potter characters such as Peter Rabbit, and Amazon's Kindle.

Copyright

It is important to examine on what basis publishers control their intellectual property. Book publishing today rests on copyright. In general terms, this is a form of protection, giving authors and other creative artists legal ownership of their work – that is, it establishes their work as their personal, exclusive property; and because it is their property they have the absolute right to sell or license it to others. It is these exclusive rights that make an author's works attractive to publishers. What the publisher wants from authors is the sole, exclusive right to publish their work and sell it as widely as possible. Without copyright protection, authors would not be able to grant this exclusive right and could not demand payment for their efforts; and publishers would not risk issuing a book which, if successful, could be instantly copied or plundered by competitors. Copyright stimulates innovation in a market economy, protects the author's reputation and is the common foundation for publishing and the other cultural industries.

For copyright to subsist in a literary work (one which is written, spoken or sung), it must be 'original', i.e. some effort, skill or judgement needs to have been exercised to attract copyright protection, and it must be recorded in writing or otherwise. Copyright exists in the concrete form of expression, the arrangement of the words, and protection in the UK endures for the author's life plus 70 years from the end of the year of the author's death. After that period the work enters the public domain. If, for example, an author died on 11 January 1928, their work came out of copyright on 31 December 1998. This is the case with the novelist Thomas Hardy. The previous period of protection was 50 years and under that system the works of Hardy had already come into the public domain at the end of 1978. When, in 1995, following an EU directive, the period in the UK was increased to 70 years, Hardy came briefly back into copyright until the end of 1998 and publishers of new editions of his work had to pay royalties to his estate. Publishers compete fiercely on the pricing of public domain classics, such as Jane Austen, on which no author royalties need be paid, and face competition from ebooks that are free to download. The term of copyright in the European Union and the USA is also 70 years. In France there is a special 30-year extension to this term for authors considered to have died for their country – 'mort pour la France': such writers include Irene Nemirovsky (1903–42) and Antoine de Saint-Exupéry (1900–44).

There is no copyright in ideas, or in the title of a work

Works created by employees in working hours – and covered, as a further safeguard, by their terms and conditions of service – are the copyright of the employer. Publishers who commission freelance editors, technical illustrators, indexers and developers ensure that copyright is assigned in writing to the publisher through an agreement. The publisher's typographical layout of the page is the copyright of the publisher and that lasts for 25 years from publication. Copyright in an index belongs to the compiler, unless assigned to the publisher; copyright in a translation belongs to the translator. Copyright exists in compilations, such as databases, provided that there is an adequate degree of originality in the selection and arrangement of the information.

Moral rights

Under the 1988 Copyright, Designs and Patents Act, authors were given additional statutory rights, called moral rights. Deriving from the practice in mainland Europe, and in particular the *droit moral* in France, they are as follows:

The moral right of paternity must be asserted by the author

Paternity

First, there is the moral right of paternity, which gives the author the right to be credited as the author of the work. This must be asserted by the author before it can be enforced. Often this can be seen on the title verso of a book – the reverse of the title page: 'The right of Angus Phillips and Giles Clark to be identified as authors of this work has been asserted in accordance with sections 77 and 78 of the Copyright, Designs and Patents Act 1988.'

Integrity

Second is the right of integrity, which is the author's right to be protected from editorial distortion of the work. An author who argues that such distortion has occurred may be asked to give proof of financial loss, and as Mira T. Sundara Rajan says,

> The case of an author whose artistic integrity is damaged, but whose work actually sells better because of intervention – for example, the addition of erotic scenes to bring excitement to a film adaptation of a novel – might have little hope of success. (2011, page 35)

False attribution

Third is the right to prevent false attribution, which prevents an author from being credited with something that they did not write.

Privacy

A final right gives privacy to individuals in the case of photographs they have commissioned, perhaps for a wedding, from a photographer who owns the copyright.

Moral rights are likely to grow in importance in an era of digital publication, which frequently involves substantial adaptation of the work of authors and illustrators. Manipulation of authors' works is relatively straightforward, increasing the risk of non-attribution and of plagiarism. Moral rights can be waived by an author, and if a publisher owns the copyright in a book, it will probably want to ensure that such a waiver is contained in the contract. The moral rights of paternity and integrity have the same duration as copyright; the right to prevent false attribution lasts for life plus 20 years.

Copyright or licence?

Should a publisher be content to negotiate a licence with an author, or should it ask the author to assign them the copyright? Theoretically the latter will give it more control over the work. Some journal publishers, for example, still take the copyright in all the articles that they publish. But most book publishers regard a licence as giving them the necessary protection that they require. The licence is a grant by the author of the rights to publish and sell a work, and also the right to stop others from copying the work. If a licence is in place which grants the publisher all the necessary rights, there is usually no need to take the copyright from the author. Hugh Jones and Christopher Benson write:

> a sole and exclusive publishing licence for agreed territories, drafted in wide terms if necessary (including a very robust clause allowing the publisher to take legal action if necessary), will probably meet most publishers' needs. It has been likened by a number of commentators to taking a lease of a house rather than buying the freehold – a long lease for all practical purposes will probably be just as valuable. (Jones and Benson, 2016, page 108)

The civil law protects copyright holders in the UK, and cases can be brought by them or the exclusive licence holder against individuals or institutions who copy texts without the necessary permission. Under a set of international treaties and conventions, UK copyright works are also protected around the world. These include the Berne Convention, which dates from 1886, and the WIPO Copyright Treaty signed in 1996. Under the Universal Copyright Convention (1952), all copies of a book should carry a copyright notice, and again on the title verso you will find the standard wording – © 2025 Angus Phillips & Giles Clark. The date given is the year of publication, and a new edition attracts a new date in the copyright line. Copyright can be held jointly, as is the case with the present book.

The copyright symbol © is required under the Universal Copyright Convention

Permissions

An author seeking to quote from a work by another author should normally seek permission from the publisher of the work, which holds the anthology and quotation rights on behalf of the author. However, the Society of Authors offers the following guidelines for quoting without needing copyright permission – all of the below must apply:

- the use is fair dealing;
- the work you are quoting from has been previously published;

- you quote 'no more than is required by the specific purpose for which it is used';
- the use is genuinely for the purpose of quotation, for example, in the context of criticism or review. Using a quotation as the header to a chapter, or in a collection of quotations, is not 'fair dealing';
- you include proper acknowledgement (generally the title and author).

How much can be quoted is open to interpretation, and the Society advises: 'A short extract may be a vital part of a work. A few sentences taken from a long novel or biography are unlikely to constitute a "substantial part", but a few lines of poetry may be' (societyofauthors.org, accessed 16 August 2023).

In the USA, the doctrine of fair use applies, and

> [under] the fair use doctrine of the U.S. copyright statute, it is permissible to use limited portions of a work including quotes, for purposes such as commentary, criticism, news reporting, and scholarly reports. There are no legal rules permitting the use of a specific number of words, a certain number of musical notes, or percentage of a work. Whether a particular use qualifies as fair use depends on all the circumstances. (copyright.gov, accessed 12 April 2024)

In order to use an illustration contained in another book, permission should be sought from the publisher or original source of the illustration (this could be a library or gallery). Obtaining permission to use material from websites is fraught with difficulty, since there may not be a satisfactory paper trail to prove who owns the original copyright.

Digital rights management

Digitization has reduced the costs of copying and distribution to next to nothing. Yet the production of ideas and information by authors and publishers is expensive in time and money. Publishers earn their living from selling ideas and information and make efforts to protect it from illicit copying. They are fearful that their work will escape into the wild on the internet from which they receive no payment. The technical means of controlling usage is broadly referred to as digital rights management (DRM), and it 'might be defined as a set of standards and technologies that allow digital content to be distributed while also being protected, managed and tracked by content providers' (Owen, 2024, page 415).

The software for DRM is problematic. DRM systems are frequently broken into by hackers – not least because of the weakness that each time a proprietary system gives someone a locked item, a secret hidden key is provided to unlock it. Hackers around the world work on discovering such secrets – they may then publish them on the internet for others to access the content. DRM can also be sidestepped by a user scanning a printed book and posting it for free on the internet. The most common forms of DRM for ebooks are those from Amazon, Apple and Adobe.

When a reader buys a printed book, under the 'first sale doctrine' there are few restrictions on its further uses;

> If you read a book, that act is not regulated by copyright law. If you resell a book, that act is not regulated . . . If you sleep on the book or use it to hold up a lamp or let your puppy chew it up, those acts are not regulated by copyright law, because those acts do not make a copy. (Lessig, 2004, page 141)

There can, however, be restrictions on the use of an ebook – the reader usually buys the book under a licence. By accessing the book over the internet, a copy is made and copyright law comes into the picture. There may be controls on the number of times the book can be read, whether it can be printed out, or on its transfer to other devices. Since the use by consumers of digital materials is defined by a licence, it may be sufficient in some cases for publishers to take the risk that they are sufficiently honest and trustworthy not to abuse their rights. Social DRM simply ensures that ebooks when sold are watermarked rather than subject to strict control. The watermarking allows users to be traced if they post up the books on pirate websites, and also for irresponsible fans to be named and shamed by fellow users. Academic publishers license materials to universities, under site licences via their libraries. The user group is clearly defined – staff and students using their institution's IP address, or users authenticated off-campus through the use of a password system. Authentication reassures publishers that any points of leakage outside the user group may be identified and halted, and helps universities to limit their liability in the case of defamation, obscenity or copyright infringement.

An institutional repository is a digital collection of research papers by members of an institution

Creative Commons

Founded in 2001, Creative Commons is an initiative to enable authors to offer their work on different terms to the usual publisher's licence. 'Every license helps creators – we call them licensors if they use our tools – retain copyright while allowing others to copy, distribute, and make some uses of their work – at least non-commercially' (creativecommons.org, accessed 16 August 2023). For example, a photographer may choose to publish their work with a Creative Commons (CC) licence that enables others to copy, distribute or display the photographs, provided that the work is attributed to them. The objective is for more people to have the opportunity to view and use their work freely.

The advent of open access publishing (based on the argument that publicly funded research should be free to use by everyone) started in scientific journals and greatly expanded the use of the Creative Commons licence. The funders of the author's research pay for its publication and typically stipulate the use of a CC licence. Bearing in mind that there are marked differences between AHSS (where the value lies in the author's argument) and scientific papers (where the value often lies in the experimental findings, which can be protected by patent), there are big issues on which type of CC licence to apply and that affects authors' rights (freedom to publish, reputation and earnings). There are different types of CC licence and their application is in a state of flux and some controversy.

- *CC-BY* allows users maximum freedom in re-using content: essentially all copying, redistribution and reuse is permitted provided the author (copyright holder) is acknowledged (that is 'attributed'). The user (licensee) can make derivative works, and potentially reuse for commercial purposes though such profiteering would be widely criticized. This is the most open licence and is usually applied to open access journal articles.

- *CC-BY-NC* is the same as CC-BY except the reuse for commercial purposes is not allowed (without first obtaining permission, as with standard copyright). This type is also applied to journal articles. It is used by publishers of open access monographs and of OER (Open Educational Resources) textbooks which need the additional revenue from the sale of printed copies; and by universities not wanting other institutions to profit from their OER.
- *CC-BY-NC-ND* additionally excludes the creation of derivative works. AHSS authors of open access monographs may wish for the non-derivative (ND) restriction in order to maintain the integrity of their work, especially when translated.

Future of copyright

Without the copyright regime, publishers would be unable to prevent works being copied at will. Books would be photocopied, printed and sold, or passed around in digital form for free, without a return for the copyright holder and their licensee. Publishers are naturally anxious about any threats to the stability of the copyright regime. They can see what has happened in the music industry, for example, and the tendency for music to be downloaded and shared for free. As technology becomes ever more important, the protection of copyright is diminishing in significance with content made available under contractual terms – whether journal articles to institutional subscribers or self-published books sold through Amazon.

'It's going to change entire industries; people have compared it to electricity, or the printing press.' Mira Murati on AI

Digital publishing and the advent of AI have added considerable uncertainty as to who controls intellectual property and its financial returns. It is in the interest of a large technology player such as Google that as much content as possible is freely available – their business model is built primarily on the sale of ads. For publishers the key is very often to build a direct relationship with their end users, so that they are not solely reliant on intermediaries such as Amazon for their sales income. Fearful of piracy, they are reluctant to relinquish DRM controls but at the same time they do need to ensure that content is readily available through legitimate channels, and that ownership is clearly identifiable to potential licensees.

Major digitization projects are carried out by commercial publishers, libraries, or technology companies such as Google. The latter has digitized out-of-copyright works in the collections of major institutions including the New York Public Library and the Bodleian Library in Oxford. Google Books has also digitized books in print from a variety of publishers, enabling searches within the titles. Links then offer ways of purchasing either the printed book or online access.

The issue of an orphan work (a copyrighted work for which the owner cannot be traced and therefore contacted) came to prominence during Google's scanning of library books in the mid-1990s. An orphan work may have gone out of print but still be in copyright. The problem of being unable to trace copyright holders hinders creativity, for example, when an author wants to seek permission from a third party to use their text or illustrations in a new work but who faces an arduous detective trail in trying to find the owner. Google proposed to establish a 'rights registry' to expedite and automate the permission process. More recently, governments in North America and Europe are focusing on the issue which becomes progressively more important for all of the creative industries in a digital world. There is a volume of text or images available on the web for which the ownership and rights are uncertain or unknown, and this creates an explosive growth in new digital orphans.

There are also authors who would like to see their work – text or pictures – more widely disseminated and feel that the present system of copyright does not adequately meet their needs. Self-publishing is relatively straightforward and the author may be looking to garner a wide readership rather than attempt to make their fortune and some may use Creative Commons licences.

The adoption of AI for content creation poses issues for copyright and there are notable differences in the IP regimes between countries. Whilst in the UK it seems possible for computer-generated projects to assume copyright, since the author is taken to be the person who arranged the creation of the work, in the USA at present copyright law does not protect an original work if it was not created by a human being. Developing a consensus across territories appears to be a pressing issue.

A controversial area is the use of copyrighted material by the tech companies to train their large language models (LLMs), and authors and publishers are pressing for some kind of collective licensing system. The doctrine of fair use is well established in the USA, whereby the copying of copyrighted works is allowed for certain purposes such as comment, scholarship and research.

Now read this

Roberto Calasso, *The Art of the Publisher*, Penguin, 2015.

Sources

Michael Bhaskar, *The Content Machine: Towards a theory of publishing from the printing press to the digital network*, Anthem Press, 2013.

Bill Cope and Angus Phillips (eds), *The Future of the Book in the Digital Age*, Chandos, 2006.

Eric de Bellaigue, *British Book Publishing as a Business since the 1960s*, British Library Publishing, 2004.

Hugh Jones and Christopher Benson, *Publishing Law*, 5th edition, Routledge, 2016.

Lawrence Lessig, *Free Culture*, Penguin, 2004.

Thad McIlroy, *The AI Revolution in Book Publishing: A concise guide to navigating artificial intelligence for writers and publishers*, The Future of Publishing, 2024.

Tim O'Reilly, 'What is Web 2.0?', 30 September 2005, https://www.oreilly.com, accessed 29 January 2024.

Tim O'Reilly, 'The Future of Digital Distribution and Ebook Marketing', Tools of Change (TOC), 2010.

Lynette Owen, *Selling Rights*, 9th edition, Routledge, 2024.
Angus Phillips, *Turning the Page: The evolution of the book*, Routledge, 2014.
Angus Phillips, 'Does the Book Have a Future?', in Simon Eliot and Jonathan Rose (eds), *A Companion to the History of the Book*, 2nd edition, Blackwell, 2020.
Angus Phillips and Michael Bhaskar, *The Oxford Handbook of Publishing*, Oxford University Press, 2019.
Michael E. Porter, *Competitive Advantage: Creating and sustaining superior performance*, Free Press, 1985.
Michael E. Porter, 'Strategy and the Internet', *Harvard Business Review*, March 2001, pages 63–78.
Simon Stokes, *Digital Copyright: Law and practice*, 5th edition, Hart Publishing, 2019.
Mira T. Sundara Rajan, *Moral Rights*, Oxford University Press, 2011.
John B. Thompson, *Merchants of Culture*, Polity Press, 2012.
John B. Thompson, *Book Wars: The digital revolution in publishing*, Polity Press, 2021.

Web resources

https://www.copyrightdoneright.org Information about copyright in the UK.
https://www.copyright.gov/fair-use/index.html The goal of the US Copyright Fair Use Index is to make the principles and application of fair use more accessible and understandable to the public.
https://creativecommons.org Creative Commons.
https://www.jisc.ac.uk Joint Information Systems Committee (UK).
https://www.wipo.int/portal/en/ World Intellectual Property Organization.

CHAPTER 5

The author

Authors have different motivations for writing, according to the type of book and the individual. Writers of poetry and fiction may be driven to write by an inner force – they just have to write. Academics have to be published in order to advance their career. Professional authors may earn their living from their books, and writing is what they do. The now various routes for self-publishing add a different dimension to authorship, and anyone can post an ebook on Amazon in the hopes of gaining a wide audience, and perhaps attract the interest of a publisher.

The reality for many authors is that the financial returns are low. A survey published in the UK in 2022 by the Authors' Licensing and Collecting Society revealed that the median (or typical) earnings for professional authors were only £7,000 per annum. For those who are successful, the rewards can be very high (in 2022 the top 10 per cent of authors earned 47 per cent of the total income received by authors), yet many writers struggle financially, have another job, or rely on their partners' income. The research also revealed that the pay for black and multi-heritage authors is around half that of their white counterparts. With the mostly low fees paid for writing newspaper and magazine articles, or book reviews, another possible route for sustaining the incomes of authors is now much tougher.

> Once upon a time you could make a living as a literary hack, the sort of person who wrote book reviews, averagely received novels and was given to wandering around the house in a stained dressing gown in the middle of the afternoon. Many of the traditional ways of grubbing around for extra cash as a writer are drying up. (*The Times*, 29 June 2018)

There are authors such as Dan Brown who are highly organized in their approach. In his witness statement for the 2006 case in the High Court regarding *The Da Vinci Code*, he said:

> Writing is a discipline, much like playing a musical instrument; it requires constant practice and honing of skills. For this reason, I write seven days a week. So, my routine begins at around 4 am every morning, when there are no distractions. By making writing my first order of business every day, I am giving it enormous symbolic importance in my life, which helps keep me motivated. If I'm not at my desk by sunrise, I feel like I'm missing my most

DOI: 10.4324/9781003403289-6

productive hours. In addition to starting early, I keep an antique hour glass on my desk and every hour break briefly to do push-ups, sit-ups, and some quick stretches. I find this helps keep the blood (and ideas) flowing. (*The Bookseller*, 31 March 2006)

The Da Vinci Code sold around 40 m copies in its first year, and has made Dan Brown a fortune. For many authors, the income earned is of secondary importance, and the pleasure of seeing their work published is a reward in itself. There is no shortage of authors who would like to be published, and in fact there is an oversupply. How then do authors set about getting published? The traditional method, in the last century, was to send your manuscript to a number of publishers, and hope that it caught the eye of the relevant editor.

After all, J. K. Rowling was rejected by a number of publishers before being picked up by Bloomsbury. What is known as the slush pile is a system seldom operated by publishers any longer, and trade publishers in the UK and the USA rely on agents to supply them with proposals. Authors look to be signed up by an agent first and many publishers will not accept unsolicited material – occasionally companies advertise an open submission programme. Agents in turn can receive hundreds of submissions each month and the chances of being taken on are slim, but first-time authors are still discovered through this route. In recent years agents have relied more on personal contacts and recommendations, and many are also closed to receiving unsolicited typescripts. The slush pile has been moved online, with authors posting their work on community sites for writers such as Wattpad. There they can engage directly with readers and gain feedback. The 17-year-old UK novelist Beth Reekles posted her novel *The Kissing Booth* on Wattpad, chapter by chapter, and started to gauge her popularity when she posted a cliffhanger, which led to hundreds of emails from readers. The book was taken on by Random House and published (first as an ebook) in 2012. The movie became a hit as a Netflix original in 2018; and the sequel appeared in 2020.

In fiction, agents will ask for a covering letter, a synopsis, and typically three chapters (or 10,000 words) in draft. If they like what they see, they will call in the remainder of the manuscript. In areas such as non-fiction and textbook publishing, publishers will want to see a proposal from the author as the first stage. This is an outline of the proposed book, which sets out the content and gives the publisher a sense of the book's commercial potential. The advantage of this system is that the author need not take the risk of writing the whole book until they have a contract in place.

Once completed by the author, the proposal is sent to the relevant in-house editor; their agent may invest time in rewriting the proposal to raise its chances of success. If there is interest from the publisher, suggestions for changes may be made before the proposal is circulated to key decision-makers in sales and marketing. The final decision on a proposal is taken at an editorial meeting attended by the relevant staff.

When celebrities or sports stars come to write their memoirs, they may require the services of ghost writers to turn their words or thoughts into a polished book. Sometimes the writer will remain anonymous, but since such a working relationship has become quite usual their name may even appear on the title page.

'In seventh grade we read the first chapter of Ralph Ellison's *Invisible Man* and I thought: here's a Black weirdo who writes; maybe there's room for a Black weirdo like me.' Colson Whitehead

FOCUS

The main elements of a book proposal

Title

This must be eye-catching and can be crucial to the book's success.

Introduction

A summary of the idea for the book, what makes it new and special, its likely market, proposed word count and illustrative content, and delivery date.

Contents

An outline of the structure of the book, fleshed out to show what each chapter will cover.

Readership and market

Who will buy the book and what is the market? The danger here is to be too general, and avoid the difficult task of saying who is likely to need, or be interested, in the title. (An equivalent danger is trying to reach too many markets with one book.) For a book on canoes, will it help someone paddle one, or build one? What is the readership for a business textbook – first-year undergraduate or graduate students?

Competition

Successful authors know the market for which they are writing – not just the readership but also competing titles. How will the book relate to, differ and improve upon the titles presently available? Existing titles on the same subject may not be a disadvantage, since they can help prove there is a market. Indirect competition could include content on the web, not just published titles.

Marketing ideas

How can the book be marketed? Ideas can include forthcoming events or anniversaries, hooks to arouse media interest, public appearances and connections with influential people, and promotional channels such as social media, podcasts, websites, and magazines.

Author qualifications

Required are biographical details of the author with relevant information such as previous publications. For non-fiction books it is important for the author to prove their credentials as an expert in the subject area of the book. Publishers may be interested in whether the author is promotable to the media, for example, in the case of a first-time novelist. An author can also display a talent for self-promotion, and they are often expected to have their own website and strong presence on social media. The novelist Anne Tyler, traditionally reluctant to give interviews, concluded that she needed to play her part in promoting her books:

> I used to think it was my publisher's job to get people interested in my books and persuade them to buy copies, but books are suffering. We need to do all we can to encourage people to see books and reading as part of their lives. If we don't, then some day kids will stop reading and that will be the end. (*Guardian*, 14 July 2018)

Additional material may also be attached, such as sample sections or chapters. There should be no spelling or grammatical mistakes in the sample material.

When considering celebrity authors for a book deal, a social media following is a requirement, as spelt out by Mark Cowne of the talent and speaker agency, Kruger Cowne:

> When we come to do book deals, the first thing the publisher says is, 'What is their following on social media?' It creates a yardstick over whether they're more popular than anyone else. Doesn't mean their followers will buy anything. It's part of the metrics. (*Financial Times*, 8 July 2023).

Most academic theses that are sent direct to editors are unpublishable as they stand, but a fraction can be turned into monographs. Theses are also published open access online typically through institutional repositories, reducing the market for any book publication. It is very unlikely that an unsolicited textbook manuscript would have the right structure to be commercial, but occasionally unsolicited ideas can be developed.

Iceland has more published writers per head of population than any other country in the world – one in ten people

STARTING OUT AND SELF-PUBLISHING

It is tough for authors to get their work published. It can take years for an author to be taken on by an agent, land a contract with a publisher and see their work published a year or so later. Agents and publishers are inundated by unsolicited submissions from aspiring authors. Many do not target their approach and fail to undertake their research on agents and publishers by using a reference title such as the *Writers' and Artists' Yearbook*. Those considering self-publishing may turn to the long-established US magazine *Writer's Digest*, and join the Alliance of Independent Authors. It is common for authors to begin their published career with smaller publishing houses, which may be less conservative in their approach to commissioning titles (and they will not necessarily work exclusively through agents). The difficulty for smaller houses is that they may not have the funds to keep authors who have become successful.

The author's perspective

Sarah Franklin, author of *Shelter*

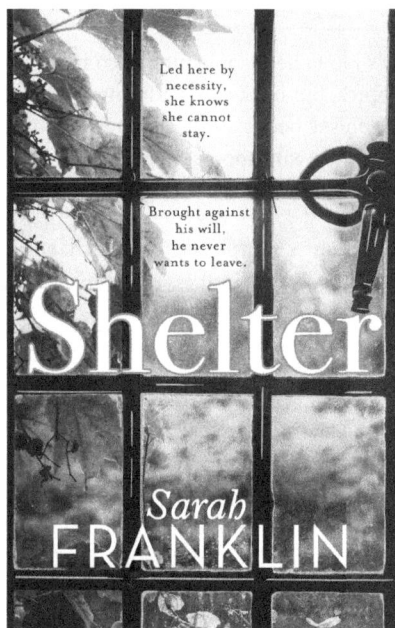

E★PERT

I'd always wanted to write a novel, but I lost my nerve somewhere in my twenties when 'real' writers seemed somehow too intimidating. But eventually, the fear of never having tried to be published overtook the fear of trying and failing.

After several years and multiple revisions, fitting in word counts around my day job and our then quite-small children (endless glamour), I had a draft of something I thought might, possibly, be OK. I checked submissions criteria, sweated over a synopsis, then submitted the manuscript to four agents, all of whom replied. Very kindly, several of them asked to see the book again when it was finished.

So after a short, sharp burst of self-pity – I'd thought it *was* ready! - I knuckled back down.

Eighteen months and a substantial fifty-thousand-word-edit later, I submitted the novel again and was offered a contract of representation from my first choice of agent. After another robust round of edits, the book was sent out on submission to editors ahead of the London Book Fair. Shortly afterwards, the rejection emails started to come in. In many ways, this was the scariest part. Waiting to see whether a life's ambition could be fulfilled, and no control whatsoever.

Ultimately, two publishers wanted to buy my novel, which led to an auction. My agent and I met with teams from both publishers and heard their plans. We also asked each team to send us editorial and marketing/PR plans for the book. In the end, we signed a two-book deal with the publisher whose editor, it seemed to me, would both work with me to create the best book we possibly could, and whose energy and commitment would translate into championing the book fiercely with the in-house promotional and sales teams. Publication was set for fourteen months later, which flew by due to the multiple rounds of editing that the manuscript went through.

The run-up to the book being published was interesting. Once editing is finished, the manuscript became very much the publisher's product.

They apply all their commercial and creative expertise to ensuring that the book's coming out through the appropriate sales channels, and that all the publicity and marketing are lined up and optimally timed. Proof copies were ready a few months before publication and my editor sent a weekly spreadsheet detailing activity in the final months pre-publication, which was hugely informative. I simply tried to make myself as available as possible.

The book's publicist set up a number of, events, which were great fun and ensured that the book (and I) got out to people beyond just friends and family. And then it was time to focus on the next book, and do it all over again ...

There are trends in publishing that affect what types of books publishers would like to acquire. In an uncertain world, with the rise of populism and concern around migration and climate change, publishers saw a reaction to this instability materialize in growing sales of serious non-fiction. There have been also strong sales across categories such as nature writing, wellness, and lifestyle. Caroline Sanderson commented:

> I think it's now almost impossible to publish a book of nature or travel writing which doesn't also grapple with the climate crisis in some way. Just as I think the market has moved on from memoirs that don't weave in bigger social themes or issues such as mental health. (*The Bookseller*, 1 June 2023)

Wattpad has a community of 85 m readers and writers

Trends in fiction have ranged from erotic fiction during the popularity of *50 Shades of Grey* to grip lit, following the success of *Gone Girl* and *The Girl on the Train*. Trends have to start somewhere, and Gillian Flynn, the author of *Gone Girl*, perceived a gap in the market: 'What I read in spades were books about men, their rage, self-harm and violence, and what that violence looked like generationally. What I felt was completely absent was anything examining how women process rage' (*Sunday Times*, 1 July 2018). Sales of ebooks are dominated by genre fiction, and digital-only imprints have concentrated on areas such as romance, sci-fi, fantasy, saga and crime.

Literary fiction has been in decline for some years and in 2017 crime fiction sold more than the category of general and literary fiction. Robbie Millen, Literary Editor of *The Times* wrote:

> Most readers want plot, suspense, action and resolution, something a lot of literary fiction does not condescend to guarantee. There seems to be a growing number of cleverly structured but empty novels that go nowhere, where plot or character play a tiny second fiddle to literary tricksiness. Besides which, so few of them have anything burning or brave to say. (*The Times*, 27 July 2018)

Subgenres in fiction abound and in the area of crime these include police procedural (Peter James) and cosy crime (Richard Osman). More generally, genres are under constant invention and reinvention, from romantasy (a mix of romance and fantasy) to dark academia. Pamela Paul writes of the latter:

> The cultural touchstones of dark academia are many and various, but the quintessential dark academia film is *Dead Poets Society* with its midnight poetry and tortured souls. Its ur-bible is Donna Tartt's 1992 best-selling novel, *The Secret History*, the story of a murderous group of classics undergrads with names like Edmund (Bunny) Corcoran and Francis Abernathy. These are stories that feature bacchanals, clandestine gatherings at night and steep ravines. (*New York Times*, 30 October 2022)

First-time novelists can be offered a two or three-book deal, which ensures they are already signed up should their first book prove to be a winner. The advance paid can also be set against all of the books. The excitement generated can be short-lived, and if an author does hit the big time straight away, this only increases the pressure on them to deliver another bestseller. It is also possible they are trapped in their agreement with a smaller publisher, unable to accept the higher terms being offered to move publisher.

A midlist author with several modestly successful titles in print in turn runs the risk that they are deemed unproductive by their agent or publisher, and passed over in favour of new authors, perhaps seen as more 'promotable' (viewed by some to mean young and good-looking). Francesca Simon describes how it took some time before her Horrid Henry children's books became successful:

> It wasn't until *Horrid Henry's Nits* was published, three years on, that the books started to attract attention. Nowadays, if authors haven't got noticed after two books, they are cast adrift. So had I begun it 10 years later, Horrid Henry would never have had a chance. (*Guardian*, 17 June 2013)

Social media stars can prove highly successful authors. The Instagram star Mrs Hinch was signed up by Michael Joseph in 2018 and by 2021 had sold over 2 m copies of her books with tips on cleaning. The rise in popularity of audio titles is encouraging authors to write books with this market in mind; and there have been some innovative fiction podcasts such as Blum, which was highly successful in Spain before launching in the UK in 2023. The actor Richard Armitage wrote *Geneva* (2022) as a digital first audiobook for Audible, and the print rights were then picked up by Faber. The rise of graphic novels and webcomics is stimulating the market for authors and illustrators. The cartoonist and illustrator Sarah Anderson produced a serial comic strip on the Tapas platform in 2019, and the gothic romance, *Fangs*, was published by the Kansas City publisher Andrews McMeel the following year.

Agents keep an eye open for potential recruits coming out of creative writing programmes. Such courses have proliferated in the USA and the UK and famously Ian McEwan was the first writer on the MA course at the University of East Anglia, run by Malcolm Bradbury and Angus Wilson. Marina Lewycka's first novel, *A Short History of Tractors in Ukrainian* (2005), was picked up by an agent when she joined the course at Sheffield Hallam University, and was published in 2005 when she was 58. The novelist Will Self commented on creative writing programmes:

> The people coming out of these courses are never going to make a living as novelists, certainly not in literary fiction though that's a somewhat suspect term. Basically writers are chasing too few readers at the moment. I think literature is morphing into something else, it's morphing into a conservatoire form, into a more privileged form in many ways, morphing into a giant quilting exercise where people read and comment on each other's writing. (*The Bookseller*, 2 May 2019)

New consultancies have developed in the UK offering writers' services. For a fee, the company offers to give the author a report on their manuscript, both the writing and the likely market, and editorial services including rewriting of proposals or full works. A full service will offer marketing and publicity support. Publishers have also developed a range of services including creative writing workshops and self-publishing operations. Novelists such as S. J. Watson and Rachel Joyce are alumni of the Faber Academy, which offers courses for aspiring writers. In 2024, the digital publisher Bookouture, part of Hachette UK, launched their Publishing Academy – a paid, online training platform for potential authors to guide them through the publishing process from concept to publication and beyond, with a focus on commercial fiction.

Self-publishing has left behind any stigma of vanity publishing – it is inexpensive in digital and cheap in print form. It can take place directly by the author or through a specialized company or self-publishing community group. Some indie authors relish their total control over the way their books are published and their retention of all rights. Ambitious authors can take to sites such as Kickstarter to crowdfund a writing project: 'The literary world was stunned in the first week of March [2022] when prolific fantasy novelist Brandon Sanderson's *Surprise! Four Secret Novels* blew past $20M in its first 72 hours to become the most funded Kickstarter project of all time' (kickstarter.com, accessed 27 February 2024).

'The first draft is not the book.' Olivie Blake

As well as posting work on community sites, writers can publish their book as an ebook on Amazon or another platform such as Smashwords. Starting from the Word file, an author can make their book available in a very short space of time. A self-published author typically receives a 70 per cent share on ebook sales, whereas through a publisher would receive 25 per cent. However, self-publishing authors have to bear at their risk and expense all the costs, such as editing, cover design, project management, marketing, web design, and the time spent on social media campaigns. The chances of securing bestsellerdom, let alone a film deal, remain slim: most indie authors sell fewer than 100 copies. They lack the investment, high street distribution and discoverability provided by publishers. But the success stories are there and in 2019 Amazon reported thousands of authors making over $50,000 from its KDP programme, and over

Hybrid authors
are happy
to work with
mainstream
publishers and
to self-publish

a thousand authors receiving more than $100,000 in royalties (aboutamazon. co.uk, accessed 16 August 2023). A fast-selling self-published title may also attract the attention of a mainstream publisher, keen to capitalize on its success. The fantasy author Olivie Blake self-published *The Atlas Six* (2020) on Kindle – it went viral on platforms such as TikTok and the author was then contracted by Tor Books. Hybrid authors pursue the twin track of being published through a publisher and self-publishing other books (sometimes their backlist). Academics too self-publish books but their work in this form does not count for career advancement.

The internet has enabled many kinds of self-publishing, for example, in the area of fanfic or fan fiction – new works written by fans of original fiction. There are many stories written about the characters from Harry Potter; Megan Ray writes: 'Traditionally marginalized groups use fic as a way to see themselves represented in stories with little diversity in the canon; a common trope in modern fan compositions recasts Hermione from Harry Potter as Black' (*New York Times*, 26 June 2023).

For print publishing, the growth of print on demand using digital printing means that print runs can be as low as a few or single copies. Services such as

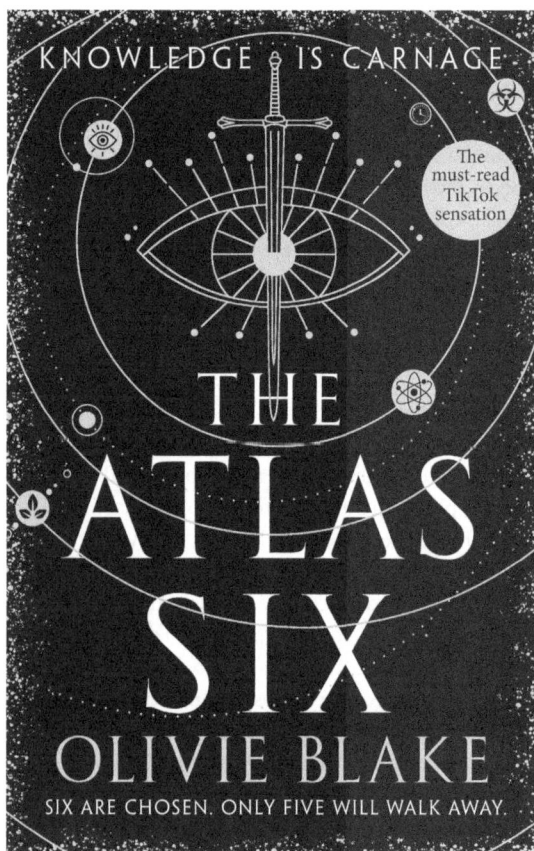

Atlas Six cover

The decision to self-publish

Rachel Abbott, bestselling self-published author – over 5 m copies sold

The decision to self-publish was an easy one for me. I had never seen myself as an author and had written my first book more as an act of self-indulgence, fulfilling a long-held ambition, than as a serious attempt to be a published author. When the inevitable rejections came from the small number of agents that I submitted to, I wasn't particularly concerned and put it down to experience. My novel was parked on a virtual shelf for several months. And then I heard that it was possible to self-publish on the Amazon Kindle.

It was early days for the technology (2011) but I had some experience of coding in HTML – something of a requirement back then if an author wanted their book to look professional (although it is no longer the case). I decided to give it a go, with neither hope nor expectation. Six weeks after publication, I became excited about the fact that I had sold six books in one day – and it was at that point I realised this was an opportunity I didn't want to overlook. I had some marketing experience and so decided to write a detailed marketing plan. Immediately the Christmas holidays were over, I sat down and worked out how I thought I could get my book noticed – because in marketing terms that is the number one priority. Awareness and visibility were the key drivers for phase one of the plan. I worked hard – fourteen hours a day for seven days a week. I did this for three months, and saw some staggering results. My novel – *Only the Innocent* – shot to the top of the Kindle chart and stayed there for four weeks, initially selling over 3,500 copies per day.

I have continued to self-publish, although in 2018 my first traditionally published title – *And So It Begins* – hit the shelves. Both publishing options are exciting, and both have very different pros and cons. As a self-published author, you retain control of everything from pricing to cover design. But you are largely on your own (although I am lucky to have a very supportive agent). As a traditionally published author, you have the backing of a marketing and PR team, and excellent editors. But of course you get a smaller cut of the proceeds.

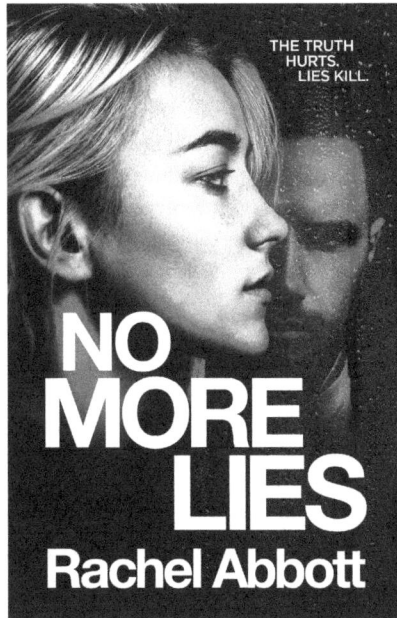

In the end, every writer has to decide on their priorities. If success to you means selling a lot of your well-written books, then as a self-published author your titles have to appear to readers to be every bit as good as every other title. This means you have to invest in a good cover designer, and your book should be professionally edited. Then, once your book is in good shape, the marketing begins. To market successfully, you have to devote time and patience, and you must work out a plan. A random approach is unlikely to work. You will probably need to build a social media presence and work hard to build and engage followers. It's not easy, but it's worth it.

Even though I am now a hybrid author with a foot in each camp, I hope my experience in self-publishing will inform my journey with a traditional publisher. Whichever route you take, it's a journey you are unlikely to forget.

AuthorHouse, KDP (part of Amazon), IngramSpark and Lulu offer authors a low-cost route to publication. Only when a book is ordered from Lulu's website is it then printed and sent to the purchaser. However, self-published authors find that most booksellers will not stock their print titles, and this remains a key advantage of the mainstream publishing houses.

Supply-funded publishing

A factor in supply-funded publishing is that it attracts scam publishers that entice authors to pay up-front for services which are never delivered. There are still such publishers, called vanity publishers in consumer markets, or predatory publishers in open access journal publishing. However, both consumer and academic publishers have occasionally sought subventions or subsidies from authors to publish certain books, which, though publishable on assessed quality, are financially too risky. This is a common model in some countries for the publication of academic theses. There is also growth in the hybrid publisher sector. Such publishers curate and select projects, carry out conventional publishing activities, invest their money but ask authors to make a contribution towards costs. An example of such a publisher is Hoi Publishing in Sweden – it is estimated that 30 per cent of Hoi's income comes from investments from its authors (Vandersmissen, 2023).

Researchers wanting to publish in open access journals which charge article processing charges (APCs) face great complexity in choosing the journal which best suits their work and career advancement while trying to comply with the myriad of funder and institutional policy guidelines and mandates, obtaining the funding, processing the charges (usually through the library) and archiving the article, including data. The arrival of transformative agreements has, however, made the process much smoother and easier.

The future for authorship

The data on author incomes suggests the life of the professional author is only becoming harder, with many having to rely on side-hustles to make a decent living. The large advances touted in the press are mostly reserved for brand authors although the debut author still commands attention with the right project. Generative AI is growing in importance in many fields and there are already books available written with the help of, or entirely by, AI programs. The author Rie Kudan won the Akutagawa Prize in Japan in 2024 with her futurist novel *Tokyo-to Dojo-to* (*Tokyo Sympathy Tower*). She said that around 5 per cent of her novel had been directly written by ChatGPT.

There is a consensus that AI may be able to do an adequate job producing genre fiction. What about literary fiction? Monica Ali suggests that:

> Perhaps literary fiction – the genre I write in – will be a harder nut for the AI machine to crack. It's less formulaic. It relies more on depth of characterisation and elegant and innovative use of language. But remember that these AIs are babies, still sucking on dummies. By the time they reach maturity, adolescence even, they may reach a level of sophistication that is difficult to imagine today. (*Guardian*, 2 December 2023)

Authors are starting to request clauses in their contracts to ensure that their works are not used to train AI programs. But it was revealed in 2023 that pirated works from authors including Stephen King and Zadie Smith have been used to train LLMs – large language models (*Atlantic*, 19 August 2023).

The industry has become tangled up with debates around what stories can be told and by whom, and Laura Hackett commented that we are lacking state-of-the-nation fiction from British novelists: 'The interesting cultural shifts in Britain, regarding class, race and gender, have had limited treatment, thanks to

'It's not difficult to write a single novel ... What's really hard is to keep on writing novels year after year.' Haruki Murakami the cult of "lived experience", in which only authors who have directly experienced injustice can write about it' (*Sunday Times*, 6 August 2023). There is no doubt that publishers have made much more effort to recruit authors from diverse backgrounds, but is there a risk that those authors feel pigeon-holed as to what they can write about? The writer Yomi Adegoke says:

> We are seeing a push towards more books written by ... minoritised authors. But does that mean those authors are necessarily given the freedom to write about anything, or is there a push for writers of a particular identity to write to that identity? (*Guardian*, 1 July 2023)

AGENTS

Literary agents are mostly located in London or New York, giving them close proximity to their main customers: fiction and non-fiction editors, mainly in adult but also in children's book publishers and other media industries. Their business is selling and licensing rights to a variety of media (not just book publishers) at home and abroad on behalf of their client authors with whom they have a contract on each book for the full term of copyright. There are many specialisms such as book-only, book-to-screen, and screen-only. Agents receive a commission on authors' earnings, typically 15 per cent on earnings from home sales but rising to 20 per cent on deals made abroad. The commission on film and TV deals tends to be from 15–20 per cent. The prevalence, power and influence of agents are very much a feature of the Anglo-American media worlds. In mainland Europe and elsewhere there are still few agents, although the numbers are growing. There are also 'sub-agents' of English language agents or publishers – not of local authors – who may earn half of the 20 per cent commission received by the UK agent. Some Anglo-American agents sell directly into foreign language markets. There are also literary scouts, who tip off agents and publishers about new authors – or established authors in other territories – in return for a fee. Some publishers suggest that their work could be overtaken by the ability of AI to summarize books.

Agents operate in an increasingly polarized market in which a small number of top-selling authors secure advances against royalties of more than £100,000, compared to the majority of authors receiving advances below £10,000. An agent may spend equal amounts of time on both types of author, but with a very different financial return. For example, if an agent secures an advance of £6,000 and charges 15 per cent commission, their share is just £900.

Agents manage lists of authors and they represent many of the established professional writers, i.e. those who derive much of their income from writing. They may also represent academics if their work appeals to a wide readership. Some agents may acquire new clients on personal recommendations from credited sources, such as media contacts and their other clients. They differ in the extent to which they are prepared to review unsolicited manuscripts from aspiring novelists. Some less-reputable agencies charge hopeful authors a reading fee while most absorb the cost paid to external readers. Agents may look to maintain a high profile on social media through which they can find new authors. In 2024, one agent suggested on social media that they were looking for the following in the YA space: 'Unconventional love stories. Heists and hijinks. Fun romps. Inventive dystopias. Genre-blending YA. Magical academies. Queer stories. Romantasy for teens. Fairytale retellings. High-stake/deadly competitions. Assassins/thieves guilds. High-concept romance w/ a speculative twist.' Agencies also launch pitch events on social media for limited periods. In 2023 United Agents promoted their Open House initiative:

> For 24 hours, United Agents Books Department will be holding an Open House submissions window to encourage submissions from groups that are under-represented in the creative industries. We guarantee that 100 – randomly allocated – submissions will receive a minimum of 100 words of personalised feedback from a member of the books department. (unitedagents.co.uk, accessed 17 August 2023)

It is now commonly accepted that authors can make multiple submissions – to several agents at once. Andrew Lownie still advises caution:

> Agents understand that authors need to make multiple submissions to agencies but dislike 'beauty parades'. It is not flattering nor encouraging to be told one is simply one of a hundred approaches. Time is limited and if one suspects the author may go elsewhere then one simply says no at the beginning. (andrewlownie.co.uk, accessed 1 February 2024)

Once an agent has taken on an author, the agent develops the book proposal with the author. It is their job to pitch the book to the right editor in the most suitable publishing house. The literary publishing house Jonathan Cape was rarely offered more commercial books, and in his memoir *Publisher*, Tom Maschler recalls being sent the manuscript for *Not a Penny More, Not a Penny Less* by the literary agent Deborah Owen. The author, unknown at the time, was Jeffrey Archer:

> She did not actually say it was a first submission but, in the manner of certain agents content to mislead, this was the implication. The aspect of Archer's book which especially intrigued me was that he himself had been involved in a con and had lost a great deal of money, both his own and others'. And now he had written a thriller about a man similar to himself, and furthermore was doing so in order to earn a large sum so that the money could be repaid . . . I found the conceit intriguing, and although the style was indifferent, decided to offer a contract. I must admit I was motivated, in part, by the feeling that Jeffrey was so obviously ambitious that he would be likely to succeed in almost anything to which he put his mind. (2005, page 200)

An agent manages a writer's career primarily from a commercial viewpoint, for example, by placing the author's work with the right publisher or fuelling competition between publishers (on major books by holding auctions); negotiating deals to secure the best terms; by submitting their own contracts to licensors weighted in the authors' favour; checking or querying both publishers' advance payments against royalties, and royalty statements, and chasing debts.

E★PERT

The role of the agent: a case study

Juliet Pickering, Blake Friedmann Literary Agency

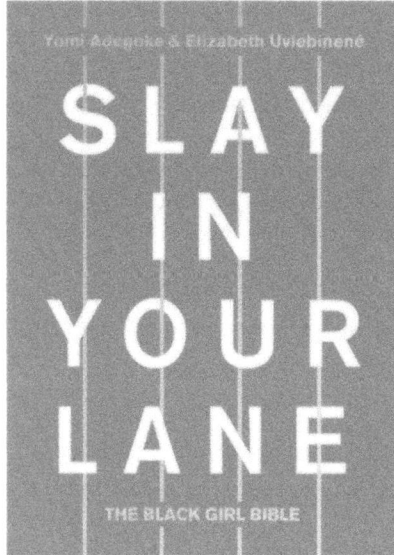

The role of the agent has evolved hugely over the last decade. We are now not only the broker between author and publisher, but as books have reached more platforms than ever, we have had to adapt our horizons and experience too.

For example, a book formerly on my list, *SLAY IN YOUR LANE: The Black Girl Bible* (2018), gathered traction across radio, TV, podcasting, corporations, and even reached into fashion outlet. There are traditional spaces for books, and an ever-growing opportunity to take books into non-traditional spaces, which the agent has to start thinking about from the point of taking on the book and the author. The success of *SLAY IN YOUR LANE* is largely due to its hardworking authors and their tireless campaign, which has led to interest far beyond the publishing industry, and to which I have to be open and responsive. From education to work to dating, this inspirational, honest and provocative book recognizes and celebrates the strides black women have already made, while providing practical advice for those who want to do the same and forge a better, visible future.

The book began as a short proposal that arrived in my inbox a few days before Christmas. It was very visual, but the authors had included a compelling and thorough chapter plan, and I knew instantly that the idea appealed (with non-fiction, agents and editors will usually know immediately whether the idea has potential for them). I met the authors soon after, and we began working together on developing the proposal into a package that we could send to publishers, sending edits back and forth for several months. For the proposal we needed a two-page overview, the chapter plan, and two sample chapters, one of which was the introduction. To add a little of the original visual appeal, we kept a couple of the images that so well reflected the writing, and emphasised our message of wanting to make black women visible.

Once the proposal was ready, it went to approximately twenty editors – in response nine offered and two others wanted meetings. With nine offers, we turned down the extra two, and focused on spending an hour with each of the bidding editors and their teams, to hear about what that publisher had to offer. The meetings varied in atmosphere and energy: some were confused by the message of the book or wanted to dilute it ('can we make this about BAME women rather than just black women?', one editor asked), but mostly we met enthused editors with marketing and publicity colleagues who had drawn up ambitious plans for how they would promote and market the book. The connection to the editor is usually most important for authors, but it's also the agent's job to know how successful their teams have been for other, maybe similar, books, and to advise our authors on their choice of publisher accordingly. At the final round of bids we had a couple of matching highest offers, but one publisher was new and fairly untested in publishing a successful book, while the other was long-established and a very solid (and exciting!) prospect. We chose 4th Estate as the best all-round fit.

From the point of the book deal, we've all worked hard to promote and spread the message of *SLAY IN YOUR LANE*, which was always intended to be a movement and not just a book, and began evolving into a 'brand' with further books planned, and conversations about development across media outlets and more. It's a best-case scenario kind of success, and this doesn't happen for every book, but it's a reminder that with success we have to be adaptable as agents, and anticipate a bigger, busier workload for our authors!

The example of the author–publisher contract summarized in Chapter 7, and weighted in the publisher's favour, shows the author granting various world rights to the publisher. Because most authors are unable to market the rights on their work worldwide, they mainly allow publishers to do so on their behalf. But an agent representing an author may limit the rights granted to a publisher, and their territorial extent, and license the rights retained on behalf of the author to other firms at home and abroad. They do this both to maximize the author's income but also in order to ensure a range of advocates for the author's work. For instance, the UK publisher's licence may apply to the English language only, and the territories (the countries) in which it has the exclusive right to publish (e.g. the Commonwealth and Europe) are listed, as well as those from which it could be excluded (e.g. the USA and Canada). An agent could then license the book in the English language to a US publisher directly. A UK publisher, within its exclusive territory, could, for instance, be granted the following rights: the right to publish in hardback and paperback; an audiobook and ebook; and to license to others – book club, reprints, second and subsequent serial (i.e. extracts appearing in newspapers after the book's publication), quotation and anthology, mechanical and reproduction, broadcast reading rights, etc. An agent would then retain, for example, foreign language translation, first serial rights (extracts appearing before book publication, thereby giving a newspaper a scoop), stage/radio/television/film dramatization, games, merchandising, and other electronic rights.

However, there is no clear-cut division of rights or territories covered – each book differs. Whilst the ebook is commonly regarded as standard to license to the publisher, an agent may wonder about keeping audio rights to sell separately. A publisher which has the idea for the book and contributes much editorial and design effort, or which is investing a large amount, for instance, in a new writer on a two-book deal, has a strong case for acquiring wide territorial and language rights and the sharing of other rights. Publishers and packagers producing highly illustrated books for the international market need world rights in all languages. A wider set of rights is needed in order to recoup the initial high costs of these books. Book packagers and some highly illustrated book publishers often try to acquire the copyright outright from authors, enabling subsequent repackaging and recycling of authors' material without further payment or author contract.

UK agents retaining rights may sell them directly to US publishers or mainland European publishers, or use overseas agents with whom they have arrangements. Conversely, UK agents may represent well-known American authors on behalf of US agents, and sometimes US publishers. Agents also sell rights to a range of media, such as to film, TV and game companies. The selling of rights from a publisher's viewpoint is described in Chapter 11; an agent's work is similar except that an agent solely represents the author.

An additional dimension of agents' work falls under an editorial heading. For instance, agents send out synopses and manuscripts for external review, comment on manuscripts and undertake developmental editing, advise authors on what they might write, and develop ideas with them. With a range of options available for storytelling, from, say, a podcast to a Netflix series, Jonny Geller of Curtis Brown suggests that the agent has become a literary manager. The different media forms offer 'a huge opportunity for us because now we can have a good storyteller tell a story and I can think, well, actually this would work better as a ten-part series and then the book' (Phillips, 2020, page 174).

Agents might be asked by publishers to supply authors; or they might initiate projects themselves for sale to publishers. In such ways, some agents increasingly take on roles which were once the province of publishers' editors. They can reflect trade realities back to authors, and arbitrate on arguments between their authors and publishers. A further role may be to manage the author's backlist, which could include moving titles between publishers or negotiating ebook deals on older titles, or helping them to self-publish ebooks.

Agents provide a degree of continuity in the face of changing personnel amongst publishers and editors. However, some authors decide to change agents or are poached by them. This famously happened when Martin Amis changed agents to Andrew Wylie, known as the 'Jackal', when selling the rights in his novel *The Information* (1995). The former agent may continue to receive commission on contracts which they negotiated. The long-established agencies manage the literary estates of classic authors whose work remains in copyright.

Agents may specialize in particular genres, such as adult fiction or YA, but not necessarily to the exclusion of other opportunities. Some agents operate from home as single-person companies and the smaller agencies are often run as nimble operations, spotting new talent. The trend in recent years has been for agencies to get larger in order to meet the needs of authors with interests across a range of media, including public speaking appearances. They may be in competition with other kinds of agents who represent celebrities and sports stars. There are medium-sized agencies consisting of several agents plus assistants, and major agencies in the UK such as Curtis Brown (owned by the Hollywood-based United Talent Agency) and United Agents. The Creative Artists Agency (CAA) has targeted expansion in the UK literary market and the parent company works across film, television, music, sports, and digital media.

A large firm has a range of agents, each of whom specializes in broad areas of books or the selling of particular rights, though each agent usually looks after a particular primary group of authors. A specialism is film and TV rights, which involves selecting books for screen adaptation, and submitting them to producers. Some of their assistants show sufficient aptitude to develop their own list of authors, and new agents come from rights and editorial staff of the publishers. The larger agencies usually have agencies on both sides of the Atlantic, and good connections in Hollywood. There are also agencies which specialize in selling particular rights, such as translation, or film and television, on behalf of publishers and authors' agents. Sometimes a package of talent (book, star and director) is offered to a film studio. Of growing importance is representing authors as speakers for events and dinners, and also for theatre appearances in front of large audiences. This latter business is threatening the ability of literary festivals to attract big names to come and talk.

Agents may fear disintermediation in an age of self-publishing, and this has led many to broaden their offer. They have followed publishers into the area of creative writing courses (e.g. Curtis Brown Creative), and some agents offer authors assistance or advice on digital marketing and self-publishing. Diversification has led some into film production or to co-invest in new digital projects. Occasionally they have established their own publishing imprints, leading to questions about a possible conflict of interest – can their advice to authors remain independent? The literary agencies are mostly based in London but smaller, one-person outfits are often based away from the capital. With the trend towards smaller advances from publishers, the business has become harder work for those smaller agencies that are not diversified across different types of media.

Now read this

Chapter 6, Commissioning and acquisition

Sources

ALCS, *Why Writers Are at a Loss for Words*, December 2022.
Alison Baverstock, *The Naked Author: A guide to self-publishing*, A&C Black, 2011.
Brendan Clark, *The IngramSpark Guide to Independent Publishing*, revised edition, 2018.
Andrew Crofts, *Confessions of a Ghostwriter*, The Friday Project, 2014.
Arthur M. Klebanoff, *The Agent*, Texere, 2002.
Tom Maschler, *Publisher*, Picador, 2005.
Haruki Murakami, *Novelist as a Vocation*, Harvill Secker, 2022.
Katie Nicoll, 'Using BookTok and Bookstagram as an Author', *Logos*, 34:1 (2023).
Scott Pack, *Tips from a Publisher*, Eye Books, 2020.
Angus Phillips, 'The Modern Literary Agent', in Alison Baverstock, Richard Bradford and Madelena Gonzalez (eds), *Contemporary Publishing and the Culture of Books*, Routledge, 2020.
Robbe Vandersmissen, 'From Grey to Great: Hoi Publishing and the rise of hybrid publishing services in Sweden', *Logos*, 34:3 (2023).

Published annually, the following guides contain useful information about publishers and literary agents.

UK

The Writers' and Artists' Yearbook, A&C Black.
Writers' Handbook, JP&A Dyson.

USA

Guide to Literary Agents, Writer's Digest.
Writer's Market, Writer's Digest.

Web resources

https://www.allianceindependentauthors.org Alliance of Independent Authors.
https://archiveofourown.org Access to fannish activity for all fans.
https://authorsguild.org US professional organization for published writers.
https://www.fanfiction.net Fan fiction from *Harry Potter* to *The Lord of the Rings*.

https://www.janefriedman.com/blog/ Jane Friedman's blog for writers.

https://feeds.megaphone.fm/howtowriteabook Podclass on How to Write a Book

https://jerichowriters.com/agentmatch/ Lists all agents in the UK and the USA.

https://querytracker.net Database of literary agents.

https://www.scbwi.org Society of Children's Book Writers and Illustrators.

https://www.societyofauthors.org UK Society of Authors.

https://www.writersandartists.co.uk Industry advice for writers.

https://writersguild.org.uk UK trade union representing professional writers.

Commissioning and acquisition

The commissioning editor in a publishing house is responsible for coming up with marketable ideas and matching them to good authors. Working for the editorial director or publisher, who manages the editorial team, the editor is a key player in the publishing process. The more senior commissioning editors will take a strategic view of their list or imprint – called list-building – while junior editors may commission within a set brief.

A distinction can be made between books *acquired* from agents or authors, where the idea often comes from the author, and those books that are *commissioned* from scratch by the editor. In the case of the latter books, the idea comes from the editor, who then goes in search of a suitable author. In textbook publishing, for example, this is the typical process for commissioning. About trade non-fiction, Anthony Cheetham of Head of Zeus, commented:

> The great thing about non-fiction is that you can make it happen; you cannot commission a novel in the same way. In non-fiction, you can say, 'I want a book on this subject, at that length', and then you find the right author. (*The Bookseller*, 29 June 2018)

Most editors remain unseen to readers, although the best editors across all types of publishing become known and respected by author communities in their particular fields. The role of editors, especially in consumer book publishing, has been impacted over generations by changes in the publishing environment. After the Second World War, editors had to adapt to the rise of authors' agents, and during the 1960s and 1970s to the impact of corporate accountants instilling financial controls. The rise of the bookselling chains in the 1980s and 1990s affected the types of books published and increased the power of sales and marketing over publishing decisions. The transition to digital publishing is having an enormous impact on editors across all field of publishing: whether it is how they connect with authors and readers – for example, they may use social media to promote a book long before publication – or in the opportunities presented to publish books in a variety of formats for an international audience.

EDITORIAL COMMISSIONING

In consumer books, editors may cover different fiction genres or non-fiction areas, or specialize in hardback, paperback or digital lists, or children's books. In

DOI: 10.4324/9781003403289-7

educational, academic and STM houses, an editor may concentrate on several subjects, spanning a variety of academic levels and markets, or on product types, such as journals or textbooks. The style and identity of each list are the outcome of the editor's attitudes and effort.

A publisher depends on its editors to provide a sufficient flow of publishable projects to maintain the planned level of activity, for example, 15–30 new books annually per editor, sometimes far less or three times more (depending on the market sector). Editors are assessed on the revenue they bring in or the overall profit, or contribution, of their books. Publishers may have electronic systems in which editors record their output in terms of titles commissioned and forecast revenue. Editors out of tune with senior management regarding the character of the books, or who fail to produce a profit, leave voluntarily or are fired. The job is high risk and exposed, especially in consumer publishing.

With some exceptions, such as in the area of fiction, editors do not assess titles for publication on their thorough reading of complete manuscripts. Most books (including some fiction) are commissioned from authors on the basis of a proposal or specimen material, or are bought from agents (see Chapter 5). Editors generally do not edit the author's work in detail – that is done by freelancers or junior in-house staff. However, senior editors may carry out developmental editing by giving authors substantive criticisms and suggestions to help them produce their best work and to shape it for the intended market (see Chapter 7).

The industry has come under criticism for the working conditions of more junior staff, especially in editorial, where alongside a busy week of editorial tasks and meetings they may be expected to read manuscripts in their own time. The novelist Keiran Goddard criticizes the attitude towards the workforce, writers included:

> Almost all novelists now have day jobs to pay the rent, snatching time to write here and there on commutes and in the stolen hours before or after work. If they manage to actually find enough time to finish writing a novel, they then submit it to an overstretched and under-remunerated editor who will have to read it at the weekend. (*Guardian*, 3 February 2024)

List-building

Publishing lists have their own identity and even within the larger groups there has been a conscious decision to keep separate imprints, each with their own distinctive flavour and editorial strategy. The small publisher feel is attractive to authors and the use of imprints assists the trade to make sense of the large number of new and existing titles. Lists may be built around fiction genres and authors (Gollancz for science fiction and fantasy), subjects (Yellow Jersey for sports books), brands (Teach Yourself and For Dummies), or design character (text only or highly illustrated). In 2023 Mills & Boon launched a new list, Afterglow, aimed at young users of TikTok:

> Afterglow is 'a trend-led, trope-filled list of books with authentic and relatable characters', with 'a generous dose of spice in every story', says Katie Barnes-Wallis, marketing director at Mills & Boon. Tropes – for example:

'If we don't like a book, we don't publish it.' Natania Jansz, Sort of Books enemies to lovers; small-town settings; grumpy versus sunshine – are key to the way younger romance fans choose books and talk about them on TikTok. (*Guardian*, 19 December 2023)

A set of titles that presents a defined genre or subject to a specific audience will have a greater value than one which simply aggregates disparate titles. Successful lists attract both authors and readers, and marketing a list is often more cost-effective with cross-marketing opportunities between titles. Lists are assets which can be bought and sold between publishers. List-builders may be asked to create a new imprint from scratch – reflecting changes in the market or strategic ambition – or to expand and strengthen an existing list. They will be on the look-out for new authors and projects, bearing in mind their list's identity, and focus, future direction and changing boundaries.

Elements of editorial strategy include:

- Market – level and readership; sales channels
- Author-led or title led
- Frontlist-driven or titles with backlist potential
- Brand
- Production values
- Digital developments

The strategy will be informed by a view of the competition and trends in the market. A programme of new editions is important in non-fiction and essential in textbook publishing, in order to refresh the list and keep titles up to date. Rebranding the list in new covers can also achieve this.

Editorial contacts and market research

Good personal contacts are paramount for commissioning. An editor's in-house contacts are the members of senior management who accept or veto projects; the people who produce the books; and those who market and sell them. But more significant are the editor's external contacts. Prime sources of new books are the firm's previously published authors – they often have new ideas, or editors suggest ideas to them which are developed jointly.

Consumer books

In consumer book publishing, editors try to establish a mutual trust with authors and their agents (often over lunch). Agents may send fiction manuscripts or non-fiction proposals to selected editors one at a time, or sometimes conduct auctions amongst several publishers on highly saleable titles. Conversely an editor may contact an agent if they are pursuing one of their stable of authors, or have an idea and want the agent to find an author. If an editor is determined to secure a book being offered, they may issue a pre-emptive bid – large enough to prevent an auction taking place. Fiction editors may find new talent by spotting people who can write well, not necessarily fiction. They may be journalists or writers who are being published poorly or in an uncommercial medium, or who have generated a following for their blog. Editors

#Merky Books is an imprint launched in 2018 by Stormzy and PRH UK with the aim to publish books that will 'own – and change – the mainstream', focusing on new works by young writers may look to pick up authors through social media, from community sites or from amongst the pool of self-published authors – the writers may come with a ready audience or already market-tested. Authors with their own podcasts are a fruitful source of non-fiction projects, for example in the area of history. Celebrity authors may have to be wooed with personal touches such as handwritten notes.

Non-fiction editors develop contacts in a variety of fields, constantly keep an ear to the ground, notice people's enthusiasms, or review the media or blogosphere for topical subjects. They remain in touch with their markets and understand the needs of book consumers, for example around portability. The German publisher Gerhard Steidl says: 'People are travelling a lot ... So if you go to Tokyo and visit a nice bookshop and find a beautiful little book, you buy it immediately because you can easily take it home in your suitcase' (*Monocle*, October 2023). Editors try to predict trends or events which will be in the public's interest (tools such as Google Trends can assist), monitor successful book categories and authors by understanding what makes them good and why are they selling, and either avoid the competition, imitate it, or attempt to find unfilled niches by developing a new twist. They write speculatively to those who have the potential to capture the public's imagination – as do agents. They could be an up-and-coming celebrity or sports star, a social media influencer, or an academic with a talent for popularization. Editors interested in television and film tie-ins keep abreast of new productions and monitor audience ratings.

Editors are often forced to play for high stakes – being too cautious is unlikely to lead to a stable of bestsellers, and will not impress management. Some brand authors are surefire winners but inevitably risks need to be taken with new authors or projects. Some bets will not work out but the aim is to more than compensate with the successes. Offering, and paying, high advances are sometimes necessary in order to attract or retain the best authors, and to be in the hunt with agents for the next high-profile book. John Thompson writes:

> an editor's relationships with the key agents are their lifeline: they simply cannot afford to screw this up. So they may find themselves deciding to bid for books, and asking for permission to bid at levels that even they feel are excessive, simply because they don't want to offend important agents and they want to be seen and known around town as somebody who bids, and can, if need be, bid high. (Thompson, 2012, page 210)

Nielsen BookScan provides publishers with sales data on their own and competitors' titles

Working with authors

Simon Winder, Publishing Director at Penguin Press

Working with authors is a delicate and complex business. There is a constant need for the editor to balance between the needs of the business and the sensibilities of the author. Sometimes these are simply not reconcilable – there are deadlines to be met, jacket designs to be approved, ruthless decisions about acceptable length, costs and schedule. But it is too easy for the editor to slip into the role of an incompetent sort of slave-driver.

E★PERT

Somehow corporate timetables and demands have to be balanced with a much more delicate and private world.

Authors who are driven along will, at a point invisible to the editor, suddenly realize that their relationship with their publisher is no longer enjoyable and, however regretfully, will simply run away, moving on to a fresh publisher. An author sometimes spends years working on a project, often in considerable isolation: the smallest thing can take on a huge importance, whether it is a specific phrase or a way of laying out the page or placing an image. The tension between an editor and an author is inevitable, but editors must not ever lose sight of the fact that one of the reasons they are being paid by their employer is to act as a reliable and truthful conduit for an author's feelings. If, for example, an author really hates a jacket design, the editor has to balance corporate needs (the deadline approaches, the art director is adamant) with an imperative to be the author's advocate. If an important manuscript is really not ready, then the editor has to act accordingly and break the bad news to colleagues and as early as possible.

All departments in publishing have important relationships which are *outside* the office and which are largely invisible to colleagues. But for the editor those invisible relationships are with agents and their authors, and in the end those relationships are based around trust, reliability and availability. Other editors are always prowling around and each has nightmares about that party or dinner, to which they are not invited, at which a competitor successfully turns an agent's or author's head. A lot can be done to fix this just by remembering to keep in touch – even if a manuscript is not due to deliver for another three years, it is really easy with a short email or an occasional lunch or drink to remind a writer, who may be having a terrible time battling with an intractable script, that you are to hand and can be talked to, shouted at, cried over pretty much any time day or night. This thoughtfulness can feel like an intolerable burden, as it sits to one side from the day-to-day rain of emails and office deadlines and is invisible to colleagues, but for some writers it can be a real life-line – they have someone to talk to and a real incentive to hit often very difficult targets – any worthwhile book is a triumph of exertion and focus. If the editor has done a good job at this stage in the process, then the editor is also much more likely to be believed and trusted by the author when the final, tricky stages of deadlines, blurbs, jackets and so on march into view, making these a lot less grim, and making the slave-driver editor a thing of the past.

Editors forge links with other firms from whom they might buy or sell to, for example at the Frankfurt Book Fair or, in the case of highly illustrated books, with packagers. UK editors are in contact with US editors and rights sales managers in order to gather market intelligence on new projects. Children's book editors have contact with agents, packagers, teachers and librarians, and if producing illustrated colour books know US and foreign language publishers with whom they might trade. Some concept books in children's publishing are planned out by the editor and an outline is prepared with ideas for story and the characters. From this outline a manuscript is commissioned from an author.

Non-consumer publishing

The educational, academic, STM and professional book editors publish for more defined markets about which more statistical information is available. This includes student enrolments, and the numbers of researchers or professionals working in specific fields. These editors, apart from reading school and college syllabuses, and the relevant journals, are engaged in direct market research and product development, especially in textbook publishing.

Quantitative research can include:

- student numbers
- number of courses in a subject
- sales figures of similar titles
- market share of the leading titles and publishers (indicated by data from Amazon).

Qualitative research covers:

- trends in the subject area
- analysis of competing titles – their extent, features, authors, strengths and weaknesses
- questionnaire results on products used and future needs
- focus group data – from students, teachers or librarians
- visiting schools or universities.

The academic and STM publishers may retain for each discipline exclusive advisers who direct new writers to their publishers. They could be senior academics or professionals with worldwide contacts. Expert general or series editors may be employed by publishers, especially in non-consumer sectors. Their task is to help editors develop and edit the books, and they usually receive a small royalty.

It is vital for editors to understand the current and future market on the ground. Educational editors see local education subject advisers, inspectors, examiners and lecturers on teacher training courses; school heads, and teachers using the materials in the classroom; and attend conferences. They need to understand forthcoming changes to the curriculum (and the opportunities they offer), and the trajectory within subjects stimulated by the views of the latest education minister. ELT editors, in addition to using UK contacts, will travel abroad and visit Ministries and Institutes of Education, private language schools, offices of the British Council, and local publishers and distributors to meet key contacts and decision-makers. College textbook editors spend several days a week visiting universities and will meet teaching staff in order to discover subject trends, find out their views on the books currently available, and flush out ideas and contacts they have, and to sell the firm's books. Academic editors may forge links with institutions, societies, and industry organizations for which they could publish or distribute books or journals. They will visit academic conferences to network and the best become well known in the relevant academic communities. Organizations and societies issue publishers with invitations to tender to publish their materials (such as journals), and competing editors will submit bids on behalf of their companies. When large US sales are anticipated, editors shape the material in

DK *My Book of the Elements* cover. An introduction to the periodic table for children aged 5–7

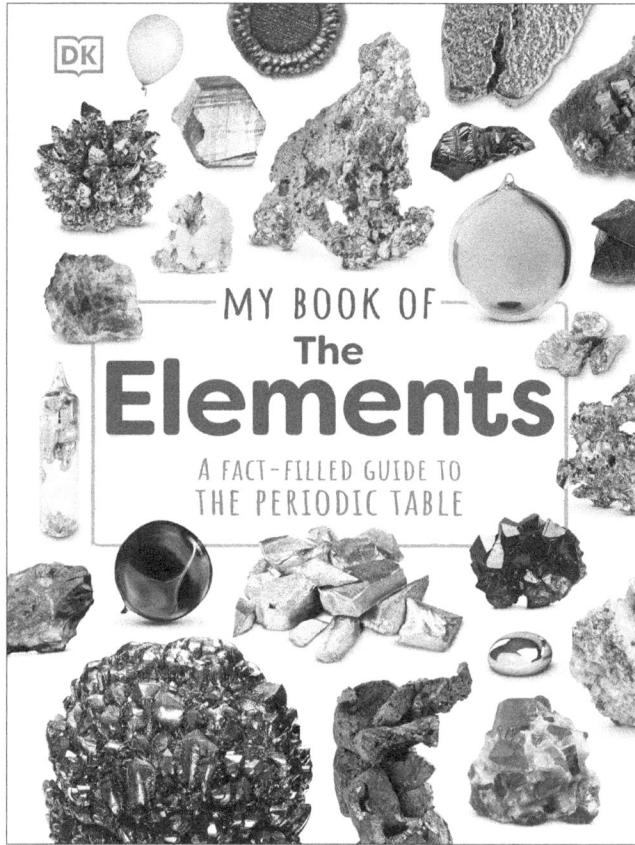

conjunction with their US counterparts and visit their sister companies. All editors receive in-house feedback from the marketing and sales departments.

The decision to publish

Many factors influence an editor's decision to pursue a new project.

Suitability for list

A title has to fit the style and aims of the list it will join, so that it is compatible with the firm's particular marketing systems and its sales channels to market. Taking on a book in a new subject area has implications for marketing and sales, not just editorial. Editors assessing new titles are also concerned with the list's overall balance, direction and degree of innovation. If a similar title is already in the pipeline, the editor may pass on a proposal.

Content

The editor's judgement of the quality and appropriateness of the content is aided by others. Fiction editors may use junior editors, or external readers, to supply plot synopses or to offer first or second opinions. Non-fiction editors may ask external readers to comment on specialist titles. Other publishers rely heavily on experts – teachers, academics, professionals – sometimes worldwide to comment on material. All these external readers are paid small fees and remain mostly anonymous to the author. The management of the peer review process is critically important in academic and journals publishing.

Author assessment

This covers the author's qualifications, writing ability, motivation and time available to write the book, public standing, reliability to deliver on time, responsiveness to suggestions and connectivity with the intended audience. Whether the author is 'promotable' is a key question for some types of consumer books. This can be interpreted as – is the author personable? – although the more cynical will say it is also a question about age and looks. There is a strong expectation that an author will have developed a strong presence on social media. There is debate about the quality of books commissioned from celebrities, for example in children's publishing, but the books are often seen as highly marketable.

Unique sales proposition (USP)

What will make this book different from others (its competitive advantage), or what makes it special – the quality of the author, a new treatment of the subject, or some differentiation by price or format? What are the special marketing opportunities through which the book could be promoted? This could be a tie-in with a TV series, taking advantage of a special sporting event for a sports autobiography, or the author's status and celebrity.

The USP defines what makes a book stand out from competing titles

Market

Understanding the main audience for which the book is intended, who would buy it, and the possible take-up at home and overseas. The sales records for the author's previous books or those of similar books may be used as a guide, along with market research regarding interest level and trends. Sometimes the rights sales potential is assessed, such as likely translation and co-edition sales. This is most relevant to trade titles. The likely international market is important now that an ebook can reach all parts of the globe before any print distribution.

Competition

The title's features and benefits compared with competing titles are evaluated. This is important for textbooks and reference titles, and for a variety of non-fiction. The strengths of competing titles should be acknowledged, not just their weaknesses. Consideration should also be given to indirect competition, such as content freely available on the internet.

New titles are the frontlist; established titles the backlist

Frontlist/backlist potential

Is the book expected to have a short life on the *frontlist*, or does it have the potential to *backlist* for a long period? If the former, the commercial opportunity needs to be sizeable.

Packaging and price

What is the best combination of packaging and price for the project? This covers word length, illustration content, size, binding style (if print) and production quality, the likely cost and the price ranges within which it could be sold in different physical and digital formats. *Digital first* could be considered for books which should reach the market quickly; *digital only* might suit a short text or a journalistic approach. The popularity of the *New Yorker* short story, *Cat Person* by Kristen Roupenian, led to book publication in 2018 for a 4,000-word tale – packaged as a 72-page book.

Investment and return

How much time and money needs to be expended on acquiring the book, such as the size of advance expected by the agent, and on developing and marketing it through to publication, in relation to its expected earnings and profitability? Would its earning power justify its place on the list? Sometimes a project may be too small in scale to be worth pursuing. Alternatively it may be worth investing in a new market where the number of readers is likely to grow, enhancing the brand of the publisher.

Risk and innovation

What are the external factors at play affecting the risk investment, such as the timing of publication in relation to the optimum time to publish, the link to topical events and their perceived popularity, and the actions of competitors? What is the downside if the expectations are not realized? To what extent is the project experimental in terms of taking on a new author, or publishing in a new area or format (print or digital), or price? Without taking risks and innovating, the publisher is overtaken by competitors.

Approval process

Some ideas are rejected by the editor, especially after unfavourable reports. Some authors are asked to resubmit in the light of the editor's suggestions. If an editor wants to take forward a project, they cannot offer a contract without the agreement of senior management. Editors sound out and lobby senior colleagues, such as the marketing and sales managers, over possible prices and sales forecasts, and the production manager over production costs. For a major investment, such as a large advance, the finance director will be consulted. The editor prepares a publishing proposal form, which covers the scope of the book, its format, its market and competition, readers' reports, publication date, and the reasons for publication. A costing or financial statement sets out the expected sales revenue, the costs of producing the book and the proposed royalties to the author, in order to show the hoped-for profit margin – provided the book sells out. For standard formats there may be a set of production scales that feeds into the costing form. Different combinations of prices and sales forecasts, and of production costs and royalties may be tried – they will reveal differing margins.

Many publishers hold formal editorial meetings at which the senior management hear editors' proposals – a lot are accepted, but some are referred back or rejected. Editors have to be prepared to pitch their proposal and demonstrate their wholehearted commitment. Tom Maschler writes:

> To publish well the publisher must be passionate about the book for its own sake . . . Once the choice is made the task begins. It is to transmit one's conviction first within the publishing house and then to the outside world. (2005, page 282)

If given the green light, the editor negotiates the contract with the author or agent (see Chapter 5), agrees or invents the book's title, and on commissioned books ensures that the author appreciates what is expected (e.g. content, length, deadline). Titling is an important skill. In a crowded book market, unusual or different titles can attract attention, for example, *The Hundred-Year-Old Man Who Climbed Out of the Window and Disappeared* by Jonas Jonasson, *A Gentleman in Moscow* by Amor Towles, or *Lessons in Chemistry* by Bonnie Garmus. This last title was originally going to be called *An Introduction to Chemistry*; the night before the Frankfurt Book Fair her agent Felicity Blunt called the author and said they must change the title because the novel was coming up as non-fiction in databases. There are concept books where the title may drive sales: an example in

The Bookseller's Diagram Prize is awarded each year to the oddest title for a book. Past winners include Bombproof Your Horse, How to Avoid Huge Ships, and The Joy of Sex: Pocket edition

the psychological thriller market is the bestseller *The Couple Next Door* by Shari Lapena. Stephen Hawking's popular science bestseller was originally going to be called *From the Big Bang to Black Holes: A Short History of Time* until 'his editor at Bantam, Peter Guzzardi, turned it round and changed "Short" to "Brief". It was a moment of inspiration that surely helped Hawking amass record sales' (*Guardian*, 14 September 2013). Internet searches drive the need for clear and explanatory titles for specialist titles. Sometimes the book 'does exactly what it says on the tin', such as *How to Run a Marathon* by Vassos Alexander. Some titles work at more than one level: the footballer Frank Lampard's autobiography was called *Totally Frank*; and Steven Norris, the former Conservative transport minister, used the title *Changing Trains*.

When signing up a new fiction writer, the editor may decide on a two- or three-book deal – if the first novel is a hit, the author is already safely under contract for the second novel. There may be an optimum publication date which would maximize sales. The book may be topical or need to be published for the Christmas market. In the case of textbooks, bound copies will be needed for inspection by teachers in time for the details to be added to the relevant reading lists – ideally they should be published by March – May at the latest.

NEW TITLE COSTING

Successful publishing is founded on contracting good books that sell, and each new book is a business in its own right contributing to the business as a whole. The decision to publish is the crux of the whole enterprise. If mistakes are made here, all efforts of management to control overheads will come to nothing. Books which fail to achieve their target sales and profitability must be counterbalanced by equal profits from other books which exceed their target.

In order to gain approval for a project, editors must prepare a costing – a profit and loss form – to prove the book's profitability. There are varying degrees of sophistication in this process, and electronic templates are now in widespread use. What is important, however, is to understand the principles behind a new title costing. The editor is not simply finding out a cost for the book, but comparing revenue and costs to maximize profitability, while working within the price constraints of the market and the formats chosen.

Net sales revenue

The publisher's net sales revenue (NSR) – also called the net receipts – is the sum of money the publisher receives after the trade discounts have been deducted. For example, a book with a recommended price of £20.00 may be sold to bookshops by the publisher at an average discount of 50 per cent. The bookshop will pay the publisher £10.00 for the book, and this is the net sales revenue for one copy.

In order to calculate the total revenue for a book, a sales forecast needs to be made. If a book is overpriced, few copies will be sold and the total revenue will

Price:	£20.00
Average discount:	50 per cent
Net sales revenue:	£10.00

Note: a more realistic discount for a trade title is 60 per cent, giving NSR of £8.00 but for simplicity the example uses 50 per cent.

be low. If a book is priced too low, the opportunity will be missed to maximize the income for a title. The art is to price the book competitively within the market, thereby maximizing sales and the total revenue. There is a more detailed discussion of pricing in Chapter 9.

The sales forecast is related to a time period. Publishers print stock sufficient for a limited period only (6 to 12 months, or for mass-market paperbacks only a few months) in order to minimize the cash outlay, costs of storage and the risk of overprinting. The planned life of a hardback may only be one sales season before the book goes into paperback – it will simply stop selling when the paperback appears. Judging the print run is a difficult art. Keeping the run low may lead to lost sales if a title is selling fast; raising the run may lead to overstocks which cannot be sold. The latter approach runs the higher risk. Ebooks offer a flexible option for satisfying the market, and when in 2013 the author of the recently published *The Cuckoo's Calling*, Robert Galbraith, was unmasked as J. K. Rowling, the immediate spike in sales was of the ebook (only a few thousand print copies had been manufactured). A US bookstore owner said: 'People who can't get it as a book are going to run and get it as an e-book. By the time the [print] books are back, two weeks from now, most people are going to have read it on some device' (*New York Times*, 16 July 2013).

While each book is sold at many discounts, according to the customer and sales channel, an average discount can be derived by working out the likely orders from different types of customer or territory. Estimates may be gathered from the sales departments or overseas branches. The ways in which an international publisher trades within the constituent parts of its group vary and depend upon in which territory it is advantageous to declare profits for taxation and shareholder benefit. For instance, by transfer pricing they may sell internally a UK-originated book to their sister US firm at a very high discount thereby increasing the profit in the USA.

Costs

The costs of producing a book usually come under two headings. The fixed costs are incurred before the printing presses roll and do not change whatever the quantity of books ordered. They may include:

- sums paid to external readers, translators, or contributors
- legal fees, for example, if the book needs to be read for libel
- permission fees for the use of third-party copyright material (text and illustrations, cover image), unless paid for by the author

- payments to freelance copy-editors, proofreaders, illustrators, and designers (for both text and the cover)
- indexing, if not done by the author, although this charge may be put against the author's royalties
- payments to suppliers for typesetting, file conversion, origination of illustrations, proofing, corrections.

The *variable* costs occur after the presses start to roll and depend on the quantity of books ordered. They include the costs of printing and binding, and the paper consumed. The quantity ordered would be the sales estimate plus an allowance for copies wasted or gratis copies given away, for example for review purposes. The total production costs are the sum of the fixed costs and the variable costs. Ebooks incur little by way of direct variable costs, and the cost of a digital copy approaches zero, but there are still the fixed costs to be covered (and any relevant sales tax to be paid). Publishers may regard the income from ebook sales as additional revenue, or try and work out what share of fixed costs should be borne by the digital edition.

The average cost of producing each print copy, the unit cost, is calculated by dividing the total costs by the print quantity. The unit cost diminishes with increasing print quantities, falling rapidly on short printings of between, say, 500 to 2,500 copies and then more slowly. The rapid decline in unit cost results from the fixed costs being spread over larger quantities. Although the per copy cost of producing the book becomes progressively lower with increasing quantities, the overall total cost still increases. Therein lies the danger for editors preparing a costing: the temptation is to reduce the unit cost by increasing the print quantity – but if the books are not sold, the publisher has sunk an even greater amount of cash into the book's production.

In the late 1990s Dorling Kindersley printed 13 m copies of its Star Wars titles – sales only reached around 3 m

The author's royalties are calculated by applying the different royalty rates to the sales forecasts for home and export markets. A costing prepared before a contract has been signed with the author will show suggested royalty rates for the title. The royalty may be based on the book's price or on the net sales revenue – the sums actually received by the publisher. To carry on with the earlier example:

Recommended price: £20.00
Average discount: 50 per cent
Net sales revenue: £10.00

If the royalty is 10 per cent of the published price, the author would receive 10 per cent of £20.00: £2.00 on each copy sold. If the royalty is 10 per cent of the net sales revenue, the author would receive 10 per cent of £10.00: £1.00 on each copy sold. A publisher looking to reduce their costs would work with royalties based on the net sales revenue. The author may not necessarily agree with this approach or even understand the difference. A good agent would push hard for the best deal.

Gross and net profit

The *gross profit* is what is left after the unit cost and royalty have been deducted from the net sales revenue.

Net sales revenue:	£10.00
Unit cost:	£4.00
Royalty to the author (10 per cent of NSR):	£1.00
Gross profit:	£5.00
Gross margin:	50 per cent

The *gross margin* is the percentage of the net sales revenue that forms the gross profit. In the above example, the gross profit forms 50 per cent of the revenue (this calculation for all products gives the gross profit in the company accounts in Chapter 4). The management may say to their editors, 'We want to see each publishing proposal attaining a minimum gross margin of 55 to 60 per cent.' That percentage represents the sum of money the publisher would have left after the production costs and royalties have been deducted from the NSR, provided all the copies were sold. The sum would, in theory, be sufficient to recover the overheads and expenses and to provide a net profit. The publisher's overall net profit is the sum left after all the costs of running the business have been deducted (again see the company accounts). Overheads for a publisher would include the costs of salaries, marketing and sales, warehouse and fulfilment, online platforms, general administration, office space, heating, lighting, and other items such as bank interest and bad debt.

The editor strives to balance the income and costs so that the desired gross profit is attained. This is called *value engineering*. If the gross profit is too low, the production costs could be trimmed (fewer pages, fewer illustrations, cheaper paper) or the author's proposed royalties reduced. Conversely, the price and/or sales estimate could be increased. But while the publisher worries about costs and margins, the end-user is concerned with price and perceived value, and does not care about the costs, the number printed or the author's effort. Reducing the production values on a book, for example by using cheaper paper or fewer colours for the cover, may harm the book's sales. The market for special editions of brand authors depends on high production values including endpapers, foiling on the cover and sprayed edges. Decisions will be made according to the type of publishing and the expectations of the market – which are high in some markets like art or cookery books. For an editor publishing a book with a limited market, there remains the fatal temptation to imagine a non-existent larger market and to increase the print-run in order to lower the unit cost.

When the publisher takes the final decision on fixing the price and print quantity, the fixed costs have already been incurred and cannot be changed. On account of the uncertainties of estimating demand, a prudent publisher favours a higher price and a lower quantity rather than a lower price and a higher quantity. If the actual demand for the book is less than expected, a price on the high side may still return a profit, whereas too low a price could lead to substantial loss. The great dangers are underestimating costs, overestimating demand, and underpricing. This leads not only to a loss on the individual book, but also can wipe out the profit on others. Successful books can always be reprinted, but at a price and quantity which again are chosen to avoid loss. Ebook editions can soak up surplus demand, and their prices can be adjusted almost in real time. If a book is likely to be added to the backlist, there may be an argument for accepting a lower than usual gross margin on the first printing, on the grounds that a reprint will have a much healthier margin. The first printing of a school textbook may attain no profit, but the hoped-for second and subsequent printings should move it into profitability. Also hardbacks can perhaps tolerate a lower gross margin, since the ebook or follow-on paperback will not have the production fixed costs to bear. A quirky trade title with no certainty of making the backlist, such as *The Book of Bunny Suicides* or *50 Sheds of Grey*, has to make its money straight away.

Other factors affecting the pre-publication decision concern the level of investment at risk, for example very high authors' advances or a large investment in a major textbook, and its duration. Several combinations of price and sales forecast print run may be tried out, including 'worst case scenarios', and the *break-even* may be calculated. A project's break-even point is the minimum quantity that must be sold to cover the production costs and the author's advance or royalty. Also included might be a proportion of the company's overheads. On some proposals, if the break-even is considered attainable, that may inspire sufficient confidence to go ahead. Some publishers calculate a project's cashflow and the interest incurred over time. From the outset to after publication, the publisher usually endures a net loss before the income surpasses the outlay. The estimated income is derived from the sales forecasts broken down over time (e.g. monthly, quarterly and yearly). Possible rights sales income, other than that from co-edition deals, usually does not enter into the early costings and thus can be regarded as extra profit. However, it may be included, especially when needed to justify paying the author a large advance.

Some publishers stop their calculations at the gross profit line while others continue and deduct direct overheads expressed as overall percentages (e.g. for editorial and marketing or sales and distribution) to reach the *net profit*. The way in which overheads are apportioned, either as actual sums or percentages, varies (see the indicative percentages in Chapter 4). To continue with our example:

Net sales revenue:	£10.00
Unit cost:	£4.00
Royalty to the author:	£1.00
Gross profit:	£5.00
Gross margin:	50 per cent
Editorial and marketing overheads (15%):	£1.50
Sales, platform and distribution overheads (15%):	£1.50
Net profit (gross profit less overheads):	£2.00
Net profit margin (as percentage of NSR):	20 per cent

The problems with the method as outlined above are that titles are allocated overheads in proportion to expected revenue (which may not accord with reality). It also focuses attention on a desired percentage rather than money, for example, a title with a 25 per cent gross margin may yet deliver much more cash than one with a 55 per cent gross margin. It is important therefore to look at the total sums involved, and not just concentrate on the percentages. A costing should also include a column showing the totals received and paid out: revenue, costs and royalties.

Recommended price:	£20.00
Average discount:	50 per cent
Net sales revenue:	£10.00
Unit cost:	£4.00
Royalty to the author:	£1.00
Gross profit:	£5.00
Gross margin:	50 per cent
Total number of copies required:	10,000
Copies sold:	9,500
Total NSR:	£95,000
Total production costs:	£40,000
Royalties due to the author:	£9,500
Gross profit:	£45,500

In the above example, the royalties are calculated on the sales, but in order to secure the book a much larger advance might have to be paid to the author. This sum is paid even if the book's sales are disappointing. If the advance paid to the author against royalties was £15,000, the overall cash surplus would be reduced by £5,500. A full costing should not only allow provision for copies given away free or gratis (as above), but also for returns from booksellers (the percentage can reach 20 per cent for consumer titles), and so should not assume that all copies are sold. A complete costing could show income from the ebook or paperback edition and projected rights income. Preparing a separate costing for an ebook is possible since they are mostly sold on the same wholesale model as for print (a discount is given against the recommended price), and there is broad agreement that royalties are paid on the net sales revenue. But the calculation is complicated by the question of what costs to apply – the marginal cost of an ebook is close to zero – and for simplicity many publishers load all fixed costs against the print edition.

Mark-up method

An alternative costing approach is the mark-up method. This traditional and simple method is severely criticized but can be used as a ready-reckoner. The unit cost is derived from dividing the quantity of books to be ordered expected to be sold into the total production costs. This is then multiplied by a factor (say, 5–8 for a trade title) to arrive at the published price. The accounts department calculate for editors the factors pertaining to different kinds of books (e.g. consumer or academic) with different royalty rates and discounts. Provided the copies sell out, the factor accommodates the firm's costs and profit. But if the published price is thought to be too high, the editor is tempted to increase the forecast print run to lower the unit cost in order to arrive, by multiplication, at a reasonable price. Conversely, the publisher may print the number it believes it can sell but fixes the price too high to absorb that number. Unless careful, the publisher ends up with unsold copies or loss-makers. The method, based on a predetermined level of activity, disregards the fact that costs do not act alike as output increases or decreases. It encourages rigid pricing and conceals assumptions. Worse, it focuses attention on the unit cost and away from the market and price elasticities.

The method can be used in reverse. The gross retail value (price multiplied by sales estimate) is divided by the factor to arrive at the desired unit cost. The book's specification could then be adjusted to match.

The use of a mark-up factor often occurs when consumer book publishers buy books from packagers. A mark-up factor (say, 6–7) is applied to the packager's all-in, royalty-inclusive, price per copy to arrive at a published price. If the publisher is translating and resetting a title, the mark-up could be 5 or 6.

Open access cost plus method

Some open access monographs are published by charging the funder of the book a book processing charge (BPC). The publisher provides a service to the funder and typically uses the cost plus method to arrive at price to be charged to the funder. All the costs in acquiring, producing, marketing and distributing the book (including the allocation of overheads) are determined, and a percentage for profit (or surplus) is added to arrive at the BPC.

Commissioning

SKILLS

No editor can simply sit back and expect marketable ideas and authors to flow in. Editors need to be creative in that they encourage and develop received ideas – or initiate ideas themselves and match them to authors. Inevitably these lead to false trails, so editors have to be agile enough to hunt the front-runners, ruthless enough to weed out the wrong projects, and tough enough to withstand their exposed position within the publishing house. Editors need a knowledge of production methods (limitations and costs), digital opportunities, and contracts, and the skill to negotiate with authors, agents and others. As the book's champion, the editor must display infectious enthusiasm and superb persuasive skills. Robert Gottlieb says, 'Publishing is the business of conveying your own honest enthusiasm for a book and a writer to the rest of the world' (2016, page 318). An editor's strength in marketing the book, in-house and externally, is imperative, and today extends to creating an audience for a book ahead of publication through the use of social media.

Publishing is a business, and it is vital that editors have financial acumen. Profitable publishing also depends on a perception of trends in markets and timing. Good editors pre-empt competitors – in textbook publishing the lead time can easily be three years. In specialist fields the work involves asking experts the right questions and being able to talk to them intelligently. The skill lies in choosing the right advisers and readers. The consumer book editors, who face great difficulty in ascertaining market needs, base their judgements on a combination of experience of what sells, having a finger on the pulse, and intuition. Robert Gottlieb again: 'Every book has its own potential readership – figure it out and reach for it, don't try to sell every book to everyone' (2016, page 318).

Backing one's own hunches takes considerable audacity and confidence, and the stakes can be high. Without a reasonable hit rate, they run the risk of losing their job.

Fundamental to book and author selection is the editor's ability to assess the quality of the proposal and of the author's writing and purpose. This critical faculty is underpinned by skills in speed reading and sampling sections of writing. Most editors will be able to assess a manuscript from the first few pages, and this skill develops with experience. Editors should be able to contribute to structural improvements, and in specialist areas appear to the author not merely as a cipher for expert readers' comments.

Authors are engaged in long spells of isolation when writing with little else to draw on but experience, knowledge and imagination. In their books rest their hopes and dreams. In their eyes the editor is exclusive to them; to the editor an author is one of many. Authors expect editors to represent their interests in-house, to get things done and so judge editors on their level of clout. Conversely editors must represent the best interests of the publisher to authors – at times a fine juggling act. Good editors persuade authors to write, often plead with them to deliver, and foster author loyalty to the house. Authors need encouragement, reassurance and praise – that, and the editor's diplomacy, are vital. Those authors who rely on their books for income (unlike teachers, or academics) centre their whole life around their writing. To some, an editor becomes inseparable from their private lives.

SUCCESS AND FAILURE

Generally speaking, publishers make very little net profit from their new book publishing programme over the first year. Their profits stem from the titles that continue to sell strongly. That said, a Christmas bestseller can still make a large sum of money, as can a title timed to coincide with a sporting event or anniversary. If a book continues to sell and the publisher has recovered all its development and marketing costs from the first printing, the gross margin and net profit increase dramatically. With the advent of digital printing and ebooks, publishers are able to lower their level of risk regarding stock. They can keep an extensive list of titles in print and respond to demand without incurring significant warehousing costs.

A vigorous and profitable publisher is in a strong position to publish books which, it is estimated at the outset, will not show a profit; indeed, there may be good publishing reasons for doing so. A book could be published for prestige purposes. A fiction publisher may believe in a novelist's long-term ultimate success, or want the author's next more desirable book. A textbook publisher may want to enter a new area and undercut competitors. A university press may be obliged to publish a great scholarly work – sometimes supported by a subsidy or grant.

Publishing is a high margin business and can be immensely profitable, but for many publishers those profits prove to be a mirage. Some authors

With the growth of digital printing, small numbers can be reprinted much more easily and this model has spread across all sectors of book publishing fail to deliver their manuscripts or submit unacceptable material. Publishers have forecast budgets and if a proposed book is not published, the estimated contribution needs to be recouped from elsewhere. It is relatively easier for a consumer book publisher to fill its list more quickly, for example, by buying from agents or from another company abroad, than a school textbook publisher. However, the consumer publishers, which pay significant sums on signature of contract, will find the advances impossible to recover if the level of sales is disappointing. All the decisions regarding the quality of a book, its market, price and sales potential are based on advance subjective judgements. Amongst the new books there inevitably lurk those that will fail to recover their production costs or the author's advance, let alone make a contribution to overheads.

Now read this

Robert Gottlieb, *Avid Reader*, Farrar, Straus and Giroux, 2016.

Sources

Diana Athill, *Stet*, Granta, 2000.
Tom Maschler, *Publisher*, Picador, 2005.
Daniel Menaker, *My Mistake*, Houghton Mifflin Harcourt, 2013.
John B. Thompson, *Merchants of Culture*, 2012.
Thomas Woll, *Publishing for Profit*, 5th edition, Chicago Review Press, 2014.

CHAPTER 7

The author contract and editorial development

Once the costing for a new title has been agreed and the book receives the green light, a contract is drawn up with the author. This chapter examines the author contract and the editor's continuing role in shaping and developing the project. Agreeing the right contract is of benefit to the author and helps to ensure the book's profitability; and a successful working relationship with the author throughout the book's development is crucial to the book's quality and commercial success.

AUTHOR CONTRACT

Each publisher – as the buyer of rights from an author – draws up its own contract, also called the agreement. The contract differs according to the book and the author, but most publishers operate with standard contracts. Commissioning editors negotiate contracts with authors or their agents, and can then adjust the standard contract to fit the final terms agreed. The publisher is usually in a position to weight the contract in their favour. Some authors sign the contract that is offered; others, or their agents, will try to improve the royalty rates and advance offered, or ask for changes to particular clauses, which may have to be reviewed by the publisher's legal department or outsourced to a contract specialist. Alternatively the agent will present their own contract to the editor.

The contract formally defines the relationship between author and publisher. Today's publishing contract can be a lengthy document as the publisher seeks to secure as many rights as possible, and the obligations of both parties are set out in detail. The full acquisition of rights will prevent problems that may occur, whether in selling a book around the world or its exploitation as a digital product. It will also maximize the income from licensing a range of rights to third parties. Although it is unlikely that a book will be turned into merchandised goods such as tea towels and duvet covers, it did happen with Edith Holden's *The Country Diary of an Edwardian Lady* and Flora Thompson's *Lark Rise to Candleford* – many years after they were first written or published.

DOI: 10.4324/9781003403289-8

A verbal agreement can be sufficient to form a contract

A contract is usually a legal document signed by both parties – the author and the representative of the publisher. The following requirements are seen as important for an enforceable contract (Jones and Benson, 2016, page 96):

■   a clear agreement,
■   an intention to be legally bound by it, and
■   some valuable consideration to seal the bargain.

If these requirements are in place, a verbal agreement may be enough to form a contract. This was highlighted by the case of *Malcolm v. OUP* (1991), when an editor offered assurances over the telephone to the author that they would publish his book. The book was later turned down by the publisher, but in court it was revealed that the author was tape recording the conversations. The court ruled in favour of the author, who was awarded significant compensation. Since that case, editors have been cautious about giving verbal agreement to publish, and most companies have tightened up their procedures so that deals are subject to a final written contract. It is rare, however, for disputes between the author and their publisher to reach court, and there is little case law in existence.

Main elements of the contract

Outlined below are the items covered in a typical contract between the author and the publisher. Of main interest to the author will be the level of the royalty and any advance. Other clauses open to argument or negotiation include any option on the author's next work, royalties for new editions (should they be increased?), payment for the index or illustrations (does the author or publisher bear the cost?), and the number of free copies for the author.

Preamble

The date, names of the parties (their assigns and successors in business) to the contract, and the title of the 'Work' (the book's provisional title) are stated.

Author's grant

The author usually grants to the publisher the sole and exclusive licence and right to publish the book (the 'Work') in volume form (print and electronic), in all languages, for the full term of copyright (author's life plus 70 years), throughout the world. By granting a licence, the author retains ownership of the copyright. Some authors, such as contributors to multi-authored books or to highly illustrated general books, assign their copyright, thereby passing ownership and all control to the publisher. The grant of electronic rights may include 'the right to publish or license the publication of the Work in all formats now known or later invented', or other similar phrase, to cover the publisher against future technological developments. Authors may be asked to give the right for their text to be used to train generative AI.

Author's warranty

The author warrants that they control the rights granted, that the work is original (not plagiarism), does not contain defamatory, libellous or unlawful matter; and will indemnify the publisher for any loss or damages. Few publishers check for plagiarism and most run the risk of a scandal if issues are discovered after publication. Frederick Studemann writes:

> 'Nobody really fact-checks,' is a common, if surprising, response you hear from publishers. Several publishers, big and small, that I spoke to this week in New York, London and Germany all said that if they had to check everything they would not be able to function. 'It's easier to fact-check a 2,000-word piece of journalism than a book of 150,000 words,' says Andrew Franklin of Profile Books. (*Financial Times*, 4 November 2023)

Competing works

The author agrees not to write a directly competing work for another publisher.

Typescript

The contract will detail the length of the typescript (preferably in words not pages), the date and form of delivery (typically double spaced, in Microsoft Word, and electronically). It will also cover the author's responsibility for supplying illustrations and the index, and for obtaining and paying for third-party copyright material (unless otherwise agreed). The publisher reserves the right not to publish if the delivered manuscript is overdue or does not conform to a previously agreed brief.

Corrections

The author is constrained from making extensive corrections to the proofs – other than those attributable to the publisher or printer – and is charged if author's corrections exceed a specified percentage (say 15 per cent) of the cost of typesetting. The author must return proofs within a certain period, usually two to three weeks.

Publication

The publisher solely controls the publication – production, design, publicity, price, methods and conditions of sale. In practice, authors may be consulted on matters such as the cover design; they may request that the contract stipulates that the cover image is not to be generated using AI. The author is given a number of free or gratis copies (typically six) and may purchase more at a discount.

Payments to the author

On the publisher's own editions, the author is normally paid a royalty expressed either as a percentage of an edition's recommended published price on all copies sold (common in consumer publishing); or as a percentage of the publisher's net receipts, i.e. the sum of money received by the publisher after discounts have been deducted (common in non-consumer publishing). The author's earnings are thus proportional to price (or net receipts) and sales. Royalty rates are quoted for each of the publisher's own-produced editions: hardback, paperback, and ebook; and sales made in the traditional home market (the UK and Ireland), and in export markets. Export rates are usually lower to take account of the higher discounts involved. As more publishers do their own audiobooks, having a royalty rate agreed is important.

A scale of royalties rising by steps of 2 to 2.5 per cent when certain quantities have been sold may be included, especially on home market sales. Royalty rates on the published price can range from 5 to 15 per cent (many authors never surpass the lower base rates). If an author has reached a higher rate on a scale (whether based on the published price or net receipts), and a new edition is produced, the royalty reverts to the base rate. When the book is remaindered, no royalties may be paid. Other provisos where lower royalties apply are stated. If royalties are based on the published price, for example, the rate applied may be reduced or based on net receipts if the publisher sells the book to a large retail chain at a high discount of say 52.5 per cent or above. A lower royalty rate may also apply to small reprints. The royalties paid on ebook sales range from the rate payable on the printed book up to the industry norm for trade books of 25 per cent of net receipts. The percentage of net receipts for audio is likely to match the rate paid for the ebook.

Subsidiary rights

The contract lists further rights granted to the publisher, which it could license to other firms, and the percentages payable (from 50 up to 90 per cent) to the author on the publisher's net receipts from the sales of those subsidiary rights. Agents will be keen to reserve subsidiary rights in order to sell them separately. If the publisher is granted under the contract US and translation rights, for example, the firms to which these rights could be licensed may print their own editions and pay royalties to the publisher to be shared with the author. However, the publisher may print bulk quantities, for example, for a co-edition partner. The publisher sells such copies at a high discount (up to 80 per cent) and the author's royalty may be based on the actual sums received (a common rate is 10 per cent). There are many other rights such as serial and extract rights; dramatization rights for stage, film, television and radio; broadcast reading rights; quotation and anthology; large print; digest condensation; and digital publishing rights, including games. There is a fuller discussion of rights in Chapter 11.

Accounting

The publisher's accounting period to the author is usually six months for general books and a year for educational and academic books, with settlement up to three to four months after. Consumer book publishers normally withhold a proportion of royalties payable in an accounting period as a reserve against subsequent returns of unsold books from retailers.

Revisions and new editions

The author agrees to revise the book when requested or to permit others to do so at the author's expense.

Reversion

The rights may revert to the author if on request the publisher fails to keep the work in print. The reversion of rights has become more complicated – print on demand and the ebook mean that a book need never go out of print. Many agents would insert a clause to ensure that the level of sale (by units or revenue) should be the determinant of whether rights can be reverted. By contrast many academic authors are only too pleased to have their works available indefinitely.

Arbitration

Arbitration may be necessary in the case of a dispute between the author and the publisher.

Option

The author may give the publisher the right of first refusal on their next book.

Moral rights

These are covered in Chapter 4.

Advance

An advance, if paid, is set against the author's future royalties. It is important to note that the advance has to be earned out before the author receives further payments for the book. Most authors receive either a small advance – up to £10,000 for a two-book deal in the case of a first-time novelist – or none at all. Big advances tend to make the headlines in the trade and sometimes the national press, for example when the Obamas received a reported advance of $65 m for two books:

> Assuming, then, that PRH did spend $65 million on both books, the publisher has a number of ways to make back its money, and then some. Industry members are confident both books will do well in hardcover, trade paperback, ebook, and audio. With Barack Obama's new book, PRH has a title that will likely be an instant bestseller and will also become a backlist mainstay. It also has the potential to become a popular choice for course adoption. (*Publishers Weekly*, 3 March 2017)

Advance payments may be staged, with separate payments on signature of the contract, delivery of an acceptable manuscript, and on publication.

In 1996 Random House in New York sued Joan Collins in an attempt to retrieve an advance paid to her of $1.3 m for two novels. It alleged that the manuscripts she delivered were unpublishable. The star of *Dynasty* won the case since the original contract only said that the manuscript should be 'complete' not satisfactory.

Publishers may seek other reasons for the cancellation of a contract and in the light of the #MeToo movement and unsavoury stories about authors appearing in the press, some publishers now seek a morality clause in a contract. 'Morality, or morals, contracts have existed in the film industry since 1921, when Universal Pictures introduced them in response to Fatty Arbuckle's trial for manslaughter, but they are relatively new in the publishing industry' (*Guardian*, 13 June 2018). Such clauses are controversial and many agents will resist their inclusion.

> Publishing executives insist that in an era when social media can unravel a reputation overnight, their ability to market a book can evaporate just as quickly. Many agents and authors, on the other hand, see the clauses as dangerously subjective, allowing publishers to dump a project based on their own assessment of a writer's conduct. (*New York Times*, 11 February 2021)

Signatures of the parties

The author and the nominated representative of the publisher will sign at least two copies of the agreement, and one copy will be kept by the author. The signature of the contract is the trigger for allocating an ISBN to the title, and the editor's dispatch to the author of the author questionnaire for marketing purposes.

Electronic rights

The publisher's 'volume rights' or 'primary rights' encompass print and electronic. Some of the far-sighted educational, academic and STM book publishers included electronic rights in their contracts with authors during the 1990s, even in the 1980s. By the twenty-first century many of the main publishers had secured electronic rights from authors on thousands of old contracts which had made no previous provision. The learned journal publishers are also free to publish electronically since contributing authors often assign their rights to the publisher, or society. Similarly, many of the book packagers and highly illustrated publishers own the copyright in the texts they publish, and in the commissioned artwork and photography, through assignments.

This issue of who owns electronic rights in backlist titles was highlighted in the USA by the case of *Random House, Inc. v. Rosetta Books* 2001, in which it was ruled that the publisher did not automatically hold ebook rights, even if it was granted the right to publish a work in book form, and if the rights were not specifically granted in the contract they were retained by the author. The inclusion of third-party material – text extracts or photographs – is sometimes an impediment to the epublishing of the backlist and of new books. The rights holders, whether publishers or picture agencies, can be resistant to granting electronic rights or will charge exorbitant fees – in effect a refusal.

Impact of agents

Where the author has an agent, the contract used may be provided by the agent weighted in their client's favour. The agent's contract typically is shorter than one from a publisher, reflecting the more limited grant of rights by the author. So-called boilerplate agreements – standard contracts – are used with the leading publishers, avoiding wrangles over the wording of standard clauses. Agents may opt to withhold many of the subsidiary rights (to them they are not subsidiary), such as serial, audio and translation, preferring either to sell the rights themselves or to negotiate if the publisher proposes a deal later. The decision may also be taken to divide up the English language territories, selling UK and US rights separately. For sought-after books the traditional view is that this should yield a higher income for the author. However, a large advance in return for world rights may trump this approach.

The death of territoriality?

Traditionally, the UK and US publishers (especially consumer) were in separate ownership and divided the world English book market between them. For books published on both sides of the Atlantic, the UK and US publishers sought exclusive market areas (closed markets) from which the other's competing editions of the same book are excluded. The US publisher's exclusive territory was essentially the USA; the UK publisher's the Commonwealth, Ireland and South Africa and a few others. The remaining areas were then non-exclusive to either – called the open market, such as mainland Europe – where UK and US editions of the same book were in direct competition. Canadian rights were exclusively retained by UK publishers on their own originated books, and by US publishers on theirs. A mainstream publisher is keen to secure world rights for a book but for some titles a broad division persists and can affect the way agents and packagers grant rights to publishers, and how publishers trade books between themselves. For example, the two separate arms of a large consumer publisher, in London and New York, may bid separately for the same title, since the rights have been divided up by the agent. A UK publisher that holds world rights can either sell its own edition into the USA through its related US firm, or license the rights to a US publisher, in which case the US publisher's exclusive, non-exclusive, and excluded territories would be negotiated. Conversely a UK publisher may buy a US-originated book from a US publisher or author represented by an agent, and its rights and territories would also be carefully defined.

This traditional territorial split in English language publishing of exclusive, non-exclusive (open market) and excluded territories is threatened by actions of governments, consumer pressure groups and internet traders. For example, Singapore legislated itself into the open market in the mid-1980s. From 1991 Australia required local publication to occur within 30 days of first publication anywhere in the world, if the local edition is to preserve its exclusivity. This measure was designed to encourage domestic publishing and boost the earnings of local authors. In 1998 New Zealand declared itself an open market. Meanwhile the availability of books from online booksellers is breaking down the influence of territoriality, with competing international editions visible to consumers. On the internet, the consumers' choice of bookseller is affected by the cost of shipping a physical book and the timing. The major internet booksellers in the UK have agreed to list only the UK edition, based on territorial rights supplied by Nielsen BookData. The presence of ebooks, often available instantaneously at a lower price, changes the equation and the consumer will also be choosing on format and device.

Whilst the UK was part of the EU, UK publishers were able to argue that the economic and political area should be treated as a single market and that it should be the exclusive territory of UK publishers. However, the UK's departure from the EU through Brexit weakened the ability of UK publishers to secure exclusive rights in Europe, undermining the argument that the UK should be considered part of Europe. It is still possible for UK publishers to buy exclusive rights in Europe but an agent may be faced with (and tempted by) the offer of a large advance for US rights with the request for Europe to be an open market (with the US publisher having non-exclusive rights). This in turn raises the fear that the UK will see cheaper US editions imported from mainland Europe. The technical issue of copyright exhaustion is also of importance – where the publisher's edition can be resold. The UK's exhaustion regime has largely protected publishers from the unauthorized importing of their own international editions, perhaps priced differently to local markets, back into the home market.

The answer to the thorny issue of territorial rights is for the publisher to acquire world rights from the author. This is easier to do in some sectors of publishing, such as educational and academic. Most of the major UK and US consumer book publishers are in common ownership and aim to be strong enough to acquire exclusive world English language rights in authors' works. This enables them to overcome legislative difficulties anywhere in the world and ameliorates any 'buying around' practices of third-party traders. However, many authors' agents still believe that they can secure better offers from different international publishers by dividing exclusive territorial rights amongst competing publishers. The collapse of territorial rights is not a foregone conclusion given the opposition from many agents.

Apart from price differentials between competing editions (which are influenced by £–$ exchange rates with the Euro and other currencies), there is also an issue around the date of release of different editions of the same title. US and UK consumer book publishers deploy the strategy of maximizing earnings through the sequential publication of a particular book in different formats and prices. For example, first publication would be in a higher priced hardback, followed by a trade paperback and a smaller-format, mass-market paperback edition. In export markets, especially the growing mainland European market, UK and US publishers will aim to pre-empt the other's competing edition in paperback while maintaining their home markets for a period exclusively in hardback. Hence UK export editions of paperbacks are available earlier on mainland Europe than in the UK, and can be bought on the airside of UK airports. Mainland European paperback importers may hedge their bets by simultaneously ordering their stock from both US and UK publishers to ensure they receive stock from whichever is the earliest. Importers also compare the prices of competing editions, and scout around for bargain-priced editions. Ebooks can quickly penetrate markets across Europe and their low prices impact on the sale of print and local translations.

PRODUCT DEVELOPMENT

Once a book has been commissioned from an author and the contract has been signed, it needs to be monitored while it is being written, and planning begins for the editing, design and production stages that are interlinked with the book's marketing. Books need differing levels of care and attention during their development. Commissioning editors may await the completed text of a novel or biography. Some authors like editors to read chapter drafts while the writing is in progress. The legendary New York editor Robert Gottlieb (1931–2023) stressed the value of a quick turnaround when reading drafts from authors, making both agents and authors happy:

I didn't do it in order to score points, though; I just couldn't restrain my curiosity. Besides, why put off reading a manuscript or doing an editorial job? You're going to have do it sooner or later, and it doesn't take more time to do it right away than after putting it off for whatever neurotic reason. (2016, page 122)

For textbook and reference projects especially, attention will be paid to word length, any co-ordination necessary if there are a number of contributors, and the use of templates during the writing process, which can help with the tagging vital for digital editions. Authors may deliver the complete manuscript on time or late, an inherent trait of many authors. The non-deliverer may have their contract cancelled. The delivered manuscript is checked for length, completeness and quality – and for any sensitivities around libel or third party content. It may be returned for revision, or accepted and passed on for production. The author may be reminded to complete the author's questionnaire which is used for marketing purposes.

Commissioning editors brief and liaise with junior editors, designers, production, marketing and promotion, and sales. Editors may write the blurb for the cover and catalogue entry, with an eye to discoverability by search engines, and may seek endorsements from experts or opinion formers. The copy may also be used as the basis for the book's advance information (AI) sheet – which is needed six to nine months ahead of publication. Although editors have no managerial control over other departments, they endeavour to ensure their books receive due attention. Commissioning editors present their books to the publisher's sales force at the regular sales conferences.

Some editors, especially those involved with complex and highly illustrated books, or major textbook projects involving digital resources, get very involved in the product research and development stages. Commissioning editors may undertake development work themselves, or hand on the work to junior editors, whose job titles could be Editor, Development Editor, Production Editor, Assistant Editor, or Editorial Assistant. Those working across print and electronic products are sometimes called Content Managers or Editors, and the word digital is now added to some traditional job titles. The editor maintains contact with the author so as to plan backwards from the proposed publication date, trying to ensure that the manuscript is delivered in good time to make smooth progress through the production process. A development editor in textbook publishing carries out survey research in association with the marketing department, organizes the external review of drafts, and helps shape the project with the authorial team from conception to completion.

In fiction publishing, an editor may work closely with the author around the development of the story, structure, and characters. When Emily St John Mandel, author of the bestselling *Station Eleven*, delivered her new novel *Glass Hotel*, she was initially shocked by the response:

My first round of editorial notes were really hard. They could be summarised as: please could you change everything, the structure, the characters, the plot. Nothing was working. I probably spent a couple of days crying on the floor of my office and then I got up and started revising. (*Guardian*, 9 April 2022)

Similar developmental editing may be carried out by a literary agent ahead of the delivery of the manuscript by the author to the publisher.

Developmental editing

EXPERT

Scott Pack, freelance editor

A developmental edit, also known as a structural edit, is a thorough and in-depth review of an author's manuscript. It examines all elements of the writing, from individual words and sentences to overall structure and style. In fiction, a developmental edit also addresses issues related to plot, characterization and other key aspects of storytelling.

In practice, a developmental edit involves annotating and correcting the author's manuscript, what we call marking up the manuscript, as well as writing an accompanying editorial report. When it comes to the writing, if a choice of word does not feel right, an editor may highlight it and suggest another. If a sentence is too ambiguous or does not flow well, again the editor can indicate that and offer an alternative. If an entire passage, scene or chapter is not working, a developmental edit will examine why and help to address it. Much of this can be written as margin comments within the manuscript itself.

With the storytelling and overall structure of the manuscript, an editor will consider and make notes on many areas, such as plot, narrative voice, pace, characterization, dialogue, world-building and so on. These will usually be presented in the form of a separate document, a sort of editorial report. Of course, the specific areas examined will depend on whether the book is fiction or non-fiction, the genre and intended audience.

An editor will also look out for any bad habits the author has – do they punctuate speech incorrectly? are there certain words they use more often than necessary? do they slip into a pattern of storytelling, or scene structure, that becomes predictable or repetitive?

These days, most editors will perform a developmental edit on their computer, or other electronic device, and will annotate the text as they go along. They may give the whole book an initial read through, or they might capture their impressions as they read the text for the first time. Whatever their approach, the end result is usually more or less the same – an annotated manuscript, with tracked changes and margin comments, accompanied by a report that explores the key issues and broader topics.

It is worth pointing out that a developmental edit is not the same as a copy-edit. It is not intended to fix typos or punctuation or grammatical issues. Although a developmental editor may pick up on these as they work through the text, it can be a waste of time to actually fix them at this stage, especially if the manuscript is likely to go through some rewrites. Of course, if an author repeatedly makes the same mistake, then an editor will point that out in their report but may not go in and correct each instance.

Finally, as with most editorial functions, the purpose of a developmental edit is to help the author make their work as good as it can be, and as suitable for its intended audience as possible. It is about enhancing the original work through advice and suggestions but it is important that an editor does not impose their own voice on to the text. The end result should be a version of the author's manuscript that achieves what they have set out to do as effectively as possible.

The case of *American Dirt* (2020) by Jeanine Cummins raised questions in the industry about who can tell which stories. A book about Mexican migrants, it was criticized for cultural appropriation because the author is white. Constance Grady wrote:

> Cummins had written a story that was not hers – and, according to many readers of color, she didn't do a very good job of it. In fact, she seemed to fetishize the pain of her characters at the expense of treating them as real human beings. (*Vox*, 30 January 2020)

Editors may be wary about taking on similar books, and also sensitivity readers are asked to work with some authors around issues of gender, race and cultural awareness. Imogen West-Knights writes of the process:

> At root, sensitivity reading is just editing. Before sensitivity readers existed, regular editors might flag elements in a text that they thought were in bad taste, were inaccurate or could be misconstrued. They still do this. But sensitivity readers are able to do it from a position of experience about a particular issue, rather than well-meaning guesswork. (*Financial Times*, 14 April 2023)

In 2023 came the news that Puffin Books was going to release new editions of Roald Dahl's books with the language edited to remove any potentially offensive phrasing. The storm of protest at this development led the publisher to backtrack and keep the original editions available alongside the revised versions. The debate as to how to deal with such issues continues and Niranjana Roy suggested:

> It is understandable that publishers might wish to benefit from their lucrative back catalogues, but there are less intrusive ways to flag language or beliefs that seem outmoded or harmful – through forewords, or back-of-the-book reading guides that can be updated as sensibilities change. Every Dahl has his day, but let readers decide when they're done. (*Financial Times*, 25 February 2023)

At the page-proof stage, the book's price is fixed across formats, as well as the number of physical copies to be printed and bound. The number printed may differ from that envisaged at the outset, and changes may have been made to the format and pricing. This could reflect feedback from major retailers, changes in the market, or a new view on ebook sales or the best way to publish the book. Editors may also make decisions on reprints and have to manage stock for their lists. In some larger companies this work is handled by sales and inventory control specialists.

Particular times of year can be good for the publication of trade books, and the publisher has to make sure the book appears at the time of the relevant sporting event, anniversary (for the subject of a biography), or the relevant season (Christmas for cookery, Spring for gardening titles). Publicity opportunities such as media exposure or festivals (e.g. Valentine's Day) may influence the date of publication. The New Year, and its associated resolutions, offers opportunities for publishers of health and personal improvement titles; beach reads are out for the

The New Year is a good time to publish self-improvement titles summer months. Hardbacks receive the most media coverage in the spring (when many of the literary festivals take place) and autumn (in the run-up to Christmas). New college textbooks should appear early enough in the adoption cycle (in the spring) so that lecturers can view them ahead of preparing their reading lists.

Illustrations can add value and this continues to be reviewed during product development. Are illustrations necessary to aid the explanation in the text – for example, in a school textbook? Are they essential in a particular market – art publishing or cookery? Can you charge more if there are many illustrations – will you sell more copies? A balance needs to be struck between the cost of illustrations and their likely added value.

Editorial project management

Planning tasks as part of the product development process include:

- a schedule for the editing, design and production stages,
- the necessary clearance for permissions for both text and illustrations,
- a brief for the text and cover design,
- copy written for the cover, and
- a budget.

Schedule

This is preferably drawn up in advance of the delivery of the typescript from the author. A copy-editor can be booked in advance, and the design and production stages can be planned around the proposed publication date. Schedules can be more or less complicated, and can be done using software or simply on a single sheet of A4. There may be a standard set of weeks allowed for different stages, but there is no formula set in stone. If a competing title is to be beaten to market, or if revenue is required within a particular financial year, the schedule may be severely shortened. If this was done with every title, however, there would be the risk that quality would suffer and there would be tremendous pressure on the staff involved. Below is a sample schedule – the audiobook will follow a parallel path through its studio production.

June to December	Picture research/clearance of permissions
January	Delivery of the typescript
	Copy-editing (six weeks)
	Cover and marketing copy written
March	Handover of typescript/illustrations to design department
	Cover proofs

April	Typesetting
May	First page proofs (three weeks for checking)
	Index preparation
June	Revised proofs and index proofs (one week for checking)
	Passed for press
July	Advance copies from the printer
	Copies into warehouse (six weeks before publication)
September	Publication (print and ebook)

Permissions

Permission may need to be sought for the use of text and illustrations in the book. Longer quotations not covered by fair usage will need to be cleared, and for anthologies of poetry or prose some detective work may be required to track down the relevant copyright holders. A freelancer may take on the work of clearing permissions for an anthology. Usually the first approach is to the originating publisher, who may control subsidiary rights. PLSclear provides a service for permission seekers who want to use content from books, journals, magazines and websites. Occasionally you will see a line in a book saying that 'every effort has been made to contact the copyright holder', and the extract will appear without permission having been granted. The publisher has made a risk assessment before going ahead.

Under the contract the author may have to clear and pay for the permissions, and the publisher will request copies of relevant correspondence. The publisher may still have to undertake picture research or brief a researcher, putting the cost of the permissions against the author's royalty. If the publisher is responsible for obtaining copyright permission, the editor or researcher writes to the copyright holders. Each illustration or table is labelled and compared against the accompanying text and caption. Caption and source copy are prepared.

Drawn illustrations are prepared from copies of those previously published, if suitably amended, or from the author's original line work, roughs or ideas. They are edited for sense and consistency before being passed to the designer or illustrator. The desired position of the illustrations is indicated in the text.

Design brief

Standard forms or memos may be used to brief the cover and page designers. The cover designer, who is unlikely to have read the manuscript, will be briefed on the market for the book and its contents: for example, upmarket commercial fiction aimed at a largely female market. For the page design, the brief may be to follow the design of another title (copy enclosed) or to create something new and distinctive. A sample chapter or two enables the design to be started on before the book's delivery. For key titles, sample spreads may be needed to help sell rights or to assist the author in writing to the correct length.

A design brief may contain the following elements, and separate consideration may need to be given to digital products:

- *the market for the book* – in the case of fiction, age and gender
- *the content* – synopsis or contents list,
- *some text elements* – with sample text (to show content, heading structure) and illustrations,
- *single or double column format* – double column format can accommodate smaller type and is often used for reference works,
- *the style of the running heads* – chapter heads are more informative than simply the book title, and
- *a similar title* – if the book is to follow that more or less closely in style.

Cover copy

The cover is needed well in advance of the printed book for promotion and sales purposes, and is still important as part of the metadata for the ebook edition. Cover copy (title, author, blurb and ISBN) may be prepared before the book's delivery by the author. Blurb writing is an important skill. In the case of fiction, it must grip the potential reader without giving away too much of the plot. Editors may ask sales or marketing to review the blurb copy for important titles, and the copy should also be written with an eye to online searches by potential customers. Review quotes or advance puffs from prominent names may be used – they may also help to position a new author in the market. *Dear Mrs Bird* by A. J. Pearce appeared in 2018 with approving quotes from authors such as Nina Stibbe and Marian Keyes. In 2023 controversy surrounded the quotes on the back of the paperback edition of Jordan Peterson's *Beyond Order: 12 More Rules for Life*. A review quote attributed to James Marriott of *The Times* read:

> "A philosophy of the meaning of life … the most lucid and touching prose Peterson has ever written." The actual phrase from Marriott's review is: "one of the most sensitive and lucid passages of prose he has written", a description specifically about one chapter in an otherwise almost entirely negative review. (*Guardian*, 1 September 2023)

'I generally love being edited. It is an honour to have someone examine your text as closely as you have.'
Anna Funder

Budget

The title costing will have estimates for the first costs of the book, including editorial and design work, and permission costs. The budget may be reviewed in the light of real costs or any change in the book's specification – page extent, number and type of illustrations.

Blurb writing

The blurb is the copy, describing a book's content, printed on the back cover of a paperback or displayed in an ebook. It remains highly important as an influence on the purchase of print books (along with an arresting front cover), and it may well be used as the basis for the description on sites such as Amazon. There it is perhaps of less importance given that potential purchasers can read customer reviews and assess the star ratings given to a book. Search engine optimization (SEO) is aided by the inclusion in the blurb of relevant key words. Some see a future for AI composing the blurb based on the text of the book.

Blurbs should be concise and all must be:

- impactful,
- intriguing,
- relevant, and
- short.

Paperbacks often make generous use of review quotes, and many new books appear with specially solicited quotes from opinion-formers. SEO-friendly non-fiction blurbs need to be concise but complete – in other words, answer all the questions you would want to ask a salesperson if you were buying the product in a shop. Bullet points can help put across the key benefits of the book; jargon should be avoided, and time taken to choose the right word. Short sentences can be highly effective.

Fiction blurbs are more emotional: you must think yourself into the story. Try to engage potential readers with the first few sentences. The first line in the blurb for Anne Tyler's *The Accidental Tourist* shows how to draw you in: 'How does a man addicted to routine – a man who flosses his teeth before love-making – cope with the chaos of everyday life?' A shoutline on the front cover can give the story in a nutshell, as with 'Twenty Years, Two People' for *One Day* by David Nicholls, or make use of tried and tested angles: 'Now a compelling film starring ...'; 'The no. 1 international bestseller'; or 'By the award-winning author of ...'

Editorial work

Although a commissioning editor or junior editor may copy-edit manuscripts in detail, this work is usually done by freelance copy-editors. There are also packagers and offshore companies which undertake the entire editorial and production process (including project management) up to the delivery of the digital files ready for manufacturing and electronic publication, although the publisher still retains direct control of the cover. *Line editing* is a hybrid of developmental editing and copy-editing.

Junior editors supervise the progress of books from manuscripts to bound copies, working closely with the production/design department, and giving information to marketing and sales people. They may copy-edit manuscripts and organize illustrations themselves; they may edit manuscripts for overall clarity and pass them to freelance copy-editors for the detailed work. They subsequently send proofs to authors and to freelance proofreaders, collate corrections and generally oversee the book's production from an editorial standpoint. Some book and journal publishers employ production editors, who are also responsible for the design and production stages, and the management of suppliers. The production department may organize freelance editing and proofreading. In illustrated book publishers and packagers, editors work alongside designers to create the book spread by spread.

In firms where job demarcations are drawn not too tightly, and where junior editors work specifically for sympathetic commissioning editors, there is sometimes also the opportunity to gain commissioning experience, usually without responsibility. This may depend on the size of the company. A common job role is that of editorial assistant, whose work ranges from administrative support to editorial work under supervision, such as proofreading, collating corrections, finding pictures for the text, applying for the clearance of third-party copyright material, and handling reprints. In consumer book publishing, junior editorial staff may write reports on new book proposals. In textbook publishing, development editors may look after the commissioning of new editions.

Editorial

SKILLS

Crucial editorial skills include the ability to get on with authors and close colleagues, and to communicate well with those in other parts of the company. Agreeing changes with authors and getting them to return proofs on time take tact, self-confidence, persuasion, tenacity and negotiation. Editing manuscripts and proofreading demand a meticulous eye for detail, a retentive memory, sustained concentration, patience, commonsense detective work and an ability to check one's own and others' work consistently. Authors often have great loyalty to both commissioning and more junior editors, and this loyalty binds them to the company.

Copy-editing and proofreading skills can to some extent be learnt from books, but added to that must be an editor's sound grasp of grammar and spelling, and preparedness to look things up. Editors should be able to place themselves in the reader's mind whatever subject knowledge they themselves hold. Good copy-editors and proofreaders are prized and valued.

The enhancement of an author's work involves not only a knowledge of current stylistic conventions and language, but also judgement on the desirability and extent of their application, recognizing when it is necessary or unnecessary to make changes. Breaking the rules for effect is not restricted to fiction. Appreciating the intangible quality of the author's voice can be important, especially in children's books.

Although an editor needs an enormous capacity to soak up detail, the ability to examine the text's overall sense is equally important. Visual awareness is valuable, especially in highly illustrated adult and children's publishing and packaging, and low-level textbook publishing. Knowledge and understanding of production processes and ways of minimizing costs at all stages are essential, as is clear marking of the text for structure. An understanding of publishing software is also important as the range of editorial duties expands.

Good editors are unflappable, they set priorities, manage time efficiently, juggle projects, switch quickly from one activity to another, and expect crises.

Copy-editing

The aim of the copy-editor, who may be the only person other than the author who reads the book before publication, is to ensure that the text and illustrations are clear, correct and consistent for both the printer and the ultimate readers. 'Good copy-editing is invisible: it aims to present the book the author would have written if he or she had had more time or experience – not, as some new copy-editors think, their own improved version' (Butcher et al., 2006, page 32).

Libel is an issue across types of publications and even fiction can be subject to a libel read by a lawyer. The copy-editor may be expected to look out for passages that are libellous:

> Any statement in a book or journal or newspaper, or any other published matter (an advertisement, e-mail or website, blog, message board for example), runs the risk of being defamatory if it contains an untrue allegation or imputation which has caused or is likely to cause serious harm to the reputation of another. (Jones and Benson, 2016, page 199)

The novelist Iris Murdoch (1919–1999) refused to have her work edited, even resisting changes to her punctuation

In the case of an unauthorized biography of a leading celebrity, a read by a lawyer may be required alongside evidence from the author to back up any controversial claims. Investigative reporting and publishing were given a boost in 2007 with the case of Graeme McLagan's book *Bent Coppers* (2003), 'The inside story of Scotland Yard's battle against police corruption'. The UK court of appeal decided that the author had acted responsibly when writing and researching the book. 'The court upheld the so-called "Reynolds defence" of qualified privilege, under which journalists can claim the right to publish material in the public interest even if they cannot prove its accuracy or it turns out to be untrue' (*Guardian*, 11 October 2007). This was the first time the Reynolds defence had been applied to a book.

The copy-editor, who is briefed on the nature and market of the book, first needs to check that all the manuscript items handed over are indeed present and that they have been clearly labelled and numbered by the author. The author is asked for any outstanding items, otherwise the book will be held up.

The work of copy-editing falls into three related processes:

- consistency,
- substantive editing, and
- structural mark-up.

Consistency

The most basic task is to ensure that the author's text is consistent in such matters as spelling, hyphenation, capitalization, agreement of verbs and subjects, beginning and ending of quotation marks and parentheses, and many other points sometimes included in the firm's editorial house style. The house style may be based on a particular reference work, for example, *The Oxford Style Manual*, or may have been developed internally. In the USA most editors use *The Chicago Manual of Style*. One advantage of following a house style is that proofreaders and other staff working on the text will have a set policy to help resolve problems later on in the production process. The style will determine whether to use -ize or -ise (the former is used in this book), how to style initials such as J. K. Rowling, and the use of single or double inverted commas.

Working on-screen, the editor can use tools such as the search facility to help with the enforcement of consistency in spelling and hyphenation. There are also software programs used by freelancers and at typesetters; and publishers may provide macros to editors that will help incorporate basic elements of house style. The danger is that some words, such as in quotations or references, are also changed by mistake. The editor must check the accuracy and relationship of parts of the text to others, such as in-text cross-references to illustrations, captions, chapters and notes; the matching of headings on the contents page to those in the text; and of citations to the reference list. The arrangement and preparation of pages about which authors may be unsure (e.g. the preliminary pages) are also the editor's concern. Each new book presents its own problems in the detailed handling of stylistic points, and decisions have to be made in regard to alternative ways of applying the rules. Editors need to be sensitive to the wishes of the author, as suggested by the 2021 winner of the Nobel Prize for Literature, Abdulrazak Gurnah, who insisted

> that words from Kiswahili, German or Arabic, which dot his prose, should not be italicised. 'It was a response to perhaps an over-energetic desire from editors to put every word they didn't know in italics. But it's not foreign in the context. So let me use italics when I want emphasis and not to say, "This is a foreign word",' he explains. 'To my astonishment, they let me do it.' (*Financial Times*, 9 September 2023)

Substantive editing

While some publishers restrict copy-editing to work on consistency, others expect editors to engage in the second parallel editorial process, which may be termed substantive or content editing. This calls for clear perception of the author's intent and sometimes restraint from the copy-editor. Where appropriate, attention is paid to discordant notes, such as obscure, incoherent, misleading or ambiguous sentences, or non sequiturs in factual passages; unintentional use of mixed metaphors or of repetition; unusual punctuation in sentence construction; paragraphing; and over- or under-use of headings. Again there are tools which can be called upon, such as the Bookalyser which helps to identify 'inconsistencies, errors and poor style' (bookalyser.com). Furthermore, errors of fact, and inconsistencies, omissions, contradictions and illogicality in the argument or plot may be found. Substantive editing may entail the rewriting of sentences, reorganization, or suggesting other ways to present material. It is important, however, not to annoy the author by making unnecessary changes. Also it is often better to present improvements as queries rather than as imposed changes.

Editors look out for abbreviations and terms unfamiliar to readers. The avoidance of parochialisms or culturally specific UK examples is especially important in books aimed for overseas markets. Books can be edited in British English, American English or even mid-Atlantic English. The avoidance of offensive – for example, sexist or racist – language or values and of corresponding stereotypes are issues which confront editors, designers and illustrators, particularly those in educational and children's publishing. It may be necessary to employ a sensitivity reader. It is also important to ensure that the level of language and the illustrations are appropriate for the intended age group.

Structural mark-up

The parallel editorial process carried out, whether the second substantive form is done or not, is to indicate to the designer or typesetter the structural elements of the text. Items so tagged or coded include the heading hierarchy (chapter headings, section and sub-section headings) and other elements (long quotations, lists, notes, captions, tables). The following shows Extensible Markup Language (XML) tagging for a chapter opening. Each opening tag must be completed with a closing tag.

<ch>40 Does the Book Have a Future?<chx>

<au>Angus Phillips<aux>

<epig>Old media don't die; they just have to grow old gracefully. (Douglas Adams 2001)<epigx>

Text that is structurally tagged is platform independent and can be published in different formats (ebook, online) or readily licensed to third parties. A further impetus on publishers (especially educational firms) to make books available in structured, digital formats is the Disability Discrimination Act (1995). There is demand from the reading impaired (not just the visually impaired) and their institutions. Text in digital form can be adjusted by the user in size, style and colour contrasts. Functionality also includes the ability to have the text read out loud using a screen reader, or the provision of extra navigational information – such as whether a line is a heading or a short sentence – and image descriptions (alt text). The Digital Accessible Information SYstem (DAISY) consortium produces technical standards for publishers. Publishers can also produce audio files for download. The Marrakesh Treaty, agreed by the World Intellectual Property Office in 2013, aimed to improve access to books for the visually impaired and print disabled. Exceptions to copyright law are allowed if they enable books to be copied into accessible formats. The European Accessibility Act (2019) requires that from 2025 e-readers must include the facility for text to speech. Ebooks must be available in accessible form, so that the text (and any non-textual elements) will work with different reading needs using assistive technologies.

A sample page
from a typescript
showing marks and
tags inserted by the
copy-editor

<number>2

<title>Slow books

<u><rhr>Slow books</u>

<u><rhl>Slow books</u>

<text>Just as the prospects for books look limited without authors, the same applies

without readers. Paul Auster says, 'If you write a story or a poem, you hope there will be a

reader,'[1] although of course there are a good many titles read by very few people. There is

a received wisdom that reading is good in itself, and offers personal and social benefits

beyond those for the economy of having an educated and literate population. If studies

show that readership of books is in decline, does this matter? What is at stake here? Are

there other ways of learning and developing our intelligence, and how can we expect books

to compete with the range of other media which compete for our attention?

Surveys suggest a fall in reading over time, in many countries, and this chapter will

examine the evidence and the reasons put forward. These include the loss of time to read,

in an often frenetic world of competing demands, and declining interest amongst newer

generations. Is the reading of books being replaced by other forms of reading, <u>for

example</u>e.g. blogs and websites? The science of reading tells us what is happening inside our

brains, and suggests that the pace of reading is faster with some digital devices.

<head1>Decline in reading

<text>The statistics regarding reading have to be treated with some caution. There is no

satisfactory set of data over a long period, and none-certainly <u>none</u> which can provide

Working method

Individuals differ in their approach to copy-editing. A common method involves
the editor quickly looking through the manuscript to gain a measure of the author
and the book. Ideally, decisions regarding the handling of stylistic points (e.g.
spelling, hyphenation, capitalization, terminology) are taken at the outset. A style
sheet is developed to aid consistency and memory, and helps the proofreading,
which will be done by a separate freelancer.

103

impulse is a short signal comprising a single value followed by zeros. The nature of the filter

response, called the *impulse response* will characterise the filter. The simplest form of filter is

called a Finite Impulse Response FIR filter, in which 'taps' are taken from successive samples,

which are then multiplied by a coefficient (a multiplicative factor) and the results are added

together to form the output of the filter. This is called 'finite' because there are a fixed number of

taps. An IIR filter, by contrast, allows feedback between the output and the input, which can

create some long-lasting results, including growth or decay over time. This is particularly useful

please give in full

for effects such as reverberation. Where the impulse-response of a physical space may be

recorded by, for example, firing a gun or bursting a balloon, the IIR filter may be used to model

the same digitally. However, IIR filters are often unstable and somewhat inaccurate, owing to the

complexity of their operation, and can easily produce feedback and other such unwanted results.

This makes digital reverberation one of the most difficult things to achieve successfully, and the

range of commercially available solutions can be quite variable in quality.

Creative uses of such filters include interpolation, in which sounds of two different types are

apparently fused together over time, and convolution, which combines two sound files / an input

and an impulse response by multiplying their spectra together to produce a new sound file.

Frequencies that are common to both sound files will tend to be reinforced and resonate together.

The filter will try to match bin content across the two spectrum. Where there is a match, the data

is preserved. Where there is no match, it is discarded (or, strictly, multiplied by zero). Among other

things, this enables the application of the reverberant properties of resonance to FFT windows

over time and thus the superimposition of the reverberant characteristics of one sound upon

another.

Where digital filters find the most direct parallel with analogue equipment is in the field of EQ,

or Equalisation. Both analogue and digital EQ are designed to make the final recorded sound

equal to the original source, by correcting inadequacies of both equipment and the recording

environment. However, it can also be a highly creative tool when used skilfully. EQ adjusts the

A sample page from a typescript copy-edited by hand

To a varying extent, house style editing and substantive editing conflict, in that concentration on one may lead to neglect of the other. Good editors may go through the copy several times at different speeds, focusing attention at various levels, moving back and forth during each examination. Editors may work on hard copy – a typical example is shown above – or on screen (using software tools), or both.

Skilled on-screen copy-editors, making good use of their computer's tools such as find and replace and macros, can work quickly and efficiently; and if they are able to present the typesetter with fully corrected and coded files that can be simply passed through the typesetting system and run out as pages, there can be genuine savings in the schedule. (Butcher et al., 2006, page 15)

During each examination editors make alterations on matters – especially those of house style – they believe to be right and defensible, but even so authors may disagree. Queries to the author are marked on the copy in the electronic file using track changes, listed separately or scanned to make a portable document format (PDF) file. Those that affect the design or production of the book are addressed to the design or production department.

If the author is contacted by telephone, email or in writing, editors need to be particularly tactful, explaining the kind of editing that has been done – perhaps by mentioning representative samples – raising matters needing assistance, and reaching agreement on matters of concern. Best practice is that the edited copy is returned to the author for checking (although some publishers are reluctant to do so if a large amount of tagging is visible), as this reduces costly and time-consuming changes at proof stage. Sometimes a meeting is held with the author – or the editor or lead author in the case of a multi-author work. By adopting the reader's viewpoint, and suggesting solutions, the editor sets out to persuade the author to make necessary changes. If the text has been edited on-screen, the edited copy forms an early proof.

Prelims and end-matter

The editor, in-house or freelance, drafts the preliminary material – prelims or front matter – the first few pages of the book. These include the pages giving the book title and author, the name of the publishing house, the copyright notice, and the International Standard Book Number (ISBN) – a unique number identifying the book. Other pages are the contents page, list of illustrations, and acknowledgements – for advice and support to the author, or for copyright material used. The author writes a Preface; a third party provides a Foreword. The cataloguing in publication (CIP) data – supplied by the British Library and Library of Congress – has to be applied for.

The usual order of the prelim pages is as follows, with variations according to the book. A right-hand facing page is called a *recto*; a left-hand facing page a *verso*. Recto pages are visually more important, but the advent of ebooks has diminished the impact of such distinctions.

- *Half-title page* (recto) – the main title without the subtitle and author's name
- *Half-title verso* – often blank, or a list of the author's previous works
- *Title page* (recto) – full title and author's name, with the publisher's imprint
- *Title verso* – copyright page with the publication history and ISBN

The other prelim pages follow. These include the dedication, acknowledgements, preface, contents page, and the list of illustrations. The prelim pages are paginated using roman numbers, switching to Arabic numerals for the introduction or the first chapter. The advantage of this system is that changes can be made to the prelims at proof stage without affecting the main pagination (which could have knock-on effects for the index). If pages need to be saved to achieve a set extent, the prelim pages can be adjusted. The pages at the end of the book, or end-matter, can include appendices, notes, bibliography and the index.

Proofreading

Most unillustrated books, or those with only a few illustrations which are easily placed, go straight to page proofs. The typesetter arranges the page breaks, inserts any illustrations, and returns proofs of pages numbered as they will finally appear. Proofs are usually sent as PDF files by email. Proofs are normally read by the author and publisher (most commonly by a freelancer). They can be checked *against copy* (compared to the original), which is more expensive, or simply read *by eye* for obvious errors. The corrections and improvements are collated by the editor and inserted using standard symbols – proof marks are set by the British Standards Institution – on one master set in paper form (the marked set) or most likely marked electronically in the PDF. Correction marks have traditionally been colour-coded (red for typesetter's errors, blue or black for author's and publisher's) so that costs can be apportioned, but this practice is not always followed. Publishers are likely to charge authors for excessive corrections. The marked set or file is returned to the typesetter for correction, and second page or revised page proofs are produced to check the author's and proofreader's corrections have been correctly implemented. Books with many illustrations integrated with the text may follow a different path. The designer may supply a page layout to the typesetter or work on the pages themselves. A sequence of page proofs is checked by the author and publisher.

Most manuscripts arrive on disk or by email, and there is no necessity to have them rekeyed. This minimizes errors at proof and if the copy-editor works on screen a high-quality version of the text is passed to the typesetter. In some companies production editors or designers prepare the digital file from which the book is published.

Index

Serious non-fiction books should have reliable indexes that anticipate readers' needs and expectations. The author is often responsible for index preparation and the cost, and either compiles it themselves or is supplied with a freelance indexer, found by the editor sometimes from the Society of Indexers. Typesetters can prepare simple indexes using standard software. Indexes are prepared from a page proof and have to be edited and typeset at great speed because the publication date is close. The professional indexers have usually passed their Society's course exams, use specialist indexing software, and may wish to retain copyright. The index is usually missed out of ebook editions given the complexity of flowable text without fixed pagination, and the availability of a search function.

'Should not the Society of Indexers be known as Indexers, Society of, The?', Keith Waterhouse

Now read this

Judith Butcher, Caroline Drake and Maureen Leach, *Butcher's Copy-Editing: The Cambridge handbook for editors, copy-editors and proofreaders*, 4th edition, 2006.
Hugh Jones and Christopher Benson, *Publishing Law*, 5th edition, Routledge, 2016.

Sources

Peter Ginna (ed.), *What Editors Do*, University of Chicago Press, 2017.
Robert Gottlieb, *Avid Reader*, Farrar, Straus and Giroux, 2016.
Jocelyn Hargrave, 'Life Before and After: Editors' work and place in the COVID-19 gig economy', *Logos*, 34:3 (2023).
New Oxford Style Manual, 3rd edition, Oxford University Press, 2016.
Lynette Owen (ed.), *Clark's Publishing Agreements: A book of precedents*, 11th edition, Bloomsbury, 2022.
Beth Richard, 'Key Issues Affecting the Inclusion of Alt Text in Scholarly PDF Publications', *Logos*, 34:1 (2023).
The Chicago Manual of Style, 18th edition, University of Chicago Press, 2024.

Web resources

https://www.bsigroup.com the British Standards Institution maintains the standard proofreading marks and symbols.
https://www.ciep.uk Chartered Institute of Editing and Proofreading (CIEP), formerly the Society for Editors and Proofreaders.
https://daisy.org Digital Accessible Information SYstem.
https://www.indexers.org.uk Society of Indexers.
https://www.nuj.org.uk National Union of Journalists.

CHAPTER 8

Design and production

Alongside the work of the editor in product development, the contribution of design and production colleagues is equally critical. Good design sells books – whether it is the cover of a novel attracting an impulse buyer in a shop, or the effective use of typography and illustrations in a school textbook. With the growth of digital products such as ebooks came the recognition from publishers that print books need to reassert strong production values around their look, feel and paper quality. Some publishers, especially in the highly illustrated book and art book markets, are actively design-led. Their design standards are used as a marketing and sales tool internationally. In the transition to digital publishing, production managers make crucial decisions about quality which affect how a book is perceived in a market of multiple formats. Through effective purchasing of services from freelancers, trade suppliers and project management companies, they ensure that work is kept to budget and schedule.

Environmental considerations have come to the fore and publishers need to ensure that books are produced and sold in a sustainable manner. The use of digital and distributed printing has grown and companies are anxious to source paper and printing with the appropriate green credentials. There are choices for a book to be made around type design and page extent, the type of paper used, and where it is printed.

Authors want publishers to market and distribute their books effectively, and they also want publishers to produce them efficiently and attractively. Some new competitors to the more established companies offer speed to market and more flexible operations. Author service companies will bring books to market in a matter of a few weeks, whilst digital only publishers and distributors are free of print-first production systems. They can offer authors faster publication and are less constrained by the economics and physical restrictions of print.

DIGITAL WORKFLOW

The previous boundaries in the design and production process have been broken down so that authors, editors and designers are much more involved in producing the final text. On highly illustrated books, designers, not typesetters, may produce the final file for the printer; at the same time the increasing sophistication of pagination software reduces the need to employ designers to hand craft the layout of illustrated texts. The requirements of digital publishing mean that the file of

DOI: 10.4324/9781003403289-9

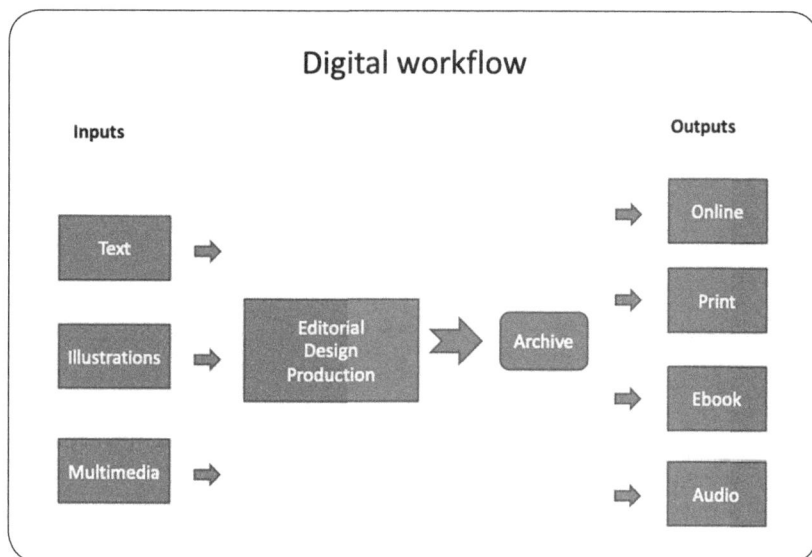

a book will be rendered to several outputs: print and digital formats. There is now an imperative to hold a properly archived version of a book so that it can be published across formats and repurposed as necessary. Re-engineering the workflow has been one of the biggest challenges and many publishers now have a digital-first strategy: the creation of a format neutral version of the book, ready to be published in a variety of digital and print forms. Audio publication involving separate studio production follows a parallel route in order to publish at the same time as the book; and some authors and publishers are experimenting with an audio first route to publication. AI-generated narrations may be suitable for titles previously not commercially viable in audio format.

Companies have changed the work and system processes of publishing content in order to move from a print-only world to a mixed print and digital world. The growing use of XML is an important part of the transition, and in Chapter 7 structural mark-up was introduced. STM, professional, and reference publishers were early adopters, but trade and educational publishers are catching up. Publishers vary in the extent to which they have changed the workflow.

At first, publishers adopted the least disruptive approach. The publisher's typesetter produced the XML file after the printed book was printed. As that could delay digital publication, progressive efforts were made to introduce structural tagging earlier and earlier. For example, the typesetter may produce the tagged file from an application such as InDesign, or before that from the copy-edited manuscript. In an 'XML first' workflow the content is tagged in Word by the copy-editor – or even the author – and then exported to XML. Underlying the XML approach is the drive towards greater standardization in the production process in order to lower costs and quicken lead times, to publish in various formats through different channels to market, and to future-proof the business. Publishers are moving from a 'cottage industry approach', where the production of each book differs, to scalable production approaches and systems. Books may be published as part of an ebook collection or merged into large, searchable databases. This is not to say that hand-crafted books do not have importance in some markets, and building value into print products has been a response to the rise of digital.

The publisher's suppliers have kept in step with the moves towards standardization and modernization of the workflow. Whilst publishers in the period after the Second World War used printers which offered a complete service from re-keying and typesetting of manuscripts through to printing and binding, by the last quarter of the twentieth century, publishers' production managers found it cheaper and more flexible to use specialist typesetters. UK publishers also used overseas printers in continental Europe and the Far East which offered lower prices, especially for the manufacture of colour books. UK printers facing a static, if not declining market, went bust, consolidated, or became part of European groups (such as CPI or Elcograf), and added digital services. New competitors from different sectors exploited digital printing technologies which enabled short-run printing or print on demand (POD). Lightning Source created by the US wholesaler Ingram pioneered POD in the late 1990s, and Amazon acquired the POD printer BookSurge in 2005 (first integrated into CreateSpace, then merged into KDP Print). Printers were forced to diversify by offering supply chain management and distribution services (including direct delivery to intermediaries and end-users), to supplement their conventional practice of delivering stock to publishers' warehouses. Advances in digital printing allowed publishers to reduce their printed book inventory and switch much of their backlist to just-in-time fulfilment of orders. Some academic publishers, e.g. SpringerNature, now aim only to print copies to order across their whole list of books. Printing in local markets – distributed printing – saves on time as well as shipping and environmental costs. Distributors serving publishers are aligning themselves with digital printers, and the growth in self-publishing has given digital printers new business.

The pre-press supplier market evolved too from the 1980s. Typesetters made greater use of computers for the pre-press production processes of printed books, and this led to a dramatic fall in the cost of typesetting per page. As digital publishing developed at the turn of the century, the typesetters, mostly based overseas, adapted and consolidated. New firms arose offering publishing solutions and they made large investments in technology to process content and data. Some of the largest, for example global companies such as Straive, Apex, Aptara, employ large and well-educated workforces in offshore locations such as India and the Philippines. From the late 1990s they digitized the printed back issues of journals into fully coded and thus searchable content. The digitization of journal back issues is mostly complete; by comparison the backlists of many book publishers have yet to be digitized in a systematic way, and the concentration has been on file conversion to ebook formats. In any case, trade publishers have less control over their IP, which is often agented and includes third-party content such as illustrations.

Academic publishers in particular have looked to strip out costs from their organization through outsourcing to service providers, which now offer a range of higher value services, including copy-editing and proofreading, permission clearance, technical drawing, design, outputs to all formats, and project management. The solutions offered now include AI-powered workflow tools that reduce costs and speed up processes. The client base of these companies is broadening out from the academic and professional publishers to include educational and trade houses. There are also specialist companies to supply content management systems within which workflow is managed and content is stored – examples are Librios in the UK, and Contiem in the USA; and others which focus on the development of e-learning solutions and digital textbooks, such as Hurix in India and Inkling in the USA.

The major trends of the adoption of a digital workflow, the output to a range of formats, standardization in processes, outsourcing to service providers (rather than to freelance copy-editors and designers), and the use of digital printing to manage the backlist of printed books, are having a major impact on the production departments of publishers. Some of the tasks (and job roles) of the print-only world are eliminated. On the other hand, the management of pre-press services, an awareness of constantly changing technologies, sound project management skills, and expertise in print buying remain vitally important.

DESIGN

With regard to the text design, the basis of the book designer's job is visual planning. They operate within technical, cost and time constraints, and take into account the views of the editor, and the production and sales departments. Their task is to transform and enhance the author's raw material, text and illustrations. The printed book should have aesthetic appeal and meet the practical needs of its users – whether for leisure, information or education. The drawing element of the job, if any, usually extends to providing blueprints or rough visuals for others (technical illustrators, artists, typesetters, image originators or printers) to execute. Design work can vary greatly according to the nature of the content.

The use of freelancers or agencies to design books or websites is widespread. They are commissioned by editors, production staff, or in-house designers. Small publishers (or self-published authors), without in-house staff, may ask a good printer to help with the design; and in some large firms issuing relatively straightforward books, editors or production controllers may design the books while commissioning the covers from freelance designers. Many titles – for example fiction, lightly illustrated non-fiction, academic, and professional books – follow pre-set typographic templates in the approved style of the publisher.

In-house staff tend to be employed by medium to large houses, designing covers or more complex illustrated books (from illustrated adult and children's non-fiction to textbooks), and by the more established book packagers. They will work in a design or production department, reporting directly to the manager. The design manager or art director, responsible for the overall brand of all the firm's books, is concerned with the deployment of in-house and external services, budgets, scheduling and administration. Senior designers may coordinate the work of junior designers; there may be design assistants; and some in-house designers specialize in particular lists. The design of book covers for most kinds of books, other than the most utilitarian, requires specific design attention which is carried out by in-house cover designers, or freelancers under the supervision of the art director. For the production of complex digital and print products, multi-disciplinary teams may be set up, consisting of editors, designers, interactive media designers, developers and project managers. Book designers and typographers need to be aware of the requirements of other outputs such as an ebook (text flow and image anchoring).

The preparation of artwork is mainly outsourced, and some publishers and packagers employ illustrators and designers on short-term contracts. Photography

Touch Press sold more than 250,000 downloads of its app *The Elements*

The cover design is usually carried out separately from the text design is normally commissioned. The design of promotional material may be the responsibility of in-house designers in marketing, or freelance designers or agencies commissioned by that department.

Design brief

The point at which a designer is first involved with a new book varies. It may occur before or after the author has completed the manuscript, the designer receiving either an edited or unedited copy. By then the book's overall parameters (for example format, extent, illustrations, binding, paper) have been planned. In some firms, editors personally brief designers while in others design meetings are organized, attended by the production team and sometimes the sales staff. The outcome may be a production specification, a budget, and the schedule. It is vital for the designer to be given a clear brief by the editor at the outset. A designer may be able to suggest alternative ideas to save money or to improve sales potential. Assuming the book is not part of a fixed format series or that a pre-existing design cannot be adapted to suit it, the designer's opening tasks are to prepare the type specification and page layout which are supplementary to the book's overall production specification.

Type specification and page layout

The type specification sets out how the main text elements should be typeset in respect of typefaces, sizes, page depth, and line lengths, and of the positioning and spacing of the elements. The elements include:

- body text,
- headings – the hierarchy of chapter heads and subheadings,
- displayed quotations – broken off from the main text,
- tables,
- captions for illustrations,
- running heads at the top of the page
- footnotes or endnotes, and
- page numbers.

The page layout is a graphic representation of the printed page – invariably of two facing pages. Layouts are based on a grid – the underlying framework within which text and illustrations are placed on the page.

> A grid is the graphic design equivalent of a building's foundations. As we read from left to right and top to bottom, a grid is generally a series of vertical and horizontal lines. The vertical lines will relate to the column widths, while the horizontal will be determined by the space that a line of type occupies. (Roberts and Thrift, 2002, page 18)

Layout and typographic style considerably affect the readers' perception of a book. The two are interdependent and should, if well designed, allow the author's work to be presented consistently and flexibly, taking into account the content, aims, character, market, and technical and cost constraints of the book. Books may require a highly tailored approach; or designers may work on a series design that

The main text of this book is typeset in Scala and is unjustified (i.e. it has no fixed margin on the right-hand side); the sidebars are in Scala Sans will apply across many titles. Book typography has four main functions (Mitchell and Wightman, 2005):

- readability – the text should be comfortable to read,
- organization – the structure of the text should be clearly communicated,
- navigation – information in the book should be easy to find, and
- consistency – the overall effect is to create a unified whole.

Factors that should be taken into account are the fitting of the author's manuscript into the desired extent; the ability of certain typefaces to cope with mathematics or foreign languages, or to ease reading by early or poor-sighted readers; and the typefaces available from a supplier. The page design may balance readability against the environmental concern to optimize the number of pages in the volume. The designer presents one or more designs in the form of mock-ups to the editorial and production staff for their comments and approval – usually specimen pages are produced.

There are a variety of typefaces commonly used in books, ranging from traditional faces, such as Bembo, Garamond, or Times New Roman, to sans serif fonts (without the finishing strokes at the ends of letters) including Frutiger, Helvetica and Univers.

Typefaces popular for blogs and web pages are Arial, Georgia and Verdana

Design

SKILLS

Designers have technical proficiency and usually a professional qualification. Underpinning design is a thorough knowledge of typography and the ways in which books and covers are put together. Mastery of software such as Adobe InDesign and Photoshop is essential, and an understanding of the capabilities of XML and HTML, and the different ebook formats. Designers need perception, clarity of thought, an ability to take a raw manuscript, to analyse it, and come up with an effective design within financial and technical constraints. They should be able to anticipate the needs of readers. It calls for a combination of imagination, knowledge and understanding of technical processes and software, and an awareness of the work of leading freelancers and of trends in book design. For cover design a creative mind is pre-eminent, combined with knowledge and an instinct of what sells.

They must be able to explain to authors, editors and sales staff, who rarely think in shape, colour and form, how they arrived at a solution, and why it is the best. They need to give clear and unambiguous briefs and instructions to other designers, illustrators, production staff and printers.

Highly illustrated work requires designers to get under the skin of a subject, to undertake research if necessary, to ask probing questions of experts and to pay due regard to ethnic or cultural sensitivities. The establishment of the all-important rapport with in-house staff and external suppliers takes time and experience to develop. The handling of artists, illustrators and photographers, some of whom can be awkward, calls for a special mixture of tact, pleading or coercion to induce them to produce their best work. Most designers work on many projects simultaneously, all at different stages in production. Thus, like editors, they need to be flexible and self-organizing.

Adobe Caslon Pro

abcdefghijklmnopqrstuvwxyz 1234567890 1234567890

ABCDEFGHIJKLMNOPQRSTUVWXYZ fi fl ffi ffl ½ ¼ ¾

At endre magna faccum velessis ad eu feuguercin henit lore et, vulla at, sequat, consenibh et wisl iustie erosto odolessequat in vel utatue duis aliquam, quatem exeriure vel ullam. Con utate te velit illumsan ullandre corperat alit nonsenim adit lutatie dunt utpatie conse facipit at velesse quismol orperci tisi. Pit veliquate dolortie molutatem ipsum vel do consequ ipsustisi. El doloborem velis autet ad te tet luptatue ming estrud esse modit laor aci tin hent dolortissi.

Adobe Garamond Pro

abcdefghijklmnopqrstuvwxyz 1234567890 1234567890

ABCDEFGHIJKLMNOPQRSTUVWXYZ fi fl ffi ffl ½ ¼ ¾

At endre magna faccum velessis ad eu feuguercin henit lore et, vulla at, sequat, consenibh et wisl iustie erosto odolessequat in vel utatue duis aliquam, quatem exeriure vel ullam. Con utate te velit illumsan ullandre corperat alit nonsenim adit lutatie dunt utpatie conse facipit at velesse quismol orperci tisi. Pit veliquate dolortie molutatem ipsum vel do consequ ipsustisi. El doloborem velis autet ad te tet luptatue ming estrud esse modit laor aci tin hent dolortissi.

Adobe Jenson Pro

abcdefghijklmnopqrstuvwxyz 1234567890 1234567890

ABCDEFGHIJKLMNOPQRSTUVWXYZ fi fl ffi ffl ½ ¼ ¾

At endre magna faccum velessis ad eu feuguercin henit lore et, vulla at, sequat, consenibh et wisl iustie erosto odolessequat in vel utatue duis aliquam, quatem exeriure vel ullam. Con utate te velit illumsan ullandre corperat alit nonsenim adit lutatie dunt utpatie conse facipit at velesse quismol orperci tisi. Pit veliquate dolortie molutatem ipsum vel do consequ ipsustisi. El doloborem velis autet ad te tet luptatue ming estrud esse modit laor aci tin hent dolortissi.

Some examples of typefaces

Typographic mark-up

Once the complete manuscript is edited, the designer may carry out the typographic mark-up, that is the addition of typesetting instructions to the manuscript or disk. Some instructions, such as the mark-up of the heading hierarchy and use of italic or bold within the text, may have been marked in copy-editing. The copy-editor may also have implemented a system of coding to mark the different text elements. The designer checks, for instance, the editor's hierarchy of headings to ensure they conform to the agreed type specification, and may want them modified. The typesetter follows the specification or style coding. However, depending on the complexity of the material, the designer may indicate the design treatment of recurring text matter which, though covered by the specification, may still need to be marked by using abbreviations or codes. Complex text (including tables) as well as displayed text, such as that of the prelims, may require specific mark-up.

Illustrations

The illustrations may reach the designer before the author has handed over the manuscript to the publisher. The designer may have briefed the author or supplied the editor with guidelines to help the author prepare drawn illustrations. Designers are usually responsible for commissioning the technical illustrators or graphic artists who execute the final artwork – often prepared on-screen in software such as Adobe Illustrator. In children's books, more traditional techniques of illustration may still be used. When many complex diagrams need to be drawn, the designer prepares an artwork specification to serve as a technical reference for illustrators. AI-generated images are not yet common in book publishing, and their use remains controversial.

Chosen freelance illustrators or artists are contacted directly, or are recruited from artist's agents, art colleges, or commercial studios. The designer, who may have developed or sometimes revisualized the author's roughs, briefs the contact about the purpose of each illustration and the style of execution (including the final size) and gives a deadline for completion; the cost is estimated in advance. Roughs may be prepared as the first stage and the designer checks that the brief has been followed; they will also want to confirm with the illustrator that the technical standard is suitable for processing and reproduction by the printer. The designer ensures that mistakes attributable to the illustrator are not charged to the publisher.

Proofing stages

With unillustrated books that go straight to page proofs, the edited and coded file (together with the type specification and grid) is sent off to the typesetter or pre-press supplier. For a book with illustrations grouped on pages, the designer provides a layout. When illustrations are interspersed with the text, the digital files are sent off with the text, or the designer instructs the typesetter to leave specified spaces for the illustrations to be inserted later. The designer may fine-tune the typography and correct any bad page breaks or layouts at page-proof stage.

With more complex illustrated books, the designer controls and plans completely the book's layout by means of a manual layout on screen, using Adobe InDesign. The designer may be involved with the final selection of photographs and advises whether they will reproduce well. The layout of a page can affect the choice, and the integration of text and illustration influences the sizes of photographs – these may need to be adjusted or cropped. The designer tunes the ensuing page proofs and any illustration proofs, spotting visual errors which authors, editors and proofreaders may fail to recognize.

It is important to establish the correct final version of the text of a book, and this issue was highlighted when the UK edition of *The Corrections* by Jonathan Franzen appeared in 2010 with hundreds of mistakes. The typesetter had apparently sent the 'last but one' version of the book file to the printer. When the book is all correct and ready for printing, the typesetter produces the digital file of the book in one or more formats such as a high-resolution portable document format (PDF) file used by the printer, a low-resolution PDF file (perhaps for use on the web), an XML file, and an EPUB file for the ebook. There may be further stages undertaken by the printer to ensure the supplied PDF is reproducible by their system (a pre-flight check), and on colour books various kinds of proofs to verify the colour reproduction. All file conversions to the different ebook formats need checking.

XML

Bas Straub, academic publisher, The Netherlands

XML is a mark-up language that is used in the digital production of books and journals – primarily in those publications where the ability to structure large volumes of content is more important than freedom in design. Whilst XML looks quite similar to HTML, with its structure of beginning and end tags (<H1>This is the main type of heading</H1>), it gives the freedom to self-define tags (<species>Homo Sapiens</species>). Due to its emphasis on function over form it is used mainly in more complex, uniform publication areas like science and education.

E★PERT

Terms

1. *Element.* XML has two different type of tags: An *element* has an opening and a closing tag, controlling the content between them. This tag can be defined by the user. An *empty-element* tag is mainly used to steer the formatting within XML:

    > Element: <species>Homo Sapiens</species>
    > Empty Element: <Line Break/>

2.   *Attribute.* Attributes are used to increase granularity as well as structure without having to create too many elements. Within the element <garden> you can have different type of plants:

> <plants category = "flowers"/>
> <plants category = "trees"/>.

3.   *Mark-up versus content.* XML can be seen simply as a database contained in a single, linear document mixing both content, as consumed by the reader, and the separate mark-up comprising all the elements; yet the tags and attributes also add value to the content.

4.   *Parser.* A parser is a piece of software that is used to translate XML into a different format. Within publishing, a parser is used to output XML into the PDF, InDesign or ePub format.

5.   *DTD.* Publishers define the XML schema they are using in a document type definition (DTD) that explains the various elements and attributes used. As an example one DTD could govern the most important heading as <H1>chapter title</H1> whereas another DTD would use <Heading1>chapter title</Heading1>. The DTD is used to instruct parsers.

Use of XML

XML is most often used in publishing production to structure content.

Formatting. The use of XML allows for more efficient production. Content is structured in Word which is converted automatically into XML. Then the XML is parsed automatically into, for instance, InDesign. For 'simple' publications like novels, as well as publications that are design-heavy, like travel guides, XML is often less efficient.

Indexing. Using elements you can tell the computer what a piece of content means. Using, for example, the element 'species' also makes for easier searching amongst a number of documents.

Enhancement. Should a text contain location coordinates these could be tagged and then linked to, say, a Google Maps location. Similar enhancing is often done in scientific publications, for example by embedding data on chemical structures or proteins into journal articles.

Updating. Using the attribution functionality allows for easy updating of a document. A publication written at the end of 2008 could, for instance, contain Barack Obama within the element <President> and the attribute 'elect'. In early 2009 the attribute could be updated to 'current' thus rending the document current again. In 2017 the attribute would then be changed, most likely for the last time, to 'past'.

Future

Currently most publications only use XML for efficient production and to aid indexing and search. Thus they use only a small part of the theoretical capacity of XML. Think of allowing a reader to select a dyslexia font for easier reading before outputting a document into a bespoke PDF formatted and optimized for their home printer. Tagging publications with greater granularity will add more value in the publications process. The possibilities of linking, merging and reusing content as well as adding value through enhancement are enormous.

Ebooks

Ebook file formats can be produced from many types of source file formats, such as InDesign or PDF, and are not dependent on an XML-early workflow. Backlist titles can be converted at relatively low cost by specialist companies or suppliers of publishing solutions. In most fields of scholarship, the PDF file, faithful to the printed and paginated page, is still favoured by researchers and teachers. The greatest disruption to traditional book design has been the introduction of reflowable text enabling ebooks to be read on a variety of screen sizes. Designers of print books concentrate on positioning and sizing text and illustrations on fixed pages in an attractive way. The typography conveys functionality and aesthetics, and it differentiates the character of one book from another. Reproduction as a PDF enables the design to be preserved when read digitally, but most ebook consumers are now happily choosing their own font and type size, and seeing the text reflow accordingly. Reflowable text makes it hard for designers to control set proportions, or the placement of illustrations and captions. The concept of the page spread, across two pages, often becomes redundant, and text and illustrations flow in a linear single column. The producers of e-reading devices may also strip out formatting by the publisher to impose their own styles, reducing product differentiation.

Designers can, however, work to ensure that the text design is flexible and capable of display on a variety of devices. They can adjust the ebook design to ameliorate features of printed books, which if carried over to an ebook would irritate readers, such as omitting blank pages or adjusting spaces around chapter headings. Usability is aided by providing navigational hyperlinks between the content page headings and the relevant point in the text, or between note cues and end-notes. The design limitations of most published ebooks are partly due to technical and commercial reasons.

There are many ebook formats in existence and publishers will rarely wish to publish for just one format or retailer. The most universal format is EPUB, which is a free and open XML standard, supporting both reflowable content and fixed-layout content, and the needs of visually disabled readers. The format is supported by the publishing industry worldwide, and by most ebook resellers and device manufacturers. Version 2 still remains popular despite the launch

E★PERT

Audio production

Barry Gibson, producer, composer, writer – Creative Director, sQuarish Productions

From tin-foil and wax cylinder phonograph (starting with Edison's 1877 *'Mary had a little lamb …'*), from gramophone-horn to hi-fi, from 78 to 45 to 33⅓ rpm, from EP to LP, from audio-cassette to CD, from PC to iPod, from tablet to smartphone, from mp3 to streaming and smart-speakers, then back to vinyl and good old steam-radio, for almost a century and a half the recorded-voice has happily floated from medium to medium. Recent substantial growth in take-up sees new business models emerging to fit twenty-first-century lifestyles and the devices in our pockets.

Oral storytelling precedes the written word (let alone the printed book) by many millennia. It's at the core of language and the sharing of thoughts. So its appearance in ever-changing formats and notions like 'Talking Book', 'Spoken Word' and 'Audiobook' provides an experience that many people happily identify with, in immediate, deep and real ways.

AI-generated human-like auto-narrations and 'voice-clones' are becoming a familiar presence and can be a fast, cost-effective way to launch audiobooks in some genres. But for many a human narrator, speaker, reader, actor, even singer – brings special abilities based on understanding to really engage each listener, as if one-to-one. Who is that right voice? 'Author-as-reader' can occasionally work well, if that person can convey their understanding of the material through a varied enough voice. But the skillset needed for narration is quite different to that of a writer. Good professional narrators (who may have experience in radio drama, TV voice-over, live theatre or ELT)

Session in progress at the Soundhouse Studios, London

will often bring a more convincingly 'natural' narration, as well as varied characterizations (if needed), expressive voice-colour, rhythmic-cadence, human engagement and an overall coherence to the recording. The key is to find a good match for the particular book, style and genre.

Where to record? Individuals such as self-published authors looking to record their own material on a small budget can sometimes achieve quite good results with limited equipment, though to do so, great care is needed with set-up in an acoustically 'dead', soundproof space free of extraneous noise such as traffic, weather, buzzes and reverberation. Some affordable microphones sound good ('dynamic' types often directional and boomy, 'condenser' mics more sensitive and nuanced) with pop-shields helping to reduce 'plosives'. Easily available audio-software includes GarageBand, Audacity, ProTools, Adobe Audition, Reaper and Hindenburg – some music-DAWs such as Logic Pro or Cubase can also be effectively set up for speech.

However, a reading (even if subtle) is a 'performance', so bringing in an experienced producer and/or sound-engineer at a dedicated sound-studio is often advisable. This provides invaluable quality control, with the extra ears monitoring the recording process for details such as mouth-clicks, thumps and rustles, as well as checking for overall continuity, energy-levels, consistency and keeping track of errors and 'retakes'. After recording, the painstaking audio-editing process can be time-consuming and needs good judgement (and sometimes careful use of plug-ins) to ensure the final recording sounds natural, clear, fluent and well-paced. Every project is different but a 'finished hour' of material might take double that time to record in studio, and sometimes double that time to edit and mix ... that's worth it if the results are brilliant for the listener!

The need for 'abridgements' to fit physical formats is not so vital with digital and there is significant demand for 'unabridged' titles, though skilled adaptations for particular user-groups (such as educational age-groups, second-language, etc.) or just to create interesting 'potted versions' can be valuable, exciting and worthwhile. For some projects a 'semi-dramatized' approach may work well, where actors other than the main narrator provide character-voices and dialogue, to give extra life and a sense of 'being there'.

Full-scale audio-dramas with sound-effects and music are a way of opening up the experience into new forms of immersive storytelling and enthusiastic new audiences, nourished by the growth in podcast-popularity. The sky really is the limit – not just for sci-fi and fantasy – and the art is to mix voices with sound-design techniques from areas such as traditional radio drama, live theatre sound, film soundtracks, binaural, surround sound, music production and computer games.

Audiobooks synced with ebooks are increasingly common – new hybrids and crossovers between audio, visual elements and extended content proliferate. In the text-to-speech and synthetic-voice world, several technology big players offer improvements in accents, pronunciation and customization. For non-fiction publishers presenting simple or complex ideas, this may help reach all sorts of listeners, including those who aren't confident readers, who have restricted vision, or who want to get away from screens. But despite the march of unlimited technology, sometimes a good story, well told by a single voice is the best solution. Special fields such as poetry still offer a wealth of new opportunities for untried approaches in audio, to reach new generations.

Whatever the genre and approach, audiobooks have the ability to fit into everyday life in a multitasking world. The focus on sound alone means that stories and experiences can be directly shared and enjoyed at any time while doing other things – exercising, driving, washing-up, holidaying, gardening, daydreaming, even working – as well as for their own sake. Audio provides a parallel world to the 'book' and, with its direct link to the imagination, the pictures are great too, because you make them yourself.

of EPUB 3 in 2011. Based on HTML5, version 3 supports rich media (audio and video), global languages, improved accessibility features, typographical and layout enhancements, user navigation and interactivity.

Highly illustrated colour books

Some print books are sold on the quality of their design and pictorial content, such as illustrated non-fiction titles and textbooks. The approach to the design of these titles is closer to that of quality magazine publishing – the designer's role is more central. The interrelationship of the text and illustrations, and the positioning of colour within the book are planned and controlled, page by page, right from the outset. Sample spreads are produced to aid the writing by the authors or contributors. Such material (supplemented with the cover and a dummy) is also used to interest overseas publishers in co-publication. The designer has a greater say over the format, appearance, art direction and creation of the book, which allows more scope to vary its grid and pace, and to provide surprise elements. Some books, including school and ELT texts, use double-page spreads on topics. Strong headlines, dramatic illustrations and extended captions (often read first) capture the interest of a bookshop browser or learner. Digital editions may be in PDF format (preserving the page design) or in enhanced ebook formats. The downloading time of large file sizes, especially when they include video, can be an issue. Textbook publishers reference the media files in the EPUB with an external URL. The interactive media is rendered only when the device is connected to the internet.

Books for international co-publication have special design needs. To gain economies in co-printing (printing two or more editions simultaneously), the colour illustrations should remain unaltered in position, whereas the translations of the text are changed on the presses. The typographic design allows for the greater length of translations (into German, for example); chosen typefaces have the full range of accents; type is only printed in black; type running around illustrations is avoided; type is not reversed out of blocks or colour or illustrations; and illustrations are not culturally specific to the UK.

Cover design

The cover or jacket protects the book, identifies the author and title, and carries the blurb. The ISBN and bar code enable ordering. The cover's main purpose is to sell. The design should inform as well as attract, be true to the contents, and be tuned to the market. The sales objective of the image is more significant in consumer book publishing (especially paperbacks) than other areas because of the importance of impulse purchase; and covers are used by the sales department to sell books well in advance of publication to wholesalers and retailers. The image must be powerful enough to attract a browser to pick the book up within a few seconds, and be typographically clear enough to be reproduced in reduced form on websites, in catalogues of the publisher, overseas publishers or agents etc. Some cover finishes cause recycling problems in the pulping of stock and affect the publisher's sustainability goals.

Cover images are usually needed at least six months ahead of publication. The designer is briefed by the commissioning editor and generates rough visuals for approval by the editorial, marketing and sales departments. The chosen treatment is developed, and illustrators, photographers and picture researchers commissioned as necessary. Designers will typeset the copy and the cover will be proofed. The author may be consulted over the cover, or need to be persuaded by the editor of the merits of the publisher's choice. Covers arouse strong passions amongst all participants, and at worst may be revised right up to publication. For important titles many different versions will be tried before the final selection is made; retailers may also be consulted and can sway the final decision. If WHSmith or Waterstones is seen as the key channel for the book, their opinion (and likely order) is of vital importance. Sometimes a retailer may request a special edition with their own covers: for example, Waterstones sold for the Christmas market an exclusive gift edition of Sarah Perry's *The Essex Serpent* (2016).

PICTURE RESEARCH

Picture research is the selection, procurement and collection of illustrations of all kinds. There are few in-house picture researchers, mostly concentrated in some of the large consumer and children's book publishers (where they may create a picture library), and educational houses. More commonly a publisher or packager will use expert freelance researchers, who specialize in particular subjects and serve a range of media. Otherwise, picture research for the text or cover may be just part of an assistant's work in an editorial or design department.

A general working specification for a book is drawn up in the editorial department. This covers the title, author, publication date, print run, book's market and its territorial extent, number of pictures required, ratio of colour to black and white, page size and picture budget. The picture researcher will be briefed by the editor or designer usually before the author has completed the manuscript, to ensure that the pictures are ready for the design stage. The brief can range from being very specific (the author or editor supplying a complete picture list citing most sources), less specific (just listing the subjects), to very vague (requesting pictures to fit the manuscript). It is vital for the researcher to clarify the brief.

The researcher may read the outline or manuscript in order to generate a list of ideas for approval by the editor and the author, or amend the picture list supplied by the author to something more feasible. An estimate of cost is produced, based on the researcher's experience, and the researcher advises whether the time and budget allocated are realistic; and potential sources are listed. The researcher cannot progress quickly with selection without knowing where to look for an image, and without a relevant set of contacts.

Sourcing pictures

The possible sources, both home and abroad, are varied and include:

- museums,
- libraries,
- archives,
- commercial picture agencies,
- photographers,
- PR departments,
- professional and tourist organizations,
- charities, and
- private individuals.

Some major collections are accessible on the web in low resolution, and there are low-cost banks of images which can be obtained under licence. Researchers consult online directories and picture source books, museum and library catalogues, guidebooks, brochures, magazines, acknowledgement lists in books, and forage in reference libraries. They build up personal contacts with picture libraries and agencies, interview photographers, visit photographic exhibitions, and form contacts abroad. They compile their own records, indexes and address books. Their knowledge accumulates with each assignment.

Picture research

SKILLS

Picture researchers require the ability to interpret the message the book is trying to convey and, during selection, to make critical judgements on technical possibilities and costs as well as on aesthetic values. An understanding of the complexities of copyright and permission fees backs up their knowledge of sources; and allied to budget consciousness are the skills of negotiation especially with commercial picture agencies. Researchers must be highly organized in their work. As one art director puts it, 'It's a fascinating job – creative as well as administrative and business-like.'

Picture researchers are only as good as their source address books and accurate visual memories. They must keep up to date and use imagination in research, not just in visualizing fresh uses for remembered pictures but almost instinctively knowing where to start looking for pictures on any subject. Also necessary are methodical thinking, the knack of finding cheap sources, and a dogged persistence to get into new areas, getting behind closed doors. It is vital to forge good relations with sources – on the telephone, in writing and face to face. Some picture researchers have a degree in fine art or the history of art; knowledge of foreign languages eases contact with overseas sources; and IT skills are essential.

Photographs can be commissioned for a project from photographers. Working to a brief, they will set up a shoot specially for the publisher. This can be expensive, with fees sometimes payable to the subject as well, but it should provide high-quality images. Often the relatives or friends of staff are called upon to act as subjects. Images may be put up online during the shoot for approval, to ensure the right images have been taken.

The criteria for selecting picture sources include the nature of the material required, such as the subject range, type of material, quality, and the service offered – accessibility, speed and reliability, terms and conditions restricting borrowing or use of material, and cost. The use of stock images will lower the cost but are likely to look cheap alongside higher-quality pictures used in competing titles. Researchers will know which picture libraries are more expensive and from which ones special terms may be sought, perhaps when selecting a number from the same source.

With the list of potential sources compiled, the next task is to request and collect the pictures by telephoning, emailing or visiting. The web has made it much easier to view sample images, and today most images are received from agencies electronically. Under a limited licence, digital files can be used to prepare sample pages, but a full licence must be agreed in order to include the images in the final publication. For non-digital images, replies are reviewed, and the incoming material is logged and labelled with sources' names. The researcher is responsible for the good care of the material, so they select suitable items and quickly return the rejects to avoid paying holding fees and reduce the risk of loss.

The researcher does the initial selection and rejection of the pictures from a large assortment. The criteria for selection include the picture's editorial content – for example, does the picture make the points or convey the impression or mood the author intended? Also important are the picture's composition, which should give the content clarity and impact, and reproducibility (tonal range, colour range and definition), bearing in mind the quality of paper and reproduction method to be used. The costs are assessed – reproduction fees, fees for digital use, print fees if buying prints, and search and loss/damage fees. Some pictures may be rejected on the grounds of cost.

Once the researcher has sufficient suitable illustrations, the cost is estimated again and a meeting held with the editor and designer to make the next selection. It might be that the researcher has to find more pictures very quickly before the final selection is made. Photographs must be ready by first proof stage to enable the designer to start the page layout. The researcher organizes the pictures for handover to the designer, and supplies the picture credit copy and information for the captions (provided by the sources of the photographs) to the editor.

The next task is to write to the sources for copyright permission to reproduce pictures, and to negotiate the fees. These will depend upon the territories and languages, print and digital formats required, the sales forecast, and the size (whole page, half page or quarter page), and whether the image is for a cover/jacket or the inside of the book. Some ebooks and online editions appear without the illustrations from the print edition in order to save on cost – the fees requested reflect the continuing anxieties of agencies about the use of images in digital publications (can the publisher control copying of the whole book or the image?). The researcher passes the suppliers' invoices for payment and calculates the total picture costs. After checking the page proofs (some sources want copies), the book is printed, and the final responsibility, if required, is to return the pictures to the sources.

PRODUCTION

The publisher's production department is the link between editors and designers and external suppliers. As the publisher's big spender, it buys the services of the pre-press suppliers and the printers which manufacture the books – and also raw materials, such as paper, if purchased separately. As publishers move further into digital publishing, the department increasingly deals with technology providers and developers, and has the responsibility for reorganizing workflows. The production department manages the pre-press technologies and the digital archive of the publisher's products for print and digital publication. In this respect, 'production' broadly defined concerns content management and is highly technical. Overall the job of production is

> to manage the conversion of inputs into outputs using a series of processes (usually provided by outside suppliers) so that the required number of books is available at the right time and to the right standard... Production management is about project management. (Bullock, 2012, page 25)

ESG

Larger companies have made commitments in the areas of ESG (environmental, social, governance) given their sourcing of work from companies around the world, often in developing nations. For example, the Hachette UK Group is part of the Lagardère group (owned by Vivendi), a signatory of the UN Global Compact, which asks companies to 'embrace, support and enact, within their sphere of influence, a set of core values in the areas of human rights, labour standards, the environment and anti-corruption.'

Sustainability is at the forefront of publishers' agendas: 'it is since 2019 that we've seen a remarkable re-evaluation of the need for sustainability in end-to-end production and distribution. The largest publishers now have designated roles and departments responsible entirely for their environmental impact activities' (*Publishers Weekly*, 19 April 2023). A global supply chain highlights the dilemma of book miles – books may be printed the other side of the world, say in China, before entering the warehouse in the UK. In the area of environmental impact, many publishers are trying to achieve carbon-neutral targets. Penguin Random House UK has declared that:

> We are already climate neutral in our direct operations, and will be climate neutral in our global value chain by 2030. Our most significant carbon footprint lies in our global value chain, in particular because of the energy intensive production process required to make paper in a paper mill. (penguin.co.uk)

Improved sales forecasts can reduce overstocks in the warehouse, and digital printing gives much more flexibility over print runs and allows printing to order. Distributed printing reduces the amount of book miles as books need not be

Making publishing more environmentally sustainable: A case study

Georgia Buckthorn, publisher of Ivy Kids, an imprint of Quarto

E★PERT

In 2021 we launched a book imprint, the kind of which has never been seen before in the UK: Ivy Kids. We aim to publish books that connect children to the natural world and tell joyful stories about our precious planet. But that's not what makes our imprint different to all the others. The real difference in in how the books are made.

All Ivy Kids' picture books, activity and non-fiction titles are printed on 100% post-consumer-waste recycled paper, as locally to where they will be sold as possible. Our UK editions are printed right here in the UK. Our European co-editions are printed in mainland Europe.

Ivy Kids sits within the Quarto Group, a global illustrated publisher, which has embraced this experimental new imprint as a way of taking first steps towards a more sustainable industry for us all. It all started in 2019, when I was working closely with a colleague on a couple of other children's imprints. It was the summer of the vast, global school strikes, inspired by Greta Thunberg. A picture book manuscript was sent to us that was a fictionalized retelling of Greta's story.

We knew we had to publish it, but to sell Greta's story without taking concrete steps to embody the message that she was communicating – that we need to reduce humanity's impact on our planetary home, and fast – felt cynical. So, we took ambitious action, finding local printers in the UK, the US and Europe, and sourcing 100% post-consumer-waste recycled paper and boards. The book was hugely successful, and it paved the way for launching the Ivy Kids imprint entirely produced in this way.

The reality of making books sustainably is complex. Right now, no other publishing company is doing this, so the demand for the 100 per cent recycled paper is low. This makes the supply chains fragile. We often run into issues such as our paper source disappearing thanks to global events. While the paper is still a niche product and most illustrated printing happens abroad, the costs are also a great deal higher, so margins are squeezed and working in a commercial

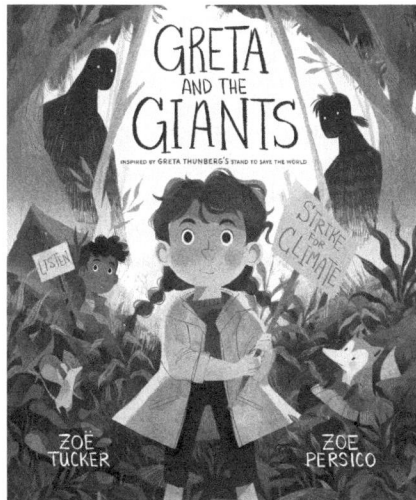

environment it can be harder to make the figures add up. However, our unique production approach has already given us the opportunity to work with significant and inspirational figures such as Isabella Tree and Ranger Hamza, and have been shortlisted for the prestigious Waterstones Children's Book Prize with *The Fairy Garden*.

Ultimately, for a truly transformed world that remains habitable for humans and our fellow living beings, we will need to reshape 'business as usual' in every sector, including publishing. As a species we cannot continue the 'take, make, dispose' relationship we have with the Earth's resources. This includes the virgin paper and other materials we use to make books. Ivy Kids is exploring the first steps of what this could look like in our industry. We hope that soon, many other companies will join us.

shipped long distances but can be printed in domestic markets. Yet there remain books, such as those in colour, where the need for cost savings will encourage the use of overseas printers.

The book's carbon footprint

The carbon footprint of a typical paperback book has been estimated at 1 kg CO_2e, printed on regularly sourced (virgin) paper and with around 60 per cent of the copies printed being sold. This figure reduces to 400 g CO_2e if recycled paper is used and all copies are sold. Mike Berners-Lee says that the 'carbon footprint of a typical paperback is about the same as watching 6 hours of TV'. (Berners-Lee, 2022, page 73). In the greater scheme of things the carbon footprint of an individual book is relatively unimportant compared to the figure for an average person in the UK of 13,000 kg (annual carbon footprint) but still publishers are keen to report on their environmental impact and look for ways to reduce carbon emissions. An important part of the work of the production department is giving attention to environmental considerations.

Organization of the production department

Within a production department, there are commonly three main levels of job.

Production manager or director

They are responsible for the purchasing policy on sources of supply; establishing standard book sizes and papers; controlling the flow of work and maintaining quality standards; contributing to the preparation of the publishing programme by planning schedules and cost budgets for forthcoming books; and responding to major technical changes such as managing the pre-publication workflow.

The manager contributes to the firm's profitability by buying materials and services at the most economic cost, by conserving the firm's cash by influencing the timing of major items of expenditure and by obtaining the longest possible credit periods from suppliers. The manager also handles the production of certain important books.

Production controller

This role is responsible for seeing books through the production stages from manuscript to receipt of bound copies and ebook publication. They may specialize in whole imprints or just part of the list, for example working alongside certain editors. This role may also be called a production editor or project manager.

Production assistant

Some people start their production careers at this level. The production assistant gives clerical or administrative support to the department. They monitor proofs and production schedules, chase editors and suppliers, and record production costings.

In some publishers, production activities are split. One section deals with the pre-press process: essentially concerned with originating the products with external suppliers, or creating them in-house; and with the maintenance of the digital archive and its internal and external connections. Another section organizes and purchases the manufacturing of printed books and journals: essentially from printers and paper suppliers; and sometimes of other non-print items, such as CD-ROMs and DVDs and their packaging.

Production and book design go hand in hand. Production staff may design the books or hire freelance designers, or in-house book designers report to the head of production – if there is not a separate design department. The production department gives the accounts department information on anticipated costs and their likely timing, details of work in progress, and materials held in stock. In a small firm an editor may carry out production duties or use freelancers or external companies which provide a project management/production service; but with increasing size a firm will employ its own production, IT and data management professionals.

Provisional estimates

The production manager supplies the commissioning editor with estimates of the costs of producing a proposed new title, and may suggest alternative production options. There is increasing use of automated costing systems that work well for standard formats, leaving production colleagues to advise on more complicated projects. The book is envisaged in broad terms, for example its format, extent, illustrative content, the quality of paper desired, and the binding style. The estimate itemizes the costs across different sales forecasts. Some costs, such as for editorial and design work, will not change with the sales forecast, and overall the unit cost will decrease as these fixed costs are spread over higher forecasts. The costs for a book include:

- the origination of illustrations,
- illustration and text permissions,
- design costs,
- editorial costs (including copy-editing and proofreading),
- typesetting and proofing,
- printing and binding,
- paper, and
- cover printing.

Once the author has signed the contract, production may advise the author, directly or via the editor, on how the text should be keyed – some publishers issue authors with style sheets in Word, or XML templates. The production controller, who gathers information from the editor or from pre-production meetings, prepares a specification – a detailed technical description of the book. The book's desired physical attributes, the amount of money and time available for its production, and any special market needs (particular typefaces, a subsequent paperback edition or co-edition) are taken into account, and the choice of production processes and materials is made. In children's publishing, ensuring physical product safety is crucial.

Print and paper buying

The specification is sent to one or more suppliers so that they submit an estimate or quotation. Although there are printers that carry out all the processes, they may not do all economically or well. The typesetting and printing specifications may be sent to different specialist firms, known as trade suppliers. A publisher usually deals with a core of regular and trusted suppliers whose technology, machinery, staff, strengths and weaknesses are known; but new ones are tried. Sometimes fixed price schedules are negotiated with major print suppliers for standard types of work, which reduces the need for quotations and simplifies estimating. Suppliers may offer discounts on titles processed in batches or during slack periods. Moreover, the long time (for example six to 18 months) books take to produce gives publishers and packagers the option of using overseas suppliers (for example in Europe, the Far East or the USA), notwithstanding the impact on their carbon footprint. Whilst the printing of monochrome books is largely carried out in the UK, most colour book printing now goes abroad. The competitiveness of overseas suppliers is affected greatly by exchange rates, but other factors such as freight, communication, and environmental costs, longer timescales, and the location of the book's main markets are considered.

Suppliers are assessed on five main criteria:

- price,
- quality of work,

- service – the ability to keep to dates, or to make up for slippage, and communication,
- capability – skills and machinery, and
- capacity – the ability to handle larger jobs/reprint quickly.

The priority given to each varies according to the type of work. For example, a small saving from the cheapest source may be outweighed if that supplier produces inferior work or misses dates. Cost savings can be achieved by sending work abroad, but other considerations may keep the work in the UK. For example a quick reprint may be needed for a bestseller in the run-up to Christmas, and a domestic printer will be much more amenable if they had carried out the original job.

The quotations are assessed, prices sometimes negotiated downwards and the work awarded. From the quoted prices, another in-house estimate is prepared. Paper is a major cost item which can account for 40 per cent or more of the production cost of the book. It is bought either by the printer, or by the publisher from a paper merchant or directly from a mill. Wood pulp and paper are world commodities priced in dollars, subject to exchange rate variations and to price instability. During periods of price fluctuations or of real or imagined shortages, publishers may peg the price by buying forward, or store paper as an insurance against non-availability for quick reprints, even though that ties up the publisher's cash and incurs storage costs. Publishers are responsive to environmental concerns, and will choose to purchase paper derived from sustainable forests (e.g. Forest Stewardship Certified) and made with minimum pollutants; others use acid-free materials to ensure that their books and journals will last. Publishers are keen to increase their use of recycled paper but this tends to be more expensive and less easy to source. In 2020 recycled fibre was 9.2 per cent of the overall paper usage for the US Hachette Book Group. There is a fine balance between using FSC-certified virgin paper or recycled paper. The carbon footprint of a book will vary according to the paper used (virgin or recycled), and whether books are recycled or end their life in landfill. The use of virgin pulp is more energy-intensive than recycling but the energy source of the mill may alter the calculation – say, if the mill sources its energy from renewables.

Paper has both weight and thickness (or bulk). Short books can be bulked out with a thicker paper; long books may need to have thinner and lighter paper. Recycled paper tends to be thinner than virgin papers. Paper may also be judged on its opacity – the degree to which image or text shows through to the other side of the page – and its colour or shade – from white through to cream or ivory. Coated papers are used for highly illustrated titles such as art books. Acid-free papers have a longer life.

There is also a range of sizes in which books can be printed (Table 8.1). A trade paperback is 198 × 129 mm (also called B format) and the mass-market paperback size is 178 × 110 mm (A format). Popular formats for hardbacks are demy octavo (216 × 138 mm) and royal octavo (234 × 156 mm). The dimension head to tail is given first in the UK, but in the rest of Europe and the USA the convention is to give the width dimension first (the US dimensions are also in inches).

The format for this book is pinched crown quarto

E★PERT

Paper and sustainability

Adrian Bullock, Associate Lecturer, Oxford International Centre for Publishing

Paper is a versatile material tough enough to be used for packaging, and soft enough to wipe your mouth with. It can trace its origins back to China at the beginning of the second century (105 CE), when paper was made using a recipe of pulp from tree bark, bits of hemp, rags, and old fishing nets. However, since the 1860s, most paper has been made from wood pulp, predominantly from softwood – coniferous trees, such as pine and spruce. These trees are used because of their longer fibres, which give paper its strength; and, because they grow best in temperate climates, most of the world's wood pulp is produced in the northern hemisphere in countries like Canada or Finland. Pulp can be produced from hardwood trees like oak or beech, but this is not generally done – their fibres are too short. This is also true of tropical hardwoods which grow in the rainforests of South America and Africa. The threat to trees here does not come from papermaking: the rainforests are being cleared, and the trees burned, to make way for cattle ranching, agriculture and mining.

Trees for papermaking are planted as a crop, just like rice or wheat; and, like a crop, they are harvested at a later date – sometimes 25 to 30 years later, or even longer. Only part of the felled tree ends up as paper: the trunk, for example, is usually turned into timber for the furniture and construction industries. For every tree cut down, at least three seedlings are planted to ensure that the paper and the timber industries do not run out of their basic raw material – wood.

Despite the predictions of a paperless world, paper consumption has, if anything, increased over the past 20 years, bringing with it growing pressure on forests, as the need for wood pulp intensifies. The Forest Stewardship Council (FSC) with its familiar tick-tree logo was established in 1993 'to promote environmentally appropriate, socially beneficial and economically viable management of the world's forests' on a global basis. FSC was soon followed by other initiatives like the Programme for the Endorsement of Forest Certification (PEFC), the Sustainable Forest Initiative (SFI), and the Global Forest Coalition (GFC) – all with similar aims.

Publishers as major consumers of paper are increasingly aware of a market expectation that they source their paper responsibly and sustainably; and more and more books carry the FSC logo with the statement that 'the publisher makes every effort to ensure that the paper used in its books is made from trees that are legally sourced from well managed and credibly certified forests'.

This is certainly a step in the right direction. But sustainability is more than just about responding to market pressure, it is about doing things differently and smartly with the future firmly in mind; and, in doing so, to come closer to the UN World Commission on Environment and Development's definition of sustainable development as 'development that meets the needs of the present without compromising the ability of future generations to meet their own needs'. There *is* more that a publisher can do to make their printed products more sustainable and a good place to start is by rethinking how their printed products are created, manufactured, and distributed, which involves looking at things as diverse as:

- their products' physical specifications in terms of format, word count/ extent, typeface and size, lines per page, number of illustrations, use of colour, binding style, and, of course, paper
- how many copies to print
- how, when, and where they are printed and distributed

When it comes to paper, the number of options might appear daunting: paper, as a natural product, has a range of physical and optical properties like weight, thickness, smoothness, grain direction, pulp type, brightness, whiteness, shade, and opacity, all of which are key factors in determining the quality and cost of the product in much the same way that the quality of the product determines the kind of paper to use and its cost.

There are a few simple strategies that a publisher can adopt to reduce the impact of their paper use on the environment. The first is to use certified recycled paper wherever possible: by using less water, energy, and chemicals during production, and by keeping paper out of landfill, the environmental impact of a tonne of recycled paper is lower than that of a tonne of virgin paper. Other strategies are to:

- reduce the paper weight (grammage, substance): lighter books use less paper, and cost less to move around. Book paper weights range from 70–115 gsm
- reduce the paper thickness (bulk, volume, calliper): thinner books cost less to move around; and they take up less room in a container, on a pallet, and in the warehouse

- print the entire book on uncoated paper: the environmental and economic gains are significant; and the problems once associated with loss of image quality have been solved
- stick to standard formats

The options are presented here rather like an *à la carte* menu from which publishers can make choices, while reserving others for later on. To implement them all at once might be a step too far, too quick. But to ignore them altogether would be irresponsible.

Table 8.1 Standard book formats (UK)

Format	Dimensions (H x W)
A4	297 × 210 mm
Demy quarto	276 × 219 mm
Crown quarto	246 × 189 mm
Pinched crown quarto	Up to 248 × 175 mm
Royal octavo	234 × 156 mm
Demy octavo (C format)	216 × 138 mm
A5	210 × 148 mm
B format	198 × 129 mm
A format	178 × 110 mm

Scheduling and project management

The production controller is usually responsible for all stages in the production of the book, following receipt of the approved manuscript from the editor. The stages include typesetting and cover development through to the final outputs; a production editor will also supervise the copy-editing, proofreading, and index preparation. All of these activities are usually outsourced to specialist freelancers or companies. The controller draws up the schedule of the internal and external operations that end with the output of the PDF file and ebook formats, and delivery of bound copies to the warehouse a few weeks ahead of the publication date. The schedule, related to those of other books, takes account of any optimum publication date, cashflow demands, the time needed for the tasks and to route material to and from suppliers. Alternatively, if the project management is outsourced to a full service supplier, the controller liaises with the supplier.

Production staff monitor progress and chase editors, designers and external suppliers to keep to agreed dates. As all the book's material passes between editor and designer, and between publisher and suppliers, it is processed by production at every stage, as are any problems with suppliers. Outgoing material is accompanied by documentation and orders; incoming material is logged, sent on to editors and designers, and return dates agreed. If the return dates are not adhered to, the machine time booked at the printers will be missed and the book unduly delayed.

Operations

Some of the large international publishers have operations departments which act as a bridge between editorial and production departments, and liaise with sales and distribution. Their work includes tracking the publishing programmes, managing retail slots, maintaining title records (including metadata) over the entire lifecycle of a book, working with overseas sister companies on their editions, and shipping and inventory control matters. The complexity is increasing with the rise of special editions, subscription boxes and retailer exclusives, multiple formats and added content.

Digital workflow management

Production is responsible for digital file preparation, file conversion to numerous formats, the checking of files (preferably including accessibility), the distribution of files and their storage and archiving in a digital asset management system. In some publishers, the pre-press processes are carried out in-house and the documents progress through the stages and staff entirely in digital form. Content management systems (CMS) were first used by journal and reference publishers faced with processing and reusing large amounts of text data. They are designed to manage the creation, handling, storage and delivery of content for publication, and subsequent re-purposing. Content is stored without print-specific formatting, and typically XML is used to tag the content using standardized templates. As digital publishing has become more important, workflows are adapted to hold content in properly archived files, which can then be used to publish products on different platforms. Journals publishers have led the way in creating a production route that enables articles to be published rapidly online.

Additional functionality includes workflow management and access control. Such systems monitor the movement of jobs through the stages, and the workloads and performance of staff. Automated alerts track the progress of files as manual or automated sequences are applied. Users of the system are given differing levels of access. Authors may be part of the process – for example journal authors may be asked to write using an XML template supplied by the publisher; they can also track their articles online through the production process via journals management systems. The Journal Article Tag Suite (JATS) develops best practice in XML tagging across the industry.

Production

Fundamental to production is a thorough understanding of current technical processes and digital developments, of machinery and materials, and of freight systems and methods of payment. More senior roles require strategic thinking as digital workflows are configured or adjusted. Most production staff have a degree or professional qualification, or equivalent professional background. Knowledge of languages is useful in a department handling international co-editions. Numeracy, computer literacy skills, the ability to see alternative options and the consideration of all components are necessary in costing titles. Project management skills cover planning and progress chasing skills – ascertaining and clarifying objectives, setting priorities, assessing strengths and weaknesses of suppliers, foreseeing crunch points, and the development of specifications and schedules. Strong negotiations skills are required to deal with a range of suppliers.

Effective and fluent communication with in-house staff and external suppliers is crucial. Production staff must be able to work with editors and designers as a team even though their priorities of tight cost control and the maintenance of dates may conflict with those of editors and designers. The role of production editor straddles the two worlds of production and editorial. Much of the work is highly administrative, requiring a good memory and meticulous attention to detail and record keeping. While friendly working relationships are formed with suppliers, production staff must never get too close to suppliers otherwise the negotiating edge is lost. Sometimes they have to be very tough, and they must have the integrity to reject any inducements.

A digital web press at Clay's

Production staff come under great pressure. As the buffer between
publisher and suppliers they receive kicks from all sides. They must buy
competitively, conserve the cash, meet the deadlines, and not make mistakes,
which can be expensive to correct. Much time is spent troubleshooting
and trying to keep everyone happy. They need to resolve problems, to think
laterally and find the best solution, to switch quickly from one thing to
another, and thrive under the strain.

Monitoring costs and quality

Many books, especially if illustrated, may change from their original concept
during the writing and design stages. A new format may be chosen or the number
of illustrations varied. Deviations from the original estimate and specification are
monitored and costed. There is a constant risk that the estimate of costs made at
the outset will be exceeded. Substantial proof corrections quickly erode a title's
profitability. Costs incurred to date are recorded and revised estimates of total costs
produced, particularly at the page-proof stage. Then the publisher normally fixes
the book's price and the balance of print/digital sales, influenced, for example, by
the actual advance orders from booksellers. Suppliers' invoices are subsequently
checked, passed for payment, or queried.

The production controller checks the completeness of material at every stage
as well as the accuracy of the instructions from the editor and designer, the quality
of illustration originals sent to suppliers, and the quality of material returned.
Technical advice is given to editors and designers to help them in their work.
Constant contact with suppliers' representatives, and visits to suppliers maintain
relationships.

Highly illustrated quality colour books may involve the production manager
or controller in approving the sheets of each section run off the press – whether
in the UK or abroad – and taking responsibility for the quality on behalf of the
publisher/packager. The printing is compared against the final proof to ensure
that corrections have been made, and that the colour quality matches the values
agreed at the contract proof stage.

Advance copies of the bound stock are checked to ensure that the specified
materials have been used, and that the binding, as well as the overall quality of
the product, meets the publisher's standards. Exceptionally if a major error is
discovered, an enquiry is held to determine who is responsible and has to pay.
Finally, all the costs of producing the book are compiled. Controllers also cost and
organize reprints and new editions; some large publishers employ staff solely for
this task. The publisher or packager owning the digital file does not always use the
original printer in which case the job is moved to the new supplier.

The printing of editions for other firms (for example, English and foreign
language co-editions) involves supplying the rights department with estimates
of costs. The costs will include printing the bulk order – or if the buyer does the
printing, the cost of supplying digital files – and costs of imprint changes – for
example, the name of the co-publisher will have to appear on the title page instead

of the original publisher's and the details on the copyright page will change; all of this makes a halt in the printing and costs money. When the publisher or packager prints foreign language editions, the overseas publishers supply the file of the translated text which is checked by production to ensure it fits the layout of the colour illustrations. Production staff may also be concerned with the purchasing of the manufacturing of non-print items and their special retail or mail-order packaging requirements.

Suppliers are chosen according to cost, technology, and quality. Significant cost savings can be achieved by outsourcing typesetting and printing to countries in the Far East. Companies in India, for example, not only offer typesetting but also IT services (digitization and tagging) and editorial and design work. It is now possible to outsource the whole process from receipt of the author's text through to the digital file for the printer.

PRODUCTION PROCESSES

Typesetting

The core business of a typesetter is text and data processing, plus other services. This could range from cleaning up authors' Word files prior to editing, XML tagging, pagination and proofing, through to production of outputs for printing copies, and for ebook and web distribution. They may digitize the backlist in whatever formats the books exist. There is a reduced role for typesetters when designers supply the finished files.

Some firms offer additional editorial and design services while others concentrate on highly technical material or text database management. The vast number of titles with no or minimal illustrations do not require designers to lay out the pages – the typesetters' largely automated pagination systems do it for the publishers. They can generally take a 100,000-word manuscript and submit page proofs to a publisher within two weeks – much faster if supplied with coded content.

Typesetters use a variety of applications, such as Adobe InDesign and (though less widely used) QuarkXPress. Only typesetters who have specialist-trained staff operate the very expensive and sophisticated programs designed especially for academic books and journals (such as Arbortext Advanced Print Publisher – formerly 3B2). LaTeX, pronounced 'laytek', is an open source program with many variants, designed by mathematicians in Chicago for authors of physics and mathematics to present papers and books full of equations. The typesetter will supply proofs as PDF files for checking by the publisher and author. The publisher will usually ask the typesetter to convert the output of its pagination systems into PDF files. From such files printers are able to output text and graphics straight to plate or press.

Reproduction of illustrations

Illustrations may be prepared or sourced in digital form and can be provided to the typesetter as EPS (encapsulated PostScript) files – from a drawing program – or as TIFFs (tagged image file format) or JPEGs (joint photographic experts group) – for half-tones. Non-digital originals of illustrations are converted to digital form.

Book printing presses cannot reproduce directly the continuous shades or tones of colour appearing in photographs or pencil drawings, thus 'the half-tone process' is used. The image of the black and white or colour original is screened, i.e. broken into a series of dots of varying size with larger, closer or adjoining dots in dark areas; and smaller, further apart, or no dots at all in light areas. When printed, the dots create the illusion of continuous shades.

Printing a full-colour image requires a four-colour process. The image needs to be broken down into four basic colours: cyan (blue), magenta (red), yellow, and black (known as key). These colours, used to put ink on to paper, are called 'CMYK', or process colours, and are subtractive primaries. Red, green and blue (RGB) are the additive primaries, used in TV screens and computer monitors. They cannot be used on a printing press. Colour separation can be done using a scanner, or a digital image can be saved as CMYK in an application such as Adobe Photoshop. In order to print a four-colour image, you ideally need a four-colour press, capable of printing all four colours in one impression. It is possible to print a four-colour image on a two-colour press, but this is less efficient and can cause quality problems. Various kinds of proofs are submitted to the publisher before the final digital file of the illustrations is accepted. If necessary, books can be printed in six colours. This process was used, for example, for Kevin McCloud's *Choosing Colours* (2007), where orange and green inks were printed after the CMYK to create a six-colour job.

Litho printing: imposition and platemaking

The printing plates on a litho press do not print one page at a time. Rather each sheet of paper, printed both sides, carries 8, 16 or 32 pages (or multiples of these), and is subsequently folded several times and cut to make a section (or signature) of the bound book. Since printers have different sized presses and different binding machinery, each printer is responsible for its own imposition: the arrangement of the pages that will be printed on each side of the sheet so that once the sheet is printed and folded the pages will be in the right sequence and position. The publisher will supply the printer with PDF files that have been prepared by the designer or typesetter. The printer then imposes the pages on to each plate – this is called computer to plate (CTP).

Online content

Low-resolution PDF files can be conveniently put on the web for either downloading or viewing within a browser. The user sees a replica of the final printed page. Journal articles are often presented in PDF for the ease of librarians and others wanting a common standard, and for publishers who are working with print-designed documents.

Structured mark-up of the text using XML, independent of any typographic mark-up, allows the text to be published in different ways. The XML file conforms to an agreed DTD (document type definition) or schema that specifies the tags and their relationship to each other. From a source XML file, the content can be published as a book, an ebook, an HTML (HyperText Markup Language) file for the web, or on a mobile device. Publishers also find it easier to sell XML data to third parties for electronic publication. Its use facilitates the online linking of elements such as bibliographic references and illustrations. The growing use of Adobe InDesign by publishers facilitates the origination of XML.

Publishers or content aggregators look to add value online by generating keywords for content, enabling online searches, and also by identifying text elements or chunks by metadata. For example, a journal publisher can use a DOI (digital object identifier) to identify an article or an illustration within the article. A DOI name can apply to any form of intellectual property expressed in any digital environment. DOI names have been called 'the bar code for intellectual property': like the physical bar code, they are enabling tools for use all through the supply chain to add value and save cost (doi.org). Industry-wide initiatives such as CrossRef enable the linking from references in online journals to the cited article (crossref.org).

Publishers with websites or online services which need regular updating or additions may opt to use a content management system (CMS) – software for managing websites. For some publishers the web is a different medium needing different design approaches, which are not based on linear textual organization and print-derived typographic design. Web pages may be prepared using HTML and supplementary content, such as animations, video clips, and sound recordings. Interactive prototypes for both websites and apps can be created using software such as Adobe XD. An example of the benefits of using a highly structured approach is the cooking database of the *New York Times*. Their database has a variety of fields for each recipe, and using finely structured data enables them to use granular HTML markup to improve their SEO as well as sort recipes by meal, occasion, diet, and cooking method.

Printing

Many books are still printed by offset lithography (abbreviated to offset or litho), but there has been a rapid growth in the use of digital printing. Offset metal plates have a flat surface which is treated so that the areas to be printed attract grease (ink) and repel water; and the non-printing areas attract water and repel ink. A plate is clamped around a cylinder on the press, dampened and inked by rollers. The plate rotates against a rubber-coated cylinder (or blanket) on to which the inked image is offset and from which the ink is transferred to the paper.

Many offset presses are sheet-fed and vary in plate size and in capabilities. There are also offset presses – known as web presses – that print on to a reel of paper. Sheet-fed presses would be the usual choice for standard printings of black-and-white books. Web presses produce a folded signature at the end of the operation. This, and their high running speeds, make them attractive for long print runs.

A digital folder, folding digitally printed work from a digital web press at Clay's

Digital printing

High-speed digital printing has begun to challenge litho printing. Digital printers do not use printing plates – instead they create the impression on the paper with an ink jet or by using toner and electrostatic charge (like in a photocopier). A number of single copy orders can be printed one after the other without the disruption of having to set up the press each time – the computer lines up the next titles. The quality of digital printing has been variable, but is now perfectly acceptable for most monochrome books and increasingly for colour work.

The choice of litho or digital printing comes down to economics. Depending on the equipment operated by the printer, litho runs are much less common below 4,000 copies. But other factors may come into play such as the quality, page extent, or format required. High end print jobs are likely to remain with litho, for example for colour work. The use of litho means working to pagination in multiples of, say, 16 or 32 pages – there no such limitation with digital. The use of litho is more time-consuming work with more stages involved. Digital printing facilitates the viability of printing a book with a very short run – for example five copies – but also genuine print on demand – where just one copy is ordered by a customer.

Digital printing is suitable for use by publishers of specialist books or for backlist titles more generally. After the initial printing (litho or digital), publishers face continuing demand. They could reprint a short run by digital printing, either to hold in stock or to supply a major customer, or print one copy in response to a firm order. Once the title moves to 'on-demand' status it need never go out of print. The manufacturing time from the receipt of an order for one book is measured in hours, rather than in the weeks taken by litho print-runs, with next-day dispatch. The automated workflow batches together different titles sharing common specifications, configures the production machinery accordingly, manufactures the batch, and then reconfigures the machinery to the next shared specification.

There are now also automated stock-replenishment systems using short-run printing, whereby printers receive direct feeds from the publisher's warehouses and produce in quantities of anything from 20 to 500. In order to work cost effectively and quickly, they may standardize sizes, paper, cover finishes and binding.

Digital printing has generated new ways of working beyond the management by publishers of the backlist and single copy orders. Wholesalers can use it to produce copies for end-users from digital files supplied by publishers. The printing of hard copies becomes 'distributed' as opposed to being centralized by publishers through their own print suppliers. This can happen elsewhere in the world, reducing the 'book miles' and carbon footprint of a title: previously a bulk order might arrive in the UK from an overseas printer, only for copies to be sent back again around the world. Publishers can customize for a teacher a pack of teaching resources drawn from a variety of titles for student purchase. Smaller digital presses are now commercially available, and these have the potential to be placed anywhere in the world, in bookshops, libraries and universities, with access to an unlimited catalogue of titles over the internet.

Binding

After printing, the sheets are folded by the printer or possibly by a trade binder. The folded 8-, 16- or 32-page sections are gathered in sequence to make up every book. Some hardbacks and some quality paperbacks, especially those printed on coated papers (including some textbooks) have their sections sewn together. With quality hardbacks, the sewn sections are trimmed on three sides (leaving the sewn spine folds intact), end papers are glued to the first and last sections (unless the text paper is sufficiently strong), any decorative head or tail bands added, strong material (known as lining) glued to the spine to reinforce the hinge with the case,

and the spine sometimes rounded. Meanwhile the case is made by gluing the front and back boards (and paper backstrip of the spine) to the 'cloth' which in turn is blocked with the title, author and imprint in gold, silver or a range of different colours. The outer sides of the end papers are pasted, the finished case dropped over the book (spine-side up), and the book squeezed. The jacket is printed on a small colour press, sometimes by another firm. This is often laminated with clear plastic film and is wrapped round the finished book. Sometimes the printed cover is glued to the case before binding to produce a *printed paper case* (PPC) or *cover to board* book.

Sewn bindings are stronger but more expensive. Adhesive binding methods are commonly used for paperbacks and some hardbacks. *Perfect* binding is used typically for paperbacks – the spine folds of the sections are cut off and the spine edge of the now individual leaves roughened. Glue is applied to hold the leaves together and to stick the printed cover to the book, which is then trimmed on three sides. The cover may have been varnished (on a printing press or special machine) or laminated. Another method, cheaper than sewing but stronger and more expensive than perfect binding, is known variously as *slotted*, *notch* or *burst* binding. The spine folds of the sections are not cut off. Instead they are perforated during sheet folding. The binding machine merely injects the adhesive to hold together the folded sections, applies the cover and trims the book.

Packing and distribution

The printer/binder packs quantities of the book by shrink wrapping, parcelling or in cartons and delivers them on pallets to the publisher's specified warehouse. Printers have traditionally delivered the bulk stock of new titles to the publisher's warehouse, which in turn ships them out to the main retailers and wholesalers. However, printers competing on service, may deliver stock directly to key customers and to individuals, and may act as retailers. In the case of print journals, for example, they may deliver to subscribers.

Now read this

Adrian Bullock, *Book Production*, Routledge, 2012.

Sources

Tricia Austin and Richard Doust, *New Media Design*, Laurence King, 2007.
Phil Baines and Andrew Haslam, *Type and Typography*, Laurence King, 2005.
Alan Bartram, *Making Books: Design in British publishing since 1945*, British Library and Oak Knoll Press, 1999.
Mike Berners Lee, *The Carbon Footprint of Everything*, Greystone, 2022.
Robert Bringhurst, *The Elements of Typographic Style*, version 3.1, Hartley & Marks, 2005.
Adrian Bullock and Meredith Walsh, *The Green Design and Print Production Handbook*, How Books, 2013.
Simon Garfield, *Just My Type*, Profile, 2010.
Chris Jennings, *eBook Typography for Flowable eBooks*, PagetoScreen ebook, 2012.
Margherita Mariano and Andrea Reece, *Print Production: A complete guide to planning, printing and packaging*, Laurence King, 2024.
Michael Mitchell and Susan Wightman, *Book Typography: A designer's manual*, Libanus Press, 2005.

Michael Mitchell and Susan Wightman, *Typographic Style Handbook*,
    MacLehose Press, 2017.
Lucienne Roberts and Julia Thrift, *The Designer and the Grid,* RotoVision,
    2002.

Web resources

https://bapla.org.uk UK trade association for picture libraries and agencies.
https://bookchainproject.com Book Chain Project provides information
    on sustainable book production, chemical safety, and labour and
    environmental standards.
https://www.britishprint.com British Printing Industries Federation (BPIF).
https://www.crossref.org CrossRef operates a cross-publisher citation linking
    system.
http://www.doi.org International DOI Foundation.
http://environmentalpaper.org/ Environmental Paper Network.

CHAPTER 9

Marketing and publicity

Marketing has a broad role within publishing and marketers play a pivotal role in many aspects of a book's publication. In an age of self-publishing, consumer publishers in particular have to be able to demonstrate to authors the efficacy of their marketing efforts and their ability to develop and manage an author's brand. Book marketers play a vital role in the changing business models of publishers. The effects of the internet and mobile technologies continue to have major implications on the ways in which books are marketed and sold. Readers can see thousands of titles in a bookstore, and on screen they see very few. The challenge for publishers is to help readers to discover, and buy, their books in a digital world of content abundance, much of it available for free.

Whilst it has diminished print newspapers and the amount of review space for books, the web has opened up many new marketing opportunities, often at low direct cost. Internet retailing has broadened and deepened book availability worldwide. The rapid rise of social media has fostered word-of-mouth recommendation – hitherto restricted to family and close friends – and the influence of bloggers, Instagrammers, and book recommendation sites has grown. BookTok has brought books to the attention of a new audience, leading to sales growth for YA and romance fiction amongst other genres. The web enables the development of vertical communities, sharing interests, who can be attracted to a publisher's books, and publishers themselves can develop such communities around their titles. Publishers commission online book trailers, author video chats and podcasts to supplement author tours. Technology reduces the cost of former print-based marketing and extends its reach. For example, trade publishers send digital proofs to reviewers and booksellers (platforms such as NetGalley and Edelweiss facilitate this process); academic publishers send e-inspection copies of textbooks to teachers. Trade publishers produce online newsletters and academic/STM publishers conduct targeted email campaigns when formerly they were restricted to posting out printed items. The power of search has given prominence to SEO (search engine optimization) and the importance of metadata – information about content from a book's cover through to chapter abstracts.

DOI: 10.4324/9781003403289-10

Technology facilitates direct to consumer (B2C) marketing and a dialogue with readers and users. Publishers can connect with individuals within the audience, to inform publishing decisions and increase marketing cost-effectiveness. The direct connection with individuals offers the prospect of being able to customize and personalize the content they wish to consume, and to predict which authors and books will succeed. The use of analytics increases the understanding of consumer behaviour and informs the effectiveness of social media and other campaigns. AI offers tools to analyse a text, write selling copy, micro-segment audiences, and hone the messaging around brands and individual titles.

Marketing staff in large publishing groups may be attached to particular companies, imprints or lists within the group. Many marketing departments consist of just one or two people who do everything, but in medium to large firms there are usually at least three levels: marketing director; marketing, brand or product manager; and marketing executive or assistant. Often in a separate team will be the function of public relations and publicity. Marketing encompasses numerous, diverse activities. Large companies employ specialists in key areas such as social media; sales support; events and exhibitions; and customer databases. The collection and management of data in all its forms and its effective application are increasingly important across all activities. A resource available across a large publisher will be market research and analytics – or consumer insight.

Senior marketing staff may first become involved at the publishing proposal stage. They will advise on product development, especially when the project is a large investment. They will be involved in a range of discussions about the book's pricing, cover, target market and the ways this can be reached; a promotional plan may be a key element in persuading a new author and their agent to sign up with the publisher. From discussions with editors and sales staff, each book is evaluated and decisions made on the promotional effort required – to support sales and for the target readership – and what publicity and media coverage should be sought. The marketing budget may be proportional to the expected sales revenue or set separately for key titles. It is impossible to promote all books equally and, especially in consumer publishing, the lead titles and brand authors receive by far the largest budgets – often proportionate to the bigger advances paid. The sizeable budgets around some titles and authors remain the domain of the large publishing groups. The key judgement for every title is deciding how much to spend to generate profitable sales that more than recoup the outlay.

Penguin Platform is a community of YA readers across social media channels

A company will develop an overall strategy for a list or set of products and services. This will involve targeting particular market segments, positioning the product or brand in the minds of customers, settling on the relevant marketing mix and PR for those customers, and establishing a budget for marketing expenditure. For significant new products or series an individual marketing plan may be prepared. Carefully considered should be how some types of marketing (e.g. through social media) are measurable whilst others (such as PR) are not.

F◎CUS

Marketing plan

There is no fixed template but a marketing plan will often contain the following elements.

Executive summary

Target market and marketing environment

Market segments, market drivers, and the results of market research. Analytical tools to be used include PEST (political, economic, social and technological) and SWOT (strengths, weaknesses, opportunities and threats). Research into reader demographics and social media analytics may be used.

Product overview

Information about the current situation regarding the company's products and competitor activity.

Marketing objectives

These should be SMART: specific, measurable, achievable, realistic, and time-bound. For example, to achieve a market share within the secondary school mathematics market of 15 per cent within three years.

Marketing strategy

Outlines the target markets, key influencers, positioning, the readers the publisher wants to reach, where they can be found, what kinds of marketing they respond to best, and what it will cost to reach them. Analysis of what size of response rate is required in order to make the campaign viable is also essential.

Specific strategies for each area of the marketing mix

The marketing mix is the 4Ps – product, price, place, and promotion. This is covered in detail later in the chapter.

Schedule and budget

Set out are the actions within a time-scale, costed through in detail.

Controls

How will progress be monitored and analysed?

Follow-up plans

What are the possible next stages?

THE MARKET FOR BOOKS

The first step in marketing a product is to understand the nature of the market. A range of data is available on the purchasing behaviour and demographics of the consumer book market. Table 9.1 reveals the factors that influence consumer book purchases in the UK. For marketers it shows the value of building author and character brands, and the impact of the cover and recommendation on a book's sales.

There is variation across the population in terms of the number of books bought. First, around 30 per cent of adults do not buy a book at all – how can publishers reach this part of the population? Generic initiatives to encourage reading are important for the industry. City Reads, which began in Seattle in 1998, encourages a whole city to read the same book. A prominent example in the UK is World Book Day, and in 2023 UK schoolchildren received a £1 book token to spend on a specially created £1 book; or they could put it towards the cost of any book. There is also World Book Night, run by the UK Reading Agency, when free books are handed out on the international day of the book (23 April; also Shakespeare's birth and death date), with a focus on giving to those who do not normally read for pleasure or who have limited access to books. On the same April date, the day of Sant Jordi, the patron saint of Catalonia, by tradition people in that region of Spain give each other a rose or a book.

In the UK, organizations such as the National Literacy Trust and BookTrust are involved in the promotion of reading and literacy. Reading for pleasure amongst both adults and children is under pressure in a rich media environment of social media, TV, the internet, and games. The co-founder of Netflix, Reed Hastings, commented: 'You know, think about it, when you watch a show from Netflix and you get addicted to it, you stay up late at night. We're competing with sleep' (*Guardian*, 18 April 2017). Examining reading amongst children in the UK in 2023, the National Literacy Trust found that just 2 in 5 children or young people enjoyed reading in their free time. Looking at the levels of daily reading, 'Fewer than 3 in 10 (28.0%) children and young people aged 8 to 18 said that they read daily' (literacytrust.org, accessed 8 January 2024). Libraries play an important

23 per cent of the UK population listens to podcasts weekly (RAJAR)

Table 9.1 Top 10 reasons for book purchase

	Percentage of responses
Like/interested in subject	28
Like/interested in the author	24
Description of the book	18
Like the series	16
Low price/on special offer	15
Front cover caught attention/appealed	14
Recommendation/review	12
Like main character(s)	12
Requested/suitable gift/recipient likes	9
Read extract/looked inside	9

Source: 2022 data from Nielsen's UK Books & Consumer Survey.

part in promoting reading and the use of books, and librarians promote books in a variety of ways, from personal recommendations to working with children and schools to champion reading. Yet there have been closures of public libraries in the UK and a precipitous fall in total library borrowings, declining from 377 m in 2001/2 to 150 m in 2018/19.

The temptation for publishers is to concentrate on selling to the heavy book buyers, those who purchase a lot of books. If they are regular visitors to bookshops, they can be reached by ensuring that the books are in stock and promoted there. If frequent purchasers online, they can be reached through social media or word of mouth. BookTok is reaching an audience of younger, mostly female readers; and for audio, as revealed by Nielsen research,

> the downloaded audiobook format 'remains particularly popular among young males, who tend to appreciate the benefits of narration, finding it easier for taking in information and learning than reading books.' Anything that can bring more men and boys to reading is something the world industry wants to encourage. (*Publishing Perspectives*, 30 November 2021)

Demographics

Table 9.2 shows book buying in the UK by gender, age and socio-economic group – all three have an influence. Travelling by public transport encourages reading, as can most readily be seen on the Underground in London. The age at which the person left education is also an important factor – those who leave later are bigger consumers of books. In the USA, book reading is strongly associated with college education: '44% of US adult citizens without a college degree said they read at least one book in 2023, compared to 73% of those with a college degree' (yougov.com, accessed 25 January 2024).

Table 9.2 Book buying in the UK – demographics

Gender, age, socio-economic group	Proportion of all books (%)	Proportion of adult books (%)
Female	60	58
Male	40	42
13–16	7	4
17–24	12	12
25–34	21	19
35–44	20	17
45–54	14	16
55–64	12	15
65–84	14	17
AB	39	39
C1	25	25
C2	14	13
DE	22	23

Source: 2022 data from Nielsen's UK Books and Consumers Survey.

When it comes to ebooks, the profile is of an older, female reader.

> It's very much a woman's world, with 75% of the most avid readers being women. Uptake in digital reading is driven by middle-aged people – approximately 77% of the most active readers are age 45 and older, with the largest single group (30%) being age 55 to 64. However, when breaking down the numbers by age, things shift slightly. While women make up the largest group of digital readers, men age 65-plus seem to have acquired the habit. (Kobo)

More sophisticated *segmentation* may look beyond the obvious demographics to psychographics, for example personalities and lifestyles. There may be consumers who like to discover new authors before others, or those who prefer to read what everyone else is reading and enjoying. On social media there develop interest groups or communities around particular genres or authors. There are generational differences around reading habits and types of content:

> Diversity and access to a wider range of voices in stories they consume is a key consideration for Gen Z overall, across all media. Seventy-nine percent of Gen Z respondents said diversity and representation is important to them when choosing books, movies or other forms of entertainment – significantly more than other generations including Millennials (66%), Gen X (53%) and Boomers (34%). In fact, 60% of Gen Z readers reported looking for books, stories or comics that highlight marginalized groups, much higher than other generations at just 40%. (wattpad.com, accessed 14 February 2024)

Developing *personas* for different types of customers or users is common across publishing sectors. For example, users of a service in academic publishing may be characterized by different personas for the author, researcher, or librarian.

Targeting

With a clear view of the market segments amongst book consumers, trade publishers can decide whether to target a particular audience. The same principles apply in textbook publishing, where 1st-year undergraduates may be chosen as the segment for an introductory text.

Decisions around targeting have implications in consumer publishing for the cover design, where any advertising is placed, and what type of media coverage (including social) is planned. The publisher of a YA novel may decide to target both a children's and an adult audience. Marketing may include advertising in London Underground stations and a targeted digital marketing campaign, based around the author's website, with teasers sent to the author's existing fans. Other ways of segmenting the market include by retail channel: there are different demographics for those purchasing books at Waterstones or in supermarkets. A book may be seen as ideal for promotion through a particular channel.

Positioning

Once the target market has been selected, it must be decided how the product will be positioned in the mind of the consumer. This process may start once the book has been signed up, with the ground being prepared within the book trade, often positioning a new title alongside existing authors. Marketers can prepare positioning maps which show how their product or brand will fit into the market. Will this be a high-value item with an air of quality, or a cheaper product with an emphasis on value? 'More for more' positioning involves creating an upmarket product or service at a relatively high price; 'the same for much less' offers a basic product at a competitive price. An example of the former would be electronic access to the *Oxford English Dictionary*, and an example of the latter would be a low-priced ebook in genre fiction. In the reference market the Dummies brand offers simplified information across a whole range of subjects.

There are three levels of brand positioning: product attributes, benefits, and beliefs and values. 'The strongest brands go beyond attribute or benefit positioning. They are positioned on strong *beliefs and values*, engaging customers on a deep, emotional level' (Kotler et al., 2020, page 253).

MARKETING MIX

For a lead title, marketers will prepare a full marketing plan which assesses the target market for the book and lays out strategies for reaching that market both through online and offline activities. Marketing activities can be placed under the four general headings of what is known as the marketing mix:

- product,
- price,
- place, and
- promotion.

Product

Marketing plays a full role in the development of new projects, from coming up with new ideas and commenting on editors' proposals to market testing new projects during their development. Consumer insight will provide information around the motivation of consumers, relevant segmentation, and how an author brand should be positioned or repositioned. Such information could lead to the creation of special editions of an author's work, aimed at their super-fans. Or the books of a brand author could be refreshed with a new cover design. For an author no longer alive, a writer could be commissioned to produce new stories: an example is the Hercule Poirot mysteries written by Sophie Hannah. Marketing will also be involved in commenting on the book's title and other textual elements to maximize search engine optimization (SEO) and discoverability; its genre or subject classification; cross-marketing opportunities with other titles; and the cover design and how it works with the target market.

Market research can inform decisions about new projects, covers and marketing ideas. Regular data on the sales of individual print titles, their demand curves, and books by category is available from Nielsen BookScan – sales rankings on Amazon are a free alternative. By 2013 bestseller data for ebooks was becoming available in the UK. Ebook charts tend to be dominated by fiction, and audio charts favour narrative non-fiction, in particular 'celebrity-penned or whistleblowy non-fiction' (*The Bookseller*, 27 October 2023). Publishers would dearly love access to the data held by Amazon and Apple – not only on sales but also on consumer behaviour and profiles. Those publishers able to build a direct relationship with their customers can collect their own information, enabling them to target new customers and design appropriate products and services. They can also stimulate the co-creation of value, with readers perhaps suggesting commissioning ideas, titles for translation, or classic books to reissue.

Educational publishers developing a new textbook will want to assess market trends in terms of student numbers in that subject, and evaluate the competition. They will conduct primary research in schools, and major new textbooks and digital media will be concept tested using focus groups. An academic publisher may seek the views of librarians on a proposed database of key texts and journal articles. The use of data analytics may show how online content is being used whether by learners in schools or academic researchers.

Brand management

As we saw in Chapter 4, consumer publishers have to direct their attention towards the creation of communities and brands which will work with consumers. Does the publisher have existing brands which will work as consumer brands, or does it need to create a new identity? Part of that effort will involve the management of key author brands. Today brands have to work in many different places, as outlined by Emily Hayward of the creative agency Red Antler:

> the principles of brand-building are somewhat timeless: have a clear idea of the story you want to tell and then apply that everywhere you show up. But the consumer is going to get bored if you're showing up the exact same way on Instagram as you are on your website. You've got to find a way to have one voice but with a lot of nuance and surprise built into it. (*Monocle*, November 2018, page 74)

Since one of the factors that influence book purchases is familiarity with the author, much attention is paid to the branding of authors (and sometimes the characters they have created), whether on social media, author websites, book recommendation sites or through their covers. Publishers build author brands but do not own those assets. Once authors develop a fan base, those readers are targeted early in the promotion of the author's next book, and are emissaries who spread word-of-mouth recommendations worldwide. All the covers for an author may receive a similar treatment, encouraging the reader to look out for and buy the next book by one of their favourite authors. Brands also affect gift purchases offering an option which lowers the risk. The case study of Robert Galbraith reveals the power of author brands:

> In April of 2013, Little Brown (Hachette) published *The Cuckoo's Calling* by unknown author Robert Galbraith. Despite the big-five publisher and solid early reviews, the book sold just 440 print copies in April. When it was revealed several months later that the book's author was none other than J. K. Rowling, the sales arc bent. ... *The Cuckoo's Calling* sold 228,000 print copies in July. (*Forbes*, 4 March 2014)

In the area of audio publishing, the brand of the narrator can be important, and some expert readers like Stephen Fry attract a loyal following. Audible, for example, has been investing in high-profile names to expand the market and also in ensemble productions. Examples of the latter are *Lincoln in the Bardo* with a chorus of voices and the immersive *1984* narrated by Andrew Garfield, Cynthia Erivo and many others. Representation is a live issue, and

> many who work in the industry still feel the tensions around casting acutely. Amid a publishing boom in literature by writers of color, nonwhite narrators are being offered more work than they once were. Meanwhile, like most narrators, they find themselves getting asked to voice marginalized characters from backgrounds that bear no resemblance to theirs. (*Slate*, 21 June 2021)

It used to be said that the brand names of publishers and those of their imprints have little impact on sales – readers do not select books on the name of the publisher. It is true that the general public's recognition of publishers is generally weak, apart from notable exceptions such as Penguin. Trade brand names are, however, important to publishers' business connections – to agents, authors and book trade intermediaries – and to media relations. The success of *Eats, Shoots and Leaves* by Lynne Truss (2003), which sold half a million copies within six months of publication, will have persuaded bookshops to take seriously future titles from Profile Books. Teachers in schools recognize publisher brands and this may influence their purchasing decisions or recommendations. Consumer branding is used to good effect for book series, for instance in language learning, reference, travel and computing guides, and in children's publishing; and for vertical communities interested in some fiction genres and non-fiction subjects. In ELT publishing, publisher brands will be an important guarantee of quality in overseas markets. In an internet world that is oversupplied with information of uncertain provenance, publisher branding should convey quality assured products and services. The risk for publishers is that users will head for content on the web that is free – perceived as 'good enough'.

Covers

Covers remain important and books without covers on Amazon do not sell well. Titling is ever important when sometimes a cover may only appear at a small scale. Covers give off messages about a book's target audience, and they help to position the book in the mind of the consumer. A good cover will encourage the consumer to pick up a book, and the consumer is then five times more likely to buy (Phillips, 2007). Mostly publishers target heavy buyers, who provide the bulk of their sales, and design the covers accordingly. Women are more likely to be heavy buyers of books, purchasing for their children, gifts, or themselves. Purchases can be classified by occasion – when the book will be read – and benefits – what the book offers to the reader. Covers can suggest a light read for the beach, an air of mystery, or a mood of passion. In general, hardback novels, which may become collectables, have elegant and restrained jackets, aimed at older groups. Fiction aimed at younger readers may go straight into paperback; and genre fiction has a strong sale in ebook form.

Regular research may be commissioned by consumer insight teams into the readers of an author and a new cover look may reflect the results. For example, research by Anita Shreve's publisher, Time Warner, found that readers associated her books with emotions and human feelings: 'her readers – mostly women, – came up with the phrase "life intensely felt" to describe her writing' (*Telegraph*, 9 April 2018). They then made sure that a new cover design put people on her covers. Sometimes a book is issued with two cover designs to capture different market segments. This happened with the Harry Potter books when it was found that they had a crossover adult market.

Add-ons

Extra value can be created with digital add-ons to the printed book, internet or augmented reality links in the text, or the bundling of print and ebook editions together. It would be rare to publish a major textbook without an associated website offering extra resources. Videos, tests, quizzes, and games may be available for educational texts, with lesson plans for the teachers. For academic textbooks, lecturers may be provided with a full course of lecture slides and, for major texts, a full range of resources including student assessment tools. Enhanced ebooks can contain rich media features such as videos, animations and quizzes.

Price

Marketing will be involved in setting the prices for new books. Factors affecting the book's possible published price include its perceived value to end-users; their ability to pay low or high prices (for example high-earning professionals); and the price of competitors' books, especially if the book can be easily compared against similar books. Sometimes a book has a uniqueness that can let it command a premium price. Other factors include whether the book will be bought primarily by end-users or by libraries or businesses; and whether there are established price norms in the market which, if ignored, could reduce sales. Trade publishers have to price with a view to discounts offered by retailers to consumers. Christmas bestsellers will have their recommended price set in the full knowledge that retailers will reduce the price considerably. A hardback priced by the publisher at £26 may be sold at up to half price by retailers if a price war develops in the market.

A *cost-based* approach to pricing is rare – this involves a standard mark-up from the unit cost of the book. *Competition-based* pricing is common and it is essential to review the prices of competitors' products. For trade fiction, pricing to market will override considerations such as the book's length. There are common price points in the market for given categories of books, such as general hardbacks, trade and mass-market paperbacks. Pricing strategies include *skimming* – pricing high a hardback before moving into paperback – through to *penetration* pricing – capturing market share for a new series through aggressive low pricing.

The raising of the recommended retail price for a book would usually lead to a fall in demand, whereas lowering the price would usually (but not always) lead to a rise in the quantity sold. Products which are thought to be *price inelastic* – changing the price has only a limited effect on the level of demand – tend to be highly specialist and professional titles. A book or database may convey need-to-know information for which an organization or professional is happy to pay a high price. Consumer books, especially paperbacks or ebooks, which may be bought on impulse, and many textbooks tend to be *price elastic* – changing the price has a greater effect on the level of demand. Price elasticities vary according to the type of book and product. It can be difficult, for example, for an editor to persuade an academic book author that lowering the price will not open the gates to a flood of eager readers.

Digital products can be difficult to price when there are no set price points in the market. Publishers may resort to cost-based approaches in order to recoup their investment, or keep prices low initially in order to encourage early momentum. The prices of ebooks may match those of printed books or be much lower, say 20 per cent. The pricing of consumer ebooks is in constant flux as they have proved to be highly price elastic, and their prices can be altered almost in real time. Low ebook pricing, often used by self-published authors, can also assist the launch of a new author by a publisher: the risk is lowered for a reader wanting to try somebody new. David Naggar, Vice President of Amazon's Books and Kindle Content, commented: 'I look at price as a tool for visibility. You can either spend a lot of money on marketing or you can invest it in a super-low price until they get the flywheel going of the recommendation engines' (*Daily Mail*, 2 September 2017). Occasional flash sales are used by retailers to capture market share. Publishers and self-publishers too may use *pulse* pricing, dropping the title's price drastically over a short period to increase demand. Larger publishers may employ analysts to work out pricing policies which maximize unit sales or revenue per sales channel. Such *dynamic* pricing is automated through the use of algorithms, pioneered by Amazon.

In the area of academic textbooks, the price points for humanities and social sciences paperback texts are lower than those for management and STM titles. Publishers may offer individual titles at different prices: a title may be published simultaneously as a high-priced ebook for multiple reader use in libraries and at a lower price in paperback for personal purchase. The use of site licences gives publishers the ability to set different prices for each title depending on the ways in which it is licensed. For example, an ebook may be acquired by a library under a perpetual access licence, or it may be licensed as part of a collection (in effect at a discount per title), or through Patron (user or demand) Driven Acquisition, or through short-term rental.

Print books and ebooks are free from VAT in the UK, but the tax is payable on digital products such as audiobooks and online content.

Place

A full view of a book's distribution and the different channels through which books are sold is provided in later chapters. From the point of view of the marketer, they need to understand fully the markets into which books are sold, both the needs of consumers and the different sales channels. The movement of sales away from physical stores to internet retailers is a key trend which has affected the marketing of books. Marketers need to assess the likely audience for a book and work out, with the sales department, how it can be made available through the relevant physical and digital channels (ebook and audio), as well as promoted to the relevant decision-makers and consumers.

Given the importance of search and discovery in the purchasing and accessing of many books online, marketers must ensure that full and correct metadata is available to all the relevant sales channels and libraries. Books with fuller metadata sell better. This includes the book's cover (vital for driving online browsing and sales), the short and long description of the content, author biography and reviews. Metadata in the virtual space substitutes for the bookshelf in a physical bookstore or the former printed library catalogues. For example, books are classified by subject category (a metadata field), originally developed to help booksellers and librarians shelve them. For specialist books, assigning an incorrect subject category can be fatal to sales and library usage. Conversely, assigning several and relevant subject categories from the specific to the more general aids a title's online visibility. A choice of subject category in which fewer books are published increases the chance that a book will achieve a higher sales ranking. Rich metadata will help to sell books through a powerful retailer such as Amazon, with its set of algorithms driving, for example, bestseller lists or personalized recommendations. Copy for web pages needs to be written with an eye to achieving a favourable page ranking on Google searches. Relevant keywords need to be identified and used as part of the copy, and links encouraged from other sites with good reputations.

Promotion

The aim of promotion is to make the media, the book trade, and consumers conscious of the company and the products it offers; and to stimulate demand. Details of the promotional spend and activities will help pre-publication orders from booksellers. The work may be divided by task. In some publishers, especially consumer, specialists deal solely with public relations and publicity, or with online marketing and community development through a presence in social media, or the development of promotional and point-of-sale (POS) material for retailers. In some academic and professional publishers, the work may be divided by product type, for example between textbooks or journals promotion. Publishers may also hire advertising agencies (especially for major projects or brand authors), freelance publicists, and specialists in social media, direct mail, SEO, and website design.

Online marketing

The development of online marketing has revolutionized promotion and the whole marketing function, offering a cost-effective means of reaching a wider international audience. The benefits of social media are recognized by publishers as they seek active engagement with readers. It is important for marketers to understand the algorithmic nature of social media: 'Algorithms determine in part which messages, which people and which ideas social media users see' (theconversation.com, accessed 25 March 2024). The number of opportunities have continued to multiply – from Facebook ads to BookTok. Publishers recognize they must have an active presence in order to drive book discoverability, build engagement, and encourage word-of-mouth recommendations – and ensure their authors are equally active. Publishers set targets for the number of followers, likes, and retweets as they harness the power of social media. A trailer for a book may be uploaded to YouTube, a viral video posted on Snapchat, a news item placed on LinkedIn, a book club started on X/Twitter, or a cover pinned to a board on Pinterest. The aim is to increase levels of engagement, not simply to publish content. For authors, when they

> interact with their followers and engage with them authentically, readers are more likely to continue reading their work, share their love of the author, and are more willing to invest when books are published. This is not to say that the author cannot successfully brand themselves on social media as solely an author, but they need to also present content that their followers can connect with in an authentic way. (Johnson and Simpson, 2022, page 12)

For significant new products or services, it will be important to engage in online communities either through the creation of one from scratch or by making use of those already well established. Book publishers can gain network effects through developing their own community sites around their books. Community sites may be built around different levels of content aggregation: imprints, genres, series, individual bestsellers or long enduring titles, such as the *Writers' & Artists' Yearbook* (Bloomsbury). The community has to have a purpose that matters to the people who the publisher is trying to reach. Sharing control is important. On the one hand, publishers create content for and about the community, and, on the other, value and stimulate the contributions and lively debates from community members. Sites are designed to attract new registrants and customers, and to retain membership. Many techniques are used, such as the marketing of events, special offers, and membership and subscription schemes. When publishers gain knowledge of readers' interests and reading habits, they can apply metadata and analytics to target them with book suggestions, thereby reinforcing the brand connection. Community sites may offer new revenue streams and innovatory opportunities for content sales, and offline and online services. From Penguin Books, The Happy Foodie offers:

> inspiring recipes from renowned cooks and chefs ... Being part of our community will give you access to exclusive interviews, features and competitions, as well as tempting deals on our cookery ebooks. We will bring you closer to the cookery writers and chefs you love. (thehappyfoodie.co.uk, accessed 8 January 2024)

Designed partly to aid discoverability of content, a community can range from a Facebook page for an academic journal through to an online game which can be played alongside other fans of a character or series from around the world. Community activities may include podcast streams and YouTube channels; and some YA publishers develop sites which include writing forums. In 2011 Orion Publishing launched the SF Gateway as a community site for sci-fi fans whilst making available ebooks of classic sci-fi and fantasy titles. Commenting about fantasy, the literary agent Max Edwards said that it is 'centred on community, as evidenced by its collectors, conventions, fan content – and most recently by the rise of subscription boxes and special editions, which have launched débuts, entrenched fandoms and sparked connections between readers' (*The Bookseller*, 17 November 2023).

Publishers of consumer books written by brand-name authors face the reality that their imprint name is a sub-brand to that of their authors in the public's mind. In order to co-ordinate the promotion, publishers may advise authors on the use of websites and social media, or offer to host their websites. Publishers embellish their own web pages, for example with author interviews and interactive material, such as activities or games linked to particular books or children's characters, and newsletters. Efforts are made to persuade readers to register through offering, for example, discounts and competitions with prizes; and readers are encouraged to share content. Community sites around content by imprint or genre will encourage sales – usually from the main retailers but sometimes direct. This has become ever more important as internet sales have grown, and physical retail diminished, and the challenge is to help consumers discover a publisher's titles.

The presence of Amazon, Apple and Google in the marketplace offers both opportunities and threats to publishers. Academic publishers have welcomed the opportunity to display their books through Google Book Search, since they believe their titles have exposure they would not otherwise receive. Readers can view sample pages and then click through to buy the book. Voice assistants and smart speakers opened another channel for book discovery.

Internet marketing does have huge potential for niche publishers. Specialist and academic titles are not widely stocked in high street bookstores. Publishers can establish specialist interest communities around their publications to whom they can directly sell their titles. For some of the well-known academic and specialist publishers, direct sales of their books from their websites grew quickly, along with sales via internet booksellers.

Word-of-mouth recommendation

Publishers have long recognized that an important influence on sales is the elusive word of mouth (WOM). The novelist Jane Rogers writes:

> Books are promoted to us endlessly, through adverts, reviews, adaptations, through glossy attention-grabbing covers in bookshops, and wild claims on jacket sleeves. They are set texts for exams; they are hyped by prizes and awards; or they are written by celebrities. But in the end, every reader knows, probably the most compelling reason for picking up a book which is new to you, is when a friend tells you, 'Read this, it's really good.'
> (2001, page vii)

Sales are generated by trusted recommendations from friends, family or booksellers. Sometimes bestsellers can appear from nowhere, such as *Captain Corelli's Mandolin* (1994) by Louis de Bernières and *The Essex Serpent* by Sarah Perry (2016). Publishers cannot guarantee a buzz around a book, but they are constantly trying to encourage it through obtaining coverage in the media (TV, radio, podcasts, newspapers), spreading the word on social media, placing extracts pre-publication, or making sure the book is stocked prominently in bookshops. A buzz is often manufactured around those books with large marketing spends,

with the aim of selling more copies and recouping the high costs. One method is to give books away, a tactic used to generate interest in Stieg Larsson by his UK publisher:

> Mark Smith, who founded Quercus in 2004, became so desperate to shift copies, which some retailers refused to stock, he gave them away to people reading in parks – and planted dozens more on the back seats of taxis and on Tube trains. 'At that stage we were giving away more than we sold,' Smith says. 'It was getting pretty nerve-racking' (*Independent*, 6 August 2010).

Editors and marketers may tweet about a book whilst it is still in development in order to attract early attention. The 'cover reveal' is a big moment on social media. Publishers will send digital proofs (ARCs or advance reader copies) to key influencers, active on social media, in order to stimulate a conversation around a new title. They may be active in smaller communities around subgenres or authors, rather than having a high follower count, but their recommendation can be invaluable. Campaigns using micro-influencers see much higher engagement rates. A book aimed at a female audience might be sent to the UK community site for parents, Mumsnet, which in 2024 had 8 million unique visitors per month (mumsnet.com). In the area of children's/YA books, bloggers are especially active. Molly Flatt suggests:

> Go for authenticity, not pure reach. When trust is at a premium, the word of one true 'ordinary' fan can carry far more commercial weight than that of a

Deckchairs for the Hay Festival, Hay-on-Wye, Wales. Held annually the festival attracts both writers and celebrities, and was described by Bill Clinton as the 'Woodstock of the mind'

huge social media 'name'. Spend time researching non-professional posters with high engagement within smaller communities. They'll be more excited to be involved in a book campaign, and the resulting buzz will have the rare ring of truth. (*The Bookseller*, 1 August 2018)

A viral marketing campaign may be planned – to spread an idea, a joke, or information.

Viral marketing, the digital version of word-of-mouth marketing, involves creating videos, ads and other marketing content that are so infectious that customers will seek them out or pass them along to their friends. Because customers find and pass along the content, viral marketing can be very inexpensive. And when content comes from a friend, the recipient is much more likely to view or read it. (Kotler et al., 2020, page 524)

The success of local reading groups represents an opportunity to influence book sales; bookshops often have their own book groups. Publishers produce information packs and web resources around leading authors to encourage reading groups to adopt their titles, including celebrity book clubs. Other influences on book sales can include being shortlisted for or winning a major literary prize such as the Booker (Table 9.3) or adaptation for film or TV. Classic as well as contemporary authors receive a boost to their sales when the latest adaptation makes it on to the screen.

The author plays a prominent part in promoting their books, from appearances at book signings, local book clubs or literary festivals, to sending out flyers with their Christmas cards and adding a link to their local indie bookshop to their website or email signature. They are expected to be active on social media, building a connection with their readers. Amongst the largest literary festivals are

The top-selling title out of all the Booker winners is *Life of Pi* by Yann Martel

Table 9.3 Booker Prize winners, 2014–2023

Year	Author	Title	Publisher
2015	Marlon James	*A Brief History of Seven Killings*	Oneworld
2016	Paul Beatty	*The Sellout*	Oneworld
2017	George Sanders	*Lincoln in the Bardo*	Bloomsbury
2018	Anna Burns	*Milkman*	Faber & Faber
2019*	Margaret Atwood	*The Testaments*	Chatto & Windus
	Bernardine Evaristo	*Girl, Woman, Other*	Hamish Hamilton
2020	Douglas Stuart	*Shuggie Bain*	Picador
2021	Damun Galgut	*The Promise*	Chatto & Windus
2022	Shehan Karunatilaka	*The Seven Moons of Maali Almeida*	Sort of Books
2023	Paul Lynch	*Prophet Song*	Oneworld
2024	Samantha Harvey	*Orbital*	Jonathan Cape

Note: * The prize was shared this year.

the ones held at Edinburgh, Hay-on-Wye and Cheltenham. The growth of theatre tours, whereby brand authors sell out large venues, is having some impact on literary festivals as they rely on the bigger names to generate revenue. Jo James, who works with a number of festivals, says:

> Festivals need those big-name, bums-on-seats venue fillers partly to cover the costs of putting the festivals on in the first place, but also they help fund festivals to put on the more interesting but less 'celeby' events – so panels on interesting subjects, discussion topics, the things that will get much smaller audiences. It's really important these discussions happen but festivals can't do them without the big names. (*The Bookseller*, 16 June 2023)

EXPERT

Communities

Naomi Bacon, Founder and director of Tandem Collective, a global marketing agency with a focus on community building, partnerships and peer-to-peer marketing initiatives

When I first launched Tandem Collective, it was a traditional marketing agency tailored for publishers, offering affordable and creative campaigns. Little did I anticipate that an experimental campaign would redefine our trajectory and establish a unique community-centric model.

Three years into our journey, we found ourselves working on a book set over four hours which you could read in real-time. It was the beginning of the bookstagram and micro-influencer boom so, on a whim, I decided to host a 'readalong' on Instagram with 20 micro-creators. Each participant received a copy of the book with specially designed question and challenge cards hidden within the pages. Every prompt became an opportunity for participants to create bespoke content, from character POV videos to thematic flatlays, shared on Instagram, and tagging the author, publisher, and other participants, transforming a solitary activity into a communal experience.

The unexpected success of this campaign, marked by exceptionally high engagement, quality content, public discussion, and increased sales, prompted a surge in demand from publishers globally. Today, over 2,000 readalongs have been executed, cementing our trademark approach to community-led campaigns. After 4 years, our process is now well-defined. Readalongers are recruited through our Friday newsletter, where an algorithm selects influencers based on a collective follower count guide (for example, a collective following of 80k for a 30 person readalong). We intentionally reserve slots for accounts with under 1,000 subscribers, fostering community growth. The scarcity of readalong slots contributes to high engagement from participants.

The readalong format has evolved over time, incorporating reading schedules, innovative challenges, QR codes to extra content, and parcels to open at different junctures which relate to a passage in the book, be it a smell or a taste or an object. We have accompanying direct-messaging groups providing an open forum for discussion. On the final night, we invite the author into the private group for a Q&A, creating an intimate, invaluable experience for the influencers as well as the author.

We are constantly reiterating the format to make the readalongs as impactful as possible, adding elements that harness the newest functionalities on Instagram and work to support the algorithm. We have tried practically every genre and now offer cookalongs, listenalongs, journalalongs, parent-child readalongs, teachalongs and we've even done a cleanalong! A big focus for us is understanding the data around this word-of-mouth marketing so we can rethink how we measure success. After each campaign, participants send us specific stats which we use to calculate an overall engagement rate. In 2023, the cross-industry average engagement rate for Instagram is 0.47% (RivalIQ) yet consistently we hit 10% or more.

We are now operating globally, running campaigns with publishers and connecting with communities in the US, Canada, Australia, New Zealand, South Africa, India and across Europe. I never expected the readalongs to become so popular with clients and community alike. The success lies in the fact that there is nothing more valuable than an engaged and self-sustaining community that will ultimately become a marketing tool in and of itself, with individuals activating people in their own network to take action, moving us one concentric circle closer to our prospective customers. Our campaigns are company-initiated but customer-implemented, encouraging a high volume of user-generated content and leading to a word-of-mouth ripple effect. This kind of marketing is so powerful because it isn't a fad, it's a human behaviour. However, we won't be able to ride the wave of the readalong forever. There will naturally be a plateau. Therefore, the team and I can never get complacent and we are constantly on the lookout for the next thing. But whatever we do, however we innovate, you can be certain that community will be at the core.

E★PERT

Marketing fiction

Professor **Claire Squires**, author with Beth Driscoll of *The Frankfurt Book Fair and Bestseller Business* and Director of the Stirling Centre for International Publishing and Communication at the University of Stirling

Publishers have always made efforts to promote, distribute and sell fiction, but the late twentieth and early twenty-first centuries were a period of marketing intensification. Campaigns for potential bestsellers combine a range of generic marketing materials (catalogues, point-of-sale, bound proofs) and targeted marketing strategies to support the journey of novels from the author to the eventual reader, with online and social media being increasingly to the fore.

The traditional marketing method for fiction – literary journalism and press coverage – still has its place, but doubts about the impact of reviews on book sales, and the diminution of review space in most national newspapers have prompted publishers to attract customers in other ways. In 1969, the Booker Prize was established by the Publishers Association, and since this date, literary prizes have had a crucial impact on book sales. Alongside the rise of literary prizes, there has been a growing meet-the-author culture, through events in bookshops, libraries, and literary festivals. The expansion of reading groups has also presented publishers with opportunities to interact with consumers, and print, broadcast and online reading groups have pushed book sales.

The post-NBA retail environment led to heavy discounting practices, with fiction featuring prominently in price promotions such as 3-for-2s. Branding, however, is difficult in fiction – titles by market-leading authors may sell immediately, with the help of the brand identity of cover design – but for most novels publishers have to work hard to differentiate their products in a very crowded marketplace.

Online selling and social media are an integral part of marketing fiction. The lower production costs of ebooks mean that publishers – including self-publishers – can experiment with new authors, titles and genres. Amazon's use of customer reviews, bestseller charts, and time-limited sales promotions, underpin sophisticated algorithmic marketing activity. Metadata and data analytics are crucial tools in this environment. Shared online reading practices, via reading communities such as Goodreads, offer the potential for rich information to be gathered on customer behaviour.

Social media sites such as Facebook, Twitter/X and Instagram provide opportunities for authors and publishers to interact directly with readers. The explosion of TikTok in the 2020s has been particularly instrumental in pushing certain genres through 'BookTok', including romance fiction, as well as reviving backlist titles. New job roles, such as communities and web content managers, cross over editorial and marketing functions. Opportunities for crowdfunding (e.g. via Unbound) and crowdsourcing of taste-making functions (e.g. through sites such as Wattpad, and fan fiction sites) bring readers themselves into editorial and marketing roles, fulfilling the role of 'prosumers'. Much remains of traditional marketing models, but – as with all other sectors of publishing – the digital environment is seeing the rapid evolution of literary marketing.

PROMOTION AND PUBLICITY TECHNIQUES

Before running through the promotion and publicity techniques that are applicable to many books, we will take a quick look at the way the marketing department of a consumer book publisher would set about promoting a major lead title. Most of the promotion budget and staff time goes on brand authors and those titles envisaged as bestsellers.

Lead consumer titles

The first priority of marketing – many months in advance of publication – is to plan and undertake trade-focused promotion. The aim is to persuade the book trade that the book will deliver a flood of customers to their stores during the set publication slot; that they will need to display it prominently and order large quantities. The central buyers of the retailers are courted – they might be invited to meet up with the famous author. They are sent early reading copies and other devices to captivate their attention, from free gifts to videos of author interviews.

Much of the marketing budget that is directed at the book trade is spent on the main retailers to ensure they place the book in the prime spots in their stores and take it as part of their promotions (for example a summer reading campaign). Other techniques designed to increase their order quantities are developed, such as a bespoke competition for a retail chain and point-of-sale material to maximize the book's presence in their stores. Marketing then follows through with their consumer-focused promotion – the big bang advertising campaign to potential readers occurring closer to the book's publication. The publisher's consumer marketing spend, which is sometimes known to the book trade in advance of their ordering, demonstrates that the publisher is backing the title to the hilt and reinforces the book trade's confidence to order large quantities. Meanwhile, the publisher's publicist has been imaginatively engineering media interest in the book and author, which manifests itself around publication, alongside personal appearances at literary festivals and other events. A social media strategy is developed which it is hoped will stimulate debate about the book and its subject-matter, or cause word-of-mouth recommendations to ripple through the population – this may start soon after signature of the contract. The editor may have been tweeting about the development of the book, and this is followed by regular updates from the author and the publisher on the book's content and associated promotional activities.

We now turn to the variety of techniques used more generally.

General marketing activity

Author questionnaire

Around the time of the delivery of the manuscript, the author completes a questionnaire, which is returned via the editor. The author supplies personal information, a biography, a photo, a blurb, a short synopsis, and the book's main selling-points and intended readership or applicability to courses. In addition they

> New authors may be positioned in terms of established writers – for example, the 'next John le Carré'

may supply their affiliations to membership organizations and online forums; details of their social media accounts; blogs or websites to which they contribute; and lists of print, digital, and broadcast media (and individuals) that might review or publicize the book. Well-connected authors will be contacted in person to gain information on media and other contacts. Other information could include relevant festivals, conferences and exhibitions.

Keywords and analytics

The identification and use of keywords in all marketing activities (such as in descriptive copy about the book, press releases and social media activity) have grown in importance to aid the discovery of books through the main search engines, social media, and retail sites such as Amazon and Waterstones. Google Keyword Planner can help marketers to build lists of words which attract relevant traffic. Words used by authors and publishers internally may not be those used by potential readers searching for a book. There is also a growing use of analytical tools, such as Facebook Analytics or Google Trends, which show interest in topics over time and the correlation with search terms. A search on the word 'dieting' or 'fitness' shows a strong peak in searches in January each year.

Metadata and bibliographic information

The book's metadata is updated throughout the book's sales life. It encompasses all the information associated with the publishing of the book, such as a title, author, formats, cover, description, subject classification, territorial rights, price, availability and reviews. It is used by search engines, social media and all intermediaries that help sell the book. It is essential for findability (when a reader already knows of the title) and greatly aids discoverability (when a reader happens upon it).

The signature of the book contract with the author usually triggers the publisher to assign to the book the product identifier, the International Standard Book Number (ISBN), from the batch of numbers assigned to it by the national ISBN agency. An ISBN is normally given to each tradable format – in print (e.g. hardback, paperback) and digital (e.g. ePub, PDF) – although not every intermediary requires that an ebook should have an ISBN.

Supplying the main bibliographers and resellers with accurate information on each new title in the standard formats (BIC UK; BASIC USA; Thema international) is essential. This can be done by using an agreed electronic format such as ONIX (Online Information Exchange).

> ONIX is an XML-based standard for rich book metadata, providing a consistent way for publishers, retailers and their supply chain partners to communicate a wide range of information about their products. It is overtly a commercial data format, is expressly designed to be used globally, and is not limited to any one language or the characteristics of a specific national book trade. (editeur.org, accessed 9 January 2024)

The supply of rich information about a book is a low-cost means of promoting the title worldwide, and facilitates its ordering through the supply chain. Within ONIX there is now the facility to add information about the physical production of the book, including what paper was used. This green metadata is becoming more important within the publishing industry as consumers ask questions about sustainability. Information given to the bibliographers – the main ones are Nielsen BookData (UK) and Bowker (USA) – nine to six months ahead of publication lists the new title on their electronic databases. MVB developed the German books in print database VLB. Their metadata platform Metabooks has since been extended to the Portuguese and Spanish language markets.

Bibliographic Data Services in the UK is a leading supplier of rich metadata about print books and ebooks to libraries and suppliers. It specializes in the promotion of new title information in MARC (Machine Readable Cataloguing), a data standard used by libraries to store and exchange information. It also supplies the Cataloguing in Publication (CIP) data to the British Library's weekly addition to the definitive British National Bibliography (BNB) and other products, accessed worldwide. You can see the CIP data (and similar from the Library of Congress, USA) for an academic book on its title-verso page.

Legal deposit is the act of depositing published material in designated libraries. Publishers in the United Kingdom and Ireland have an obligation to deposit published material in the six legal deposit libraries, which collectively maintain the national published archive of the British Isles. The six libraries are the British Library, Bodleian Library (Oxford University), Cambridge University Library, National Library of Scotland in Edinburgh, National Library of Wales in Aberystwyth, and Library of Trinity College, Dublin.

The publisher's in-house metadata includes each title's current status (future or actual publication dates), current prices by format, production specifications, covers, its coding by product category or subject, related products, and additional information on each title built up over time (such as long and short promotional and contents copy, reviews received and association with other media releases). More extensive metadata will cover contractual matters, such as the rights held and the rights available for sale or licensed to others. The advantage of such a database is that it is a central repository of definitive information about the publisher's titles. It allows the publisher to retrieve and manipulate information in forms most suited to the intermediaries and end-users, in print and online (especially for the web catalogue).

Advance information sheet

Marketing will prepare the book's advance information (AI) sheet, which contains bibliographic information (title, author, format, extent, illustrative content, hardback/paperback, ISBN, planned price and publication date); a synopsis and the cover blurb; and a biography of the author. For a consumer title there will be information about the planned marketing and PR activities. The above are the book's features, and it is important that the AI also sets out the book's benefits – i.e. what it will do for the purchaser or reader in the context of the book's use. A dictionary will help someone with their studies or to work more effectively in business. A travel guide will enable someone to make the best of their weekend away, giving them the key information and guidance they need. Is there a key benefit – the book's unique selling proposition (USP)? For example, for a non-fiction title, is it written by the leading expert in the field; for an educational title, does it match the latest curriculum requirements? The key benefits can be difficult to identify when a book is coming into a crowded market, but the exercise is even more crucial.

The book's description is repurposed in style and in length for different audiences and the places where it is read – this exercise can be facilitated using artificial intelligence (AI) tools such as Jasper. In various forms the description appears as the cover blurb; web copy for Amazon; a Facebook post; or a sales proposition for the media or trade buyers. Use is made of bullet points and lists, feature structures and summary first techniques, and keywords may be tested for SEO.

The AI is sent well ahead of publication (preferably around nine months before) to all the people who help sell the book: the publisher's sales force and overseas agents, booksellers, wholesalers and aggregators.

> In order to write effective copy, a useful acronym to remember is AIDA: attention, interest, desire, action

Cover

The cover is another promotional item used by the publisher's home and export sales departments, wholesalers, library suppliers, internet booksellers and overseas agents. Produced well ahead of publication – preferably six to 12 months – it will be used to secure advance orders from bookshops. Books sell better on Amazon if they appear with a cover, and dummy front covers may be used when the book is first listed, ahead of the completion of the final version. The cover blurb is written by the editor, marketer, or an in-house or freelance copywriter.

Catalogue

Catalogue preparation is a major task: it involves gathering book information from all round the firm, updating it, collecting illustrations, copywriting, briefing a designer, sometimes print buying, and carrying through all the production stages, as well as database management. Publishers have worked towards the abolition of printed catalogues and stocklists, on the basis that the information can be accessed online. This has met with mixed success with some publishers retaining print versions – these can also be sent digitally as PDFs.

Reviews

Consumer reviews – whether on Instagram or a site such as Goodreads or Amazon – are increasingly important and encourage sales. This trend is more prevalent amongst younger consumers:

> One in three online purchasers have looked at other readers' online comments/reviews before buying a book, rising to 44% among

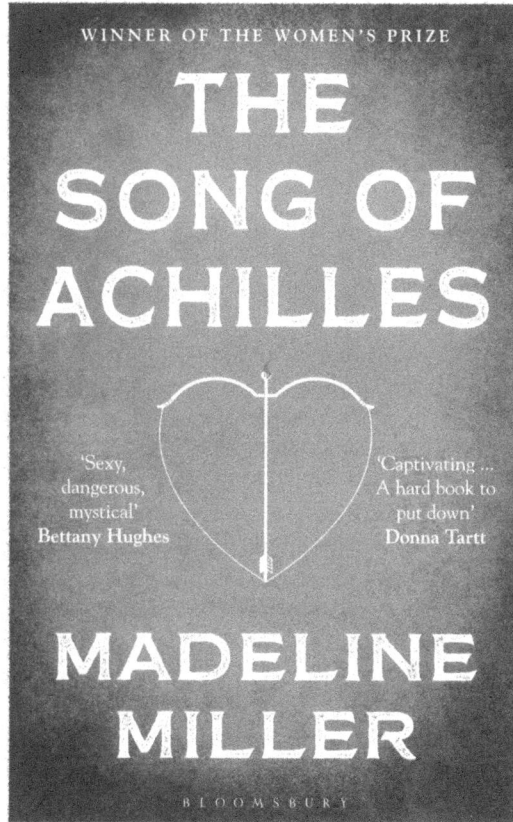

Sales of backlist titles such as *The Song of Achilles* have been boosted by BookTok

16-24-year-olds. People who bought non-fiction books online are more likely to have read other readers' reviews, perhaps looking to gain some assurances that a non-fiction book will be trustworthy before making a purchase. (Mintel, 2022)

Investment in paid search or SEO helps to direct consumers towards community websites or social media (e.g. Facebook pages) set up by the publisher. There has been controversy about paid-for rave reviews on Amazon, commissioned by self-published authors, and click farms which will generate automatically likes on Facebook pages. Traditionally there has been a strong books community on Twitter but with the change to X, this generated uncertainty over its future with some users leaving the platform.

Attention is paid to influencers on social media, book recommendation sites, bloggers, and BookTubers. Reviews from Goodreads may prove more effective with prospective purchasers than those from the national newspapers. Authors can go on a blog tour, being reviewed in turn by a series of influential book bloggers. Some BookTubers, with their own channel on YouTube, have attracted large and loyal followings for their reviews; and the success of BookTok has propelled backlist titles to sales success, such as *The Song of Achilles* by Madeline Miller, first published in 2011.

Reviews on Amazon may be written by enthusiastic readers or friends of the author. There has been controversy over 'sock puppets', fake personas used by publishers and authors to write reviews both good and bad. The crime writer Stephen Leather admitted that he used sock puppets to write positive reviews of his own books, and another crime author, R. J. Ellory, admitted giving rival authors poor reviews and low ratings. In 2023 a debut fantasy author, Cait Corrain, was caught leaving bad reviews of other authors:

> In a TikTok, the author Xiran Jay Zhao detailed Corrain's months-long pattern of leaving one-star reviews through fake Goodreads accounts, mostly on the debut works of first-time writers of color, while leaving positive reviews on her own forthcoming book. (*Time*, 13 December 2023)

Reviews in newspapers can still be crucial for biographies or academic works, for example, where potential readers may want to gauge the quality of the work ahead of their purchase. Overall such reviews have declined in importance in their influence on trade book sales, and the column inches available for review coverage has shrunk in print. Cal Revely-Calder, Literary Editor of the *Telegraph*, said: 'to cater for a predominantly online audience, we've dissociated our online and print schedules: reviews run online throughout the week and a selection go into print' (*The Bookseller*, 6 November 2023).

It is essential to maintain an up-to-date and comprehensive database of suitable reviewers. Then for each title a review list is prepared, tailor-made, taking account of the author's ideas and contacts. Review copies may be bound, uncorrected proofs, digital proofs, or printed books. They are sent out with a press release or email, with details of the title and its publication date, or perhaps a letter from the editor singing the book's virtues.

Public relations

Public relations (PR) includes generating free publicity and furthering a company's brand image with authors and the media. By comparison to the big budgets elsewhere in the marketing department, publicists operate with little direct expenditure. Engineering free publicity in the print and broadcast media is vital in consumer book publishing, and spreads word-of-mouth knowledge about the book. This can also come from encouraging debate and discussion in the blogosphere or on social media. For titles which do not receive marketing expenditure, PR can propel sales, and smaller publishers will use it to compete effectively with the major players. On some major titles prior to contract, the publisher's innovative publicity ideas (and promotional spend) may persuade the author to write for their particular company, rather than for competitors. Publicists can develop strong bonds with authors, and become close friends.

Table 9.4 Top podcasts 2023

Globally	UK
The Joe Rogan Experience	The Joe Rogan Experience
Call Her Daddy	The Diary of a CEO with Steven Bartlett
Huberman Lab	That Peter Crouch Podcast

Sources: Spotify and Edison Research

The publicist, also called the press and PR officer, is in constant contact with press and magazine editors, journalists, bloggers, podcast researchers, radio and television producers. The credibility and trust developed with these contacts are crucial and will be lost if an author is pitched who then turns out to be poor or inappropriate. With so many books and authors competing for media space, a book or author has to be carefully positioned in the marketplace. At the manuscript stage, the publicist targets the market, and formulates a publicity and media plan to commence six months before publication. A key part of the task is to meet with the author/agent/editor and discuss their book, interests and promotional ideas in order to identify what is new and exciting, and why the media should care about it, such as the back story. The publicist identifies the appropriate media that would be interested in the book, and helps them to come to a decision to cover the title by suggesting suitable angles, bearing in mind their media schedule. The stimulated coverage should occur around publication, unless there is a breaking news agenda. Coverage is gained from features, press releases, and launch parties (mostly for well-connected authors); and promotional activities which authors may be obliged by their contract to fulfil – tours, literary festivals, signing sessions, podcast, radio and television appearances, accompanied by the publicist. New authors may need coaching in media awareness and interview techniques. Around the time of publication, authors will appear in newspapers and magazines outlining their typical day or answering questionnaires about their likes and dislikes.

Publicity timeline – 12 months up to publication

A digital campaign is planned using specially created social media or the author's own online presence. For the launch of *A Street Cat Named Bob* by James Bowen in 2012, a Twitter account was set up for the ginger street cat with the starring role in the book, as well as a Facebook page for the book. This success was followed up with a book deal in 2018 for Zelda, a cat with a constantly curious look, and 80,000 followers on Twitter. Zelda's owner, who is behind the Twitter account @CuriousZelda, said:

> I'm thrilled that my cat managed to get a book deal. As she is currently unable to hold a pen, I'm honoured to share Zelda's wild ideas with more people than ever, working with the creative, cat-loving team at Sphere.
> (*The Bookseller*, 16 August 2018)

Authors themselves may come up with innovative ways to promote books.
For her collection of stories *No One belongs Here More than You* (2007),
Miranda July created a website with messages written on the top of her
refrigerator – the site was viewed more than three million times in just one week
(noonebelongsheremorethanyou.com, accessed 15 February 2024).

Signing sessions, competitions for booksellers, and joint promotions with
booksellers, especially the main chains, are arranged in close conjunction with
the sales department. Sales staff are warned about any impending coverage so
that they can inform the booksellers who are thus more likely to stock the book,
which in turn sells more copies. Major TV or film tie-in titles receive cross-media
promotion involving the link-up between the publisher and the media company
for mutual benefit. Film and TV adaptations work wonders for the sales of classic
authors as well, increasing their sales by three or four times.

Other PR involves informing the trade press (in print or online) about
the company and forthcoming titles, distributing proofs or finished copies to
influential people (this includes podcast researchers and opinion formers with
a huge following on social media), entering titles for literary prizes, helping to
plan and attend exhibitions (including the publisher's own sales conferences),
and sometimes answering queries from the public, teachers, librarians and
booksellers. For important authors merchandise may be created and given away
as part of the effort to create a buzz around a new title. For a new title by Sally
Rooney, *Beautiful World, Where Are You* (2021), her publisher in New York, Farrar,

PUBLICITY TIMELINE –
12 months pre-pub to publication.

12–9 months	6 months	5 months	4 months	3 months	6 Weeks	Pub
Author to have submitted the author Q&A to editor/publicist. Broadcast pitching to Radio 4 – Book of the Week/Book at Bedtime Pitching for major literary festivals such as Edinburgh, Hay, Harrogate. Publicity to introduce themselves to the author (if not already done) and PR strategy/feature ideas to be discussed.	Proofs to go out to Long Lead reviewers and influencers for endorsement to use on the final jacket. Event planning to begin. Early word of mouth and journalist lobbying to begin with hand selling of proofs.	Pitches for reviews and features begins for long lead magazines – following proof mailings. Pitches to the trade media for profile interviews - to run 3 months ahead of publication. Contacting book shops/libraries for events.	Events, launch – venues and budgets etc., to be clearly established. Early schedules to be drafted. Author/agent expectations – early plans to be circulated with initial ideas. Titles without physical proofs to be added to Netgalley for digital review for bloggers, Instagrammers, and endorsers.	Proofs to go out to the literary editors, relevant features editors, radio producers and the newsprint weekend supplements. Pitching for interviews and author written features in short lead media and broadcast – for TV, radio and podcast interviews to run on publication. Events to go on sale – book and ticket preferred.	Finished copies to be sent out to targeted review list to include bloggers and short lead media. Publicist to follow up with all recipients. Further interviews, features and short Q&As to be confirmed. Publicist will begin to have a much clearer picture of how the campaign will be shaped and what coverage will be anticipated. Broadcast interviews confirmed. Final draft schedule to be circulated to author/agent/editor	Final schedule to be confirmed and sent to editor/author/ and agent. Last minute interviews to be confirmed. Events, interviews and author tours to take place. Reviews to run across all media. 6 weeks post pub Post campaign analysis Debrief with author & agent Ongoing push into summer reading & Xmas gifting if needs be.

Timeline created by Louise Swannell, Publicity Director, Headline

Straus & Giroux, 'distributed yellow bucket hats and tote bags (featuring the novel's cover illustrations, by Manshen Lo) to celebrities, journalists and other so-called literary influencers. They have been encouraged to post about the book using the hashtag #BWWAY' (*New York Times*, 2 September 2021).

News stories can be a good way of getting books on to the front page, or into the radio or television. For a major dictionary, for example, stories will be given to the press about the latest words to enter the language, such as in 2021 when a selection of words of Korean origin were added to the *Oxford English Dictionary*:

With the international success of Squid Game, Parasite and BTS, it should come as no surprise South Korean pop culture is represented in the list as well.

hallyu, n. – The increase in international interest in South Korea and its popular culture, represented by the global success of South Korean music, film, TV, fashion and food.
K-drama, n. – A television series in the Korean language and produced in South Korea.
manhwa, n. – A Korean genre of cartoons and comic books, often influenced by Japanese manga.

Korean literary wave

Barbara J. Zitwer, Literary agent in New York

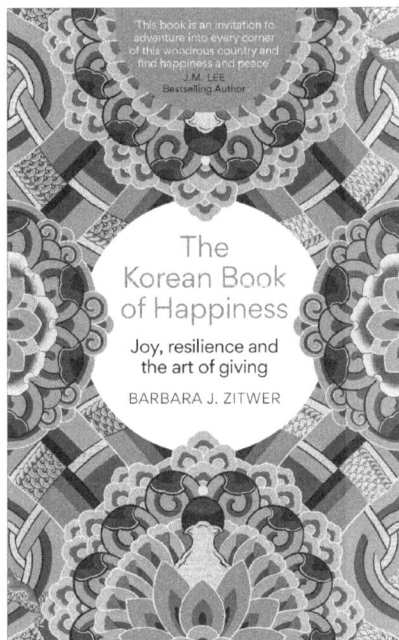

E★PERT

Today, I see Korean books on the lists of so many global publishers and their popularity continues to grow. But when I sold my first Korean book in 2005, little did I know that this was the beginning of a new era for global literature. Before then, no one had ever heard of Korean books. Most English language publishers had no Korean books on their lists. Now, everyone does! How could anyone ever predict the phenomenon called Hallyu (the Korean wave) and the growth of Korea's soft power?

Then there came the film *Parasite*, the survival show *Squid Game*, and the TV drama *Pachinko*, based on the book by Min Jee Lee. Together their success shed more light on Korean literature and helped K-authors. Now Netflix has invested millions in Korea and seemingly every Hollywood producer is in partnership with a Korean film company.

There have been many literary success stories. *Please Look After Mother* by Kyung-sook Shin tells the story of a mother who goes missing in a Seoul subway station; this bestselling book won the Man Asian Literary Prize in 2011. Han Kang won the Booker International Prize in 2016 for her novel *The Vegetarian*, and in 2024 she won the Nobel Prize in Literature (the first female Asian writer to do so). An acclaimed debut novel, *Love in the Big City*, by the bestselling young star of Korean queer fiction, Sang Young Park, was longlisted for the 2022 Booker International Prize.

Yet that jumbo-size, mainstream, big money novel from Korea has remained elusive. Yes, there has been BTS's *Behind the Story*, but the band's global celebrity and fanbase are responsible for the book's success, not necessarily its literary merit. My agency's directive is to find new authors, many never published before. After nearly 15 years of working with established Korean authors, I needed to expand and grow. I was excited to bring the western style of agenting to Korean writers, who could benefit from first-hand relationships with their editors. As of yet, there has been no Korean John Grisham or Gillian Flynn in terms of sales and hype. I was determined to find that biggest jewel in that diamond mine.

That is when I met Sue Park. She shared my vision and joined me in a new Korean adventure. Together we launched a new literary agency, the Charm Agency, which is based in Korea and represents new Korean writers. I think the future of Korean literature lies in the hands of young, independent-minded authors, author-centric literary agents, and new publishers. The new wave of Korean publishing people is changing the industry for the better. They are entrepreneurial, globally minded, and free-thinking. They are learning how to patiently grow, build, and plan careers for authors. So they too can create a global success akin to that of Stieg Larsson's series *The Girl With The Dragon Tattoo*!

Serial rights

In consumer book publishing, publicity staff may sell serial rights to their contacts in the press and magazines. Extracts or serials should appear around book publication and produce income and publicity

Marketing

An interest in the firm's books and the ability to identify the editorial reasoning and sales potential are necessary. Creativity is important in the area of promotional ideas, as well as an understanding of the relationships between costs and expected sales in maximizing the profit potential of each title, within budget. Marketing is a strategic activity, and knowledge is required of competitive behaviour and the market environment. Familiarity with social media, an understanding of its algorithmic nature, and knowledge of how it can be used to best effect are required, and web, data and IT skills are desirable. Technical skills include the ability to use email marketing and social media management programs, and the messaging abilities to reach audiences in appropriate and engaging ways. There are now specialist roles in the areas of social media, website management, community development, consumer insight and data analytics. Good personal relations inside the company (particularly with editors) and outside the company (for example with authors or the media) are vital, as are administrative and planning skills. Qualifications can be obtained through the Chartered Institute of Marketing (CIM).

The development of promotional material and online content engages SEO-friendly copywriting, editorial, production and DTP skills. PR work involves a high level of enthusiasm, living on one's wits, exchanging favours with the media, establishing a rapport and trust with all kinds of media and authors, knowing when to hype and when to hold back, being able to talk oneself in and out of situations fast, having supreme self-confidence, and a high tolerance of rude people and working anti-social hours.

SKILLS

Paid-for promotion

Point-of-sale (POS) material

Eye-catching material – posters, display kits, copy holders, presenters, brochures, badges, etc. – is designed to focus booksellers' and readers' attention on major books, series or brand authors; to make shops more enticing; and to capture display space both at home and abroad. Produced mainly for consumer books (but sometimes for major reference books and textbooks), most is declined or thrown away by booksellers. Nevertheless, it shows the publisher's commitment to the book and assists advance selling to the book trade and customers abroad. Sometimes a publisher may provide major retailers with spinners or special shelving for a series, but books are usually displayed on tables or standard shelving in the larger shops within the retailer's set of categories.

Media advertising

For most books, the high cost of advertising in the press, magazines, online, or on television or radio, or by poster would not be recouped by the sales generated. It has to be used very selectively, and short-lived, large-scale consumer advertising is restricted to major consumer books. In times of budget restrictions, advertising spend is often readily cut. The large publishers spend most of their budget on press and outdoor advertising, especially adverts on the London Underground and buses. Although its effectiveness is intangible, it encourages the book trade to buy and display the book and pleases authors and agents. Non-fiction, academic and STM publishers advertise selectively in specialist magazines and websites, and journals (especially their own) – ostensibly to sell books, but also to please authors and attract new ones.

Outdoor advertising for books includes ads on London buses.

The main tasks involved in advertising are conceiving selling ideas from editorial concepts, relating advertising to the other promotions, copywriting and working with the designer or agency, negotiating the best rates and positions, and maintaining tight budgetary control. Paid-for advertising on social media – for example, Facebook ads – is another tool to aid discoverability and word of mouth.

Direct marketing

The preparation of email campaigns direct to targeted specialist audiences forms a large part of the work of promotion staff in educational, academic, STM and professional publishers. The relevant audience could be teachers in schools, university lecturers and librarians, or business and legal professionals. Alongside any mailed subject catalogues (and to some extent reviews) it is the main promotional means by which these groups can learn about new and related backlist titles (monographs are normally promoted only once). Other promotional material includes flyers or showcards which authors can distribute or display at conferences, exhibitions or other events.

Analytics/consumer insight

The role of data analytics has grown with the explosive availability of data. If the publisher does not collect data, it cannot be analysed. The monitoring and analysis of consumer actions and behaviours inform marketing efforts, product development and business strategy. Digital marketing especially lends itself to scrutiny. For example, the design of emails may affect response rates; the timing of tweets may maximize re-tweets and consumer engagement. AI tools enable marketers to analyse response rates, customer behaviour, and purchasing history, and then predict how likely recipients are to open an email or click through to purchase. They can then send out highly targeted messaging. There are also tools available to monitor social media activity in relation to a publisher and its authors and books, and to measure levels of engagement. Marketers must have an understanding of the algorithmic nature of social media and how the algorithms differ between platforms – and be ready for changes in the algorithms. The platforms themselves offer analytics to measure data and for example for TikTok marketers can track follower growth, views, likes, comments, shares, watch time for videos, and the location of audiences. Table 9.5 shows the usage in 2023 of social networks across the world – X/Twitter had 666 m monthly active users and does not feature in the top 10.

Direct contact with customers allows the recording of traffic and referrals, and the assessment of publicity campaigns by channel. Readers' activity on a publisher's website can be monitored to assess where they come from, what is their behaviour and how they are converted to do something, in order to collect and segment information about them. Different versions of web pages can be trialled using A/B testing, comparing their performance. Publishers that have built strong direct contacts with large numbers of customers, say teachers in schools, use customer relationship management (CRM) systems to segment their customers and to plan marketing activities. In addition to data analysis, publishers also conduct qualitative research. For example, academic

> The average smartphone user unlocks their phone 150 times a day

Table 9.5 Worldwide monthly users of social media platforms (2023)

Platform	Number of users (m)
Facebook	3,030
YouTube	2,491
WhatsApp	2,000
Instagram	2,000
WeChat	1,327
TikTok	1,218
Facebook Messenger	1,036
Telegram	800
Snapchat	750
Douyin	743

Source: *Statista*, October 2023 figures.

publishers may research personas of the diverse needs of identified groups such as researchers, librarians and students; and educational publishers research through focus groups or interviews the learning needs of students and their user experience.

Textbook promotion

Lecturers' reading lists, which may be available on the internet, are a key determinant in a student's choice of books. Teachers and academics are unlikely to prescribe a book for student use unless they have examined a copy first. Inspection copies can be ordered or downloaded from the publisher's website – most publishers have moved to giving access to a digital version. The teacher, having placed the order, is asked to supply comments on the suitability of the book. If the book is adopted for student purchase, the lecturer is asked whether it is the core text or to be used alongside other titles, or merely recommended, and to fill in the number of students on the course and the name of the supplier. Some publishers will send unsolicited free print copies of textbooks to influential teachers. Any feedback and response rates are used for market research. In academic publishing the information is passed to the sales staff, who contact lecturers directly and alert the campus booksellers (if relevant) through which books are purchased and the library, which may order copies. The global pandemic pushed the direction of sales towards ebooks, given the importance of having texts available to students off campus. Textbook publishers of all levels build databases of adoptions (institution, course, student numbers) for subsequent follow-up and targeting. In school textbook publishing the schools ordering class sets directly are recorded.

Direct sales

Most print books are sold via booksellers (including Amazon) to end-users. Some booksellers, especially the specialist, sell by mail order and may produce email newsletters or their own subscription boxes. Consumer publishers rarely solicit direct print orders because until recently most were unable to identify readers and addresses, and many of their books are priced for the retail outlets, too low for their distribution systems to supply one paperback book cost effectively by mail order. Publishers may use Amazon or other distributors to sell direct to consumers. However, in so doing, the publisher passes the important customer data to the retailer. Readers of ebooks are usually tied to a particular retailer's ecosystem, and this discourages direct purchases from the publisher. There are companies, notably Harlequin in the area of romance, which have built a direct relationship with their consumers and have a high proportion of their ebook sales from their website. The development of a community around content also encourages direct sales.

College textbook publishers, in response to declining campus sales and the growth of internet purchasing, have attempted to encourage direct purchase by offering incentives to students such as all-you-can-eat offers on digital textbooks with a monthly subscription. The publishers of specialist online services sell directly to defined professional markets (for example legal, accountancy, finance and business), although some of their print products pass through booksellers and library suppliers. The academic and STM publishers likewise actively solicit direct orders – or through intermediaries – of high-level books from academics, scientists and professionals. Publisher displays at conferences can also be an effective method of reaching these markets. The schools market is ideal for the direct marketing of books and new media, since schools may buy multiple copies with repeat purchases direct from the publisher. Discounts are given by quantity rather than to any intermediary.

The database of contacts is of prime importance. It should be accurate, up to date, and appropriate for the product. Lists may be gathered from firms which specialize in constructing lists in educational, academic and professional areas, from associations, journal subscribers, and conference delegates, and from authors. In time, the best lists are the publisher's own, built from successive sales and recorded and coded into the publisher's own database or customer relationship management (CRM) system. In the UK lists must be held in accordance with the General Data Protection Regulations (2018). While email provides a highly cost-effective method of mailing, companies must ensure that its use stays within the law. The advice from the Information Commissioner's Office in the UK is that:

> You will often need a person's consent before you can send them a marketing message. If you do need consent, then – to be valid – consent must be knowingly and freely given, clear and specific. It must cover both your particular organisation and the type of communication you want to use (e.g. call, automated call, fax, email, text). It must involve some form of very clear positive action – for example, ticking a box, clicking an icon, or sending an email – and the person must fully understand that they are giving you consent. (ico.org.uk, accessed 5 September 2018)

Now read this

Alison Baverstock, *How to Market Books*, 6th edition, Routledge, 2019.
Philip Kotler, Gary Armstrong, Lloyd C. Harris, and Hongwei He, *Principles of Marketing*, 8th European Edition, Pearson, 2020.

Sources

Daniel Bunyard, 'Why We Buy Books', *Logos*, 31:2 (2020).
Miriam Johnson and Helen A. Simpson, *Social Media Marketing for Book Publishers*, Routledge, 2022.
Kobo, *How the Best Readers in the World Read*, April 2016.
Mintel, *Books and E-books*, 2022.

Angus Phillips, 'How Books Are Positioned in the Market', in Nicole
    Matthews and Nickianne Moody (eds), *Judging a Book by Its Cover: Fans,
    publishers, designers, and the marketing of fiction*, Ashgate, 2007.
Al Ries and Jack Trout, *Positioning: The battle for your mind*, McGraw-Hill,
    2001.
Jane Rogers (ed.), *Good Fiction Guide*, Oxford University Press, 2001.

Web resources

www.bic.org.uk Book Industry Communication (UK).
https://bisg.org/ Book Industry Study Group (USA).
https://www.bookmarketingsociety.co.uk Book Marketing Society.
https://editeur.org EDItEUR standards organization.
https://www.goodreads.com Site for readers and book recommendations.
https://literacytrust.org.uk National Literacy Trust (UK).
https://themanbookerprize.com Man Booker Prize for Fiction.
https://publisherspublicitycircle.co.uk Publishers Publicity Circle (UK).

CHAPTER 10

Sales and distribution

While it is the job of marketing to understand the needs of the market and promote books to the relevant audiences, it is their colleagues in sales who stimulate the visibility of products and their demand through the various channels to market. Sales is a powerful voice in decisions around what books to publish, and how they should be published. Sales staff realize income by sustained and regular face-to-face selling to key intermediaries. The roles within sales, distribution and marketing continue to be transformed by changes in the retailing of printed books and ebooks through intermediaries, and by the rise of direct marketing and attempts by publishers to sell to end-users. A combination of the dominance of the internet booksellers (i.e. Amazon), the shift of bookselling chains to central buying, and the decline of independent bookselling, has led to a change in focus of sales staff in recent years. Publishers maintain key roles selling to the main accounts, have drastically reduced the number of field sales representatives (reps) who visit bookshops, and have created new in-house roles in direct selling, website/platform development and data analytics. They also use third parties such as sales and merchandising agencies. It is also important for publishers to ensure that their books are listed online with sufficient metadata, and to deploy search engine optimization as a way of attracting purchasers. As we saw in Chapter 9, data about products helps to drive sales through the relevant channels.

In the area of print and ebook distribution, the larger publishers run their own operations. Small and medium-sized enterprises (SMEs) usually use third parties – larger publishers or independent distributors. Publishers typically derive most of their sales revenue from a small number of customers, and small revenue from a great number. This so-called Pareto effect suggests that 20 per cent of customers might account for 80 per cent of total sales.

Rights sales are covered separately in Chapter 12

SALES

In consumer publishing, a big order from a supermarket can still put a book amongst the bestsellers, and high street booksellers remain important for the visibility of books. But Amazon has taken market share for print and come to dominate in the area of ebooks. The internet provides a route to sell the 'Long

Tail' – the books that are not regularly stocked in bookshops (see Chapter 12) – and smaller publishers have found they can compete effectively online. Customers searching online for a relevant title can come across slow-selling backlist titles as well as the current bestsellers. Since independent booksellers rely on the trade wholesalers, many have lost face-to-face contact with publishers. However, they may deal with selected publishers from which they receive higher discounts than from wholesalers.

With western markets relatively mature, publishers look to other world markets to boost sales of English language editions. Export sales staff will make visits to key markets and use local distributors and agents. If the market offers potential, the company may set up its own office, which may be a sales and marketing office or possibly a full local publishing company. Publishers may also have joint ventures – companies set up in partnership with domestic publishers. This would normally be where the local laws do not allow wholly owned foreign investment, or where local company expertise is necessary to penetrate the market. Alternatively the English language publisher may want to sell the rights to their books (see Chapter 11) or enter into co-publication deals – where they co-operate with domestic companies on particular projects.

Sales forecasting and inventory control

Sales forecasting and translating it into the actual number to print of a book at the outset, especially one of expected high sales volume, are part of the risk decision for the publisher. The view of the sales department is critical. Too high an initial print run would lead to a large stock write-off if the book does not sell; printing too few and being unable to fulfil demand quickly enough on reprint would lead to lost sales and antagonize the book trade and readers. For consumer book publishers, the all-important Christmas market of short intensity is the most difficult to predict, with surprise and often quirky bestsellers popping up each year. In the UK, on Super Thursday (in late September or early October) hundreds of hardback Christmas titles are published (often three times the monthly average).

In theory, the sales department of a consumer book publisher should receive the orders from the book trade three months ahead of publication – in practice, orders often arrive after the publisher has set the print run quantity. Therefore the publisher has to forecast. The management of the sales department has conventionally based their forecasts on judgement and experience, historic data of the firm's similar books, and the conversations they have held with the book trade's senior buyers. More recently they have the aid of forecasting software, either the publisher's own or supplied by specialist firms; and historic and real-time data of actual book sales made through retailers, as supplied by Nielsen BookScan. Publishers are increasingly using analytics to work out the optimum combination of price and revenue, and may opt for a short initial run so that they can gauge the likely level of demand. The ability of printers to deliver smaller quantities quickly has also ameliorated the publisher's risk of over-stocks, while print on demand and ebooks enable books to remain available without inventory costs.

The model for audiobooks is mostly for them to be sold as individual, downloaded titles, even when part of a subscription, and publishers are keen to avoid if possible a streaming model – such a 'pooling model' gives publishers a percentage share of the total revenue based on usage. The arrangements will vary according to the bargaining power of the parties involved. In 2023 David Kaefer, vice-president of business affairs at Spotify, said that the streaming service was working with publishers in different ways: 'there is a pooling model for a segment of our partners and generally its partners who are slightly smaller scale ... some people, particularly larger providers, wanted to do something different' (*The Bookseller*, 9 October 2023).

The international college textbook publishers, academic and STM publishers face the challenge of managing stock levels in their warehouses throughout the world and the shipping of stock between them. For example, the UK sales office in the early new year would have forecast the adoption demand of a college textbook in the UK and northern Europe to be purchased by students in the autumn and would have the stock (printed overseas during the summer) to meet that demand. But what if, in September, at the critical UK buying period, another publishing centre overseas receives an unexpected and large direct order from an institution, likely to be repeated annually thereafter, which they cannot fulfil? The stock earmarked for the UK and Europe is immediately shipped out of the UK to the overseas centre, dangerously lowering the UK stock levels. But they may have other warehouses elsewhere with small quantities of available stock from which they can replenish the UK.

How sales data can inform publishing decisions

Suzy Warnock, Analytic Publisher Account Manager, Nielsen Book Research

E★PERT

Having access to reliable weekly sales data on print books in the UK can help publishers to:

- Contextualize their performance with that of the wider market, looking at gains and losses overall and within specific genres to better understand their market position.
- More accurately predict sales for new titles by looking at competitor or previous titles in a series, helping to decide print runs and minimize returns.
- Identify and track emerging trends.
- Monitor discounting behaviour by seeing the average sales price of a given book, author, or publisher, which can be compared to RRPs to see which areas of the market books are being most heavily discounted.
- See the direct impact on books sales of marketing and publicity campaigns; awards nominations and wins; TV and film adaptations; social media and other media.

Here is an example of the impact a TV adaptation can have on book sales: in 2022, the first season of the Netflix adaptation of Alice Oseman's *Heartstopper* Young Adult Graphic Novel series aired. See the graph of the Children's

Four-weekly trend

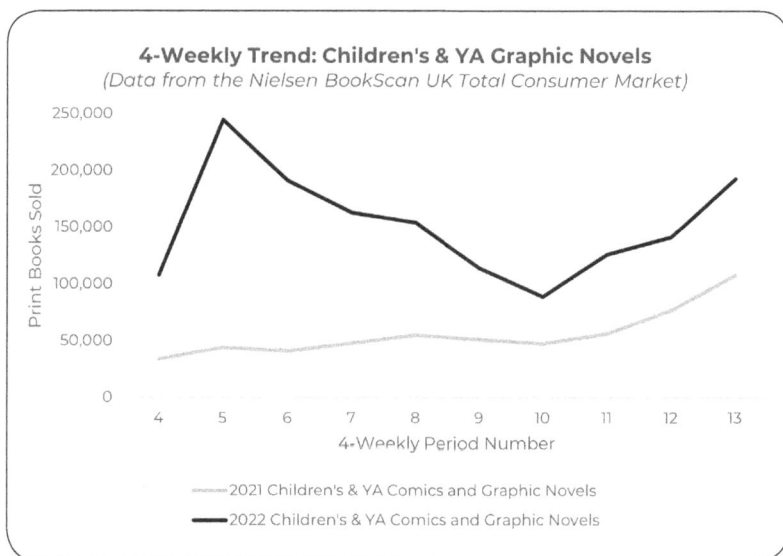

4-Weekly Trend: Children's & YA Graphic Novels
(Data from the Nielsen BookScan UK Total Consumer Market)

Print Books Sold

250,000

200,000

150,000

100,000

50,000

0

4   5   6   7   8   9   10   11   12   13

4-Weekly Period Number

2021 Children's & YA Comics and Graphic Novels
2022 Children's & YA Comics and Graphic Novels

and Young Adult Comic and Graphic Novel genre by four-weekly period, beginning in the four weeks leading up to the series premiere in April.

In the four weeks following the release of the Netflix series (period number 5), 64 per cent of the books sold in the Children's & YA Graphic Novels genre were from the Heartstopper series, compared to 22 per cent in the four weeks before the release. This boosted the volume sales in the overall genre 127 per cent between periods 4 and 5, compared to a 31 per cent increase in the same period in 2021 when no such media releases occurred. Seeing how an adaptation can influence sales can help publishers make decisions when managing rights negotiations.

Many factors, from social media trends to pricing changes, can influence book purchasing. The chart shows the genres in highest value growth in 2023 vs. 2022.

Growth in value

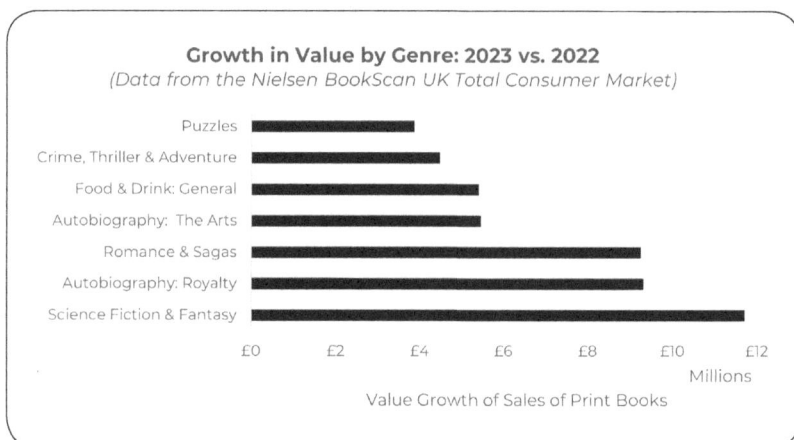

Growth in Value by Genre: 2023 vs. 2022
(Data from the Nielsen BookScan UK Total Consumer Market)

Puzzles

Crime, Thriller & Adventure

Food & Drink: General

Autobiography: The Arts

Romance & Sagas

Autobiography: Royalty

Science Fiction & Fantasy

£0   £2   £4   £6   £8   £10   £12

Millions

Value Growth of Sales of Print Books

Looking at growth in value versus growth in volume can help understand changes in pricing and which categories are most affected in fluctuations in both RRP and discounting rates. Though most of these categories did also see corresponding growth in actual unit sales, not all did – Arts Autobiographies sold 7.5k fewer print books in 2023 than in 2022, while Crime, Thriller & Adventure sold 389k fewer. Understanding pricing changes in the market can help ensure a publisher does not either over- or under-price their titles.

The large increase in the value of the Science Fiction and Fantasy genre was partially helped by trending titles on popular social media app TikTok; the highest-selling book in this genre for 2023, Rebecca Yarros' *Fourth Wing*, had 1.3 bn views for its relevant hashtag on TikTok (January 2024). However, the success of a new release can be due to many factors which can be difficult to isolate. Look also at backlist title *It Ends with Us* by Colleen Hoover, first published in 2016. This title saw a 9500 per cent increase in UK print sales in 2021 compared to its publication year for the equivalent time period (August–December) after it began to be widely discussed on TikTok. This helps contextualize the potential power of social media virality. Seeing the measurable impact of such trends can help publishers allocate resources when planning marketing campaigns and strategy. It can also encourage promotions and re-releases of relevant backlist titles to capitalize on current trends.

It is important to look at the individual titles driving growth within a genre. Whilst some trends can spark wider interest in similar titles and boost the whole genre, other genres may not see the same pattern. Prince Harry's *Spare*, which accounted for 97 per cent of sales of Royal Autobiographies in 2023, was a high-profile release from a public figure. If the sales of *Spare* are taken out of Royal Autobiographies, the remaining category sales actually fell 75 per cent in value year-on-year, suggesting its success did not help to boost the rest of the genre, and it may not be a good strategy to publish a similar book hoping to emulate the success. Compare this to Science Fiction and Fantasy, which saw 17 per cent growth, even after taking out the top title *Fourth Wing* and its sequel *Iron Flame* (vs. 24 per cent with them included).

Analysis of sales data can help understand the real impact of external factors and help in decision-making when developing marketing campaigns, supporting acquisition pitches for new titles and determining wider publishing strategy.

Roles in the sales department

The sales director, usually supported by a UK sales manager and an export sales manager, plans and organizes the sales effort, and negotiates the terms of trade with the main customers. At the most senior level, the negotiation of terms imposed by Amazon, Apple and others is exceptionally difficult and fraught. The sales management comments on editors' new book proposals – forecasting sales and advising on pricing. They are involved in decisions on covers, discussions around marketing campaigns, and the management of stock, especially of key

titles. In consumer publishing, the sales management may use the technique
of dynamic pricing for ebooks, for example lowering prices for a limited period
to stimulate titles showing a decline in sales. The large publishing houses now
employ specialists in pricing and analytics.

Key account managers will present all new titles six months ahead of
publication to the buyers of key accounts, and discuss the plans for promotions to
be run by the publisher and retailer. Co-op promotions to increase book visibility
may be based around special price offers, summer reading or back-to-school
campaigns; under James Daunt, Waterstones took the decision to end taking co-op
payments:

> Deals would be made with publishers – 'effectively driven by the amount of
> money that publishers would pay you to take a book,' says Daunt – and every
> branch would be loaded up with the same titles. To create better bookshops,
> Daunt realised that he had to stop allowing publishers to buy space in them.
> 'We said no, we won't be paid a penny, which we're not, now.' (*New Statesman*,
> 10 July 2017)

There are changing policies amongst the chains when it comes to the delegation
of buying decisions to branch buyers, and James Daunt has been keen to give
more decision-making for Waterstones to local shops. Bea Carvalho, Head Fiction
Buyer there, says:

> We don't dictate what each Waterstones shop promotes, we give them the
> tools to champion what they choose. There's a balance between big sellers
> across the market and a local slant. Scotland and the North are very strong
> on crime, for instance, while city centres do better on literary fiction.
> (Booksellers Association, 2022)

Overall the chains buy centrally and scale out order quantities to their branches.
Scale-outs will always apply to major new books and promotions but the local
managers might still have the ability to increase orders. Supermarkets buy
centrally from publishers and stock may then be delivered via wholesalers.

Another sales role is the manager who undertakes so-called 'special sales' to
customers beyond the traditional book trade, such as to non-book wholesalers,
non-book and discount retailers (e.g. The Works), direct sales companies,
newspapers and magazines (for example cover mounts), and sometimes to
remainder or promotion book imprints. Some publishers operate vendor-managed
inventory systems for them. In academic, STM and professional publishing,
special sales encompass direct supply deals made with institutions and
businesses, such as bulk sales of textbooks to universities. Special editions may
be customized and printed for companies to give away to staff or their customers.
Pharma companies purchase reprints of journal articles for distribution to medics.
Furthermore, some STM, reference and directory publishers sell advertising
space in their journals to supplement their income; and on their websites (though
advertising revenue is much lower than in print).

The licensing of content (ebooks, journals and databases) to libraries
(public, school, university and corporate) is exceedingly complex. The large STM

publishers license their content directly. Other publishers use one or more of the aggregation companies supplying the library sectors, through which the licensing and distribution are controlled – the licensing and loan usage models are under constant evolution.

In medium to large publishers the UK market sales manager (supported by in-house staff) runs the sales force. Small publishers may not be able to afford the high cost of employing their own reps, in which case they will normally hire the services of a freelance sales force. If a publisher employs its own full-time reps, each one will cover a discrete area (a territory), and is supplied with a car, a laptop/tablet, and receives expenses and a salary. Some publishers, more often the consumer firms, pay bonuses for exceeding sales targets. The reps usually live in their territories and meet together with the in-house staff only at the sales conferences (two to four times per year), where they learn about the new books, promotional plans and priorities. The reps are sent or can access all the promotional material (advance information sheets, jackets and covers), publicity and marketing details, and feedback orders and reports on their activities, and on the response of customers.

If the publisher chooses the freelance option, they will expect to pay between 10 and 15 per cent commission on their net sales. The freelance sales force will work in exactly the same way as an in-house sales team, and will expect the same level of information and sales material. The downside of this arrangement is that the reps will be selling in many other lists and so the publisher will not necessarily be given any special treatment. Equally there are no hidden costs, and the more the team sells, the more they earn.

The management of the sales channels is vital. Each channel to market offers different sales prospects and margins. Some imprints, brands or individual titles are more suitable for some channels than others. Furthermore the management of the channels is affected by the publisher's distribution arrangements. Whilst physical retail has been in decline, accounts are managed with the growing number of internet retailers and distributors, and aggregators supplying products to institutional and corporate markets, some of which are specialist. In order to sell the publisher's books, internet retailers need to be supplied over six months in advance with rich and correct metadata. For important titles pre-orders on Amazon may open a long time in advance of publication.

Terms of sale

Publishers sell books to retailers on the following terms. The definitions are open to variation, but the important distinction is between firm orders and sale or return. The risk for publishers is lower with firm orders, while the risk for booksellers is lowered if there is the guarantee that they can return unsold stock. If a book is returned to the publisher, the bookseller usually pays for the return delivery, unless otherwise agreed.

Firm orders

On firm orders the bookseller agrees to accept the books, to pay for them (preferably on one month's credit, unless otherwise agreed) and not to return them for credit. Powerful booksellers will request a higher discount on firm sales and are likely to be more cautious on the quantity ordered. Firm orders are typically used by publishers on direct bulk sales to organizations (e.g. education and corporate).

Sale or return

Most booksellers will want to operate on the basis of sale or return to ensure they are not left with unsold stock. Within a specified period they can return books (provided that they are in saleable condition) for credit, or in exchange for other books. The bookseller's account is invoiced at the time of supply, and payment is due at the expiry of the agreed credit period (which could be between 30 and 90 days).

The terms of trade between publishers and their customers – discounts, credit periods and levels of returns – are subject to regular negotiation. As the large retailers have gained in strength, the consumer publishers essentially trade with them on a sale or return basis on longer credit terms. Discounts are discussed in more detail in Chapter 12.

Ebooks

An ebook is sold under licence from the publisher to either the intermediary, which then licenses to the end purchaser, or directly to the consumer. The problem of returns is solved with the sale of ebooks, but there have been issues to be sorted out around the terms of trade. The wholesale model was prevalent with set discounts given to intermediaries, but in 2010 Amazon switched over to an agency model with the larger publishers. This gives the publisher more control over pricing but has strengthened Amazon's margins.

Selling in and selling through

It is important to realize that sales staff do not merely walk into the head offices of the chains or into individual shops with a bag of new titles to sell, authorize the return of unsold books and leave. In a rapidly changing world, affecting publishing and retailing, and of changing consumer preferences, the retailers must concentrate their time and effort on marketing and selling the right titles to their customers. The role of the rep or key account manager extends to representing the constituent parts of the publisher – the sales and marketing departments, and the editorial thinking behind projects – to the retailers, and helping them market and sell to their customers effectively.

Key account managers will discuss forthcoming titles with the major booksellers, looking to push those books most suitable for each. Sometimes a book is seen as, for example, a Waterstones title, one that could do especially well in their shops. Promotional plans will be discussed, both those planned by the publishers and suitable promotions being run by the bookseller (a sizeable prize would be securing a title as a Waterstones Book of the Month). Promise of a decent spend on marketing can be required to get a title taken seriously by the major chains. While a retailer may bear the cost of a promotion themselves, more often extra discount is required from the publisher to secure a place for a book in a promotion, and co-op payments may be required from the publisher to secure a prime position in a Christmas campaign.

A consumer publisher's senior in-house staff see the main book buyers twice a year around nine months ahead of the main seasons – in February/ March for September to January titles, in August/September for the February to August titles. They prioritize the lead titles which are part of major promotions, discuss other new books and important backlist. Monthly presentations to the key accounts follow, around five months ahead of publication. Frequency of presentations varies among publishers. What has changed the practice of selling in is the widespread use of sales data. Booksellers can check on an author's track record, and will not be impressed by wild claims by the publisher. When they are unsure about a new title, they will want to check the author's previous sales to firm up their opinion.

Those field reps who do visit individual accounts will keep a file on customers, listing their interests and opening hours. By appointment, they visit mainly booksellers – the branches of the chains and significant independents – any wholesalers or library suppliers within their areas, and other outlets which justify the high cost of calling. Tablets may be used to display covers and marketing materials. Reps rarely carry finished copies, apart from exceptions such as children's illustrated books. A high level of connectivity allows the reps to provide current information on stock availability, order status, and sales history, and to send information, such as orders and reports, back to their publishers in the evening. Reps may tweet or blog about their favourite titles; they can also use social media to pick up on trends to pass on to buyers.

A rep's aim is to obtain advance orders (or subscriptions) on forthcoming books usually three months ahead of publication from all the main bookshops, in time to inform the print run decision. As most independents place orders electronically, and not through the reps, the reps want the orders to be sent to their publishers, not via higher discount wholesalers. During a call they will cover the new books to be published in a certain period. However, smaller and infrequently visited bookshops may be sold new books post-publication.

The meeting with the bookshop buyer takes place in an office, the stock room or on the shop floor. The first few minutes are spent discussing trade gossip and the shop. Reps provide the main contact between booksellers and publishers, and should be able to supply the most recent information on all the firm's titles and to determine what information would be useful, and what marketing and promotions the bookseller could use.

The rep usually leads off with a major, strongly promoted title. The prime aim is to put the buyer in a positive buying frame of mind. Two to three minutes are spent in presenting a lead title. Showing the cover and the AI (advance information sheet), the rep talks about the book and author, covering such aspects as its contents, what part of the market it is aimed at, why it is good, previous books by the author, the promotion, and sometimes the competition. Although more time is devoted to the main titles, the rep generally has under a minute per title, just one or two sentences, to sell it. One approach is to have a key positioning line, which helps place the book in the mind of the buyer. The 'new Harry Potter' is overused, but similar lines can be created. If the book is of local interest or is

Advance orders are called subscriptions

SKILLS

Sales

Common features of all good sales staff are their energy, self-motivation and discipline which get them out of bed very early, and help them work long hours. They need a strong knowledge of print and digital markets, and competitor activity. On meeting buyers of differing levels of seniority, sales staff need to be alert and make a good first impression. Listening and watching they adjust their selling style and procedure to a buyer's character and mood. They need to be flexible, pitching their style within a range from soft to hard sell, and sense when – and when not – to talk. They are part amateur psychologist, part actor. Strong negotiation skills are required, especially when dealing with key accounts, and they should present their firms honestly, be diplomatic and have authority. When a buyer asks for special terms, or some other favour, a sales manager must be able to make decisions which are best for the company but at the same time attractive for the customer. Their marketing and customer service skills give the publisher a competitive edge.

A good field rep knows the books and the customers' businesses and their customer profiles, interests and systems. Although reps are given priorities, their skill is to determine which books are best for their area and each outlet, and what size of orders is suitable. They gain the confidence and respect of buyers by recommending books that prove themselves. Educational and college reps (also called consultants) must have a lively interest in education and the ability to get on well with the kind of people in those professions and understand their attitudes, mindsets and the conflicting pressures they work under. Overt hard selling is inappropriate. Rather they need to be able to talk about the problems faced by teachers, the kinds of materials used, and the ways a teacher likes to use them, and then have to be able to suggest and promote suitable products – as well as demonstrate online and other resources. In the higher education sector they need to understand the purchasing systems of the institutions, as well as give sales presentations and product demonstrations.

going to receive other publicity, this is mentioned. Mention of participation in an online book club, for example, will guarantee a good subscription. Vanessa Di Grigorio, a sales rep for a number of publishers in the USA, wrote on her blog:

> my job is to pick out what books will work for certain stores, and which books deserve to be highlighted. My job is to get people excited. In a way, you could say that my job is to talk to people about books – a lot. (publishingcrawl.com, accessed 22 January 2024)

Reps keep records of orders, so that they can remind buyers of orders placed on authors' previous books.

Training is usually required to sell well, both in negotiation and interpersonal skills. To avoid diluting the buyer's interest, the rep, aware of his or her buying pattern and customers, concentrates on those titles likely to sell in that particular shop – retailers' customer profiles differ greatly. There is a common understanding between an experienced rep and a good buyer with regard to the titles and order quantities that can be sold in that particular shop. Weak buyers need help. A good buyer is often aware of the books before the rep calls and can estimate within a few seconds the number of sales. But a buyer may want a larger quantity than the rep had in mind or conversely may place an order which the rep feels is too low. Knowing that the book is selling well elsewhere or sensing that the buyer does not appreciate some aspect, the rep mentions that and suggests a higher quantity. If the rep is trusted, the buyer may increase the order. Part of the persuasion may involve the rep in allowing greater freedom on returns within the firm's overall policy. But selling too many copies which are merely returned eats away at the bookseller's and publisher's margins, and erodes the trust between rep and buyer. Aside from environmental considerations, it is a waste of time for both the bookseller and the publisher.

Backed up by attractive POS material, the rep tries to persuade the bookseller to mount special window or instore displays to increase visibility. They will receive emails from head office with news of media coverage which is relevant to titles on the list. Reps may offer proof copies. The bookseller may ask the rep to arrange an author signing session in the shop, and will negotiate any cost attached. Reps also feed back promotion needs requested by customers or promotion ideas used by other publishers which could be emulated; and occasionally reps make editorial suggestions. They may also chase debts and support marketing on author events.

Academic and STM sales

Academic sales forces are smaller than those of consumer book publishers. Reps visit a limited range of bookshops, such as campus stores, which stock their titles, and may call on specialist mail-order booksellers and library suppliers which supply books to home and export markets. Additionally they may visit campuses in order to identify courses and the lecturers who make the decisions to recommend textbooks. While to a limited extent they encourage academics to order personally, or through their library, monographs and reference books (and sometimes journals and online services), their main thrust is to secure textbook adoptions. Using the promotional material and occasionally bound copies, they present the most relevant texts to individual lecturers who, if interested, are followed up by email and are sent inspection or gratis copies of the physical edition, or access to a digital edition. Mostly rep visits have been replaced by emails inviting lecturers to order inspection copies directly.

Reluctant buyers are eventually triggered into building up their stock by the students. Only a small number of booksellers stock monographs and high-priced reference books. Such books are supplied by bookshops in response to orders, and largely these sales have transferred to the internet. Academic reps also sell titles more dependent on retail exposure – these may be used by students as background reading or for reference. Examples are OUP's series of Very Short

Introductions and their Oxford Paperback Reference titles. A crucial aim is to get bookshops to stock and display the books – otherwise sales are lost. Booksellers are encouraged to distribute promotional material and to mount special displays at back-to-college time. Another activity is setting up and attending exhibitions at academic conferences. Large firms employ full-time staff solely for hundreds of conferences worldwide. Against the background of the decline in campus bookstores and the reluctance of booksellers to hold stock of academic titles, conference exhibitions provide an opportunity for academics to see the publishers' main titles.

The sales staff of the major journal and book publishers concentrate their efforts on negotiating with their main customers: the research intensive universities, through their librarians, and library consortia throughout the world. Throughout the world there are regional differences in the ways university, college and corporate libraries purchase books and journals but there is convergence. Academic libraries place orders for books through distributors and wholesalers rather than deal directly with large number of publishers. Amazon is increasing its sales of printed books to libraries. In the USA many books were traditionally purchased through approval plans, whereby the library works with the intermediary or vendor to work out the kinds of books that are appropriate for the institution. The vendor applies that filter to the new book output of the accredited publishers and presents to the library the subset of titles which the library may approve and purchase or decline. The library gains administrative savings over expensive title-by-title acquisition, and receives a small discount; and the selected publishers gain predictable sales. Approval plans peaked at the turn of the century.

ScienceDirect from Elsevier offers articles from over 4,900 journals and 35,000 books

Publishers supply most of their ebooks (in PDF and XML ePub formats) directly to libraries, either via their own platforms, or those of other larger publishers or platform providers. The major publishers owning extensive book aggregations have their own platforms. Their platforms were originally developed for journals and databases but subsequently they added ebooks. The larger publishers offer their platforms and services to smaller publishers. A publisher's platform offers it far more customer data than that supplied by third parties, the freedom to control its own business models and flexibility on how its content is used. The cost of developing platforms used to be prohibitive for smaller publishers: now platform vendors enable them to operate affordably their own customized platforms to sell content directly.

Publishers also make indirect sales to individuals and libraries via Amazon, wholesalers and through the academic aggregators that host ebooks on their platform from a range of publishers, thereby providing a consistent user experience. For libraries the aggregators offer a high level of integration with library management systems which aids their efficiency. The major US companies EBSCO and ProQuest reach institutions worldwide. Not-for-profit JSTOR (ITHAKA) and Project MUSE (which concentrates on AHSS) are well established in the US market; and in the UK Askews & Holts. The wholesale and library supply market (print and ebook) has consolidated nationally and worldwide in order to derive benefits of scale. The aggregators, dependent on securing titles from publishers, use additional DRM constraints to allay their fears of misuse or loss of sales, such as limiting the number of concurrent users viewing a book, or restricting copy and pasting. Such restrictions irritate users and librarians.

Publishers accustomed to a focus on the marketing and selling of stand-alone printed books, from which they received no subsequent revenue, are adapting to digital post-purchase and usage-driven marketing and selling deployed earlier in journals. The publishers (and content aggregators) offer libraries numerous ebook acquisition models and most libraries use a range of models. Many librarians use perpetual access, title-by-title purchasing, of ebooks that reflects their traditional role of forming their own and stable collection. Publishers create collections of academic content – typically defined by subject and time of publication, and usually excluding textbooks – and offer them to libraries on subscription. Collections offer libraries the ability to access large numbers of titles at a discounted price, generate usage even of older titles and are kept up to date. Such bundles of content are like the Big Deals offered much earlier by the journal publishers. Subscriptions to collections provide recurring revenue to the publisher, serve to lock in libraries to the publisher, strengthen the power of the large publishers and squeeze out smaller ones. Under patron-driven acquisition (PDA), or in the US, demand-driven acquisition (DDA) models, the library selects the range of books to be viewed and usage parameters trigger purchase or rental: thus the library purchases only the books used. There are other evidence-based models deployed by publishers which aid librarians' return on investment. However, some publishers became wary of DDA and similar models; also librarians were anxious that their role in curating the libraries' collections was being diminished.

Schools publishing

School textbook publishers and some children's book publishers employ a core of full-time educational reps supplemented with term-time reps – often parents or ex-teachers. The role of the rep has expanded to that of a consultant to schools, moving from simply selling to an advisory role involving consultative selling, relationship building and problem-solving. The large publishers have separate sales forces covering primary and secondary schools, and possibly the further education sector. Additionally, they may appoint specialist advisers (ex-teachers) in the major subject areas. They provide product training for sales reps, give talks to teachers and promote to local advisers. A rep of a large company may cover just two counties while one in a small company may have to cover a whole region. During term time reps usually visit two to three secondary schools per day or up to five primary schools. Large primary schools warrant coverage similar to a secondary school. The number of schools visited per day is related to their proximity. In those schools which manage their own budgets, reps encourage direct orders to the publisher, offering incentive discounts on sizeable quantities if necessary. Reps promote the use of digital products and services, and their role in this area becomes one of a consultant, advising on which resources work well.

Market research includes the regular feedback of information such as teachers' suggestions, the response of teachers to their own and competitors' books, information on competitors, buying policies, local authority guidelines affecting purchases, and gaps in the market. Sometimes reps suggest ideas for books to the commissioning editors, give advice to teachers who are considering authorship and discover new authors.

INTERNATIONAL SALES

There are various ways of organizing export sales staff within a publishing house. In small firms the sales director may be responsible for home sales and for export arrangements, spending perhaps one or two months abroad annually. In larger firms there is a separate export department headed by an export sales manager, who reports to the sales director. An export manager may be supported by office staff. In still larger firms, there may be an international sales director in charge of staff such as regional sales executives or area export managers, who look after all the group's lists in specific territories. They are usually responsible for all export sales within their territories and for the arrangements and relationships made with the distributors and booksellers. As an alternative the sales team can be organized by list or imprint but this is less economic as it means several people are travelling to the same part of the world.

Territories are usually roughly divided by continent: Europe, Asia, India, Middle East, Africa, Australia, Canada, South America, and the Caribbean. The USA can be handled in many different ways but trade publishers will aim to sell rights, rather than their own edition, into this lucrative market. Larger houses will have several people covering the world; smaller companies may only have one person, who inevitably has to prioritize the most appropriate markets. The major players may well have their own companies in Australia, Canada, India, or South Africa, and the sales role becomes more one of product manager. Fast-growing markets such as India and China are of great strategic importance.

Publishers of all types price their books primarily on their biggest market (usually but not always the home market) and that sets the basis for pricing in export markets. However, if an overseas country, such as the USA, is the main market, then the book is priced primarily on that territory. Pricing for export markets is complex and requires constant review as exchange rates (and rates of VAT) vary. Pricing a printed book to make it affordable and saleable in a poorer overseas market runs the risk that arbitrage traders will sell it in higher priced markets, including the home market.

A characteristic of staff in international sales is that they are usually expected to spend anything from three to six months abroad. For example, medium and large UK publishers may employ sales representatives who cover parts or the whole of Europe or other areas of the world. Broadly, the larger the company, the smaller the geographical area covered by each representative; but compared to the home market their territories are vast and their calls to importing book trade customers far less frequent. They are either home-based, travelling regularly, or resident overseas. Some of the major publishing groups station their nationals in small offices in countries outside the fields of operation of their overseas firms. They are mainly concerned with promoting the firm's books, liaising with and supervising arrangements made with local distributors, opening up the market and, when appropriate, employing local representatives. The export-orientated ELT divisions of major publishers typically have their own export sections deploying all of the above methods. Publishers may also employ full-time local nationals in some areas to represent their interests.

Penguin India, started in 1987, publishes a range of fiction and non-fiction books, predominantly by Indian authors. It also publishes in local languages

International sales

The ability to speak preferably two or more languages is invariably required, but is not a top priority: most customers can speak English to some extent. But linguistic ability enables you to understand and relate that much better to the market and customers. Fluency in one or more of the European languages such as French, German, Spanish and Italian, and semi-fluency in some are ideal. Standard Arabic and Chinese are sometimes particularly desirable for certain firms. Export sales staff have a commitment to publishing and exporting, and have to enjoy working with books. First and foremost sales people, they have a burning desire to ring up the till, to increase profitable turnover. Most of the personal skills required for selling to the home market are paralleled in export selling; but exporters face the complexities of understanding many different and diverse markets and need an appreciation of the political, social, economic and cultural factors pertaining to each country, as well as a sensitivity to and enthusiasm for the market. Good exporters are able to sell and adapt to different environments and situations fast; they are good at building up relationships with key customers. Sales staff must like travel, and have the self-motivation to work far away from headquarters, take high-level decisions, and cope with loneliness on overseas trips.

SKILLS

The Rizzoli bookstore in the centre of Milan

Export arrangements

The staff numbers of export departments are paradoxically far smaller than the home sales side because much of the work of promoting and selling books is carried out abroad. The international publishers with world rights in an author's work have greater control to set published prices and uniform publication dates in different parts of the world. Those publishers without world rights may be in competition with other publishers in some markets. International sales staff of UK publishers who are selling into open markets, for example Europe, will be keen to publish UK trade and ebook editions ahead of the equivalent US publisher's editions. There is mixed evidence, depending on the market, as to the impact of translation deals on the sales of English language editions. For example, Dutch publishers will rush to translate a potential bestseller ahead of the arrival of the English edition in their market. In Germany it may be the success of a novel once translated which encourages sales to those wanting to read the original English language edition. By contrast, sales of the English edition of *Fifty Shades of Grey* fell in Slovenia once a translation was published.

English-language exports into Europe have grown in recent years, and bookstores there have been expanding their English sections. Yet there is another side to this success, and it may in fact be reducing the chances of translation deals in some markets, which in turn will harm authors' incomes. Also continued growth in reading in English is affecting domestic publishing industries and the prospects for books in local languages.

The main export arrangements are as follows but ebooks can be sold directly to customers right around the world. The growth of distributive printing – printing physical copies to order in local markets – also offers publishers a new way of supplying markets without the need to hold stock locally. Local distributors increasingly offer printing facilities to their clients.

Sister companies and branches

In countries where there are firms connected through ownership with the originating publisher, such sister firms usually have the exclusive right to distribute. For example, Oxford University Press has a number of branches around the world. Nevertheless, certain titles or whole lists may be licensed to, or distributed by, other firms. Some US-focused consumer imprints of major international publishers are distributed in the UK by independent distributors such as Turnaround. Branches or sister companies may develop publishing operations aimed at their own domestic market and for export throughout the group.

Exclusive market

A stockholding agent may have the exclusive distribution rights for the publisher's output within a certain export territory. The agent services the orders originating from customers within the territory and collects the money. Normally the agent carries out the promotion and sales representation as well. Such agents may be wholesalers, booksellers, importers or branches of other publishers. Sometimes, exclusivity is restricted to part of the publisher's output or important named customers within the territory deal directly with the publisher.

Non-exclusive markets

In countries not covered by the exclusive stockholding agents or the publisher's overseas firms, the publisher deals directly with the local book trade. However, non-exclusive distribution arrangements may be made with certain local 'preferential' stockists (such as wholesalers) which receive more favourable terms from the publisher. The local booksellers can order either directly from the publisher or from the stockist. Some stockists also promote and sales-represent the publisher's books.

Sales on commission

Freelance agents can be appointed to promote and represent the books in specified countries – usually but not always in open markets, and carry many publishers' lists. Those representing publishers in the UK are based in the UK or abroad. They receive a commission of between 10 to 15 per cent on net sales revenue from the territory.

Terms of trade

The agents, wholesalers and booksellers trading in the books receive discounts from the exporting publisher, usually off the publisher's recommended price, in the same way as in the UK. The discounts are often very high to allow pricing to the local market. They then add their costs and profit which can result in book prices being higher than those in the originating publisher's home market. However, this situation is now changing as consumers are able to compare prices around the world and choose the most favourable option. Customers' credit periods in export markets are longer (90–120 days from date of invoice) but can extend to six months or more from slow-paying parts of the world. They also have to allow for import duties and freight costs, which often fall to them to pay. Wherever possible, firm sales are made, and rarely are books actually returned from export markets. Publishers will ask for a POD (proof of destruction) and then credit the customer accordingly.

There are different terms that apply to the shipping of books:

- *free on board* (FOB) – the publisher delivers the books free to the buyer's appointed UK shipping agent. Buyers within a country may co-ordinate and nominate a UK export company that will consolidate orders.
- *ex-warehouse* – the customer bears the cost from the publisher's (or printer's) door. This is a common basis for trading.
- *cost, insurance and freight* (CIF) – the publisher bears all the costs up to their arrival in a port or town. In return for saving the customer cost and (if the goods are sent air freight) time, the discount and credit period may be cut back.
- *on consignment* – the customer pays only on sales made and has the right to return unsold stock. This may be used for substantial orders.

Other export sales, not directly instigated by the publisher, are made by the UK and US export wholesalers, booksellers, and library suppliers. The largest are internationally based and promote, sell and distribute books worldwide – such firms are major 'home' customers of academic and STM publishers. An alternative arrangement is to work with such companies to help them promote the books in export markets. Sales can then be correctly recorded in the publisher's accounts as export. Some end-users seeking the cheapest source of supply (especially libraries) 'buy round' the publishers' arrangements by ordering books from suppliers which ignore exclusive territorial markets. Furthermore, internet bookselling of print and ebooks has broken down national frontiers for the trade of different kinds of books in different languages.

Promotion and personal selling

Communication with the international network is vital. Retailers and intermediaries must be persuaded to concentrate on promoting and selling the firm's titles rather than those of others. Constant contact takes the form of the supply of information through mailings, email, telephone calls and overseas visits. The AIs, catalogues, sales documents, covers, and point-of-sale material cascade on to the local network who use that material to publicize the publisher's titles within their markets. Originating publishers and the distributors operate online systems through which information on titles can be accessed by trading partners worldwide. Some agents prepare their sales documentation from information supplied while others use material produced by the originating publisher. They adapt the titles' metadata as necessary. For example, the original book description may be too difficult to understand by readers whose English is their second language. Agents may generate free media publicity, secure reviews, mail catalogues, conduct email and social media campaigns, sometimes place advertisements, attend exhibitions and operate a textbook inspection copy service.

The originating publisher may also send promotional material to booksellers, libraries, British Council offices, academics and professionals, send books for review to learned journals, send complimentary copies of textbooks to influential people and operate an inspection copy service from the UK. The promotional efforts of publisher and agent may overlap. Of equal importance is the quality and regularity of the response from agents and representatives. They provide feedback on their activities and on market conditions, and specific feedback on individual titles, such as requests for more material.

Overwhelmingly, however, export sales are generated by personal selling. The publisher's senior sales staff give presentations to agents and main customers on their visits to their offices, at book fairs, and in their own countries. Their trips may last two, three or more weeks, and encompass half a dozen countries and up to 30 to 40 customers. They primarily sell to agents' sales managers or directors concerned with imports and may brief the agent's reps at a conference. They discuss all aspects of their trading relationship and assess agents' effectiveness. The reps need to develop an excellent knowledge of their markets in terms of pricing and what genres, subjects, and authors work well. This knowledge can also feed back into commissioning decisions.

Sales reps may be working directly with customers in certain markets. They try to get subscriptions for new books, do not overlook the backlist, respond to complaints and collect debts. When appropriate they supply promotional copy for inclusion in the catalogues of wholesalers or retailers, check orders in order to avoid expensive distribution mistakes, and sometimes co-ordinate booksellers' ordering. Academic reps may call on lecturers and librarians in order to secure textbook adoptions, facilitate inspection copy orders, and encourage booksellers to carry out joint promotions and exhibitions. ELT reps promote and sell courses directly to private language schools, state schools and to government agencies.

While some bestselling series sell well across international markets, other titles may have variable patterns of sale. What goes well in one country may not work in another market. Book formats and covers may have to be varied to take account of international differences in taste and societal norms. International sales staff view titles with their markets in mind, and may join both editorial and covers meetings.

Export sales are a success story for the UK publishing industry and in 2022 they represented 60 per cent of total sales across books and journals.

Table 10.1 UK exports 2022

Sector	Top three export markets
Consumer	Australia, USA, Germany
Schools and ELT	Spain, UAE, Egypt
Academic books and journals	USA, Germany, Australia

Source: Publishers Association (2022).

DISTRIBUTION

The distribution of books and journals in digital and print formats, and new media products, is massively complex and critical to the publisher's role of getting its product into the customers' hands at the right time, and if in print, in the right quantities. The key aspects of print distribution (sometimes called logistics) are:

- customer care,
- accuracy in order fulfilment,
- speed and reliability in dispatch,
- physical protection of the product,
- economies in dispatch, and
- credit control

Failings in these areas lead to lost sales, diminished retail display, increased cost to the publisher and loss of confidence by bookseller and reader; improvements give the publisher a competitive marketing edge.

It is acknowledged that the system in the UK for the distribution of physical books is highly efficient, helped by the relatively small size of the country. Even so, book distribution is an enormous challenge and exhibits unusual characteristics. Many other kinds of goods produced by manufacturers (often on continuous production lines) are supplied directly to wholesalers and then on to the retailers. But publishers hire printers to manufacture the books which are usually delivered to the publisher or its distributor. Printers may also distribute new books direct to retailers and wholesalers. In material handling terms, book distribution presents extremes, ranging from one or more copies or other media products up to a container load. Publishers face the return of unsold books from the UK book trade (typically in the range of 10–20 per cent of sales), which are credited accordingly; and if the books are damaged or of low value, they destroy them.

Publishers carry an enormous range of new and backlist products. In the main, publishers supply retailers – individual shops or their centralized warehouses – directly. Despite the growth of the wholesalers, book wholesaling in the UK is concentrated mainly on consumer books. The customers for books extend beyond the retail trade – to schools and to individuals needing single copies (for review and inspection if not digital, and mail-order sales). Publishers receive massive numbers of small orders, the profits from which may not cover the distribution and credit cost. For some publishers, referring direct sales from individuals to internet retailers, which pay affiliate fees, is more cost-effective than fulfilling such orders themselves. Yet physical stores demand faster and more reliable distribution in order to compete against internet retailers and other kinds of products. UK publishers export vigorously and distribute to most countries from the UK via a myriad of arrangements and carriers.

Industry standards

The foundation stone on which all book trade electronic transactions and information systems are based was the introduction in 1967 of the 10 digit standard book number (SBN). By 1970 it had become internationally accepted. In 2007 it was extended to 13 digits to make it consistent with the European Article Numbering (EAN) system (now international) used to identify many kinds of products and from which bar codes are generated. The ISBN incorporates in the following sequence the prefix of the 'book' product identifier 979; the country or region or language group (e.g. English-speaking countries either 0 or 1, French 2, German 3); the publisher identifier (the larger the publisher's output and demand for ISBNs, the smaller the number of digits are assigned to it); and the unique identifier of each book or edition. The last digit is a check to ensure the preceding digits are correct. ISBNs are used by publishers to identify tradable products such as different print and ebook formats, audiobooks and CDs. ISBNs are obtained by publishers from the national ISBN agencies: in the UK operated commercially by Nielsen and in the USA by Bowker. The digital identifier for journals is the International Standard Serial Number (ISSN).

> Over 3 m ISBNs were issued in the USA in 2022

A comparative measure between national industries is new title production per capita of the population. Some countries with smaller populations score highly by this measure. By region the following are the countries with the highest ratio (Nielsen BookData, 2023, page 9):

- Africa: Tunisia, Nigeria, Ghana
- Asia: Japan, Republic of Korea, Singapore
- Europe: Slovenia, Iceland, Netherlands
- Latin America and the Caribbean: Brazil, Argentina, Chile

In the UK by the early 1990s, most main bookshops had installed electronic point of sale (EPOS) systems which read the bar codes on books. The collection of EPOS data from the UK general retail market by Nielsen from the late 1990s aids stock management during the rise and fall of a title's sales. EDItEUR is the international book trade standards body that coordinates the development of the infrastructure standards for EDI and other e-commerce standards for book and serial transactions, bibliographic and product information, digital publishing, and rights management and trading. It is supported in its drive towards electronic ordering, invoicing, information gathering and transmission, by BIC (Book Industry Communication) in the UK and the BISG (Book Industry Study Group) in the USA. For the publishing industry and the intermediaries, three main areas of standards are of importance.

Product information

First, the development of standardized product information – a classification system whereby publishers describe the bibliographical details of their products consistently – and the technical and procedural standards whereby they electronically communicate that information and its updating to others, such as to the bibliographic providers, wholesalers and retailers (see Chapter 9).

Supply chain

The second area relates to the supply chain (print and digital) and cover bar codes; B2B ecommerce transacted through electronic data interchange (EDI); and the standardization of the authorization procedures for returns in order to reduce costs. The UK Industry Returns Initiative (IRI) has led to returns requests being sent by booksellers electronically, with credits taking place automatically when stock is returned. There is no precise data, but the IRI is believed to have made reductions in the cost of returns. Under the IRI no returns are authorized until three months after publication or once 12–15 months have elapsed since the title was supplied to the shop.

Digital publishing

As publishers license and sell their products online either via intermediaries or directly to end-users from their digital warehouses, there is a need for common standards to facilitate electronic copyright management in order to trigger payment systems. For instance, an intermediary may want to print on-demand a publisher's title or to customize a product including chapters from a range of book sources, or a researcher may want to follow up an electronic journal reference in an article from another publisher's journal server.

The classic digital identifiers – the ISBN and ISSN – are the basis for electronic rights management systems at the macro level. One problem around ebooks is that this system has not necessarily kept pace – for example, a self-published ebook could be published on Amazon's Kindle Direct without an ISBN. Every product on Amazon is allocated the Amazon Standard Identification Number (ASIN) which for books is the same as the ISBN. However, many self-publishing authors do not want to pay for ISBNs and thus their books are not recorded in the statistics based on ISBNs of titles published. Also each ebook edition (say, Kindle, ePub, or PDF) is often given a separate ISBN, making the tracking of sales data more difficult. The Association of American Publishers sponsored the concept of a micro-level identifier – the digital object identifier (DOI) which is now promoted by the DOI Foundation (doi.org). The idea behind DOI is that it is a simple or dumb number which can be attached by the publisher to an object, such as a journal article, book chapter, or illustration – whatever the publisher considers could be reusable or tradable. The publisher maintains a continually updated directory, which acts as a routing system where the dumb number is associated with the publisher's internet address. The publisher's database stores the most accurate information about the DOIs such as the copyright ownership, terms and conditions of sale and prices. The journal publishers were amongst the first publishers to deploy DOIs, but the take-up in other areas has been slow.

Warehousing and distribution

There are three main types of distribution arrangement: *self-distribution* by a publisher to retailers; *fulfilment only* of the orders generated by the publisher; or *full service distribution*, which outsources the whole publisher-to-book-buyer transaction, including dispatch, invoicing and credit control. The major publishing groups run their own distribution and place the facility away from the headquarters, while the very small publishers with insufficient turnover to attract a distributor have to do it themselves from their office or garage. Amazon runs a consignment scheme called Advantage, which can be used by small publishers or authors who self-publish. Publishers set the list price of the printed book, off which Amazon receives a 55–60 per cent discount and has the right to sell it at a discount to its customers, and Amazon keeps in stock quantities as low as two copies. At the end of each month, Amazon pays the publisher for sales in the previous month.

Small and medium-sized publishers either distribute themselves or commonly use independent distributors (such as in the UK, Central Books or Turnaround for consumer titles, Marston Book Services for academic and STM). They may use larger publishers which offer their services to smaller publishers: examples are Macmillan Distribution and Bookpoint owned by Hachette. Penguin Random House announced that it will close its third-party distribution service, Grantham Book Services, in 2025. They may use wholesalers such as Gardners in the UK, and Ingram in the USA, which also act as distributors worldwide. The major distributors also offer print on demand and local offset printing.

Publishers may use a mixture of services, supplying direct sales themselves but using third parties for trade and export sales. Third-party distributors offer to publishers the complete service of bulk storage, invoicing, customer service and cash collection, and delivery for which they charge around 12 per cent of sales: less for larger publishers and more for smaller publishers. Such distributors have extended their reach, for example to beyond the physical and internet book trade to libraries, schools and universities, and to members of the public, in home and export markets. They increasingly offer additional services to client publishers, such as sales representation, marketing, print on demand, ebook distribution and negotiation with aggregators, hosting a white label website (a plain copy of the publisher's site), and platforms. Global ebook distribution has become increasingly complex and difficult to manage. Publishers may operate their own digital warehouse (Digital Asset Distribution, DAD) or outsource it to a distributor or specialist company, such as Gardners, Ingram (CoreSource), or Vearsa, etc. Some distributors also offer to publishers Digital Asset Management (DAM) which includes a complete audit trail to ensure the publisher knows where its content is at all times.

The supply chain for books

Books can be supplied directly from the publisher or through a distributor or wholesaler (see the figure for the physical supply chain). Smaller bookshops source the majority of their stock from the wholesalers, which offer a next-day service. The trend is towards fewer and larger distributors. Size gives to the distributor the turnover to invest in expensive electronic book handling and warehouse systems, the ability to bulk up order values, greater leverage in debt collection, and the securing of lower rates with carriers.

Short-run printing and print on demand are embedded in book distribution. They reduce the need for the publisher to hold speculative inventory and enable slow-moving backlist titles to remain in print. Indeed for some specialist or academic titles, journal back issues, or ebook originals, the need is removed to hold any stock at all. The publisher may export and import via printing in the sales market. A book is produced in response to an order, or an agreed minimum order is kept in stock, and the publisher's POD supplier dispatches it direct. David Taylor, Senior Vice President of Ingram, comments about their operations:

> Ingram's growing global network of wholesale distribution points linked to state-of-the-art print-on-demand allows publishers to get books to their readers in ever more effective and innovative ways. Simultaneous global publishing in multiple markets and formats is a powerful tool for publishers to use – and they are increasingly doing so. (menschpublishing.com, accessed 22 January 2024)

Third-party distributors serving publishers may have their own POD facilities or have alliances with such printers.

Some publishers have built their own platforms for the delivery of online content; others use third parties. High levels of investment are required to develop

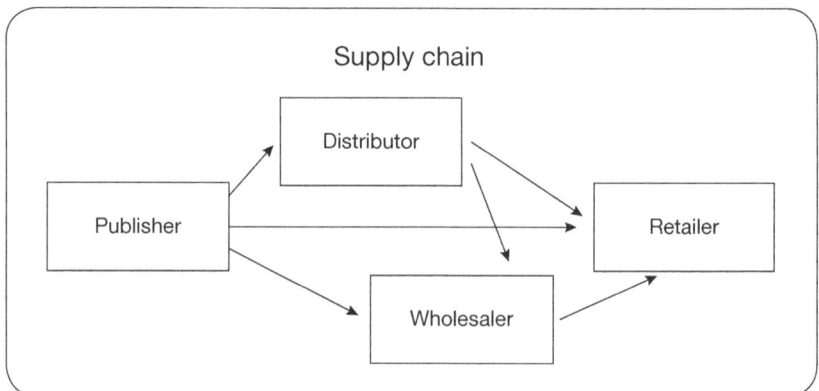

Supply chain

online services and, for example, it is estimated that Elsevier spent £200 m on the establishment of their platform ScienceDirect. For ebooks, publishers may distribute through a third party, or opt for direct supply. In practice most consumer sales in the UK go through Amazon. Libraries prefer ebooks on a common platform and there are companies such as OverDrive (school and public libraries) or ProQuest (academic), that will supply content from a variety of publishers. There have been efforts to develop direct sales of digital textbooks, and for example VitalSource makes content available digitally to HE students, faculty and institutions.

The distribution of physical books

The 'trade side' of distribution is concerned with processing received orders, raising invoices, credit control, and documentation. Once orders are received, the invoice is raised, and the documentation, labelling and physical distribution begin. There are many standardized codes which tell a customer a book is unavailable for various reasons. The Standard Address Number (SAN) and Global Location Number (GLN) are identifiers of a physical location of a bookseller and are an essential part of EDI and other ecommerce transactions. New books or reprints not yet in stock are recorded on a 'dues listing' and dispatched when available unless otherwise instructed. Export orders need additional documentation to comply with the receiving country's import regulations and taxes; there can also be censorship of titles in China or in countries in the Middle East. On orders to mainland Europe some publishers invoice in euros or local currencies and offer banking arrangements. Pro-forma invoices may be sent to new or unsafe customers – with a non-existent or poor credit history – before the books are dispatched. Most publishers supply books to UK booksellers carriage free, whereas booksellers in Europe will pay their own carriage.

The warehouse includes the bulk store of books and journals (and of any raw paper reserves), into which deliveries are made from printers, and a 'picking' area where titles and back-up stock are positioned for easy location (new books and fast-selling titles in prime sites). The invoices may include the location of titles in the order in which they are 'picked'. The collated orders move to the packaging and dispatch area. Dispatch involves knowing the most economic, speedy and reliable method (road carrier, shipping, air freight, post) and negotiating bulk deals with carriers. If the publisher bears the cost, the incentive is to lower costs to increase profitability; when the customer pays (for example on FOB export orders), the incentive is to assist them to save money, a marketing service. For the internet retailer Amazon, they may choose to supply an order from their own warehouse or from third-party wholesalers.

Looking into the future, we may see publishers abandoning their own warehousing and distribution, preferring to concentrate on core competences in editorial, sales, and marketing. Investments in digital platforms and services will bring a greater reward.

Now read this

Chapter 12, The sales channels for books in the UK.

Sources

Booksellers Association, *Annual Review*, 2022.
Nielsen BookData, *International Publishing Data*, IPA, 2023.
Publishers Association, *Industry Insights*, 2022.

Web resources

www.bic.org.uk Book Industry Communication (UK).
https://bisg.org/ Book Industry Study Group (USA).
https://www.booksellers.org.uk The Booksellers Association (UK and Ireland).

CHAPTER 11

Rights sales

The author–publisher contract sets out the scope of the publisher to license various kinds of rights to other firms. These rights allow the licensees to exploit the book across different dimensions – by media, territory and language. Rights sales can be important to a publisher since the income attracts little by way of direct costs and the share retained by the publisher is often simply extra profit. To be compared directly to sales income, the revenue from rights sales should be multiplied by a factor of six to eight. In consumer book publishing, where the contract is frequently drawn up by the author's agent, there may be a more limited grant of rights to the publisher – for example, agents may choose to retain film and TV rights, audio rights, first serial rights and translation rights to handle themselves.

It is difficult to obtain absolutely accurate figures for rights revenue, but some statistics are issued in the annual UK Publishers Association's *Industry Insights* report, which cites figures from a wide range of publishers and literary agents. Reported gross rights revenue generated by publishers in 2022 totalled £481 m (the equivalent figure for 2017 was £283 m); a further £520 m was generated by literary agents. Licences to the US and Canadian market that year included £28 m for co-edition sales with £45 m from reprint licences granted by publishers and £109 m from reprint licences handled by literary agents. Foreign language co-edition deals in 2022 totalled £153 m; foreign language licence deals handled by publishers generated £126 m, with a further £109 m from licence deals handled by agents (Publishers Association).

RIGHTS WORK

The selling of rights may be done by editors and sales staff. However, medium to large publishers normally employ specialists to sell rights actively. A small department may consist of a rights manager and assistant; a larger one has staff specializing in certain areas of the list or regions of the world. A publisher may choose to use subagents abroad (for example in mainland Europe, the USA, China and Japan), who receive a commission of, say, 10–15 per cent on rights sales made.

In the pre-digital age, there was a clear distinction between a sales department which sold printed copies to intermediaries (i.e. distribution) and

DOI: 10.4324/9781003403289-12

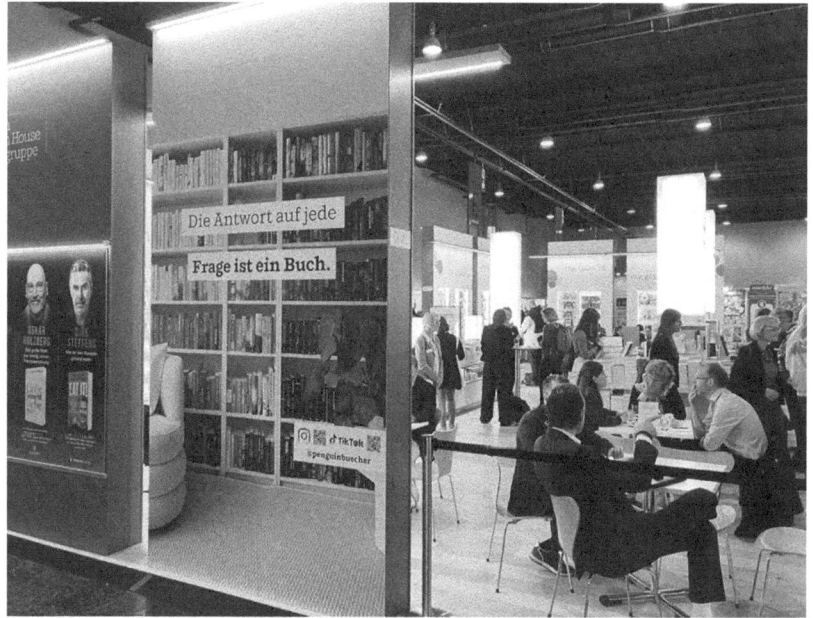

a rights department which licensed rights to other firms (mainly publishers). However, ebooks and other digital resources are often sold via intermediaries and those arrangements are now usually undertaken by the sales department. Former distinctions and demarcations between rights and sales are breaking down, as are the ways publishers organize the activities.

Publishers face a perennial question as to whether they would make more or less money by licensing a book to a local publisher (for instance in the USA) or distributing the book into that territory themselves. For example, a motivated local publisher operating under a rights deal may sell more copies but may pay a royalty or (if importing printed copies) pay a lower price per copy to the originating publisher; in contrast, the originating publisher under a distribution arrangement may sell fewer copies but receive a higher price per copy. A further complication arises with ebooks. In the former, print-only world, editions of English language consumer books would be published at different times in different territories (i.e. countries) by different publishers. With ebooks, even though territorial rights can still be maintained under contract with internet retailers (at least in theory), consumers would not understand their inability to buy an ebook in their country when it is evidently published elsewhere. A lack of availability also fuels piracy. Ebook publication is expected to occur at the same time throughout the world. Thus, a UK consumer book publisher holding world English language rights might have been unable to sell print rights to a US publisher, but it might publish itself the ebook in the USA. UK agents face the same difficulty. They may have withheld US rights from the UK publisher, but have been unable to find a US publisher. This has prompted some UK agents to publish ebooks in the USA under their own arrangements in the hope that they might make an eventual sale to a US publisher.

Many large publishers maintain separate contracts departments which put into the contractual detail the outcome of the agreements reached with authors, agented authors and with publishers from whom they have bought rights; some may also handle contracts with licensees, although in many companies these contracts are handled by rights sales staff. There are also independent contract specialists who offer their services to publishers and agents. Rights staff may also check and monitor the contracts made between the publisher and authors, and offer their expertise on copyright and media law.

Separately colleagues in a permissions department may carry out more reactive work, which involves responding to requests for copyright permission to reproduce limited amounts of material (such as extracts of text, tables, technical illustrations) from the firm's books in other publications or media. Many companies now have online forms through which requests should be completed. Usually granted is a non-exclusive licence to reproduce the material for a particular use, with due acknowledgement, for a specified edition, quantity and language either throughout the world or for more limited territories. The applicant is charged a fee, usually equally shared by the originating publisher and author. Publishers' Licensing Services (PLS, UK) and the Copyright Clearance Center (CCC, USA) offer permission management services to publishers.

The Copyright Licensing Agency (CLA) in the UK facilitates the collection of fees from educational and other organizations wishing to copy extracts for class sets, coursepacks and other uses. Such 'collective' – or 'secondary' – licensing schemes are used by publishers when it is not possible or practical for them to license users directly. The money collected is usually shared between the publisher and the author. There are similar schemes throughout the world, such as the Copyright Clearance Center (CCC) in the USA, that have reciprocal arrangements with each other. In Germany in 2016 the Federal Supreme Court ruled that monies received through the collective licensing societies by publishers should be given in their entirety to authors. As a result three years' worth of payments had to be handed over to authors, with payments totalling several hundred million euros.

Many books may have no significant rights sales income, but some consumer titles earn significant amounts while some may depend on rights deals for their viability. Where agents are involved, they may well seek to sell international rights for key assets themselves and retain other rights, thereby limiting what the publisher can sell. For example, a publisher buying volume (essentially print, ebook and possibly audio) rights for a specified territory will not be able to sell translation rights unless they are specifically added to their licence for the agreed territory. By contrast, the non-consumer publishers will aim to acquire all rights, throughout the world, from their non-agented authors. As the major publishers consolidate their position worldwide, they gain the capability of publishing books themselves in foreign languages through their subsidiary companies, rather than licensing translation rights to others. The major educational and academic publishers have the ability to sell their products digitally and directly to end-users without the use of intermediaries.

Rights work involves close contact with the editorial, production, promotion and sales departments, and also the royalty and accounts departments. Selling to customers, who are mainly commissioning editors or directors of other firms, has to be carried out in a regular and personal way, and good negotiation skills are required to finalize deals and contracts. Travel includes attending the major rights fairs of Frankfurt, London, and Bologna (traditionally for children's books, but now with a wider brief for adult trade titles). Staff who sell books of international appeal, such as highly illustrated colour non-fiction, travel widely and frequently, making sales trips to countries in addition to their attendance at relevant fairs. There is a great deal of paperwork – correspondence, maintaining customer mailing lists, and record keeping – and after fairs and sales visits considerable follow-up is required. Rights managers have to keep track of trends around which countries are likely to be fruitful sources of business – for example China and the Middle East have assumed greater significance. The Sharjah International Book Fair in the United Arab Emirates has grown in scale and importance. In Europe, there are variations between countries in terms of the number of books bought per head of population. Those countries with a tradition of cheap paperback publishing are likely to have higher sales per capita; a strong public library sector may depress consumer sales. A notable trend is the growth of reading of books in English with a high level of penetration in countries such as the Netherlands and Scandinavia; books in translation have to compete with the editions in English.

As in other areas, rights selling is aided by technology. For example, there are specialist rights, royalty and agency software providers such as Bradbury Phillips (owned by knk) and RightsZone, and rights components of larger systems such as Biblio3 and Klopotek, which enable rights staff to keep track of their submissions and sales and can automate many procedures such as chasing customers for decisions and payments. Virtual market-places for the trade of rights, especially foreign, extend reach and discoverability, such as PubMatch and Frankfurt Rights. As content is chunked into ever smaller units, whether chapters or pictures, there are software solutions for tracking their sale, ownership of the rights, and royalties payable.

Selling by rights staff may be done by telephone or email, and since the pandemic years of 2020 and 2021 there is increased use of video calls via Zoom, Microsoft Teams, etc. Rights sellers use a variety of tools, such as specialist rights websites, email alerts for new titles, advance information sheets, sample pages, catalogues and selective rights guides; material can also be shown to customers on tablets. However, for high-quality illustrated books customers still want to see physical materials. For publishers selling translation rights of fiction, for example into English, sample chapters will often be required.

The rights department may get involved with a title before the author has signed the contract. An editor may ask the rights manager to assess the title's rights sales potential, particularly if that affects the author's advance, or the viability of the book depends on rights sales. This can be particularly important for highly illustrated books with significant origination costs, where co-edition sales may be required.; in such cases, the originating publisher prints copies for their licensees. Sample covers and page spreads are shown at Frankfurt or Bologna to gauge the likely interest in a proposal. Around the delivery of the manuscript, the titles are assessed and a strategy is drawn up regarding the choice of possible

customers, and how and when they will be approached. There are many kinds
of rights and the deals struck are both intricate and varied. The main subsidiary
rights are described in the following pages. Sometimes, approval from the author
or their agent is needed before deals are concluded, and it is any case a courtesy to
keep them informed.

Book fairs

Lynette Owen, Copyright and Rights Consultant

Book fairs are key events in the publishing world calendar, providing a
meeting-place for publishers, agents, distributors and retailers to pursue their
business on a face-to-face basis; authors may also attend for book launches
and cultural events. Some book fairs admit the public, who can attend literary
events and in some cases purchase books at a discount.

Rights trading is a major feature of many book fairs. Although this
business has also been traditionally conducted year-round by letter, telephone
and email, book fairs provide a focus for new titles on offer. The fairs were
substantially affected by the COVID-19 pandemic and were abruptly cancelled
in 2020; some returned in person or as hybrid events in 2021 and by 2023
the situation had returned to normal. Cancellations and the bans on travelling
led many rights sellers to resort to contacting customers virtually via online
platforms such as Zoom and Microsoft Teams, planning appointments
on and around the original scheduled fair dates. This way of working had
some advantages (e.g. meetings longer than the traditional half-hour) but
also disadvantages – demonstrating material for illustrated books was

E★PERT

cumbersome and it proved difficult to establish new relationships or gauge customer reactions online; having to contact customers across multiple time zones often led to Zoom fatigue. In particular, both sellers and buyers bemoaned the absence of serendipitous encounters. Despite this, more contact with customers via video calls has continued post the pandemic.

The key fairs for rights business are: Frankfurt, held in October and covering all types of publication and featuring exhibitors from all over the world; Bologna, from 2024 to be held in early April, traditionally covering children's books but more recently extended to adult trade titles; and London, from 2024 to be held in mid-March.

Other fairs in western Europe have varying roles: Salon du Livre (in Paris in March) and Göteborg (late September) are largely cultural events, whilst Liber (held immediately before Frankfurt and alternating between Madrid and Barcelona) is primarily a forum for Latin American publishers to meet Spanish publishers.

In central and eastern Europe there are now many fairs, although most are 'selling fairs' for local publishers to sell books to the visiting public. The Warsaw fair, held every year in May, provides a rights forum, whilst the Moscow International Book fair (early September) provides an opportunity to meet many Russian publishers who do not always attend western book fairs. The rather oddly named Non/Fiction fair is held in Moscow in late November/early December and is rather more upmarket, with book launches and discussion panels. Fairs have also been established in Prague, Budapest and the Baltic states. In the Balkans there are fairs in Belgrade, Bucharest and most recently in Thessaloniki.

In the Middle East the Cairo Book fair was long the major event as a sales fair, but in recent years Abu Dhabi (late May) and Sharjah (early November) have established themselves as rights market places; each offers a subsidy scheme for rights deals, with Abu Dhabi funding the cost of rights purchase and Sharjah the costs for translation. The Riyadh International Book Fair (late September/early October) has also added a rights focus. Further afield there are book fairs in Calcutta and Delhi (sales rather than rights events), Seoul (June), Beijing (June) and the Shanghai International Children's Book Fair (mid-November). In Latin America, Guadalajara (late November/early December) is being strongly promoted as a rights event.

Literary agents and publishing rights staff start work on book fairs early and appointments are planned and confirmed many weeks before the event itself. Traditionally, many literary agents arrived in Frankfurt before the fair commenced to hold appointments in their hotels; however, since 2016, Frankfurt has opened LitAg, the agents' centre, and a new Publishers' Rights Corner on the day before the fair itself starts. Many overseas publishers arrive ahead of the London Book Fair and visit publishers and agents in their offices. Random callers at book fair stands may be accommodated, but prebooked appointments are now the order of the day.

Rights sellers attend book fairs armed with information and material on existing and forthcoming projects and work under considerable pressure; usually no more than half an hour is available for each appointment. Traditionally, sellers remain based on their own stand or in an agents' centre, whilst buyers move around the fair from meeting to meeting. The physical conditions at some fairs can leave much to be desired! A rights appointment will usually start with a discussion of any outstanding business, followed by a presentation of new projects; the rights seller will aim to select titles appropriate to the customer and may be switching languages from appointment to appointment. Projects may be offered on the basis of an exclusive option (more common for academic and professional titles, where the potential buyer will need time to obtain specialist reviews), multiple submission to more than one potential buyer, or a full-scale auction where would-be buyers will have to compete with each other on the basis of terms set by the seller.

Although rights trading is conducted all year round and has been much facilitated by email, social media, Skype and more recently video calls and the rise of online rights trading platforms such as PubMatch and FrankfurtRights (formerly IPR License), book fairs remain extremely important as much rights business depends on personal relationships, knowledge of the taste of the potential buyer (particularly important in trade publishing), face-to-face discussions and occasional serendipitous discoveries. Deals may be finalized for projects submitted before the fair, and new deals started which may be finalized weeks or months later. Business is often extended beyond a full working day at the fair with breakfast meetings, receptions and dinner after the fair; publishers are social animals and many a deal has come about as a result of a chance encounter in less formal circumstances than a fair appointment.

The period after a book fair is usually extremely busy, and traditionally the onus is on the rights seller to follow up with each customer promptly after the fair, confirming what has been agreed, drawing up contracts for any deals finalized at the fair and providing any information or sample material promised to the potential buyer. For educational, academic and professional titles, decisions tend to be taken some weeks or months after the fair itself – for trade titles, decisions may be made more quickly.

In the age of the internet, the future value of book fairs has sometimes been questioned, but particularly in the aftermath of the pandemic years, most publishers agree that they remain hugely important events and that 'virtual' events are not an adequate substitute for regular personal contact and the buzz of a well-run book fair.

SUBSIDIARY RIGHTS

Reprint rights

With the emergence of consumer book publishers that publish both hardbacks and paperbacks (so-called "vertical publishing"), the selling of reprint paperback rights by originating hardback publishers to separate paperback publishers is now rare. But a small or medium-sized publisher, while capable of selling a trade paperback itself, may not be able to sell a mass-market paperback edition demanding different distribution channels. Thus, it could access that market by licensing that edition to a larger publisher. The *No. 1 Ladies' Detective Agency* by Alexander McCall Smith was first published in 1988 by Polygon, a small Scottish publisher, before appearing as an Abacus paperback in 2003. Similarly a mainstream publisher might buy the print rights to a self-published work, as is the case with Colleen Hoover: 'She got her start self-publishing and has continued to do so on occasion, but has also struck deals with multiple publishers, sometimes selling print rights and keeping the ebook rights' (*New York Times*, 21 June 2023).

> An offset fee is payable in order to reproduce the original setting of a book

The key features of such deals are as follows. The seller defines the rights granted, i.e. the exclusive right to publish a particular kind of edition in specified territories is stated; and the duration of the licence is set out (for example eight years). The buyer prints its own edition and pays royalties on copies sold to the originating publisher. These royalties are shared between the author and the originating publisher. A rising royalty scale – the royalty rate increases when sales reach a certain figure – and the size of the advance (representing a proportion of future royalties) are negotiated. The advance payable is usually split, with part payable on signature of the contract and the balance on publication; it is shared with the author in a proportion agreed in the rights section of the author–publisher contract. The buyer may pay the originating publisher an offset fee, not shared with the author, for the right to reproduce the typeset text, or alternatively pay for duplicate digital files of the book.

North American rights

The USA is by far the largest and richest English language market. Agents, on behalf of authors, and book packagers may retain US rights or North American rights (the USA plus Canada). But if held by the publisher and the book is not to be sold via the publisher's North American firm or through a distribution arrangement, the rights may be licensed. Sometimes US publishers may also request Spanish language rights for their territory.

Selling to US editors is carried out at a distance or personally when they visit the UK en route to the Frankfurt or Bologna Book Fairs, or at such fairs. The London Book Fair has grown in importance over recent years. Sometimes the rights manager visits New York to see a number of publishers. UK-based scouts acting on behalf of US publishers may be used; and UK editors are also in contact with US publishers. The submission method may be simultaneous – the chosen editors from several different US houses receive the material at the same time – or occasionally full-scale auctions are held. Editors may be given the proposal, manuscript, or proofs. Depending on the stage reached, the rights manager uses the author's previous sales figures, the jacket and blurb, pre-publication quotes, the UK subscription order, reviews and details of other rights sales to stimulate interest.

There are essentially two types of deal. In the first, a reprint deal, the US publisher manufactures its own edition, pays royalties and an advance which are shared by the UK publisher and author – for trade titles, usually the larger share goes to the author, for example 75–80 per cent – in effect the UK publisher acts as the author's agent. For academic titles, the share may be 50/50 or 60/40 in the author's favour. Additionally the US publisher may pay for duplicate digital files of the book, or perhaps of the illustrations only. Alternatively, they may pay an offset fee at a rate per page. This type of royalty deal also tends to be used on most fiction and on some illustrated books of considerable US interest. It may also be used if the US publishers needs to make (agreed) changes to the text, for example Americanizing the terminology and spelling.

In the second type of deal, the UK publisher co-prints the US edition together with their own UK edition, substituting the US publisher's imprint and ISBN. This is an English language co-edition. The bound copies are sold at a marked-up price per copy; and the author's royalty of, say, 10 per cent of the UK publisher's net receipts is usually included in the unit price paid by the US publisher. This type of deal can apply to any illustrated consumer book, and could also be used for academic books published by UK firms without a strong US presence. However, the $–£ exchange rate will affect the viability of co-edition sales to the US market. Proprietary co-editions can be made with retailers, for instance, a UK children's book publisher may customize a book for Walmart or Costco.

Whichever applies, the US publisher is granted an exclusive licence, sometimes for the full term of copyright, but usually for a shorter period with provision to renew. The UK publisher is obliged to supply the material by a set date, and the US publisher has to publish by an agreed deadline date. Contractual limitations are essential to forestall premature release of an ensuing US paperback or remainder, which could jeopardize export sales of a UK paperback. The price paid or the royalty rates, and advance, are negotiated as well as the exact territories. The US publisher, which is granted exclusivity in the USA and its territories (US publishers also commonly request Canada), is excluded from the UK publisher's territories (e.g. usually the UK, the Commonwealth countries and mainland Europe, although the latter markets can prove a bone of contention), and has the non-exclusive right to distribute their edition in other countries (the "open market"). The US publisher may be granted other rights within their agreed market, such as book club or serial rights, and pays a proportionate share of revenue from such sales to the UK publisher. This is in turn shared with the author in the proportion agreed in the subsidiary rights section of the author–publisher contract. With some co-edition deals the US publisher may be territorially limited to North America, and the subsidiary rights granted may be fewer.

SKILLS

Rights

Rights staff preferably know French or German, and if concerned with co-editions, Italian and Spanish as well. But negotiations are mostly in English. However senior, the work can involve much administration.

The essential prerequisite for selling is knowledge of the books, potential markets and customers. Editorial insight into the firm's new titles alongside lateral thinking aid the assessment of rights prospects and their worth, the drawing out of salient points and the realization of sales revenue. With highly saleable titles, skilled judgement is needed on the kind of approach and its timing to selected customers.

The perception of customers' needs entails an understanding of the way they run different kinds of businesses – for example their product range, markets, business models, and financial structure – in different cultural, political and economic contexts. It is also important to recognize personal interests and tastes – especially in fiction and children's publishing – and national reading trends. Dealing with small numbers of senior people regularly and personally demands the development of good and close relations. Sales skills encompass the enthusiastic promotion of titles in writing, on the telephone and in person, even when there is scant information available on a new title. Where customers are in competition or when time is short in co-printing, they have to be pressured and manoeuvred to clinch deals quickly.

Negotiation skills allied to experience, numeracy and fast thinking help a rights person to tell if a customer is offering too low an advance or too little in a co-printing deal. Traditionally, most rights contracts are issued by the seller, but in some cases (digital licences and deals with some large US trade publishers), the contract may come from the buyer. The full implications and catches in customer contracts must be spotted and adverse clauses removed or modified. Where physical or digital elements are supplied, a knowledge of production processes and terminology is required. As so much of the job involves remembering and recording which books are on offer and who is looking at what, a meticulous, methodical mind which registers fine detail is essential. The consequences of selling the same book twice in the same territory are horrendous, although this is less likely given the use by many publishers of rights managements systems.

Long working days precede and follow the major fairs, such as Frankfurt, at which customers are seen in back-to-back, half-hourly appointments during the day, and informally into the evenings, over a week. The job calls for immense stamina and a strong voice box.

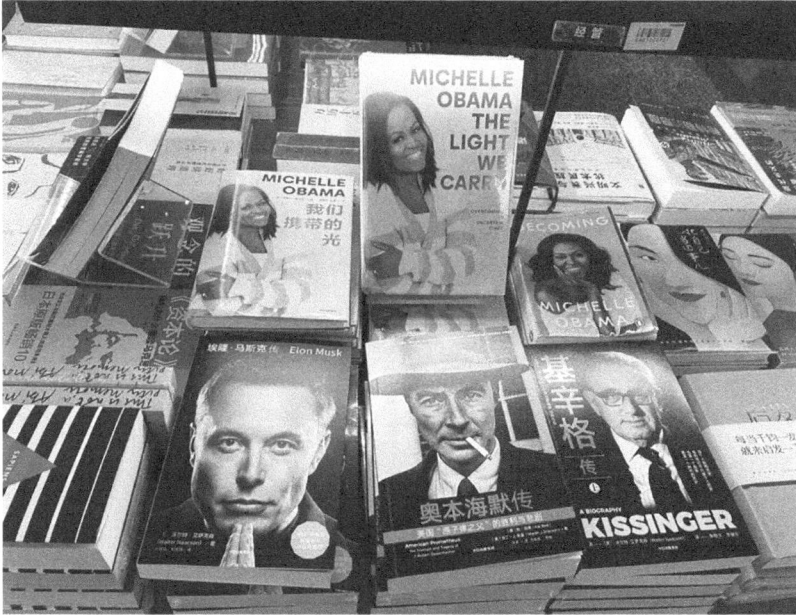

Table display in Page
One bookstore in
Beijing

Translation rights

With the globalization of publishing, sales of translation rights have continued
to grow. For UK publishers, translation sales lead the way into emerging markets
such as Eastern Europe, the Baltic countries, South America, and Asia, and help
fend off piracy. Acquiring translation rights gives the licensee the right to publish
a work in a particular language. In the case of adult consumer books, translation
rights (for some or all foreign languages) are often retained by agents. But if they
are held by the publisher, the titles are promoted abroad by email, telephone and
video calls, and personally at major book fairs or through sales visits.

   For trade titles, appropriate publishers within a language market area are
selected and sent material simultaneously. Depending on the direction of translation
(from and to which language), a sample translation may be required of a few
chapters. AI can facilitate translation of the whole book but authors and agents are
keen to exclude the use of AI for the published translation and have this written into
any contract. Academic titles take some time to be reviewed and are often offered to
only one publisher at a time on an exclusive option basis. Foreign language editions
may increase export sales of the English language edition owing to the book's
increased exposure, but there is also an argument that the translation rights for
adult titles should be withheld – for example in European markets with a high ability
to read English, such as the Benelux countries and Scandinavia – to encourage the
sales of the English language edition (by contrast, children's books would best be
read in the local language). Continental European publishers will want to race their
translations of consumer titles through to capitalize on the original publication
and to avoid loss of sales from purchasers of the English edition. They also have to
contend with the English language ebook, which may be competitive on price.

International
Translation
Day is 30
September –
the feast of St
Jerome, the
patron saint of
translators

The time-travelling novel has sold over 1 m copies worldwide

Before the coffee gets cold

TOSHIKAZU KAWAGUCHI

For many titles, the translation deal will be on the basis of a licence where the foreign publisher translates and produces the book, and pays royalties and an advance to the original publisher. There may also be a charge for the digital files of any illustrations to facilitate production of the translated edition. The advance is usually lower than for English rights, and some publishers work on an advance equivalent to half of the royalty likely to be earned on the first print run. Occasionally a lump sum is requested to reproduce a set quantity. This can be a good arrangement for those territories where print runs are small, book prices are low and the customer may not be able to provide accurate or regular data on the number of copies sold. The purchasing publisher is granted an exclusive language licence for a particular edition, and other rights, for a set period and may be granted rights for that language throughout the world. Practice varies as to whether the deal includes ebook rights in the local language, and for countries where there are concerns about piracy, the rights are often refused. Sometimes, on a consumer book, a Spanish, Portuguese or French publisher is excluded from Latin America, Brazil or Quebec, respectively, since rights can be sold separately in different territories for the same language. The author receives, say, a 50 per cent share of the royalties if academic, or up to 80 or 90 per cent if popular trade. There

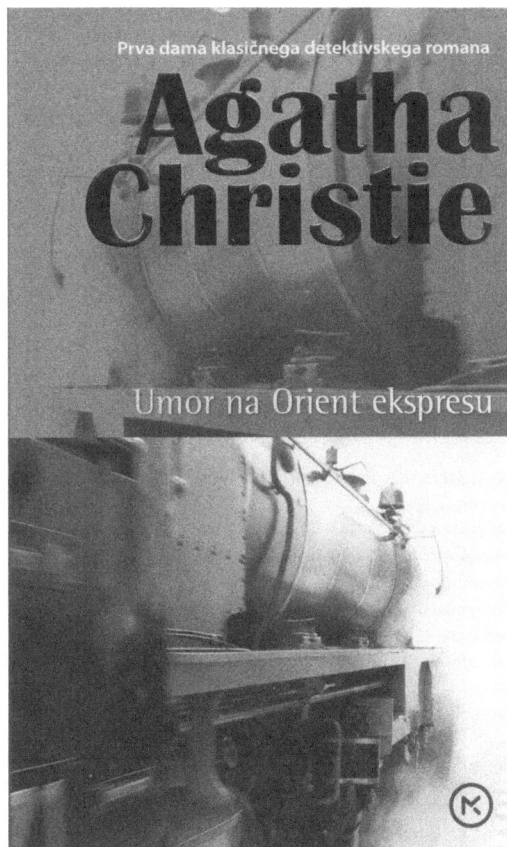

The Slovenian edition of Agatha Christie's *Murder on the Orient Express* (Mladinska Knjiga). Her books have sold over 2 bn copies worldwide and she is believed to be the most translated author

are some novelists whose sales in translation greatly exceed their English language sales – for example the US novelist Jonathan Carroll. The rewards to academic authors from translation are usually in terms of prestige and the dissemination of their work, rather than financial, but for textbooks the cumulative effect of lots of small deals over a number of years is to aid both longevity and profitability.

UNESCO has a historical database of translations which can be consulted online (see Tables 11.1 and 11.2). A search on the Index Translationum reveals the most popular *original* languages, with English heading the table. This clearly gives UK and US publishers an advantage when it comes to selling translation rights. Table 11.2 shows the top *target* languages, into which translations are made. What is often commented on is the imbalance in the number of translations from and into English. The website Three Percent showcases translated literature and its name derives from the low proportion of books published in the USA which are works in translation. In the UK in 2022, translated fiction represented 3.3 per cent of overall fiction sales (study for the Booker Prize Foundation, thebookerprizes. com, accessed 14 July 2023). Remarkably 14 out of the 30 top-selling fiction titles in translation were translated from Japanese; and the study did not include sales of graphic novels such as manga from Japan.

Table 11.1 Top 10 translated languages, 1979 to 2019

Original language	Number of translations
English	1,266,110
French	226,123
German	208,240
Russian	103,624
Italian	69,555
Spanish	54,588
Swedish	39,984
Japanese	29,246
Danish	21,252
Latin	19,972

Source: http://www.unesco.org/xtrans, accessed 14 July 2023.

Table 11.2 Top 10 target languages, 1979 to 2019

Target language	Number of translations
German	301,935
French	240,045
Spanish	228,559
English	164,509
Japanese	130,649
Dutch	111,270
Russian	100,806
Portuguese	78,904
Polish	76,706
Swedish	71,209

Foreign language co-editions

The alternative to a translation licence deal, which is used for many highly illustrated colour books and children's picture books, is for the foreign language publishers to supply the digital files of their translated text to fit around the four-colour illustrations. This type of licence is called a foreign language co-edition. Several language editions are then printed together by the original publisher or packager in order to gain economies of scale. The printing press usually has five cylinders carrying the printing plates. Four cylinders carry the plates which print the four-colour illustrations (made up of yellow, magenta, cyan and black), and the fifth cylinder carries the plate of the text printed in black outside the areas of the illustrations. The press operator changes the fifth plate for each language edition printing. Publishers who specialize in co-editions therefore ensure that all the text that needs to be substituted appears on a separate black plate, and avoid reversed-out text such as white lettering on a dark background. The ordered quantities, carrying each publisher's imprint, are usually supplied royalty inclusive. Digital colour presses allow production of shorter runs.

English and foreign language co-edition deals are central to the work of rights staff of highly illustrated adult and children's publishers and packagers. For example, the publication of a children's picture book may depend upon co-editions to make it viable, and accordingly the content may need to be sensitive to cultural

The Bologna
Children's Book Fair
is the leading fair for
children's books

differences. There also needs to be attention given to any potential issues that
could make translation harder, such as rhyming text. The translator Lawrence
Schimel points out the example of the labelling of illustrations of vegetables in a
picture book:

> The labels were sized to correspond to the length of the names of the
> vegetable in English. Unfortunately this posed a challenge: *peas* is a very short
> word in English, but its Spanish equivalent, *guisantes*, was not going to fit
> on that tiny label, nor was *remolacha* going to work on the label for *beets*. The
> publisher had to go back to the artist to make each label the same size, large
> enough to fit foreign variants. (*Bologna Show Daily*, 27 March 2018)

A co-edition deal may be preferable in those markets where there are concerns
over copyright protection – there is a guaranteed and secure sale of a defined print
run, retaining full control over the artwork, intellectual property and production
quality. Rights staff usually initiate deals well in advance of publication with
English language publishers and book clubs (although the latter have virtually
disappeared in the UK) using the book's contents, and mock-ups of the jacket
and blads (sample sections) of selected double-page spreads. The co-printing
of foreign language editions may follow because their publishers may translate
from the finished text and layout. The English and foreign language co-printing
of illustrated children's books with minimal text can coincide. Negotiations with
customers on the price paid per copy, the timing of the deals and their combined
printing can be critical for a book's viability.

A blad is a
sample printed
section

Co-editions may be combined with TV tie-ins, own-brand titles and
sponsorship deals. The complexity of these deals, involving close contact with the
production and shipping departments, makes it hard for authors' agents to enter

this form of rights selling. The late Peter Usborne, the founder of the children's publisher Usborne, commented about co-editions:

> You have to invest in each of the books you produce – you have to create something that is more expensive than your partner can afford to create so that they will buy it from you rather than making it themselves. (*The Bookseller*, 19 October 2007)

Digital rights

The licensing of electronic rights became important for publishers in some areas, such as reference and academic publishing, as a staging point whilst they set up their own digital platforms. If smaller companies do not have the resources and skills to establish digital services, they will look to sell to third parties. Even for bigger players, the sale of electronic rights on a non-exclusive basis may provide useful external income. Customers could be media companies, such as those producing games, rather than other publishers, and the possibilities of the internet and mobile technology continue to be explored. In China and Japan, for example, hand-held dedicated readers are produced for reference works such as dictionaries. The *Oxford English* Dictionary, or smaller lexical works, are licensed by OUP to numerous platforms and devices, including for Kindle ebooks. The licensing of content for training LLM models is an area under development, and in 2024 Wiley reported a \$23 m deal with a tech company for access to academic and professional book content. When asked by *The Bookseller*, 'The firm confirmed it offered "no specific opt-out for authors on these licensing agreements" should they not wish to participate' (30 August 2024).

A non-exclusive licence allows a publisher to enter into similar agreements with other third parties

Journal and reference articles and whole books may be licensed to aggregators, such as EBSCO and ProQuest, which offer curated collections from a variety of publishers to academic or public libraries and other institutions. Academic publishers offer site licences for their own electronic services to institutions such as universities – the licence outlines the conditions under which the service is to be used. In the USA, libraries have formed consortia to negotiate the terms for access to online databases. In the UK the Joint Information Systems Committee (Jisc) arranges licences for databases and ebooks on behalf of UK higher and further education (jisc-collections.ac.uk). Access will be passworded and there may be limits on the number of concurrent users for an ebook. Universities have also negotiated off campus access, using authentication systems such as Shibboleth or OpenAthens. Responsibility for this type of arrangement may vary – in many companies it is handled by sales staff, in others by rights staff. It is vital for each publisher to have a clear policy on whether these arrangements are classified as sales or rights deals, as this affects which payment clause in the head contract with the author applies.

The ebook is now usually regarded as a form of distribution rather than as part of the sale of electronic rights. Publishers selling electronic rights, for example in reference content, datasets or images, will protect themselves by granting short-term, non-exclusive or narrow exclusive licences, in particular languages, limited to specific formats or platforms, with performance guarantees and advances. Licensing on a non-exclusive basis means that new companies,

technologies and business models can be tried out. Strict controls on the use of
the publisher's brand may be written into the contract to minimize any damage to
its reputation. In the days of the dotcom boom, sizeable money up front could be
on offer for the right content but those sums are now far harder to negotiate. The
publisher may prefer fixed annual fees to royalty deals based on untested business
models. Alternatively they may enter into joint ventures in which costs and income
are shared in agreed proportions, for example to develop apps or APIs (application
programming interface) with developers. Publishers seeking to sell electronic
rights need to ensure that they hold their content in a suitable form such as XML.
Such files can be returned from the typesetter or planned from the outset. Extra
value will come from higher levels of structure and metadata in the content for sale.

Serial and extract rights

Selling serial rights is granting the right to a newspaper or magazine to publish
extracts from a book. Serial rights can be valuable in the case of celebrity or
political memoirs, with first serial rights the more important because they appear
before the book's publication, and can offer a national newspaper or magazine
a scoop of some kind. These rights are sometimes but not always retained by
authors' agents. The second and subsequent serial rights appear after the book's
publication and may be sold to a succession of regional or evening newspapers, or
magazines, at rates equal to or above that paid for original articles of comparable
length, or for zero on the basis that the coverage will stimulate sales of the books.
The author's share of first serial rights (often as much as 90 per cent) may be
offset against the advance, so as well as providing valuable publicity for the book,
the sale of such serial rights could be valuable financially. In some consumer
book publishers, the marketing department sells serial rights instead of the
rights department. The sums payable for serial rights have declined significantly,
matching the long-term decline of print newspapers, which now aim to invest
more in developing additional online content.

First serial
rights are more
valuable since
the extracts
appear before
the book's
publication

Film, TV, merchandising, audio and games

Books make an invaluable contribution to other media industries. For example,
research for the Publishers Association showed that:

> Between 2007–2016, 52% of the top 20 (by domestic box office gross) UK
> produced films were based on published material. These films grossed
> £1.5bn in UK box office revenue and £22.5bn globally ... On average, these
> adaptations earnt 44% more revenue in the UK than films based on original
> screenplays, equating to an extra £5.4m per film. This rises to 53% globally,
> equating to $91m extra per film. (publishers.org.uk, accessed 29 January
> 2024)

Film rights to
*Tomorrow, And
Tomorrow, And
Tomorrow* by
Gabrielle Zevin
were sold for
$2 m in 2021

Publishers are mostly unfamiliar with selling rights to film and TV production
companies. Such rights are usually withheld by the author's agent, and the
agencies have specialist colleagues for this area; the larger agenting firms have
developed considerable expertise. Usually production companies will acquire, for

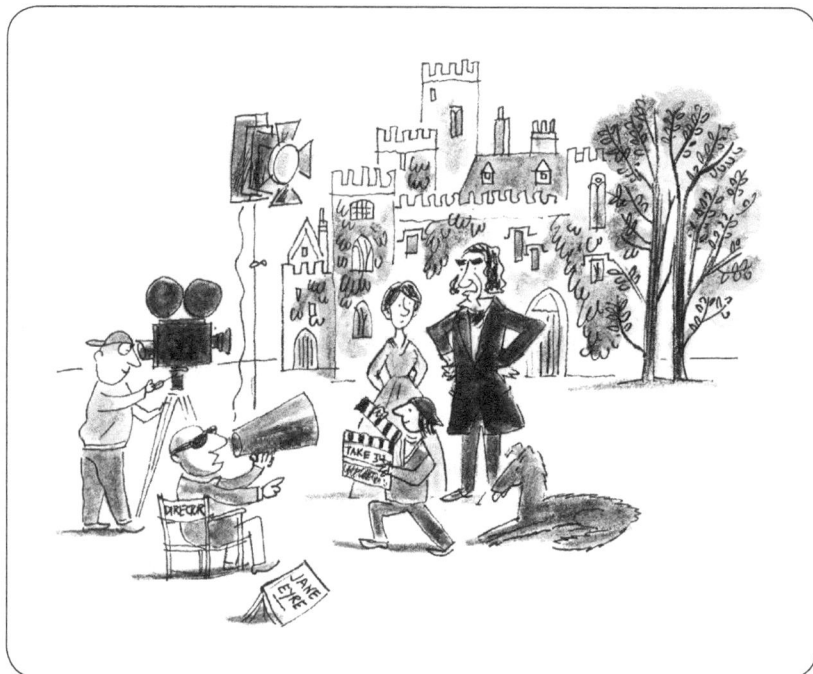

a fee, an option in a novel, which gives them the right to come back within a fixed period and purchase the full rights to take a film into production. Lynette Owen comments on the chances of a work making it on to the screen:

> between 5 and 10 per cent of options are exercised and of those perhaps one in ten finally proceeds to production; television options have a higher success rate than film options. Options should be paid for rather than granted free of charge; however, the income is usually modest. (Owen, 2024, page 355)

Preferred partner arrangements with production companies enable the sublicensing of film and TV rights (rights for merchandising and games may often be included in those arrangements) and in turn the acquisition of the rights to publish books of upcoming programmes and films. The Harry Potter films were an incredibly successful franchise generating approaching $8 bn at the box office. As new media and formats arise, partners may work together to exploit cross-media opportunities spanning the publishing, film, merchandising and games industries. One example was the partnership between the Tolkien estate, Amazon, HarperCollins, and New Line Cinema to develop a television series based on *The Lord of the Rings*. The success of streaming services such as Netflix, AppleTV+, Disney+ and Amazon Prime has had an impact on the film industry, as commented on by Rob Long:

> Whole categories of films – mysteries, romantic comedies, adult dramas – are no longer part of any studio's yearly releases into cinemas. As an agent told me a few weeks ago, 'If there's any way you can turn your screenplay into a ten-episode series, do it.' (*Spectator Life*, 22 September 2018)

Audiobook rights can be licensed exclusively in two forms: abridged and unabridged. The main trade publishers operate audio divisions which either produce their own audiobooks or license titles from agents or other trade publishers without their own audiobook lists. There are independent and specialist audiobook publishers as well as the dominant player, Amazon's Audible. Unabridged audiobooks used to be produced largely by specialist publishers supplying public libraries, which may also publish large print books – another right available for licensing. In recent years unabridged editions became the main offer: digital downloads are not constrained by the capacity of a physical format. Books can also be licensed for reading or dramatization on radio. The use of high-profile narrators and the availability of different formats – CDs, digital downloads, and streaming to voice-controlled speakers such as from Google, Amazon and Apple – have stimulated sales of audiobooks. They have proved popular with a younger audience, familiar with podcasting and keen on multitasking. They are also especially suitable for the US market, given the long distances involved in travel by car there.

The audiobooks of the Sherlock Holmes stories, read by Stephen Fry, run to nearly 72 hours of listening time

Other rights

Examples of other rights include condensation, promotional reprint rights (low-cost editions for a mass market), large print, rights for the visually impaired, including Braille and Moon (tactile reading systems), and English language paperback licensing rights to export territories. Material may also be licensed for use in customized textbooks for college course or in coursepacks (although in the UK the latter arrangements are normally made via CLA).

Many trade author–publisher contracts still refer to the grant of book club rights to the publisher by the author. However, in the UK, the book club sector (which sold books to customers at a discount by mail order) has almost disappeared in the face of competition from discounting by retailers and direct sellers, both terrestrial and online, and for many people the term book club is now more often associated with reading groups. The Folio Society specializes in offering special editions of titles in handsome decorated bindings, but no longer requires the purchase of a minimum number of books a year.

Now read this

Lynette Owen, *Selling Rights*, 9th edition, Routledge, 2024.

Sources

WIPO, *Contracts in Publishing: A toolkit for authors and publishers*, 2024.

Web resources

https://www.audiopub.org US Audio Publishers Association.
https://www.cla.co.uk Copyright Licensing Agency.
http://www.copyright.com Copyright Clearance Center (CCC).
https://www.literarymarketplace.com Directory of US and Canadian book
    publishing.
https://www.pls.org.uk Publishers' Licensing Services.
https://www.publishersmarketplace.com Publishers Marketplace (USA).
http://www.rochester.edu/college/translation/threepercent/ Three Percent
    is aimed at those interested in discovering contemporary international
    literature.

CHAPTER 12

The sales channels for books in the UK

Publishers operate through a variety of sales channels, and the choice of channel will depend on the sector in which they operate. The sales success of consumer books, for example, may depend on retail exposure and an important purchase prompt is being visible in the shops. High street booksellers remain vital to the visibility of books but the decline in physical retail, and the rise of internet sales, challenge publishers to make their books discoverable to those consumers who do not regularly visit a physical, or 'bricks and mortar', store. Also, as with many other products, consumers may use the high street store to discover a title and then purchase it online. Survival for physical bookshops has involved broadening their range of stock beyond books to include stationery, gifts and games. For ebooks and audiobooks, the trajectory is towards access being through subscription and streaming services. Nearly half of all readers of ebooks (46 per cent in 2022) are doing so on subscription; and over half of audiobook listeners (57 per cent) are signed up to a subscription platform (Mintel, 2022).

Table 12.1 shows the top sources for book purchasing in the UK. Over time the trend has been for the share of the internet to grow, and for chain bookshops, independents, bargain bookshops and book clubs to suffer a decline. The previous growth in supermarket sales went into reverse – this has had implications for the fortunes of more commercial fiction and non-fiction. For comparison, in 2005 the market share of internet retailers matched that of supermarkets, at 8 per cent. There is naturally a mixed purchasing pattern across channels, and purchasers of ebooks will still buy books from physical stores. Comprehensive statistics

Table 12.1 Top five retailers used to buy print books in 2022

	% of book buyers
Amazon	59
Waterstones	33
WHSmith	24
Independent bookshop	21
The Works	19

Source: Mintel (2022).

DOI: 10.4324/9781003403289-13

for books are hard to put together as there are segments of the market such as self-published titles, where there is no published industry data.

The UK book trade has seen a great many changes over the last 30 years. These include the collapse of the Net Book Agreement in 1995 (the official end came in 1997), which led to price discounting, and the development of large chains on the high street. Smaller shops have closed and medium-sized businesses have been swallowed up by their larger rivals – for example, Waterstones acquired Blackwell's in 2022.

The late twentieth century saw the arrival of the superstore concept from the USA – large, welcoming shops with a wide range of stock (typically 50,000 to 80,000 titles) and coffee shops. The first Borders superstore opened in Oxford Street in 1998; and Waterstones in Piccadilly in 1999. Both Borders and Waterstones were badly affected by the growth in sales through the internet and supermarkets. In 2007 came the news that Borders had sold their UK operation to the serial entrepreneur Luke Johnson and his private equity firm, and the chain closed for business in 2009 (the US company closed in 2011 with the loss of over 500 stores). Waterstones also struggled and was forced to close some of its bookshops in both 2011 and 2013, but on its return to profitability after severe cost cutting looked to expand again. The supermarkets became so significant to consumer publishers that in 2007 HarperCollins launched a new mass market list called Avon. Called 'channel publishing', the list was to target supermarket sales of three popular genres – chick lit, romance, and crime/thrillers. Supermarkets can call the shots, as they do in other product areas, demanding large discounts as well as payments to remain preferred suppliers. Publishers have responded to the consolidation of book retail not only by changing what they publish but also by forming larger groups, which can offer a constant supply of likely bestsellers.

The independent bookshops had a torrid time, faced with price discounting not only in the high street chains but also online and by the supermarkets. By 2017 the number of independents had fallen to 868 shops – compared to over 1,400 in 2007, and more than 1,800 in 1997. In 2012 their market share by volume was only 3 per cent. The ones that survive have sought to make a niche for themselves by offering excellent service (effectively hand-selling to customers), holding author events, hosting book clubs, prompt ordering, and stressing their place in the community. By 2022 the number of independents had risen to 1,072, a 10-year high, falling back slightly to 1,063 in 2023. Just as consumers are being encouraged to buy from local suppliers in other product areas, the independents are emphasizing their value in an increasingly homogenized high street. The value of local bookshops was also recognized by book buyers who experienced the temporary closure of much retail during the global pandemic. Publishers stress the importance of physical retail for discoverability, as Stephen Page, Executive Chair of Faber & Faber, says: 'Online retail is good at getting you stuff you already like; it's not good at letting you collide with something you've never thought of. That's what bookshops do' (*Monocle*, November 2018). Other outlets of significance include the airport terminal shops, especially at Heathrow and Gatwick, which sell enormous quantities of paperback fiction, travel and business books (flight delays are a boon for sales).

ONLINE

In the UK online bookselling means Amazon. With an international brand, heavy
discounting on a large range of titles, 24/7 access, and features such as giftwrapping,
the internet bookseller has built up a powerful presence in the UK market. Members
of the Amazon Prime service have free one-day delivery on physical titles. Kindle
Unlimited offers, for a monthly subscription, access to millions of ebooks and
thousands of audio titles. Audible is the leading platform for audiobooks.

The complete selection of books on Amazon dwarfs what can be found
in any terrestrial bookshop, opening up a window for smaller publishers and
self-published authors, who will struggle to get their titles into the chains, and
for backlist titles. For specialist and academic titles the main supply route is now
through Amazon; the same is true for many self-published authors. The concept
of the 'Long Tail' was coined by Chris Anderson in relation to books and music.
Usually books that are not selling in sufficient numbers are returned to the
publisher. Yet the internet provides a means of marketing and selling these titles.
If we add up this Long Tail of slow-selling books, Anderson suggested that it could
add up to a greater source of revenue than the bestsellers prominent in bookshops.
Although the theory has attracted some criticism, for example that the web seems
to amplify the blockbuster hits, the idea does strike a chord with publishers, which
have seen internet bookselling open up a new channel for backlist books which
had disappeared from terrestrial retail display. The book return rates are much
lower, and the internet provides a good route for the fulfilment of low-value single
book orders (often fulfilled through print on demand).

The original model was for Amazon to source books from the wholesalers,
avoiding the need for a large investment in warehousing. By 2017 the company ran
16 of its own distribution centres, enabling it to provide a fast supply of bestselling
lines; by 2022 there were around 24 such fulfilment centres. Many titles are still

supplied from wholesalers and dispatched in Amazon-branded boxes. Working practices at Amazon's distribution centres have come under criticism.

> The asymmetry of power between Amazon and its workers relies on the latter's isolation. Managers are fed real-time data on every aspect of the logistics chain: packing rates, the number of items moving through the facility, the optimum destination for each. Employees, by contrast, are given only one piece of information: how fast they are performing in comparison with their colleagues, a metric sometimes expressed graphically in the form of racing cars. (*Guardian*, 29 July 2023)

Amazon has also come under attack for the amount of tax it pays: in 2020 it paid £492 m in direct taxation on sales in the UK of £20.63 bn.

For some, online purchasing will never match the experience of browsing in their local or high street bookshop, but especially for those without ready access to a bookshop, the internet provides a convenient and cost-effective method of obtaining books. There is the added convenience of ebooks for either study or leisure reading – when you have finished a thriller late at night you can simply download the next title in the series straight away.

Amazon has so far held off competition from new or existing players in the book market. Play.com started to find a place in the market selling from its offshore base in Jersey, but changes to the tax arrangements on products which attracted VAT (it was selling DVDs and similar goods tax-free) forced it to become a marketplace for third-party sellers and it abandoned books. It is now owned by the Japanese company Rakuten (which also purchased the ebook retailer Kobo).

The supermarkets have their internet operations but have not created a compelling offer in the area of ebooks – Sainsbury's pulled out of the ebook market in 2016. Based in Gloucester, the Book Depository aimed to service the Long Tail. Rather than hold stock, it met customer orders from the optimal source – publisher, wholesaler or distributor – and offered free delivery to many parts of the world. Its independent status came to an end when it was purchased by Amazon in 2011. The US retailer Barnes & Noble brought its Nook device to the UK in 2012, backed up by its own website, only to depart the market in 2016. Direct sales of consumer books from the websites of publishers remain minimal.

The arrival of bookshop.org in the UK in 2020 offered independents a virtual shop front and a 30 per cent return from sales without having to handle customer service or shipping. A customer making a purchase nominates an independent bookshop to receive the payment; if no bookshop is named, then 10 per cent of the cover price goes into a general pot to be distributed amongst booksellers. By January 2024 the online bookshop had generated over £3 m for local bookshops.

Digital downloads of audiobooks are available from a variety of websites including iTunes and Audible (Amazon). In 2022 Audible reported sales in the UK of £226 m – this compares to sales in 2017 of £97 m. Spotify has started to include audiobooks in its streaming service and is planning a large expansion in this area.

Online content

In sectors such as professional and journals publishing, the model for publishing has shifted from the delivery of books and printed journals to the supply of content online. Educational publishers produce online subscription services for schools. Many publishers will sell through third parties and use rights sales to take advantage of online markets, but the largest players have built their own platforms to sell directly to their markets. Companies such as ProQuest and EBSCO offer sales channels for publishers, providing journals, ebooks and databases to libraries, companies and other institutions.

THE CHAINS AND SUPERMARKETS

There is no doubt that bookselling has become much more professional in the last 30 years, and there are high street shops which offer a good range of stock amongst pleasant surroundings, with added value from coffee bars, attractive areas for children, and a range of events taking place. Some shops have aimed to become destination stores – welcoming and lively in their approach.

The chain booksellers differ in their character, and have aimed to develop distinctive brands. The general retailer WHSmith operates two core businesses: Travel, with nearly 600 stores at, for example, airports, railway stations and motorway service stations, which totally dominates the travel hubs; and High Street, with over 500 stores on virtually all of the high streets in the UK. The book selection differs between these businesses but overall it is estimated that 'around

WHSmith opened its first bookstall at Euston Station on 1 November 1848

The book tree at St Pancras International station in London, in partnership with Hatchards and Penguin Books, on display at Christmas 2023. The tree had 270 bookshelves and audio listening booths

Waterstones dropped the apostrophe from its name in 2012 in order to provide 'a more versatile and practical spelling'

£1 out of every £5 spent on books in the UK is through WHS' (*The Bookseller*, 22 September 2023). The retailer attracts all demographics but parents of children aged 5 to 15 are an important part of the customer base. The chain was voted the UK's worst retailer in a 2018 survey but authors rallied to its defence, given it attracts many readers intimidated by more upmarket bookshops. The discount book, stationery, crafts and toy seller, The Works, has rapidly grown to a chain with over 500 shops. About a third of its turnover comes from bookselling, instore and online, and it has a family-oriented product offer.

Waterstones, owned by the Russian oligarch Alexander Mamut from 2011, was acquired by the hedge fund Elliott Advisors in 2018. In 2023 it turned in a profit of £12 m (£42 m in 2022) on revenues of £453 m (£400 m). There are around 320 shops and an average-sized Waterstones store has a range of 30,000 individual books, with 200,000 titles in the largest store. During the 1980s Waterstones competed fiercely with the Dillons chain of shops, opening well-designed branded stores, typically carrying a much larger range of stock than traditional bookshops. The two chains were brought together by their parent company HMV, which acquired Dillons in 1995 and Waterstones in 1998. They were viewed as upmarket booksellers, exemplified by their wide range of hardbacks and trade paperbacks and the depth of backlist titles stocked. However, the size of these stores became dwarfed in the late 1990s by the opening by Waterstones and Borders of flagship superstores carrying upwards of 150,000 titles. The demographic for Waterstones is skewed towards men, and its customers tend to be affluent and more likely than average to be from the AB socio-economic group. To some astonishment from the book trade, in 2012 the retailer announced a co-operation with Amazon in the area of ebooks:

> After previously describing Amazon as 'a ruthless, money-making devil', Waterstones's managing director, James Daunt, announced in May that he was teaming up with the US internet store and would sell and promote its Kindle tablets and e-readers in the UK's premier book chain. (bbc.co.uk, accessed 5 January 2024)

However, it stopped selling ebooks in 2016 and under Daunt's leadership the chain moved away from discounting offers, ended the practice of receiving payments from publishers for in-store promotions, and gave greater autonomy around stock to individual shops. The rate of returns was dramatically reduced.

James Daunt has his own small chain of upmarket shops (Daunt Books) in London and the Home Counties: 'the shop's cloth bags are de rigueur for London literary locavores' (*New York Times*, 26 September 2013). The Foyles chain, famous for its large shop in Charing Cross Road (first opened in 1906), was bought by Waterstones in 2018. The academic-orientated Blackwell's chain was taken over by Waterstones in 2022 – it has 16 outlets including its flagship store in Oxford, which boasts the world's largest room with books on display for sale. One issue for academic shops is how to attract footfall outside the two peak sales periods of the autumn and the New Year. Some campus shops now stock stationery, music, and gift items.

How the chains operate

The largest chain dedicated to books, Waterstones, operates centralized buying, that is book buyers at head office select titles presented to them by the publishers' sales or key account managers. This usually prevents the publishers' sales representatives from selling titles directly into their branches. In 2009 the chain opened its own distribution hub at Burton upon Trent, to receive books from publishers before distribution around its stores. As required, for example to source books from smaller publishers, the company also uses the wholesalers. WHSmith is its own wholesaler – it operates centralized buying from publishers and owns its own warehouse at Swindon, which receives stock from the publishers and then distributes the books to its branches. The chains have central marketing departments which organize, often in collaboration with publishers' sales and marketing staff, consumer advertising, in-store promotion, and author signings in the branches.

Supermarkets and other non-book retailers

Other kinds of big retail chains, such as the supermarkets, buy centrally and receive their stock either directly from publishers or via wholesalers. The supermarkets often offer massive discounts on bestsellers, usually up to 50 per cent of the recommended price. In general the supermarkets make larger margins on books than they do on the purchasing of food. Although the supermarkets' share of the overall book market is limited, their share of sales can be important for some bestsellers, which explains why they can ask for discounts as high as 65 per cent or more. Specialist merchandisers stock the shelves in supermarkets and monitor stock levels.

Books are available in many other kinds of retail outlets, which the publishers reach through wholesalers. For example, the merchandising wholesalers serve convenience general stores, ferry port outlets, and garages. They will check and replenish stock of mass-market paperbacks, and remove slow-selling titles for destruction. Books are sold through garden, DIY and leisure centres, and specialist shops such as computer stores and toy shops. In 2019 the retailer HMV went into administration and was then bought by the Canadian billionaire Doug Putman. The chain has around 100 stories in the UK and books are part of the offer alongside music, film and technology products.

WHOLESALERS AND INTERMEDIARIES

Trade wholesalers

Many of the independent bookshops stock from 12,000 to 20,000 titles. Most purchase their stock from the large trade wholesalers, which offer next-day delivery. Gardners, owned by the Little Group and based in Eastbourne, stocks around 500,000 titles at any one time (and 3 m ebooks), supplies many of the large trade retailers and supports independent bookshops through such initiatives as the online Hive service (hive.co.uk). Ingram, which operates in many countries including the UK, performs a similar service in the USA. Waterstones buys many of its books from small publishers through the wholesaler. Another large wholesaler, Bertram Books, went into administration in 2020. Wholesalers can also act as distributors for small publishers, and they have installed POD facilities and digital warehouses for ebooks as additional services.

From the late 1980s, the trade wholesalers revolutionized the speed and efficiency of book distribution through their supply to the independent bookshops, which were faced with a myriad of publishers' invoicing systems, and publishers' warehouses which could be slow and inefficient. The wholesalers' growth was grounded in their focus on customer service to booksellers. They offered the convenience of dealing with just a few invoicing systems, rather than those of dozens of publishers; of online bibliographic information systems (including marketing and purchasing advice); of online ordering; and of consolidated orders with fast and reliable delivery. The wholesalers became the booksellers' stockroom. If the trade wholesalers had restricted their ambitions to the independent booksellers, they too would have faced eventual decline. But they extended their reach into serving the retail chains and supermarkets, entered the school library supply market and began to export. At the end of the 1990s, they received a fillip from the emerging internet booksellers, such as Amazon UK, which initially drew their stock from the wholesalers.

Book market information

The retail outlets summarized above account for most of the UK retail sales of books. The publishers sell their new titles directly to the retailers (or via wholesalers). But the data of actual sales made by the retailers to their customers is of critical importance to the retailers, wholesalers and publishers. The installation by retailers of electronic point of sale (EPOS) systems, reading the bar codes on covers when sales are made, enables the retailers to monitor the rate of sale of titles and to control their inventory (by reordering the titles which sell or by returning unsold titles to the publisher). The effect of EPOS installations was that booksellers placed smaller orders more frequently (provided that a title was stocked in the first place) and expected faster deliveries. There are various commerce service companies that link publishers to the thousands of booksellers worldwide and which facilitate ordering, such as Pubeasy and Teleordering in the UK and Pubdirect in North America (all owned by MVB).

Nielsen BookScan collects the sales data by title from almost all of the different kinds of book retailers from across the country and from internet booksellers, and produces various bestseller charts which are published in *The Bookseller* weekly and in other media. Bestseller lists for ebooks became available from 2013 using data from publishers. Data is also sold to interested parties. Thus, for example, publishers can monitor not only the sales performance of their own titles – their rise and fall – but also that of competitors. Publishers armed with that information are in a far better position to respond to the needs for quick reprints or not. However, the data cannot help publishers' sometime over-optimism or misjudgement of printing too many copies of a new title at the outset, or that of booksellers' stocking too many copies in the knowledge that they can return unsold stock.

Returns and overstocks

The return of unsold print books to publishers from retailers and wholesalers is an expensive and wasteful characteristic of the book business. Around 14 per cent of books (by sales value) are returned to the publisher, and book wastage still accounts for 20 per cent of production in trade publishing. Books that are returned are usually pulped. This has rightly raised ecological concerns – is it right to have such a culture of wasteful distribution within the book industry? Publishers have a long history of ridding themselves, albeit quietly, of their mistakes in printing too many copies. When a title's sales are insufficient to cover the cost of storage, it may be pulped or remaindered through bargain outlets.

Some publishers never remainder in the home market so as not to damage their brand and sales of full-price stock. The greater usage of short-run printing has reduced the need to remainder. The promotional book publishers provide bargain chains with a ready supply of newly created low-priced books. Such publishers and the remainder dealers have their own London fair, organized by Ciana each September.

A book's 'end of life' forms part of a publisher's sustainability plan, which can include stock donations to, for example, Book Aid International and to schools; or stock sold to second-hand booksellers such as the World of Books (Wob), the largest in the UK.

Library suppliers

The public, academic and corporate libraries are supplied by booksellers and library suppliers. The UK public library market has been difficult and long gone are the days when library sales supported hardback runs of new titles. There has been continued consolidation amongst the main library suppliers. Following the collapse of the Net Book Agreement, the public libraries sought higher discounts – above 30 per cent – through collective regional purchasing consortia, while still demanding a large amount of bibliographic selection support and book processing from the suppliers such as Askews and Peters. In 2007 Gardners purchased Askews, followed by Holt Jackson in 2008, in a consolidation of the wholesaler and library supply market. The library suppliers export, especially academic and STM titles, sometimes under tendered contracts, to national and regional government libraries, and university and corporate research libraries. Ebooks are sold or rented through the ebook platforms run by the library suppliers, for example VLeBooks from Askews and Holts.

Discounts

The level of discounts given by publishers to booksellers and other retailers is a marketing cost to the publisher. It determines the amount of money the publisher actually receives from sales made by the retailer. The trade publishers, highly dependent on retail exposure, give booksellers the highest discounts. Most sales in a bookshop are made within the first 20 to 30 feet of the entrance, and this is the prime location where offers to consumers are displayed. Some retailers ask publishers for especially high discounts to participate in their promotions, and perhaps for additional sums (co-op payments) to secure window or table displays and prominence in catalogues or bestseller charts. Co-op payments are also demanded by some internet retailers to increase a book's visibility.

Under the wholesale model, publishers sell their books to retailers and intermediaries at different discounts off their recommended retail prices (RRP). They aim to keep their discounts secret and by law must not collude with rival companies. The main factors affecting discount levels are:

■ the type of book – hardback, paperback, ebook; consumer or non-consumer,
■ the role and value of the intermediary in the supply chain,
■ the balance of power between buyer and seller,
■ historical precedent, and
■ the size of order on a particular book or group of books.

For some publishers, the best discount is zero. The intermediaries are cut out of the supply chain entirely or are dealt with on low, or 'short', discounts. For example, the learned journal publishers may grant a discount to the subscription agents of 0–5 per cent. The highly specialist publishers producing very high-priced information products sold directly to professional markets may grant a discount of 10–20 per cent on an order received from a bookseller. The school textbook publishers may grant a discount of 17–20 per cent to a school supplier such as a bookseller, specialist school contractor or local authority purchasing organization. In such examples, the publishers generate the demand themselves, and can supply end-users directly – the intermediaries provide a convenient service to the end-users. If schools are supplied direct, a discount of 10–15 per cent may be offered as an incentive, based on the size of the order or as part of a special offer (for example, if orders are received by a certain date).

The standard discount to booksellers for academic books is 30–35 per cent; college textbook publishers offer discounts of up to 40 per cent. The publishers argue that they have achieved the adoptions through their own promotion. The terrestrial booksellers argue that they are physically stocking the titles for student purchase and displaying other titles that they might buy. Textbook discounts have risen to some extent from the pressure exerted by the chains, especially Waterstones and Amazon. However, the retailers' leverage on the textbook publishers for increased discounts is far less than on the consumer publishers. The major publishers are resistant and are building their direct supply capabilities.

In consumer books, the discounts are more varied and are the highest in the world. They average around 60 per cent for print titles across fiction, non-fiction and children's. For ebooks they can reach 65 per cent. A small publisher might give a discount of 40 per cent to Waterstones and 55 per cent to a wholesaler, but the question then arises as to how widely their titles will be stocked. To get shelf space a larger publisher will offer higher discounts and could be willing to pay for its titles to be prominently displayed front of store. These co-op charges (now abandoned by Waterstones) can amount to many thousands of pounds, and can be asked for by other retailers such as the supermarkets. In the case of the bestseller sections displayed in-store by WHSmith, the featured books are not necessarily there just because of their sales success. In 2022 it was reported that WHSmith asked one publisher for '£2,000 in exchange for promotional space, including a position in the fiction chart – for as long as sales warranted it – and the book of the week slot' (bbc.co.uk, accessed 4 January 2023).

The terrestrial retailers argue that their expensive display space generates the sales for the publishers; smaller publishers become frustrated by their inability to access the system. In order to survive, they have found new routes to market through Amazon or direct sales.

For terrestrial booksellers their largest continuing capital investment is in their stock displayed. While their margin (expressed in the form of the discount) negotiated with suppliers is crucial, their gross margin and profit are greatly impacted by the stock turn (the time it takes to sell the stock). Before the advent of Amazon, booksellers tried to turn their stock at least four times per year. Over time, the focus on stock turn progressively led to the reduction in the stocks of the slower-selling titles, such as academic and specialist non-fiction, the sales of which moved online.

> The Folio Society was founded in 1947 by Charles Ede, with the dream of publishing beautiful books that would be affordable to everyone

OTHER SALES CHANNELS

Direct sales

A proportion of children's publishers' sales and a very high proportion of educational publishers' sales do not pass through retailers. Furthermore, some publishers, especially those issuing specialist academic and professional titles, or highly niche trade titles, may sell them directly to end-users by conventional means or through the internet, and there are other sales channels available, such as sales at special events or fairs.

Children's books

Children's books sell well when displayed face out alongside other kinds of products, whether in the multi-product WHSmith chain, or amongst groceries or toys, where parents are likely to have their children in tow. They are available in supermarkets, toyshops, and internet retailers. Like the educational textbook publishers, children's publishers also supply their books directly to schools when their books are used to support the National Curriculum.

The school is an important outlet for children's books, providing a setting where children's books leap through the adult sales barrier and important word-of-mouth recommendations amongst children themselves take place. School book fairs have grown enormously and involve the supplier (Scholastic is the largest seller) providing the school with upwards of 200 titles displayed face out on special mobile bookcases. The school benefits from a sales commission or free books.

Book clubs

FOCUS

Sales to book clubs are handled by publishers under rights deals. Book clubs conventionally occupied a major segment of mail-order sales to consumers. The only prominent book club in the UK still in existence is the Folio Society, founded in 1947, which specializes in handsome illustrated hardbacks in a range of bindings. Founded in 1966, Book Club Associates (BCA) was a major player in book publishing when there were fixed prices and few alternatives to the high street shops. It found it difficult to retain members in the face of new retail competition offering deep discounts. For example, Amazon emails information about new or discounted titles to customers with the relevant profile. Previously owned by Bertelsmann, BCA became part of the Webb Group in 2011, before its parent company went into administration in 2012.

Celebrity book clubs came to the fore from 2004 when chat show hosts Richard and Judy made book recommendations to viewers. Even after the cancellation of the show, the club lived online in partnership with WHSmith. Other celebrities run book clubs and Reese Witherspoon was declared queen of the book clubs by the *Guardian* in 2022: '*Where the Crawdads Sing* by Delia Owens has now sold nearly 1m copies in the UK, according to Nielsen BookData, the majority long before this year's film adaptation – and many due to the Witherspoon effect' (12 December 2022).

Used books

Worthy of note in any discussion of the sales channels for books is the second-hand or used book market. Oxfam has over 100 specialist bookshops, alongside its sale of books in its other retail outlets and online. A survey by the Publishers Association in 2023 found that a third of respondents pass used books on to charity shops (publishers.org.uk, accessed 25 January 2024). The internet has revolutionized the search and sale of second-hand books: Amazon sells second-hand copies through its Marketplace scheme; and AbeBooks (acquired by Amazon in 2008) lists millions of new, used, rare, and out-of-print books from thousands of booksellers.

Publishers and independent booksellers are concerned about the impact of second-hand print sales on the sales of new books, and authors of course receive no royalties on sales past the initial purchase. World of Books is unusual in that it pays royalties to authors through a collective scheme on used book sales. Textbook publishers have to issue new editions on a regular basis to counteract the attractions for students of buying second-hand books. There is also concern about the sale of used books described as being like new. These could be unwanted review copies or returns that have found their way into the second-hand market. There are other channels for used books, including initiatives such as BookCrossing, which encourages readers to leave books in a public place to be picked up by others. Started in 2001 BookCrossing asks readers to tag a book before releasing it 'into the wild', enabling the book's progress to be tracked (bookcrossing.com). Similarly Book Fairies started on the London Underground and subsequently went worldwide.

Sources

Chris Anderson, 'The Long Tail', *Wired*, 12.10, October 2004.
Jeff Deutsch, *In Praise of Good Bookstores*, Princeton University Press, 2022.
Laura Miller, *Reluctant Capitalists: Bookselling and the culture of consumption*,
    University of Chicago Press, 2006.
Mintel, *Books and E-books*, 2022.
John B. Thompson, *Merchants of Culture*, Polity, 2012.

Web resources

https://www.booksellers.org.uk The Booksellers Association represents over
    95 per cent of the bookshops in UK and Ireland.
https://www.nationalbooktokens.com Book tokens were first introduced into
    the UK in 1932.

Glossary of publishing terms and abbreviations

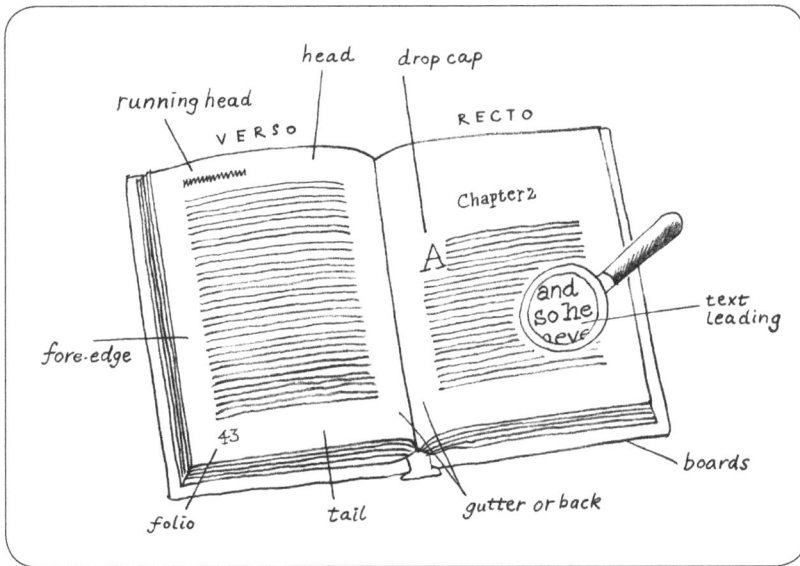

AAP Association of American Publishers

Add-on Extra value added into a product, for example a DVD in the back of a printed book

Advance Sum paid in advance to the author in anticipation of the author earning royalties from sales of their work. Advances may be paid on signature of contract, delivery of the typescript, and on publication

Advance copy Printed copy available ahead of publication. Advance copies are sent to the author and used in marketing

Agent A literary agent may act on behalf of an author and negotiate the contract for a book with the publisher

Aggregator An aggregator will license the rights to distribute content online from a variety of publishers

AGI Artificial general intelligence

Agile An approach to innovation: small teams are formed to produce new products or processes, working to a short time-scale

AI Artificial intelligence

Airport edition Export paperback edition of a book sold airside at airports ahead of the main paperback edition

AI sheet Advance Information sheet containing essential bibliographic and marketing information

APC An article processing, or publishing, charge

AR Augmented reality

ARC Advance reader copy – sent out to bloggers and influencers

BA Booksellers Association of the United Kingdom & Ireland

Backlist A publisher's established titles; *compare* frontlist

BIC Book Industry Communication

Big Deal A large bundle of journals sold by a publisher as one package

Blad Sample printed section

Blockchain A decentralized database of transactions that is difficult to alter, making it highly secure. It underpins the use of crypto currencies such as bitcoin

Blurb The selling copy that appears on the back cover or front jacket flap of the book

Book club Traditionally a mail order bookseller; now more usually a reading group

Booktuber Book reviewer, or other content creator around books, with their own channel on YouTube

Born digital Products originated in digital form

BRIC Shorthand for the economies of Brazil, Russia, India, and China

Bulk A paper's thickness

Bundling Ebooks, for example may be packaged up into bundles of titles for sale to institutions such as university libraries

CIP Cataloguing in Publication

CIVETS Shorthand for the second wave of fast-growing economies of Colombia, Indonesia, Vietnam, Egypt, Turkey and South Africa

CLA Copyright Licensing Agency

CMS Content management system

Co-edition An additional part of the print run sold to a third party. There are both English and foreign language co-editions

Consumer insight Market research into consumer behaviour

Co-publication Joint publishing agreement between two or more companies

Copy-editing Editing the author's manuscript with regard to style and consistency to eliminate errors and improve the text for the reader

Copyright The protection which gives authors and other creative artists legal ownership of their work – it establishes their work as their personal, exclusive property. The period of copyright in the UK and the USA lasts for 70 years after the death of the author. © is the copyright symbol

Cover-mount Special edition of a book attached to the front of a magazine, or bundled with a newspaper

Creative Commons (CC) Licence Licence facilitating open content such as text and images

CRM Customer relationship management

Crossover title A children's book with an adult market

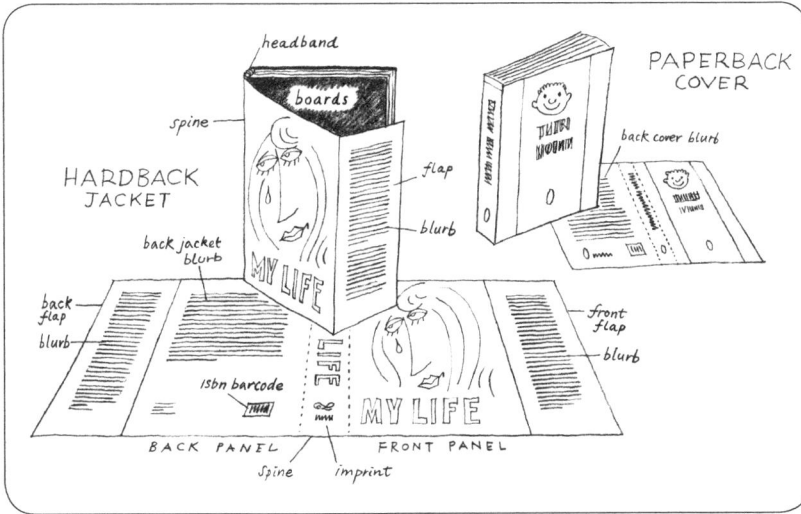

HARDBACK JACKET — headband, boards, spine, flap, blurb, back jacket blurb, back flap, blurb, Isbn barcode, MY LIFE

PAPERBACK COVER — back cover blurb

BACK PANEL / Spine / imprint / FRONT PANEL, front flap, blurb, MY LIFE

Crowdfunding   Sourcing online the funding for a new project from a range of backers

Crowdsourcing   Sourcing online the content for a project from a range of creators

CSR   Corporate social responsibility

CTP   Computer to Plate

CUP   Cambridge University Press

DAD   Digital Asset Distribution

DAM   Digital Asset Management

Depreciation   Reducing the value of stock in the company's accounts

Digital nomad   Freelancers who are location independent and often keen to travel whilst working

Digital rights management (DRM)   The technical means by which the access to digital content is controlled

Discount   Publishers give retailers a discount off the recommended price to encourage them to list or stock their titles

DK   Dorling Kindersley

DNB   *Dictionary of National Biography*

DNF   Did not finish (a book)

DOI   Digital Object Identifier

DTD   Document type definition

Dummy   A mock-up of the final printed book, mainly used for selling illustrated books to retailers or overseas customers

Ebook   Electronic book; a vanilla ebook echoes – or is a straight transfer from - print; an enhanced ebook has added value such as audio and video

EDI   Equality, diversity and inclusion

EDItEUR   International standards organization for the book trade

EFL   English as a foreign language

ELT   English language teaching

Embargo   Restriction placed by a publisher on a book to prevent it either being sold or covered in the media prior to its official publication date

EMEA   Europe, the Middle East and Africa

ESG   Environmental, social, and governance

Fang   The technology giants Facebook, Amazon, Netflix and Google; also FAAMG – Facebook, Apple, Amazon, Microsoft and Google

Frontlist   A publisher's new titles; *compare* backlist

GLAM   Galleries, libraries, archives and museums

GLN   Global Location Number

Goodwill   Assets that contribute to a publisher's competitive advantage, including its brand and employees

Grip lit   Psychological thrillers exemplified by *Gone Girl* and *The Girl on the Train*

Hackathon   Sprint event or competition seeking innovative projects or concepts

House style   The set style imposed during the editing of a text – elements include spelling, grammar, capitalization and hyphenation

HSS   Humanities and Social Sciences

HTML   HyperText Markup Language

Hybrid author   Author working with mainstream publishers and self-publishing

Imprint   A list of books within a publisher's overall publishing programme

Indie author   Author self-publishing their works

Influencer   A high-profile user on social media who leverages their following in support of products and brands

Institutional repository   A digital collection of research papers by members of an institution such as a university

Intellectual property (IP)   A publisher's IP includes its copyrights, licences and trade marks

IPR   Intellectual property rights

ISBN   International Standard Book Number

ISSN   International Standard Serial Number

Jisc   Formerly termed the Joint Information Systems Committee, Jisc is funded by the post-16 and higher education councils of the UK

JPEG   Joint Photographic Experts Group; a standard format for images

Licence   A licence gives a publisher the sole, exclusive right to publish an author's work and sell it as widely as possible. The publisher also licenses a book to other publishers, for example for translation. A *non-exclusive* licence enables the publisher to sell content – for example for digital use - to a number of companies

Licensed publishing   An exclusive licence granted to a publisher to exploit in book form a product or character

List-building   Taking a strategic view of commissioning in order to create a new publishing list or expand the present publishing programme

Litho   Offset lithography. This form of printing is still common for long print runs

LLM   Large language model

LMS   Learning Management System

Long Tail   First proposed by Chris Anderson in 2004 in *Wired* magazine, the idea that there is greater total value in the long tail of less popular products than in the more widely available hits

Machine learning   An application of AI where computers learn and improve from experience

Mag7   Magnificent Seven group of companies: Apple, Amazon, Alphabet (Google), Nvidia, Tesla, Meta (Facebook) and Microsoft

Manuscript (MS)   The author's version of the work; *also* typescript. It was originally handwritten

MARC   MAchine Readable Cataloguing

Marketing mix   Product, price, place and promotion

Mass market paperback   'A format' paperback – 178 x 110 mm; *compare* trade paperback

Metadata   Data about data. This enables content to be categorized and found more easily in online searches

Middle grade   The part of the children's fiction market aimed at those aged 8 to 12

MINT   Shorthand for the economies of Mexico, Indonesia, Nigeria and Turkey

Moral rights   Additional to copyright, these statutory rights granted to the author are the right to paternity, the right of integrity, the right to prevent false attribution, and the right to privacy

NBA   Net Book Agreement (UK)

NBI sheet   New book information sheet – also known as AI

NSR   Net sales revenue

OA   Open Access

OEBF   Open Ebook Format

OED   *Oxford English Dictionary*

OER   Open Educational Resources

ONIX   ONline Information eXchange

Online marketing   Use of the internet for marketing. Activities include the use of social media, search engine optimization, email marketing, and website promotion

On-screen editing   Copy-editing on screen rather than on a paper print-out

Ontology   The structure of a set of data

OUP   Oxford University Press

Overheads   The ongoing costs of running a business, for example office costs and salaries

PA   Publishers Association (UK)

Packager   Separate from a publisher, a packager supplies an edited and designed book for the publisher to market and sell

Paper mill   An organization confecting articles for submission to journals

Patron-driven acquisition   Free access is given to content, for example a set of ebooks, and payment is then triggered by usage past a certain threshold

Pay per view   Pay as you go model for content, e.g. purchasing a single article from a journal or a chapter from a book

PDA   Personal digital assistant; also patron-driven acquisition

PDF   Portable Document Format

Peer review   The evaluation by reviewers of an academic author's work

POD   Print on demand. Digital printing enables the economic printing of short runs. True print on demand is the ability to print single copies to order

Podcast   An episodic series of audio files; derived from i*Pod* and broad*cast*

POS   Point of sale

Positioning   Placing the product in the mind of the consumer

Post-print   Journal article as revised after peer review; *compare* pre-print

POV   Point of view

PR   Public relations

Predatory journal   An open access journal that solicits articles for publication for a fee from the author; there is little or no peer review despite the claims made by the publisher around quality

Pre-print   Commonly accepted as the version of an article submitted to a journal, before peer review; *compare* post-print

Print run   The number of copies printed of a book

Production values   The quality of the paper, design, printing, binding and cover of a book

Proofreading   Reading proofs of a book in order to spot mistakes missed at the copy-editing stage as well as any errors introduced in the design and production stages. Proofs can be read against the original copy or by eye (with no direct reference to the original version)

Proposal   A document outlining the content and market potential of a proposed title

PS   PostScript

Puff   Endorsement used on the book's cover, ahead of the book being reviewed

Readathon   Book readers read together over a fixed period

REF   Research Excellence Framework, UK

Returns   Unsold books sent back to the publisher by the retailer

RFID   Radio Frequency Identification

Romantasy   The fiction genre of fantasy romance

Royalty   The share of the income from a book paid by the publisher to the author; royalty rates will vary according to format and the source of the income (e.g. from subsidiary rights)

SAN   Standard Address Number

Scanlation   The scanning of comics by fans and their translation into another language

Schema   The structure of an XML document

Serial rights   The right to sell selections from a work to a newspaper or magazine. *First* serial rights cover extracts before the book's publication; *second* serial rights are for extracts published on or after publication

Shelfie   Photo taken of your bookshelf

Smart content   Content with an added layer of semantic meaning

STEM   Science, Technology, Engineering and Mathematics

STM   Scientific, Technical and Medical

Subscription box   A monthly delivery, often a special edition of a book, in return for a subscription. There may also be merchandise (merch) such as a mug or stationery included; this bookish merch might be revealed in a video of the unboxing

Subsidiary rights   Rights a publisher can acquire in addition to the volume rights of publishing their own edition – examples of subsidiary rights are translation rights and serial rights

TBR   To be read (of a book)

TIFF   Tagged Image File Format

Trade paperback 'B format' paperback – 198 x 129 mm; *compare* mass market paperback

Trade publishing Publishing of books that are sold through the book trade; also known as consumer publishing

Trope An element in the plot of genre fiction, such as the love triangle

Unicode An encoding system which gives a unique identity to each character

USP Unique sales proposition – what makes a book stand out from the competition

VAT Value Added Tax

Version of Record Published version of a journal article with the final formatting

Viral marketing Spreading a marketing message using social networks

VLE Virtual Learning Environment

Wasting Disposing of unsold stock

Web 2.0 The second generation of the Web in which users upload as well as download

Widget Mini Web plug-in with sample content that can be emailed or copied on to the user's social networking pages

Wiki Collaborative website. The name derives from the Hawaiian word *wikiwiki* – quick

WIPO World Intellectual Property Organization

WOM Word of mouth

XML Extensible Markup Language

YA Young adult fiction

Select bibliography

The relevant sources and suggestions for further reading are given at the end of each chapter. This list pulls together key texts and resources.

Journals and periodicals
The Author
The Bookseller
Learned Publishing
Logos
Publishers Weekly
Publishing News
Publishing Research Quarterly
Scholarly Publishing

News services
BookBrunch
Publishing Perspectives

Industry databases and information resources relevant to publishing
Mintel
Nielsen BookScan
Outsell

Industry data is also available from these websites:

https://bisg.org Book Industry Study Group (USA).
https://www.booksellers.org.uk Booksellers Association (UK).
https://publishers.org Association of American Publishers.
https://www.publishers.org.uk Publishers Association (UK).
https://stm-assoc.org

Books

Diana Athill, *Stet*, Granta, 2000.

Phil Baines, *Penguin by Design: A cover story 1935–2005*, Allen Lane, 2005.

Phil Baines and Andrew Haslam, *Type and Typography*, Laurence King, 2005.

Naomi S. Baron, *How We Read Now*, Oxford University Press, 2022.

Alan Bartram, *Making Books: Design in British publishing since 1945*, British Library, 1999.

Alison Baverstock, *How to Market Books*, 6th edition, Routledge, 2019.

Alison Baverstock, Susannah Bowen and Steve Carey, *How to Get a Job in Publishing*, 2nd edition, Routledge, 2023.

Alison Baverstock, Richard Bradford, and Madelena Gonzalez (eds), *Contemporary Publishing and the Culture of Books*, Routledge, 2020.

Michael Bhaskar, *The Content Machine: Towards a theory of publishing from the printing press to the digital network*, Anthem Press, 2013.

Michael Bhaskar, *Curation: The power of selection in a world of excess*, Piatkus, 2016.

Robert Bringhurst, *The Elements of Typographic Style*, version 4.0, Hartley & Marks, 2013.

Adrian Bullock, *Book Production*, Routledge, 2012.

Judith Butcher, Caroline Drake and Maureen Leach, *Butcher's Copy-editing: The Cambridge handbook for editors, copy-editors and proofreaders*, 4th edition, Cambridge University Press, 2006.

Roberto Calasso, *The Art of the Publisher*, Penguin, 2015.

Jen Campbell, *Weird Things Customers Say in Bookshops*, Constable, 2012.

Richard Charkin, *My Back Pages*, Marble Hill, 2023.

Clayton M. Christensen, *The Innovator's Dilemma: When new technologies cause great firms to fail*, Harvard Business School Press, 1997.

Brendan Clark, *The IngramSpark Guide to Independent Publishing*, Graphic Arts Books, 2018.

Suzanne Collier, *How to Job Search in Book Publishing*, Bookcareers, 2025.

Bill Cope and Angus Phillips (eds), *The Future of the Book in the Digital Age*, Chandos, 2006.

Bill Cope and Angus Phillips (eds), *The Future of the Academic Journal*, 2nd edition, Chandos 2014.

Robert Darnton, *The Case for Books*, Perseus, 2009.

Caroline Davis (ed.), *Print Cultures*, Red Globe Press, 2019.

Simon Eliot and Jonathan Rose, *A Companion to the History of the Book*, 2nd edition, Wiley-Blackwell, 2019.

Gérard Genette, *Paratexts*, Cambridge University Press, 2010.

Peter Ginna (ed.), *What Editors Do*, University of Chicago Press, 2017.

Robert Gottlieb, *Avid Reader*, Farrar, Straus and Giroux, 2016.

Albert N. Greco, *The Business of Scholarly Publishing*, Oxford University Press, 2020.

Albert N. Greco, *The College Textbook Publishing Industry in the U.S. 2000–2022*, Palgrave Macmillan, 2023.

Frania Hall, *The Business of Digital Publishing: An introduction to the digital book and journal industries*, 2nd edition, Routledge, 2022.

Miriam J. Johnson, *Books and Social Media*, Routledge, 2021.

Miriam J. Johnson and Helen A. Simpson, *Social Media Marketing for Book Publishers*, Routledge, 2022.

Hugh Jones and Christopher Benson, *Publishing Law*, 5th edition, Routledge, 2016.

Margherita Mariano and Andrea Reece, *Print Production: A complete guide to planning, printing and packaging*, Laurence King, 2024.

Tom Maschler, *Publisher*, Picador, 2005.

Nicole Matthews and Nickianne Moody (eds), *Judging a Book by Its Cover: Fans, publishers, designers, and the marketing of fiction*, Ashgate, 2007.

Thad McIlroy, *The AI Revolution in Book Publishing: A concise guide to navigating artificial intelligence for writers and publishers*, Future of Publishing, 2024.

Laura Miller, *Reluctant Capitalists: Bookselling and the culture of consumption*, University of Chicago Press, 2006.

Michael Mitchell and Susan Wightman, *Typographic Style Handbook*, MacLehose Press, 2017.

Simone Murray, *The Digital Literary Sphere*, Johns Hopkins University Press, 2018.

Lynette Owen (ed.), *Clark's Publishing Agreements: A book of precedents*, 12th edition, Bloomsbury Professional, 2022.

Lynette Owen, *Selling Rights*, 9th edition, Routledge, 2024.

Scott Pack, *Tips from a Publisher*, Eye Books, 2020.

Angus Phillips, *Turning the Page: The evolution of the book*, Routledge, 2014.

Angus Phillips and Michael Bhaskar (eds), *The Oxford Handbook of Publishing*, 2019.

Angus Phillips and Miha Kovač, *Is This a Book?*, Cambridge University Press, 2022.

R. M. Ritter, *New Hart's Rules: The handbook of style for writers and editors*, Oxford University Press, 2005.

R.M. Ritter, Angus Stevenson and Lesley Brown, *New Oxford Dictionary for Writers and Editors*, Oxford University Press, 2005.

Matthew Rubery, *The Untold Story of the Talking Book*, Harvard University Press, 2016.

Mike Shatzkin, *The Shatzkin Files*, Kobo Editions, 2011.

Kelvin Smith and Melanie Ramdarshan Bold, *The Publishing Business*, 3rd edition, Bloomsbury, 2024.

Claire Squires, *Marketing Literature: The making of contemporary writing in Britain*, Palgrave Macmillan, 2007.

Iain Stevenson, *Book Makers: British publishing in the twentieth century*, British Library, 2010.

Simon Stokes, *Digital Copyright: Law and practice*, 5th edition, Hart Publishing, 2019.

Michael F. Suarez and H. R. Woudhuysen (eds), *The Oxford Companion to the Book*, Oxford University Press, 2010.

Mustafa Suleyman and Michael Bhaskar, *The Coming Wave*, Bodley Head, 2023.

Mira T. Sundara Rajan, *Moral Rights*, Oxford University Press, 2011.

The Chicago Manual of Style, 18th edition, University of Chicago Press, 2024.

John B. Thompson, *Books in the Digital Age*, Polity Press, 2005.

John B. Thompson, *Merchants of Culture*, Polity Press, 2010.

John B. Thompson, *Book Wars*, Polity Press, 2021.

Maryann Wolf, *Proust and the Squid: The story and science of the reading brain*, Icon Books, 2008.

Thomas Woll, *Publishing for Profit*, 5th edition, Chicago Review Press, 2014.

Gabriel Zaid, *So Many Books: Reading and publishing in an age of abundance*, Sort of Books, 2004.

Index

Note: For citations relating to diagrams, graphs and photographs, page numbers appear in *italics*. For table citations, page numbers appear in **bold**.

*For Product Safety Concerns and Information please contact
our EU representative GPSR@taylorandfrancis.com Taylor & Francis
Verlag GmbH, Kaufingerstraße 24, 80331 München, Germany*